THE LONG WAY TO LOS GATOS

by Verne R. Albright

Drawings by William E. Jones

An Adventure Involving a Witch Doctor, two Bandil Gangs, a Smuggler, a Bullying Sheriff, a Television Camera Crew, a Revolution in Nicaragua and a Beautiful American Girl Named Emily.

AMIGO PUBLICATIONS

Published by
Amigo Publications, Inc.
1510 Dove Meadow Road
Solvang, California 93463

ISBN: 0-9658533-2-2

Library of Congress Catalog Card Number: 99-97139

Albright, Verne R., 1999
The Long Way to Los Gatos / by Verne R. Albright

First Edition 1999

Printed in the USA

Table of Contents

Prologue	Be Careful What You Wish For	5
Chapter 1	Pablito	12
Chapter 2	The Bullfighter	18
Chapter 3	Three To Get Ready	30
Chapter 4	Four to Get Ready Again	39
Chapter 5	The Bishop's Blessing	46
Chapter 6	Onramp to the Royal Road	52
Chapter 7	The Phantom of La Viña	60
Chapter 8	Beyond Olmos, Almost	66
Chapter 9	From the Frying Pan into the Fire	76
Chapter 10	Gambles that Failed	86
Chapter 11	The Worst Form of Unlucky	99
Chapter 12	Honest Juan's Slightly Used Horses	113
Chapter 13	Two for the Road	124
Chapter 14	Borderline	134
Chapter 15	The Smuggler in the Mirror	143
Chapter 16	The Andes	150
Chapter 17	My Friend the Witch Doctor	158
Chapter 18	Turkey Day	169
Chapter 19	Tschades of Tschiffely!	177
Chapter 20	True *Cold War* Spirit	187
Chapter 21	"Stop Him! He's an *Americano!*"	197
Chapter 22	The Outsider	212
Chapter 23	The Last of the True Gentlemen	222
Chapter 24	*Sure Shot* and Friends	238
Chapter 25	Where Hemispheres Meet	245
Chapter 26	A Man, A Plan, A Canal, Panama	258
Chapter 27	Empty Jail Cell	265
Chapter 28	The Pores Pour	276
Chapter 29	Bellying Up To The Bar	281
Chapter 30	The Way to San José	295
Chapter 31	The Peak of Death	303
Chapter 32	Emily	309
Chapter 33	Going the Wrong Way and Loving It!	318
Chapter 34	If It's Tuesday, This Must Be El Salvador	327
Chapter 35	Hello. Goodbye.	338
Chapter 36	Decisions, Decisions	343
Chapter 37	"Your Horses Will be Confiscated!"	351
Chapter 38	The Great Escape	358
Chapter 39	Home Stretch	365
Chapter 40	Finish Line!	370
Epilogue	Even the Best-Laid Plans	379
Appendix	Heaven's Gait: A Profile of the Peruvian *Paso*	382
Glossary	Spanish Terms	388

Acknowledgments

There have been two previous editions of this book. This one is by far the best. The main reason is Russell Robe, a man who read a previous version when he was looking to publish a series of books based on adventures in Latin America. He showed me how to take the very same events and upgrade them from a documentary into a first-class adventure story. Russell's contribution to this book was significant, and I'm very grateful for it.

Many helpful comments and suggestions were also contributed by Mimi Busk-Downey, Pat Albright, Earl Hoppes, Jeanne Shiroma, Christie Gasparri, Lionell Griffith, Dr. Deb Bennett, Sylvia Reusser and my wife, Laurie. Without their help, this book wouldn't have been the best it could have been.

William E. Jones was kind enough to permit reproduction of a selection of the wonderful drawings he did almost thirty years ago for a previous version of this book, *Horseback Across Three Americas*, which he published. My profound appreciation also goes to Ruth Riegel whose editing and proofreading didn't stop there. Her many suggestions in other areas were invaluable.

Thanks to each and every one of you.

Finally, a few words about a man you'll meet near the end of this book. John DeLozier was among the best friends that life ever gave me. He was also among the best friends the Peruvian breed will ever have. It troubles me that so many people have forgotten his contributions, and this seems like a good place for me to say so.

Verne R. Albright
March, 1999

THE IMAGES IN THIS BOOK

The photographs in this book were taken – mostly by newspaper photographers – in 1966-67. In order for them to appear on the following pages, they were electronically enhanced from yellowing magazine and newspaper originals that were over three decades old.

Be Careful What You Wish For

For several days, I had been growing uneasy about the health hazards I faced. Posters recommending inoculation against malaria had fed this concern. I'd seen them in every town since the Ecuadorian border. In the next large city I reached, I went to the local office of the Peace Corps, and spoke with a North American [1] nurse.

"I'm not supposed to treat or give medical advice to Americans," she said crisply. "I'm only authorized to work with the local poor."

"Can you recommend a doctor?" I asked.

"We're not allowed to recommend doctors," the nurse continued in the same tone of voice, "and to tell the truth, there aren't many I could recommend in good conscience."

I thanked her for her time and turned to go.

"What are you doing in Loja?" she asked.

"I'm just passing through."

"Doing what?"

"Going to the States on horseback."

"Oh, God!" she said. "You're traveling through this country on horses? I hope you're being very careful. You have no idea of the diseases they have here. What are you doing for food?"

"Buying it where I can," I answered. "I'm being careful."

"Listen, I can give you a gamma globulin shot for protection against hepatitis," she volunteered. "I'd also advise you to take precautions against malaria, typhoid, tuberculosis and bubonic plague. Do you read Spanish?"

"Pretty well, I guess."

"Well, then, here's a pamphlet that tells you how to protect yourself from cholera."

Though I knew tuberculosis to be a terrible disease, I was accustomed to hearing about it. But typhoid! Malaria! Cholera! Bubonic plague! I thought they had been consigned to history books and horror stories. These latest threats were added to a long list of dangers I faced, including bandits and avalanches. Briefly, I wondered how I had gotten myself into this mess. Then I remembered. I had been looking for adventure! As a youngster, I was chronically bored, and boredom sows not only the seeds of mischief, but also those of mischief's close cousin, adventure. During the first ten years of my life, my family moved ten times to new homes in seven states.

Instead of making me long for continuity, all that uprooting and replanting made me restless for change whenever things stayed the same for very long. We were never in one place long enough for me to get past being an outsider. Annually, I went through a hazing at the hands of my new schoolmates, and the fact that I was exceptionally tall made it all the worse. Periodically, I reached the point where I looked forward to our next move in the hope that life would get better if I could just start all over again.

According to my mother, horses were the only thing that claimed and held my interest while I was growing up. As a small child, I begged for horse books, and in time, I began to beg for a horse. When our family settled down in Reno, Nevada, my long-standing request could finally be granted. I was about ten when I got my first horse. Trixie was a sorrel-colored mustang mare and had been born wild. Her energy and aloofness made her different from all the domestically born animals we saw when my dad and I went horse shopping.

I joined a youth group sponsored by the Washoe County Horsemen's Association. On a regular basis, I participated in various horse activities, and my favorite was an annual hundred-mile ride, which took us into the wilds for three glorious days. To me, *that* was pure, unadulterated heaven. I had never found as much enjoyment in any other activity.

Over the next few years, I sprouted to a whopping six-feet, nine-inches, and in the process, I outgrew Trixie. I sold her and bid her farewell in the same casual way I had said good-bye to towns and people throughout my childhood. It didn't seem like a big deal at the time, but when I saw how long it took to find her equal, I learned a valuable lesson.

Shortly thereafter, I bought a quarter horse mare named Miss Rosetta. My new mare was phlegmatic and calm, a disposition that soon made me long for Trixie's energy and enthusiasm, a quality I'd later come to know as *brío* in Peruvian *Paso* Horses. My flagging interest in Miss Rosetta evaporated completely when I unexpectedly made the Reno High School varsity basketball team during my junior year. I had played very little basketball and was clumsy. Growing like a weed, I was constantly trying to cope with height so new that I wasn't yet used to it. The coach, however, had a logical justification for my presence on his team.

"When a boy is built that close to the basket, he's liable to come in handy," he told a local newspaper reporter.

After selling Miss Rosetta, I concentrated on this interesting new challenge. In my senior year, I stopped growing and finally came into my own. That year Reno High made it all the way to the State Championship game, losing by only three points, and I was named to several All Star teams. But after basketball season, boredom became an unwelcome guest once again.

I went to college for a year in Portland, Oregon, but it wasn't for me. My tolerance for dull routines was exhausted. I hungered to head out in search of adventure, and I left college without ever looking back. The summer after my abbreviated college career, I got married and accepted a job offer. The man I had worked for during high school was being transferred to a huge, new store, and he successfully tempted Anne and me to Salt Lake City, telling us that my experience would qualify me to manage a department.

The new store's grand opening took place a month before Christmas, and I was assigned to manage the toy department. I had to learn fast and move fast, and I loved it. The letdown came on a predictable date, December 26th! Boredom again. I began to wonder what line of work might be interesting and exciting all year round. That led to intriguing thoughts of working in some unfamiliar foreign land.

John Cooke, a geologist and the father of an ex-girlfriend, had worked outside the United States for much of his life, and I discussed my prospects for an overseas job with him. He gave me a letter of recommendation and the names of employers to contact. I filled out applications and sent them to exotic places around the world, but nothing ever came of it. In desperation, I finally decided to take the bit between my teeth.

"If I were to just show up someplace, looking for work, where would I have the best chance to find it?" I asked John one afternoon.

"Peru," John responded. "I have a friend in Lima who can help you get settled and situated there."

Just like that, I was out of the toy business. My wife and I spent half our savings on a one-way ticket to Peru. If I found a job, the other half would bring Anne and our three-month-old daughter to join me. Otherwise, it would bring me back home.

During the flight to Peru, I met a lady who offered me a job teaching English at Lima's *Instituto Cultural*. Full of optimism that I could find something far more interesting, I declined. Two weeks later, I was face-to-face with the prospect of running out of money and returning home defeated. That was the last thing I wanted. I found Peru fascinating and felt certain that adventure could be

7

found there if I could just arrange for more time. So I became an English teacher and sent for my wife and daughter. Supplementing my income with private English lessons, Anne and I began saving money for whatever new experiences might come our way. After a couple of months in Lima, we met Hillary Dunsterville and LuBette Herrick, two women who had driven to Peru from far-away New York. Their goal was the southernmost tip of South America. Unfortunately, their Jeep station wagon developed serious mechanical problems by the time they reached Lima, and the cost of repairs represented a potentially fatal blow to their budget.

While Hillary and LuBette waited for repairs to be completed, they stayed at the boarding house where Anne and I were living. With surprising speed, Anne, Hillary and LuBette became friends, and the three somehow concocted a wild idea: Anne, our daughter and I should join LuBette's and Hillary's adventure-in-progress. Our contribution toward expenses was as attractive to them as the prospect of excitement was to us. With some wood and canvas, I constructed a collapsible tent on the Jeep's roof. There my wife, our baby and I slept during a memorable three-month trip to Santiago, Chile, via the Peruvian highlands, Bolivia and Argentina.

Hillary and LuBette later found corporate sponsors, permitting them to reach their original goal in Tierra del Fuego. By then, however, Anne and I were no longer with them. Our savings had run out, and we had taken a freighter back to the United States.

George Jones managed a finance company in San Francisco, and I went to work for him not long after returning from South America. He had set some money aside and was on the lookout for ways to invest it. Repeatedly he asked if I'd seen anything in South America that might be profitably sold in the United States. Over a period of time, I suggested a number of items. One by one, George decided against them, giving the impression that he enjoyed our hopeful conversations as an end in themselves. Whenever he got the chance, however, George asked for more ideas, and we amused ourselves while he dreamed of enterprise and I dreamed of adventure. Then, one fateful day, our conversations dramatically shifted gears.

"You know those horses I told you about, the Peruvian *Paso*s?" I said. "There should be a huge market for them."

"What makes them so special?" George asked, sitting up straight, sensing potential profit.

Before I'd finished, George knew as much about Peruvian *Paso*s as I did. To my astonishment, he set up a petty cash fund and gave me the go ahead to explore this latest idea. Gradually a concrete plan evolved, beginning with the importation of a single animal to serve as a sample. The next step would depend on how much interest our sample could stir up.

I was soon on my way to Peru, feeling a heavy burden of responsibility. If we were going to sell *Paso*s, people would have to be impressed by the horse I was about to buy, but I knew nothing about Peruvian horses. Fortunately, a breeder named Fernando Graña took me under his wing once I got to Peru.

Two months later, George Jones had his first look at *Malagueña and the breed she represented. Soon he was almost as vocal about Peruvian horses as I was. Our efforts led to further trips to Peru, and within a couple of years, the number of purebred Peruvian *Paso*s in the United States stood at over a hundred. To assist in the breed's promotion, George and I founded the American Association of Owners and Breeders of Peruvian Paso Horses. He served as its first president, and I as the second. By then, I was twenty-three, and it was the first time I'd done anything that didn't become boring, no matter how long I stayed at it.

My favorite among our promotions involved the importation of a mare named *Marinera, especially chosen to compete in cross-country endurance races. George and I sold *Marinera to an experienced endurance rider named Julie Suhr. I became obsessed with following their progress. The pair did well, but I suspected that other Peruvian *Paso*s might do even better.

Remembering those hundred-mile rides of my youth, I ached to get involved in endurance racing, but I weighed too much, and my weight consisted of height, not girth, meaning there was no hope of dieting it away. That train of thought triggered the idea of linking North and South America by horseback. The more I thought about it, the more the idea appealed to me. Here was a way to promote the Peruvian breed as well as live life to the fullest. Furthermore, if I played my cards right, the adventure could continue beyond the end of my journey. The best of my horses could be entered in California's grueling, hundred-mile Tevis Cup endurance race. [2]

"You need to see a doctor. Your imagination is out of control with *Paso*-promotion fever."

With those words George Jones greeted my brainchild. When I mentioned the idea to others, I found George's reaction comparatively optimistic. No matter! I swore that George and the rest of the doubting Thomases would eat their words.

My mind tended to dwell on the positives. I knew such a ride was achievable, remembering that A. F. Tschiffely had ridden two *Criollo* horses from Buenos Aires, Argentina, to Washington, D. C. in the early 1930's. Despite many changes since those days, I was positive that such a trip could still be made and that it would produce publicity. Tschiffely's ride had stirred up a great deal of media coverage for the Argentine *Criollo* horse. Could a similar trip do less for Peruvian *Paso*s?

"It's a lame idea, Albright. You're standing on your head and declaring the world upside down!"

Good old George. He certainly could coin a phrase! To tell the truth, I had doubts, too, but I drew on my experience to generate enough confidence to proceed. Those hundred-mile rides during my youth had taught me the ins and outs of long distance riding. If I could ride a hundred miles as a youngster, all I'd have to do, as an adult, was to string together the equivalent of seventy such trips.

I also took confidence from that Jeep trip with Hillary and LuBette. Getting a vehicle across several borders had taught me about dealing with Latin America's inevitable red tape. I'd also learned a fair bit about the terrain, the people, the food and the local customs. There wasn't much left to consider. The cause seemed noble. I was physically and emotionally capable of such a journey, and well-chosen Peruvian *Paso* horses certainly would be. There was nothing left but to do it. Two minor details immediately conspired to destroy my cherished plans: time and money!

Above all, I wanted to enter the 1967 Tevis Cup race, meaning that I needed to reach California at least two months beforehand to provide enough time for special conditioning and feeding. Even if I left immediately, that would give me no more than eight months. Seven thousand miles in eight months was out of the question.

But there were alternatives. Already I knew I'd have to ship my horses around the impassable jungle between Panama and Colombia. Why couldn't I also have them transported on other occasions? Deadheading [3] trucks would probably carry us for almost nothing, and train transportation was remarkably inexpensive in South America.

Even without the time limitations, the idea of riding all the way was unrealistic. George had made it obvious that he wouldn't contribute to this venture, and my savings wouldn't last a day beyond eight months. I'd have to provide only for the horses and myself – my wife and I having gone separate ways – but I had only two thousand dollars at my disposal.

There was no hope of preparing a budget. Even the Wall Street Journal didn't publish the current cost of such things as hay in Guatemala, grain in Panama, horseshoes in Costa Rica, dinner for one in the highlands of Ecuador and paperwork for horses to cross ten borders. All I knew was that some of my money would be spent for supplies before I left ... some would be used for airfare to Peru ... the bulk would go toward buying horses ... and expenses incurred along the way back to California would consume the rest.

Two good friends, Joe and Pat Gavitt, suggested that I end my ride at their ranch in Los Gatos, California. That was the logical place. Joe and Pat raised Peruvian horses, and Pat's size and experience made her an ideal "jockey" for whichever horse I entered in the Tevis Cup.

Beyond the purchase of supplies, my only preparation was to write Tuco Roca Rey, Secretary of Peru's national *Paso* horse breeders association. Besides alerting the Association of my impending arrival, I wanted to announce my intentions. I hoped Peru's breeders would be enthusiastic about my plans. After all, I would desperately need their support and assistance.

Peruvians being as they are, I knew I wouldn't get an answer to that letter, but I hoped that, under Lima's overcast skies, Tuco and his associates would soon be preparing for my arrival.

---

[1] Residents of Central and South America consider themselves to also be "Americans" and refer to people from the United States as "North Americans."

[2] An annual hundred-mile horse race between Lake Tahoe and Auburn, California.

[3] Trucks are said to "deadhead" when they make a return trip without a load.

CHAPTER 1

Pablito

"I guess it's time to say good-bye to the sun. I wonder how long it will be before I see it again."

The Peruvian schoolgirl next to me pressed her forehead against the window, trying to keep the bright, golden orb in view as long as she could. Her comment had come as our Boeing 707 jet began its descent into the thick cloudbank that hangs above Lima in August, and it was prophetic. I was not to see the sun nor feel its warmth for many days.

As we dropped beneath the dense layer of clouds, the arid, Peruvian coast gradually came into view below. I could see a farmer laboriously plowing a small, rocky field with a team of oxen. Then the plane passed over a cluster of oil derricks with plumes of flame burning off the natural gas.

Next we were parallel to a highway where ancient-looking cars made their way along the asphalt and burros were being ridden on the shoulder. The scene was close enough for me to make out that young boys rode the burros. The lads sat on their mounts' rumps behind large clay urns, one hanging on each side of every burro. From experience, I knew they were bringing water to houses that had no plumbing.

The schoolgirl was watching the same scene. She had spent most of our international flight excitedly telling me about her summer travels in my country. Now that our flight was almost over, she politely asked what brought me to Peru. Her dark brown eyes lit up with amazement when I told her.

"I wish I were a boy, so I could have an adventure like that!" she said wistfully.

That was almost exactly the response I had gotten from a fellow passenger on my connecting flight to Los Angeles. She had been an executive-type who was amazed at first, then quite enthusiastic.

"Sometimes I wish I were a man, so I could have an adventure like that," were her parting words.

Half an hour after landing in Lima, I had successfully navigated my way through immigration and customs. Having battled at least a half-dozen porters for the right to carry my three duffel bags – and therefore not hand out a tip – I emerged from the airport terminal building. A throng of people was crowded around the doorway congesting the sidewalk and street. Some waited for friends or family, but most were selling something. The calls of hucksters drowned out all other sound. There were shoeshine boys, youngsters offering to carry suitcases, taxi drivers, salesmen for Lima's finer hotels, tour guides and entrepreneurs of every stripe.

I knew better than to take one of the taxies parked there. They were the expensive tourist kind. Around the corner were the *colectivos*, a much-less-costly form of transportation. *Colectivos* were cars that carried up to five passengers on a predetermined route. For a standard fee, one could get off (or on) anywhere along the way.

When the driver discovered I could speak his language, he asked what brought me to Peru. Pleased with the opportunity to brush up on my rusty Spanish, I told him. In response, he dutifully went through the increasingly familiar stages of reaction, moving from disbelief to amazement to enthusiasm. Finally he declared: "If only I were young again, so I could have adventures like that." The other passengers all nodded in agreement.

Neither the executive-type lady nor the schoolgirl nor the cab driver nor his passengers had expressed the slightest doubt about my eventual success. Nor had anyone else to whom I'd spoken since leaving the States. *Latinos* consider it impolite to rain on another person's parade. It was unsettling to have people automatically assume success was the only possible outcome. Everyone seemed to underestimate the difficulties, and the implications troubled me. If I succeeded, would it be considered a small accomplishment? Should I fail, would it be seen as having disgracefully fallen short of an easy goal?

In the Miraflores district, I left the *colectivo* and hailed a cab. From there it wasn't a long drive to the offices of the National Association of Owners and Breeders of the Peruvian *Paso* Horse (*Asociación Nacional de Criadores y Propietarios del Caballo Peruano de Paso*), as the group's name translates into English. The *Asociación* was headquartered in a beautiful clubhouse complete with meeting rooms, offices, a bar, a dining room, a kitchen and a courtyard with an exquisite fountain at its center.

A short time later, I was shaking hands with more than two dozen of Peru's most prominent breeders. They had gathered for their customary Monday evening dinner, and I was immediately invited to join them. After dinner, Tuco Roca Rey pulled out my letter. He read it aloud, and everyone present proclaimed his willingness to be of help.

It amused me to see how carefully Tuco had filed my unanswered letter, covered with notes he had written to himself. Past experience had taught me I wouldn't receive a written response, but there was

13

little doubt that when I arrived, I'd be well received.

Whenever I was with the members of the *Asociación*, I felt as if I was leading a double life. For one thing, I was mingling with a social class far more wealthy than any I could have approached under normal circumstances, in Peru or the States. I think the barrier was broken by my obvious enthusiasm for their beloved Peruvian *Paso* horses.

Back when George Jones and I were preparing to import our sample, I had gotten the address of the *Asociación* from the Peruvian consul in San Francisco. I wrote and persistently followed up about six times before the Secretary finally responded. He answered none of my questions but politely invited me to visit them the next time I was in Lima. This I did, and I was warmly received. Thus began a relationship that left me feeling welcome to show up on the *Asociación* doorstep at any time.

Further evidence of my double life was that I went by an alias in Peru. Years earlier, during my first visit, the *Asociación* members had found my name difficult to pronounce. Their solution was to christen me with a new one. From then on, I became known as Pablito, the diminutive form of Pablo. Given my stature, there was typical Peruvian irony in giving me a nickname that would normally be bestowed upon a small boy.

Following dinner, everyone at the *Asociación* was anxious to offer advice. I had feared that these busy men might not be able to find time to aid me with my project. However, I soon found that my old friends were looking forward to seeing their breed participate in my overland trek to California.

The rest of the evening was devoted to eating, drinking and energetic discussions of my upcoming journey. By popular demand, I unpacked my gear and spread it out on the huge, oak conference table in the main meeting room. It was an exhibit that duly impressed my audience.

Carlos González, the Association's immediate past president, was the first to see my display. Like an excited schoolboy, the massive man, affectionately called *el gordo* (fatso), herded everyone into the meeting room to see and appreciate the wonders I had brought. For the rest of the evening, he made sure that no one – including late arrivals – missed my display.

Being horsemen, these gentlemen were especially impressed with such items as my Navajo saddle blankets, nylon halters and high-quality horse brushes. After declaring that my horse blankets would provide little protection from the torrential downpours in the highlands, one man was amused to see handsful of water run off because of the water-repellent coating.

Everyone, without exception, handled the Bowie knife, removing it from its sheath and marveling over its size and design. The bottles of water-purification tablets brought the expected remarks.

"You *gringos* have such weak stomachs," Carlos González teased with a delighted grin.

One of the other gentlemen had never before had a close look at Levi's blue jeans, and he exclaimed: "These pants are made of canvas!" Carlos Luna, a professor at the La Molina College of Agriculture, suggested that I should have brought feed bags for the horses. Fernando Graña was quite unhappy to see my western-style cowboy hat.

"This will never do," he said without a trace of amusement on his face. "If you're going to ride Peruvian horses, you should have a proper Peruvian *sombrero!*"

Otherwise, my gear was heartily approved by all, and an appointment was made to further discuss my needs at breakfast the following morning.

In those days, I stayed at boarding houses when in Peru. They were generally the most economical accommodations available. Meals were included, and tasty food was served at a community dining table, where the other residents, usually from distant places, had interesting tales to tell.

When the hour was late and the clubhouse nearly empty, I said good night to Tuco Roca Rey, intending to seek lodging at a nearby boarding house. Bone tired, I looked forward – at that late hour and after my long trip – to sleeping in a comfortable bed. Tuco, however, had a better idea. Perceptively sensing my need to economize, he took me aside, as the last members were leaving for home, and pointed to my sleeping bag.

"If you're going to sleep in that thing for eight months, Pablito," he said, "this is a good time for you to start conditioning your body. From now on, you can sleep right here on the meeting room floor."

Next he nodded in the direction of the kitchen.

"You can buy your food at the market and cook it in there."

Finally, he gestured toward the bathroom.

"And in there is a sink where you can wash yourself and your clothes."

After everyone had left, I unrolled my sleeping bag and dedicated myself to the task of "conditioning my body." To tell the truth, the tile floor seemed awfully hard, but I told myself it was probably as comfortable as most places I'd sleep during the coming eight months.

The next morning, when Fernando Graña, Tuco Roca Rey and Carlos González arrived for breakfast, we sat down for a meeting. I announced that I intended to make the trip with two mares I hoped to purchase at Casa Grande, an *hacienda* north of Lima.

My three advisors politely insisted that it would be difficult to find suitable mares because Peru's breeders used them mainly as incubators. Thus most mares – aside from the best (and most expensive) show prospects – were ridden infrequently and hadn't learned to tolerate hard work. On the other hand, I was informed, geldings had a centuries-old reputation for *resistencia*. It had always been Peru's geldings that were called upon to do the work. In fact, Peruvians seldom referred to castrated male horses as geldings, preferring to call them *caballos de trabajo* (work horses).

To my surprise, Casa Grande's horses were also considered unsuitable. Fernando Graña pointed out that these particular animals lived their entire lives at sea level in the broiling heat of the desert. There they became accustomed to working in sand, where the going was cushion-soft and level. Consequently, they were unaccustomed to horseshoes, cold, rain, altitude and steep climbs in rocky, uneven terrain. Considering the specific challenges posed by the terrain ahead of me, *don* Fernando suggested that the better choice would be geldings from Cajamarca, a city in the Andes at an altitude of 7,000 feet.

"Horses raised in Cajamarca have gigantic lungs, huge hearts, legs of iron and hooves of steel," Carlos González added with a few dramatic gestures to make sure I knew he was being theatrical.

Graña insisted that this reputation was well-deserved and suggested I consider a certain gelding belonging to a breeder named Juan Miguel Rossel.

"His name is Huascarán. He's gray, seven years old, tall, strong, completely sound, healthy and half-brother to Relicario, the horse Hugo Bustamante rides to fight bulls," Graña advised. "If I were buying a gelding, I would choose this horse based on his beauty alone."

"I doubt I could afford a horse like that," I said, ever the realist.

"Juan Miguel is a good friend of mine," Graña offered. "I'm almost positive I can negotiate a special price for you."

"In that case, let's give it a try," I said gratefully.

Fernando Graña was the quintessential man of action. He moved faster than any other Peruvian I've ever met, and he immediately picked up the phone and called Juan Miguel Rossel. During their conversation, he became so enthused that he negotiated a tentative deal for me to buy both Huascarán and his half-brother, Lucero, a black said to have extraordinary energy.

This was subject to my approval, of course, but Fernando had negotiated such a good deal that it would have been very difficult to say no. Once translated from Peruvian *soles* into dollars, the price appealed to me, especially considering that it included transportation from Cajamarca's remote mountain location to any destination of my choosing. Fernando recommended Jorge Baca's farm near the city of Chiclayo, which he thought would be a good starting point for the ride.

"If you're in a hurry to get started," Graña said, after he'd hung up the phone, "I can call back and have the horses shipped right away."

My first major decision was upon me, and I found it difficult. I had several times bought horses for clients who authorized me to make a selection for them in Peru while they stayed behind in the States. But I, myself, had never bought a horse sight unseen.

"If it turns out you don't approve of my choices," Graña reassured me, trying to make my decision easier, "I'm sure I can help you arrange a trade with one of the breeders in the Chiclayo area."

"What more could I want?" I said with a smile.

Immediately Fernando picked up the phone and closed the deal. Then Fernando, Carlos and Tuco hurried off to their respective businesses, leaving me alone and feeling emotionally drained. A whole lot had been accomplished, and the morning was still young!

CHAPTER 2

The Bullfighter

That evening, I sat in on a board meeting at the *Asociación*. After dealing with their agenda, the directors endorsed my ride by unanimous vote. Plans were made for providing me with letters of introduction to government officials and *Paso aficionados* along my route. There was discussion of setting up a ham radio network so my ride's progress could be followed. Lastly, we reviewed the red tape that had to be cut before I'd be able to leave Peru with Huascarán and Lucero. The directors volunteered to help me through that daunting maze of paperwork. To save time, photographs, bills of sale, veterinary certificates and other preliminary papers would be prepared in Cajamarca before my new horses left for Chiclayo. These documents would be rushed to me in Lima, and I'd immediately apply for my export permit. One of the directors was an exporter, and he had bad news. There had recently been a stiff increase in the taxes on all goods exported from Peru. These would add significantly to the cost of my paperwork.

The following day, I had lunch with Juan Miguel Rossel, the breeder of Huascarán and Lucero. A tall, dignified gentleman, he was in Lima to spend a few days at his city house. We spent a leisurely afternoon looking at photos of my new horses and their relatives. If I'd had to choose endurance horses from photos, I couldn't have done better. I was so completely pleased that I also bought a third horse. My newest was a bay named Inka (spelled with a k as a variation on the word Inca) who was half-brother to both Huascarán and Lucero, all three having been sired by a stallion named Genio.

According to the photos I saw, Huascarán was every bit as handsome as I'd been told. All three of my new horses looked exceptionally well-built. Their legs were straight and clean, free from blemishes, injuries or swelling. Their pasterns, the bones immediately above the hooves, were strong and well-angled. Their chests were broad, and their bodies were deep and round, with well-sprung ribs. There was lots of lung capacity, as one would expect with horses born, raised and worked at high altitude.

The photos teased rather than satisfied. I wouldn't know anything *for sure* until I saw my new horses in the flesh and tried them out. I itched to start working with them. Juan Miguel's schedule called for all three to be in Chiclayo within two days, but it would be a good deal longer than that before I finished my paperwork in Lima.

Every day for the next week, I walked over ten miles, going from the Ministry of this to the Ministry of that, trying to satisfy the requirements for an export permit. I came to regard those walks as the second phase of my conditioning program. First, the bed of nails (well, tiles actually), then the Lima Death March! Psychological conditioning was also under way. I was being prepared for an eight-month battle with Latin American bureaucracy. Everything was subject to delays, and endless details consumed my time. I was foiled in my every effort to get things done.

One of the most frustrating cultural challenges in Latin America revolves around different definitions for the word *mañana* (literally: tomorrow). *Mañana* means "the next day" to me. To Peruvians it seems to mean "a more convenient, indefinite, future time."

Most of us are apt to put a few things off, but in Peru, it's an art form. This has much to do with the way Peruvians order their priorities. They know how to enjoy life. The idea is not to keep the nose constantly to the grindstone. A good portion of that can wait until *mañana*, and ... well, there's always another *mañana* to follow.

One day, I called on a Ministry of Agriculture official to get his signature. He took the papers I brought and told me they'd be signed and ready to pick up at noon *mañana*. The following day at noon, I couldn't get past his secretary.

"This has been a very difficult day, and he wasn't able to sign your papers," she told me. "Please come back *mañana* at 11:00 A.M."

The next morning at 11:00 sharp, I was there.

"Could you please come back in an hour?" the secretary asked me, explaining, "The boss is out of the office right now."

I came back in an hour and found another secretary on duty. She told me that the boss had just left for the day.

"It's a shame you couldn't have been here an hour earlier," she said. "He could have seen you then."

When I explained that I had indeed been there exactly one hour earlier, she looked a little sheepish and told me to phone at 2:30. I phoned at 2:30.

"I'm sorry," I was informed, "but he won't be here until 4:00. You can pick up your papers then."

At 4:00 I was back at the office.

"You have the worst luck," the secretary said, "He's not here. Can you come back *mañana*?"

That did it! I decided to make *today* so unpleasant that nobody would want to run the risk of dealing with me again *mañana*. By the time I was finished, my startled listener knew everything there was to know about my opinion of people who waste my time. I must have been loud – but convincing – because suddenly the boss calmly walked out of his office and promised my papers in two hours. Two hours later, I had them. It was a small victory as I still needed signatures from over a dozen other officials, but it was a step in the right direction.

Instead of visiting a single office complex, I had to travel miles between Ministries spread all over the metropolitan area. The signatures had to be collected in a certain order, and thus I had to go back and forth, often calling on the same Ministry two or three times in a single day. For this privilege, I was charged a fee every time I turned around. I even had to get one paper stamped and signed by the Secretary of the Navy. They must have thought I was exporting seahorses!

L.P. Hartley, an English novelist, once wrote: "The past is a foreign country, they do things differently there." Since Peru was a foreign country living in the past, they did things *very* differently! While the rest of the world was promoting exports, Peru went its own way, merrily erecting roadblocks that discouraged them.

To make matters worse, people on the streets acted as if they'd never seen anyone six-feet, nine-inches tall. They probably hadn't, but that didn't make their reactions any more tolerable. It was not only youngsters who couldn't resist staring, laughing, jeering and honking whenever I left the protective confines of the *Asociación*.

My stay in Peru's capital was not without compensations, however. I found Lima fascinating. It was the focal point for the nation's politics, economy, industry, transportation, culture and communications. There are few cities as important to their nation as Lima is to Peru. Not counting the metropolitan area, the city had a population of two million, compared to fourteen million in the entire country. By comparison, that made Lima the equivalent of a single American city inhabited by one and a half times the population of California! It was where things happened, *if* they happened.

Some of my most enjoyable moments in Lima were spent with Tuco Roca Rey. He had an impish sense of humor, surprising in such a dignified man. The first time I saw this delightful quality, he was dialing a phone. In those days, Peru's telephone system was unimaginably antiquated. The most irritating inconvenience was the eternity that elapsed between picking up the receiver and getting a dial tone.

One day Tuco inadvertently dialed a wrong number. He realized his error before he finished and stared at the old, rotary-style phone with mock horror. Knowing he was now obliged to break the connection and wait again for the dial tone, he elegantly pantomimed the act of punishing his dialing finger with a ferocious bite.

An accomplished amateur bullfighter, Tuco had fought in the company of some of the greatest *toreros*. At lunch, he showed me photographs of himself, in traditional bullfight attire, dueling the brave bulls. Many times afterward, I was told he was talented enough to have been a professional, but his family wouldn't permit it

Tuco had an air of Spanish aristocracy, and there was an Old World elegance to everything he did. One day, as we were walking on a crowded downtown street, he suddenly stopped and fixed his gaze on something down the street. I looked up to see a crew of workmen on a scaffold, scraping paint from a building. Dust and flakes were cascading down on passers-by in the narrow street below, covering them with a thin white layer.

Tuco put two fingers to his lips and produced a loud whistle. The workmen looked down, saw him and immediately stopped working. We waited until the blizzard of debris had stopped and then walked past the scaffold. As soon as we had passed, the debris again rained down. Not a word had been spoken. The mere sight of Tuco had convinced the workmen to grant us a special favor not enjoyed by others.

One afternoon, following a sumptuous lunch, Tuco took me to the cockfights. One wave of his hand, and the man in the box office refused my money, insisting I was a guest of the establishment. Seating was on a first come, first served basis, and Tuco had made sure we arrived early enough to get me a seat right next to the pit. Once I was settled in, Tuco excused himself and went backstage to mingle with the owners, trainers and handlers of the day's star attractions.

As the grandstand filled, I was delighted to see several Peruvian *Paso* breeders among the spectators. It had been two years since I'd seen them, and the happy reunions were a pleasant prelude to the fights. Adding to the wonder of the moment was the strumming of guitars and the lyrical voices of two young men who serenaded a group of pretty *señoritas*. Magical moments like those were hard to come by in my homeland, and I looked back with gratitude on the day when I had decided to seek adventure in Peru.

At last, two cocks, one red and one white, were carried into the ring. Their handlers armed the birds by tying long, razor-sharp knives on their legs, next to the natural spurs. The sight of the deadly knives inhibited the little enthusiasm I had for what was about to happen. I had seen cockfights before and hadn't managed to develop an appetite for them. I didn't enjoy seeing such proud and beautiful birds tear at one another until one (or both) had died. Still, this sport was part of the culture in which I found myself immersed, and I was curious to know what made it so popular.

Understanding enhances appreciation, and I had the good fortune to wind up sitting next to someone who knew the sport well. Javier La Rosa was a *Paso* enthusiast I'd known for some years. I joined him, moving back a few rows from my original seat, and we mutually enjoyed our ensuing conversation. Mostly we discussed my ride, but when the fights began, it was as if I wasn't there. My attempts to encourage further conversation went unheard, or at least unheeded.

"You don't seem to enjoy cockfights," Javier commented during the first intermission.

"All I see is a flurry of feathers," I answered. "I don't understand what everyone finds so interesting."

"Well," Javier responded, "you have to put yourself in the place of the cocks. Watch the way the opponent moves. Consider how you can defend yourself and how you can attack. Pretty soon, you should begin to see everything that happens. With time, you may even get a feel for what will happen next."

The next two feathered gladiators were, once again, a red and a white. A short while into their contest, the white rooster gave a startled jump, and the crowd (excluding myself) simultaneously jumped as well. Javier turned to me and tapped his finger against his ribs.

"The red one just got the white one, right here!" he exclaimed.

I hadn't seen anything, and to tell the truth, I doubted that Javier's senses were that much keener than mine. Everything had happened very fast. How could anyone have followed the details? Then I gave a startled jump myself. The white rooster had collapsed, and I could see blood staining its feathers exactly where Javier had indicated. So much for my doubts! I resolved to pay closer attention to the next fight.

But the next fight was about to be postponed, and a spellbinding drama was ready to unfold. While his opponent strutted about, crowing and prematurely declaring victory, the white rooster was gathering his strength for one last effort. Suddenly, the apparent loser jumped to his feet and inflicted a cavernous cut in his adversary's chest before collapsing again. Blood draining from his wound, the red cock slowly joined his fallen opponent, sitting on the sand. Both fighters were down, but neither had lost, for neither was dead.

The signal that a fighting cock has died is when its head drops and the beak enters the arena's sandy floor. Before the eyes of frenzied spectators, two beaks were slowly descending as both lives slipped away. There was bedlam as each spectator encouraged his favorite to stay alive a little longer. Then the white cock's beak came to rest in the sand, followed, a split second later, by the winner's beak. There was a resounding cheer after which wagered money changed hands. I thanked Javier for his coaching and resolved to be more attentive during the next fight.

"Don't expect anything like that again," Javier smiled. "*That* was one of the best fights I have ever seen."

During the following week, word of my ride got around, and the media took an interest. *The Peruvian Times*, an English-language magazine, asked me to write a series of articles and send them in from various points en route. Also, Lima's newspapers got wind of my plans, and reporters called on me at the *Asociación* almost every day.

On Tuesday afternoon, a newspaper photographer came, asking if he could take some shots of me with a horse. We went across the street to the *Club Hípico*, in search of a *Paso* horse with which I could pose. Hugo Bustamante, the famed Peruvian bullfighter, was there. I had often heard of him because he fought from horseback and used *Paso* horses. Graciously, he offered me the use of one of his stallions. After the photo session, I was introduced to Relicario, Bustamante's best bullfighting horse and half-brother to my three geldings. I was thrilled to be offered the chance to ride such a magnificent horse and have seldom been as thoroughly impressed. Relicario could outmaneuver anything I'd ever ridden.

As I rode in a circle around him, Hugo played the role of the bull and made numerous charges. The horse reacted immediately with no guidance whatsoever from me. I could see how he'd survived his many encounters with deadly fighting bulls.

Hugo Bustamante was much younger than I had expected, and he turned out to be a simple and relaxed man whose company was tremendously enjoyable. He let me, a stranger, ride every one of his famous bullfighting horses and spent the rest of the afternoon talking with me about my ride. As we parted company that evening, he invited me to be his guest at an amateur bullfight the following day.

The next morning, I was delighted when Hugo invited me to ride in the same truck that would carry him and his horses to the bullfight arena. The day's event was being held to raise money for various police and military charities. Unfortunately, Hugo was not scheduled to fight a bull, but he was participating in a pre-fight exhibition of Peruvian *Paso* horses.

The Peruvian Army – grateful for Hugo's free appearance – had promised to send a truck for his horses. Due at 11:00, the truck had still not arrived at 12:30. When it finally came, it turned out to be a troop carrier, completely unsuitable for horses because it had a low canopy over the bed and benches permanently attached to the floor around the perimeter of the cargo area.

"Those look like leg-breakers to me," Hugo muttered, looking at the knee-high benches.

Rather than risk injury to the horses, Hugo enlisted another fellow and me to help him ride his three horses all the way across Lima to the *Plaza de Toros*.

I knew adventure would be easy to find in Peru, I happily told myself.

The crosstown ride was great fun, for a while. In Lima's outskirts, we rode on park-like median strips that divided the spacious avenues. Surrounded by beautiful trees and with lush grass beneath, we casually talked and laughed. But as we neared the downtown area, we were obliged to focus our attention on our surroundings. The median strip was gone. The roadway was becoming ever-narrower and the buildings ever-taller. Deafening noise reverberated harshly through the narrow, canyon-like streets.

Vehicles contributed most of the racket since functioning mufflers were a rarity. The rules of the road seemed to demand constant honking. The whistles of policemen, directing traffic, tried to create order from the chaos, but, instead, they added to it.

Peru's laws encourage drivers to be aggressive. Cars are granted legal right-of-way over anyone who might gather enough courage to venture into the street. Drivers won't come on the sidewalk to chase a pedestrian, but they consider anyone between the curbs to be fair game. Leniency was not extended to horses, either.

All in all, not the easiest of circumstances for riding an unfamiliar horse, I thought to myself.

I really liked the three-and-a-half-year-old, green broke, bay stallion I was riding. He was strong, energetic and sensible. Despite the competition for his attention, his ears were always cocked in my direction, and his constant priority was to please me. There were times when the noise was so loud that I couldn't hear myself when I'd cluck to him. But he always heard, and his ready responses got us out of more than one tight spot.

Hugo rode Relicario, and the third rider was aboard a gelding that had recently been brought from Cajamarca. It took us only forty minutes to negotiate five miles of city streets and arrive at the Plaza de Acho, oldest bullring in the western hemisphere.

"I have another rider available," Hugo said, looking at me, "but if you wish to ride in the exhibition with us, you're welcome."

"I appreciate the offer, but I'd rather watch. Afterward, I can ride one of the horses back to the *Club Hípico*, if you want," I responded, turning the little bay stallion over to Hugo's waiting rider and heading for the grandstand.

At that hour of the afternoon, the sun's rays slant out of the sky and over the stadium walls at a sharp angle. The most-expensive seats in the circular stadium are in the shade. The least-expensive are exposed to the afternoon sun. That particular afternoon, though, it was impossible to tell which were the better seats. Thanks to typical August weather, all spectators, rich and poor, enjoyed shade under overcast skies.

The only event that starts on time in Peru is a bullfight. If the opening ceremony is late, the crowd will vent its frustration by whistling, stomping and finally throwing objects into the arena. Apparently there's no leniency for charity events because the spectators were heaving seat cushions into the arena by the time the show finally started.

Prior to the actual bullfight, the police presented a series of special exhibitions. The crowd's enjoyment, however, was expressed with laughter, which was not what had been intended.

First came the trained police dogs. It took the bloodhound ten minutes to track down the "fugitive," who was only fifty feet away and half-exposed from his hiding place. Next, the German shepherd attack dog couldn't be made to let go of the "criminal," and the two had to leave the arena still attached to one another. The dog's two hapless trainers carried the animal, carefully coordinating their progress with that of the man whose padded arm was clenched between vice-like jaws. The spectators launched a second barrage of seat cushions into the arena. Considering that the seats were concrete, it seemed a poor method of protest, but the crowd couldn't resist showing its displeasure with the tedious pre-fight display.

Next there was an act featuring police motorcycles ridden in intricate formations, until the leader fell off his bike. By that time, respect for law and order was rapidly disintegrating, and the crowd was howling with laughter. Then the mood turned more respectful in anticipation of the equine performances, of which there would be two. The first would be the mounted police drill team on trotting horses, and the second was to feature a drill by the *Paso*s. What the crowd didn't know was that a not-altogether-friendly rivalry had broken out while the two drill teams were offstage in the warm-up arena. One thing led to another, and ultimately, one of the troopers called the *Paso*s "silly and insignificant." A challenge was issued (and accepted) as to whether the trotters or the *Paso*s would receive more applause that afternoon.

Composed of soon-to-graduate cadets, the police drill team entered the arena, carrying the weight of a dual responsibility. They were determined to rescue police dignity after the fiascoes that had preceded them. In addition – thanks to one of their brash members – they needed to outperform the *Paso*s, which would enter the arena next.

The competition for crowd approval began with the cadets tense and their horses behaving badly. The drill formation was constantly disrupted as one horse and another had an attack of nerves. One trooper was unceremoniously thrown. On foot, he tried but had no chance to catch his frantic mount. The errant equine blindly dashed about, disrupting the drill team's routine. Two of the fallen trooper's comrades left the formation to fetch the free-lancing equine, but they accomplished nothing.

Ever the showman, Hugo Bustamante suddenly appeared in the arena, unsummoned, and flawlessly guided Relicario into position for a spectacular capture of the wandering trotter. As the first of the afternoon to accomplish what he'd set out to do, he received a thunderous ovation. Hugo prolonged his moment in the sun by side-passing Relicario around the circumference of the arena in such a way that he faced the crowd at all times. The reins had been dropped on Relicario's neck, and Hugo was guiding the gray stallion with only his legs. With one hand, he led the riderless trotter, and with the other, he held his *sombrero* high above his head.

Discouraged, the mounted police left the arena in disarray, probably thinking unkind thoughts about whomever had insulted the *Paso*s and provoked Hugo's little revenge. The Peruvian *Paso*s entered the arena as the last trotter left, and they were the sensation of the opening ceremony. In fact, they brought the house down. Even the bullfights that followed didn't excite the crowd as much.

Later that evening, we rode Hugo's horses back to the *Club Hípico*. When I noticed that the two stallions were showing the effects of a long, hard day while the gelding was still fresh and alert, I hoped it was a good omen for *my* three geldings.

As pleasant as these diversions were, I wasn't able to completely enjoy myself. Always, I was painfully aware that my limited time was on the wing. After having been in Lima nearly two weeks, I still didn't have my export permit, and the end of the paperwork was nowhere in sight. It was time for a change of strategy.

I decided to depart for Chiclayo immediately. My paperwork was far enough along to proceed without me. It would take longer without my shepherding, but I hoped to gain more time than I lost by having my horses ready to go when their export permit was finally issued. When I presented this idea to the directors of the *Asociación*, they agreed it was for the best. Tuco kindly offered to see my papers through to completion and to send them to me in Chiclayo.

My last afternoon in Lima was spent in the company of Hugo Bustamante and his lovely wife. They took me to lunch at a charming restaurant and afterward invited me to their home where Hugo showed me movies of his most recent bullfights. Having grown to like Hugo very much, I found myself wishing I could somehow prolong the day, but like all good things, it had to end. Hugo and I finished our last day together with an exchange of good-byes and mutual wishes of good luck in front of the *Asociación*.

I hailed a taxi. The night was humid, and I broke into a sweat as I quickly loaded my baggage into the trunk and back seat. Augmented by acquisitions made in Lima, such as a saddle, my baggage had become more than I could carry in a single load. Until I had a packhorse, it would be cumbersome to deal with.

On our way to the bus station, the cab driver didn't offer conversation, and neither did I. Torn between conflicting moods, I was leaving good times with good friends in familiar and comfortable surroundings. Ahead were uncertainties, hardships, unfamiliar faces, hostile terrain and the possibility of failure. It was exciting to be on my way, yet I was sorry to be leaving. However, I wasn't gone quite yet, and by the time my bus finally departed, I no longer had even the slightest regret about bidding Lima good-bye.

The taxi deposited my mountain of baggage and me on the curb in front of the bus station. There, less than an hour before the scheduled departure of the bus to Chiclayo, I found the front door locked, the lights turned off and no buses in sight. I waited on the sidewalk, figuring someone would soon open up. Suddenly, I was afflicted with a raging thirst, which sorely tempted me to visit a soda fountain down the block. But I stood fast, fearing that if I stepped out of sight, my baggage would disappear on the backs of street urchins who loitered nearby.

My height brought forth the usual number of unoriginal comments, and I slid into a dark mood that intensified as time continued to pass and the bus station remained closed. After forty long minutes, a clerk from a nearby bus depot approached me.

"Did you know tonight's bus is cancelled?" he asked, pointing to the locked door behind me. "They won't have another for twenty-four hours."

"That's impossible!" I told him, pulling my ticket from my pocket. "I just bought this ticket a few hours ago."

"Nonetheless," the clerk replied, "my company has tonight's only bus for Chiclayo, and it's getting ready to leave. If you're interested, we have a seat available."

Of course, the newly offered seat was more expensive than the one I'd already bought, but as a special favor, the clerk offered to accept his competitor's ticket as a partial payment.

"You must hurry, *señor*," the clerk warned. "Our bus will be leaving very soon."

Having delivered his sales pitch, the clerk jogged back to the tiny depot from which he'd come. With no time to lose, I made three trips back and forth, moving my baggage. I was frantic with fear that someone would steal something from one of the bus stations while I was at the other.

Once my bags were safely inside the second depot, I was overcharged for my ticket and then charged an exorbitant excess baggage fee. The clerk could see I wasn't happy about all the money I had to shell out, and he tried to appease me with the breathless delivery of good news.

"I have saved seat 1-A just for you, *señor*, right next to a pretty nurse."

I scrambled aboard the bus, just as it was leaving, and promptly discovered I had just paid a premium price for the last ticket on a half-empty bus. Too tired to care, I dropped into seat 1-A. As promised, it was right next to a nurse, and she was pretty, especially considering that she was at least sixty years old!

"I wish I had been born a man so I could have wonderful adventures such as yours," were the last words I heard from her before I fell asleep.

Their work done ... mine just beginning (see page 66).

CHAPTER 3

Three To Get Ready

The next morning, I woke up twelve hours north of Lima. I'd slept fitfully, for 1-A was located in the first row of seats directly behind the windshield. Throughout the long night, the glare of oncoming headlights had repeatedly pierced my eyelids, bringing me back from my dreams to a hard, uncomfortable seat. After dawn, my further efforts to sleep were fruitless. I struck up a conversation with the driver. When he heard what I was doing in his country, he had a predictable reaction.

"I wish I were single again, so I could do what you're doing."

As we neared Chiclayo, I asked the driver if he could possibly drop me off at Jorge Baca's farm, known as *La Quinta*, located in Reque, a village just south of the city. That small favor, I explained, would save me the trouble of traveling all the way into town and then having to backtrack.

The driver wasn't familiar with *Señor* Baca's farm but said he'd be happy to let me off in Reque. A short while later, he steered the big bus over to the side of the highway, stopped and opened the door. He got out and motioned for me to follow. We were in a small, rural settlement that appeared to have a population only slightly larger than that of the bus we had just exited.

"This is Reque," the driver announced. "Anyone here should be able to direct you to La Quinta."

He pulled my belongings from the baggage compartment, wished me good luck and drove away. I looked around and noted the differences between this world and the one left behind in Lima. The sky was clear and blue, giving me my first look at the sun since that young Peruvian schoolgirl bade it farewell high above Lima. The surrounding countryside was green with agriculture, a pleasant change from the monotonous gray desert that encircles Lima. Most of the people in sight were Indians, who seemed as amazed by my height as anyone else, but who chose to be respectfully silent about it.

Stashing my two hundred pounds of gear behind some roadside brush, I set out in search of Jorge Baca's farm. With a few mumbled words and a profusion of hand gestures, an old Indian woman directed me to La Quinta, which was half a mile down the highway. Had I known that earlier, I could have disembarked right at the entrance.

Three times I made my way to the front gate of the Baca homestead, carrying portions of my bulky baggage and being harried by numerous stray, half-wild dogs. During the next several days, I would see many coyotes as I rode in the surrounding countryside, but none looked half as wild as the local curs.

After watching me stockpile my possessions at La Quinta's entrance, one of the farmhands approached to ask my purpose. I explained. Uncertain as to how he should handle the situation, the man politely asked me to wait while he went for instructions. Quite some time later he returned with a wheelbarrow and helped me load my baggage into it. He accompanied me to the house, where *Señora* Baca waited on the porch. She seemed uncertain as to who I was and why I was there. The puzzled look on *Señora* Baca's face was unchanged after I had explained, but she invited me inside for a breakfast of rice and fried eggs. While I ate, she sent a farm hand in search of her husband, at work in the fields since before dawn.

I had met Jorge Baca two years earlier at a horse show in Lima. He'd been on holiday, enjoying himself so much that I didn't expect to find him as serious and hardworking as he was at his farm. He was friendly as ever when he finally arrived at the house that morning.

"Pablito!" was Jorge's loud, enthusiastic greeting as he came toward me with arms outstretched in anticipation of the backslapping embrace with which Latin American men greet each other. "How good it is to see you again. What brings you to La Quinta?"

Surprised by this question, I paused to gather my thoughts.

"Didn't the *Asociación* notify you I was coming?" I asked.

"No," he replied, "I haven't heard from them for months."

"What about the horses?" I asked, panic tugging at my sleeve. "Were three geldings from Juan Miguel Rossel delivered here last week?"

"Yes, but I have no idea why they're here and have been waiting for someone to tell me."

At a loss for words, I stammered and stumbled through a short explanation of the situation. Like everyone else, Jorge was amazed and enthusiastic, but he stopped short of saying that he wished he could have such an adventure himself. More important matters required his attention.

"I have some things to do at the milking barn, Pablito," he said, politely excusing himself. "Please make yourself at home and feel free to use any of the facilities. You and your horses are welcome to stay at La Quinta for as long as you like."

Almost as an afterthought, Jorge pointed out the stables where my horses were housed, and then he turned to go. The rest of the day was mine, and I intended to use it for acquainting myself with my future traveling companions.

There were ten stalls, side-by-side. Though the surrounding desert was already growing hot, the stable area was cool and shady, thanks to a number of gigantic, leafy trees that grew in an orderly row in front of the stalls. I walked up to the first stall, opened the door and looked inside. It was empty. The stalls had eight-foot-high walls, made of adobe brick. These had no openings, except for the doors. Thus the occupants were hidden, and I'd have to keep opening doors until I found my horses. I started for the second stall. Not far away stood row housing for the workers. Several children were standing in doorways, watching me.

"Are you looking for the horses that arrived last week?"

The speaker was a boy, about ten years old and bolder than the rest.

"Yes," I answered. "Do you know where they are?"

"In there," he said, pointing to the fifth stall.

"Thank you," I said with a smile. "What's your name?"

"Pablo," he answered.

"Then we have the same name, but my friends always call me Pablito."

Pablo looked me up and down, probably wondering how the diminutive could possible apply to *me*. Chuckling, I opened the door he had indicated and found all three of my horses inside.

"Do you know why they're all together like this?" I asked when Pablo came closer.

"They went crazy when they were separated," the boy explained, relishing the chance to be of service. "We couldn't sleep because they were calling to each other. My father put them together to keep them quiet."

"I'm sorry you were disturbed."

As soon as possible, I intended to put my horses in separate stalls, for safety's sake and to better appraise their eating habits. But I'd do that in the early morning, when the resulting ruckus would be drowned out by La Quinta's generators and other heavy machinery. By bedtime, hopefully, the horses would be adjusted and calm.

It wasn't possible to see much while my three geldings were huddled together in the stall's corner. To get a good look, I'd have to catch them and lead them outside, one-by-one. Unable to further delay the gratification of my curiosity, I started with the one I most wanted to see. Huascarán was named after the highest peak in the Peruvian Andes, named in turn after an Inca emperor's brother. It was a fitting name. The tall, handsome gray was a mountain of a horse with a regal bearing. Having been reserved for his previous owner's exclusive (and infrequent) use, Huascarán was not in particularly good condition. However, his flesh was hard as a rock, even without work. He did everything with energy and struck me as the kind of horse that loves to get out on the trail and go. When I briefly longed him in a large circle around me, I found his gait to be exceptional in its speed and grace. By the end of the day, he became my favorite.

Lucero, dull black in color, was the smallest. Instantly my eyes were drawn to his most commanding feature, his incredibly ugly head. Lucero's name had come from the white marking which ran down the ridge at the center of his face. Beneath that marking, he had the bulging, convex profile of a sheep, an unattractive conformation known in the States as a "Roman Nose." As I later discovered, a "sheep's head," as it's known in Spanish, is thought by Peruvians to indicate strong Barb ancestry and, therefore, great endurance. Probably because of his homely appearance, I greatly underestimated Lucero at first. With time, though, I came to appreciate his virtues. This was especially true when I rode him in rugged terrain, which he could negotiate more speedily than either of his half-brothers.

The Peruvians had taught me to evaluate a horse first from the ground up and then from the hindquarter forward. This directs the attention first toward the parts that contribute most to a horse's performance. With both Lucero and Inka, I did things backwards. I started with the head and received a shock that distracted me from going much farther, at least on that first day!

As soon as I had led the quiet, bay-colored Inka from the stall, I noticed his left eye was discolored. I quickly passed my hand back and forth in front of the eye and got no reaction. Further tests immediately confirmed that he had no vision in that eye. He was half-blind, hardly a small matter! Because their eyes are positioned farther apart and closer to the side of the head than a human's, the loss of an eye can make a horse dangerous. On top of that, I'd be selling all three horses after our arrival in the States, and half-blind horses aren't high on most people's wish list.

"I'll see you later," I said to Pablo after returning Inka to the stall.

"Aren't you going to ride the horses?" he asked, disappointed.

"Tomorrow," I answered.

Today I had to figure out what to do about a certain half-blind horse. Already I was getting over my surprise and growing angry. Why hadn't I been told about Inka's defect before I bought him?

"I'm sure Juan Miguel didn't know," Fernando Graña affirmed when I spoke with him by telephone. "No doubt he will insist on adjusting the price."

"That still leaves me with a problem," I declared thoughtlessly.

As soon as the words were out of my mouth, I regretted them. I'd managed to sound as if I didn't appreciate Fernando's assistance and considered him obligated to solve my problem.

"If you want my advice," Fernando continued, graciously over-looking my unintended rudeness, "I think you should try the horse for a few days and keep him if you find him satisfactory."

I said nothing while considering Fernando's counsel.

"I speak from experience," he continued. "I once had a one-eyed polo pony that was one of my best ever."

I thanked Fernando for his kindness and patience.

"Later, if you want," he offered, ever-helpful, "I can try to arrange a trade with one of the breeders around Chiclayo."

When he came in from work and joined me for lunch, I unbur-dened myself to Jorge Baca. His advice was straightforward and simple: "If you can find anyone who wants him, you should trade." Four days later, Jorge Baca changed that advice, but first he told me the tale of a hazardous trip he'd once made in the Andes. He had prepared two horses, but at the last minute, one took sick. A friend wanted to loan him a replacement, but Jorge declined because the animal had sight in only one eye. He didn't relish the idea of tack-ling such treacherous terrain on a handicapped mount.

The friend forced the issue, and Jorge reluctantly took the horse with him. In a surprising turn of events, he wound up riding the half-blind horse – by preference – and leading his own perfectly good animal for most of the trip. Jorge's tone revealed that he had been observing Inka and liked the horse as much as I did.

Being half-blind, Inka had compensated by developing his other senses to an exceptional degree. A number of times, I tried to sneak up on his blind side, but he never failed to detect me there. He watched the trail like a hawk and, in general, performed better than most horses with normal vision. Despite his impaired eyesight, he was as sure-footed as any of my three geldings. I was never able to make him stumble, slip or walk too close to anything. After four days at La Quinta, I ceased considering a trade. I was equally pleased with my other two horses.

Judging by outward appearances, it wasn't terribly obvious that my new horses were brothers. Beneath the surface, though, they were very much alike. All three had similar personalities and preferred the same feeds. Mysteriously, they even spooked at the same things.

On my second day at La Quinta, I took Inka, Lucero and Huascarán – one-by-one – for test rides. None seemed concerned by the many unusual things we encountered. Along came twenty burros, almost invisible beneath mountainous burdens of freshly cut alfalfa. Not one of my horses batted an eye. We passed mules stacked high with firewood. No notice taken. Next more burros, this time loaded with sugar cane so long that it noisily dragged the ground behind them. Boring. We passed creaking, groaning, ox-drawn wagons. Yawn.

Then a peculiar thing happened. Inka spotted a wagon parked next to the trail and decided his life depended on turning around and heading in the other direction. Under duress, he finally sidled past, and I forgot all about the incident until three hours later, when Huascarán reacted exactly the same way. Nothing had bothered him until we reached that wagon. Then all hell broke loose! This phenomenon repeated itself on cue with Lucero, three hours later. The next day it was a water pump sitting quietly by the side of the trail, after we'd passed other pumps that had been noisily operating. Every now and then, there was something that had the same unsettling effect on all three. It was like a paranormal phenomenon designed to puzzle and amuse me.

My first real challenge was getting the horses to eat grain. Peru's working horses weren't accustomed to such luxuries. Grain was too costly to be used as animal feed. Furthermore, there was a long-standing Peruvian notion that pampering would spoil working animals. For my purposes, however, I deemed grain absolutely necessary. It contains nutrients not found in hay, and its vitamins and minerals come in a more concentrated form. My horses would have to eat grain, especially if they were to arrive in Los Gatos ready for the rigors of the Tevis Cup. Nonetheless, they refused to try it.

At that point, Jorge Baca became the second to suggest that I should have feed bags. He pointed out that these would be useful along the trail and assured me they were the best way to introduce horses to a new feed. The technique, he explained, was to leave them on for a few hours at a time, waiting for the wearer to eventually try the contents.

With my own two hands and some canvas, I stitched together three functional – if not beautiful – feed bags. Each was essentially a canvas sack with a headband. Occupied by a ration of grain, the bags were placed on the horses' heads by virtue of a strap that passed behind the ears, offering each a clean meal that his companions couldn't steal.

First, I tried whole barley, the only grain besides corn that was readily available. It was the first time I'd seen barley that hadn't been crushed or rolled. The kernels looked much the same as oats, but there was a big difference. Barley was hard as rock and equally indigestible. As a result, the horses would scarcely try it. When they did, the kernels emerged in their manure without noticeable alteration. I responded by soaking each day's ration in water and then crushing the kernels to make them more easily eaten and digested. Initially I did the crushing between common stones, but a better method was brought to my attention.

At most of Peru's highly picturesque farms, one will find museum-quality artifacts being used as decorations. At La Quinta, I was shown an oversized, corn-grinding mortar and pestle manufactured by Indians, probably before the arrival of the Spanish. At Jorge Baca's suggestion, I tried it on my barley. It worked wonderfully.

However, crushed barley didn't prove as popular as I'd hoped. At that point, I was in unexplored territory, never before having been around horses that didn't consider grain to be a special treat. I next tried corn. There were two varieties: white and yellow. The white was softer and didn't require crushing, but according to Jorge Baca, it wasn't as nutritious. I fed a mixture in the hope my horses would grow accustomed to eating both, since one or the other would be available throughout Latin America.

White, yellow or mixed, it didn't matter. Corn proved no more appetizing than barley, even when I added sugar for flavor. Finally, I was able to purchase oats, which would have been my first choice if I had been able to find them sooner. The oats were of poor quality and the horses ate them sparingly, but for the first time they displayed some interest in learning to eat from their feed bags. This isn't as simple as it might seem. The wearer must figure out how to get at the grain hanging inches below his muzzle. It took a while for my geldings to discover that their heads had to be lowered until the bottoms of the bags rested on the ground.

Once motivated by feed bags full of something they craved, the three horses quickly mastered this new dining technique.

Unfortunately, that wasn't the only thing Huascarán mastered. He soon learned to remove his feed bag without my help, thereby frustrating my efforts to make him try corn. His preference was oats, period. That worried me because oats might not be available where we were going.

The grain I was able to buy in Chiclayo had been threshed the old-fashioned way. Kernels were separated from stalks by the hooves of oxen or by being bashed with stones. Either process left behind such foreign objects as sand, bits of stone, dead insects, and pieces of manure. Due no doubt to the German part of my heritage, I felt obligated to pick out the unwanted material. It was time-consuming but, I told myself, preferable to colic.

While watching my efforts to nourish my ungrateful beasts, young Pablo advised me to try feeding them the long, yellow seed-pods from the *algarrobo* tree. Many Peruvians feed these to their livestock, he explained, and the pods are readily eaten because of their sweet taste.

Later that afternoon, I located some *algarrobo* trees and filled a sack with dried pods that had fallen on the ground. Lucero and Inka both loved the *algarrobo*, but Huascarán steadfastly refused to try it. It was the first such difference of opinion. Until then, if one had enjoyed or refused to eat a particular food, the other two would follow suit. I preferred it that way. The greater their agreement on such matters, the easier life would be on the long trail ahead.

Before dawn the following Sunday, I was jarred awake by men stampeding past the house. Loud voices communicated tremendous urgency, but the words flowed too quickly for me to understand. I pulled on my trousers and boots before stepping outside. No one was in sight, but frantic voices came from the corrals near the milking barn. I hurried in that direction, stumbling repeatedly in the pitch-blackness.

The milking yard was filled with chaotic activity. Lanterns, carried by farm hands rushing back and forth among the cows, cast a flickering light. When my eyes adjusted, I saw that several of La Quinta's Holstein-Friesian cows were grotesquely bloated. The stricken cows were groaning, loudly and repeatedly. Pairs of workers were prying bovine mouths open and pouring medicine down unwilling throats. Other men worked in larger groups, trying to keep the most seriously afflicted cows on their feet and moving. I had no idea what was happening, but I knew that horses must be kept walking during attacks of colic, and it seemed obvious that the same must be true of bloated cattle.

One cow suddenly dropped to her knees, her breathing labored and loud. No amount of tugging on her halter and beating her with sticks could get her back on her feet. Her eyes soon glazed over, and she rolled onto her side. Blood trickled from her mouth and nostrils. I heard someone say that nothing could be done to save her. Another cow dropped with a thud. After vaulting the fence, I was at her side before she could roll over. I grabbed her ears. Someone else grabbed her tail. A third man prodded her with a stick. Together, the three of us performed the miracle of getting her back on her feet and keeping her walking until the veterinarian arrived.

The vet glanced around and came our way at a run. He carried an instrument made especially for such emergencies. It was essentially an oversized ice pick with a detachable metal sheath surrounding the blade, except for the tip. With a single thrust of this device, he punctured our cow's side and stomach. When he withdrew the ice pick, a rush of air hissed out through the metal tube left behind to prevent the wound from clogging. Immediately the excruciating internal pressure was relieved.

The vet removed another sheath from his pocket and slid the ice pick into it. He then moved on, performing the same operation on other cows. Almost as suddenly as it had started, the crisis ended. One cow was dead, and several had holes in their sides. I still had no idea what I had just witnessed.

At breakfast, *Señor* Baca explained. His cows ate freshly cut, green alfalfa every morning. They normally received this in conjunction with dried rice straw, which prevents the alfalfa from fermenting and causing bloat. With no rice straw available that particular morning, one of the farm hands had fed only alfalfa, with the consequences we had just witnessed.

Freshly cut alfalfa was also the staple of my horses' diet, and I resolved to supplement it with small portions of rice straw. There was no reason to believe that Huascarán, Lucero and Inka would suffer bloat since it's the cow's multiple system of stomachs that permits feeds to ferment and gases to collect. Nonetheless, freshly cut alfalfa was a significant change from my horses' previous diet and had provoked mild diarrhea. Rice straw would help prevent both the diarrhea and the dehydration that follows.

CHAPTER 4

Four to Get Ready Again

"Have you ever heard the expression: 'In Peru, the medicine arrives after the patient has been buried?'" Jorge Baca asked me at breakfast, two mornings later.

Having had my fill of Peruvian inefficiency, I laughed, not entirely in good humor.

"Has something happened?" I asked.

"I'm afraid there's bad news from Lima," he said somberly.

"What now?"

"I received a phone call this morning from the *Asociación*," Jorge continued. "There are problems with your export permit. Your horses have to be inoculated again for glanders, sleeping sickness and one other disease ... I don't remember which, but I wrote it down for you."

"They already had those shots, in Cajamarca, just before they came to Chiclayo," I said. "I gave the Ministry of Agriculture in Lima a certificate to prove it."

"Nonetheless," Jorge insisted gently, "you must now have the shots administered by the government veterinarian from Chiclayo, get a certificate from him and send it to the Ministry in Lima."

"Well, it's stupid, but it's not a big deal," I said. "I'll take care of it today."

Then Jorge dropped a bomb.

"All the paperwork you completed in Lima will have to be reprocessed. You have to do everything again, inoculations, photographs, applications, all of it. It will be at least two more weeks before your export permits are ready."

"Two more weeks! I can't believe it! All that work for nothing? Why?"

I was outraged, but what could I do other than channel my anger toward once again cutting every strand of red tape I'd already dealt with during those frustrating days in Lima? Spirits somewhat dampened, I turned to the task at hand. It was frustrating, almost beyond my capacity to endure, especially since no one could explain what had gone wrong. I would have gone mad, had it not been for my long, quiet rides in the Chiclayo countryside.

It was during those relaxing excursions that I discovered my horses to be closer in quality than I had first thought. It wasn't that I had overestimated Huascarán. Instead, I had underestimated the others. All I needed to do was point any of the three down the trail. With very little prompting, they performed like high-powered machines, steady and strong, straight and true. All except the free-spirited Lucero, that is. He moved at a steady pace and was certainly strong, but riding him was sort of like driving a car with too much play in the steering. If I didn't constantly tend him, he would veer off in any odd direction, merrily on his way to nowhere in particular.

I came to appreciate not only the energy and stamina of these horses, but also their intelligence. In one short lesson they learned to travel as a threesome, with me in the lead riding one and leading the other two single file. Though this was something they'd never done before, I was soon able to ride any of them while leading the other two.

From time to time, Jorge Baca remarked that Huascarán was a "conceited" horse. At first, I thought it a rather strange observation, but it was consistent with the fact that he was the only one of my horses to ever defy me. Bigger than any other *Paso* horse I'd ever seen, Huascarán was incredibly powerful, and I suspected that his former handlers had more than once surrendered to his will or hesitated to impose theirs.

There was sometimes a haughty look in his eyes. I first saw it when he persisted in removing his feed bag, despite all my efforts to the contrary. I saw it again the afternoon the government veterinarian performed the required physical examination, inoculations and worming. Long before the vet had finished, Huascarán grew unhappy with being poked and prodded. He pulled back and nearly unearthed a sturdy hitching post. My countermove was to tie him to a very substantial tree. His counter-countermove was to pull back and break his thick cotton lead rope. I spliced it, but by the time the vet had finished his work, Huascarán had snapped the rope a second and third time, making enough noise to attract young Pablo from his nearby home.

After the vet departed, I found a thicker rope and again tied Huascarán to the tree. I left him there for an hour or so, rather than reward his misbehavior by returning him to his stall. While I was cleaning stalls – and with no one closer than thirty feet – Huascarán proceeded to snap his new lead rope four times. Each time, Pablo informed me, and with color rising in my cheeks, I spliced the rope and retied my big, gray gelding. Confident of the imminent victory of brains over brawn, I tied him several different ways. Every one of *my* brilliant ideas fell prey to *his* brute strength.

When there were no more significant lengths that could be tied together, I exchanged that rope for yet another. This time, I fashioned a nerve line, passing the rope behind Huascarán's ears before running it through the halter ring. Then I tied him, content in the knowledge that the next time he pulled, the pressure would be applied to a very sensitive area. Anxious to see his reaction, I didn't have to wait long. He soon pulled back, and when the rope was taut, he responded to the unexpected pain by surging forward. I glanced around and discovered that Pablo was no longer spectating. Then I checked to be sure no one else was close by. Satisfied that there were no observers, I stepped closer to Huascarán.

"I hope you've learned your lesson," I muttered under my breath.

Huascarán had learned no such thing. The rope was unbroken, but his resolve seemed unbreakable, as well. After a brief rest, he pulled back until the rope was tight, but not painfully so. Then he violently slung his head from side to side, struggling so mightily that he slipped out of both rope and halter. Nighttime interrupted our test of wills. Huascarán had won the first round, but I was determined to teach him humility.

Round two lasted a full day. Huascarán broke the metal snaps on all my leadlines and destroyed another length of rope. When I tried high-test nylon cable I'd brought from the States, he broke it more times than I cared to count.

"I hope *you've* learned *your* lesson," the look on his face read at the end of the day.

On the third day, my initial strategy was to apply the top of my boot to his stomach every time he pulled back. The result was that he stood quietly when I was nearby but leaned back and broke his rope as soon as I walked away. That afternoon, I went into town, bought fifteen feet of towrope and attached an extra-heavy-duty metal snap designed to hold a bull. Huascarán proceeded to shatter the metal snap. When I tied the towrope directly to the halter, he broke the halter and then a second one, also.

Using the towrope, I made another nerve line so that pressure again came to bear behind his ears when he pulled. He fought it until he turned the noose upside down, cutting off his wind and obliging me to free him. Finally, I did what I should have done in the first place. I made a lasso of the towrope and passed the loop around Huascarán's body, just behind his front legs. Next I passed the free end of my heart rope between his front legs and through his halter ring before tying it to the tree.

Once again Huascarán pulled back with that sly look in his eyes. His expression changed the instant the lasso tightened around his chest, but he wouldn't give up. I was so angry by that time that I was hoping to see his eyes bug out. He disappointed me by giving up before that happened. For the rest of the day, I couldn't make him pull, no matter what the provocation. Huascarán had finally been convinced that he had to stand tied. His basic attitude, however, seemed little improved, and the look in his eyes showed his resentment.

The following day, I gave each of my horses his first lesson as a packhorse. With Huascarán, I feared another battle, but he accepted the packsaddle and baggage without protest or resistance. Likewise, Inka was his usual cooperative self. That left only the mistrustful Lucero, and I fully expected to have trouble with him. Even so, I got more than I bargained for. Lucero became agitated the instant he saw the packsaddle and duffel bags. He allowed the packsaddle to be cinched in place, but when the heavy bags were placed upon it, he went crazy. Before I had a chance to finish tying down the cargo, he exploded and made a mad dash for the wide-open spaces, dragging me until I had to let go. The snap and catch rings on both duffel bags broke, allowing their contents to be scattered from one end of La Quinta to the other. Fortunately, nothing was beyond repair except for a can of Sterno, which popped open and spilled its contents. The only other casualty was my tin cup, which was altered to a shape more suitable for begging than drinking.

After Lucero emptied the cargo bags, he jumped a fence and charged blindly into a small reservoir. Distracted, he didn't see the water until he was in so deep he had to swim. Before I could catch him, I had to corner him in the water. Ready for a second try, I led my black gelding back to the stable area and blindfolded him. When he felt the weight of the bags, Lucero made a series of blind leaps, ridding himself of them once again. Unable to see, he bumped into a tree and ricocheted, nearly trampling me underfoot before I stopped him. Terrified, he had skinned his forehead and one foreleg and was trembling uncontrollably.

As a last resort, I tied up a foreleg, left the blindfold in place and managed to get the cargo tied down. When I was ready, I removed the blindfold and let Lucero do his worst, which wasn't much with only three legs on the ground. An hour later, I untied Lucero's foreleg and permitted him to lower his fourth hoof to the ground. By then, he was at the point where he would tolerate the cargo but couldn't be trusted with it. There was no telling when he might suddenly decide to bolt again.

Frequently I went into Chiclayo, and when I got to know the people there, I couldn't decide whether I hated them or loved them. One minute, I'd find myself hoping to never see another Peruvian, and the next, I'd regard them as the finest people on earth. One particular afternoon, my opinion soared to new heights. When I asked a shopkeeper for directions to the Indian market, he insisted on closing his business long enough to guide me there. I bought a hundred pounds of oats, then caught the bus back to La Quinta. My fellow passengers saw me struggling to load the sack onto the tiny, overcrowded bus and immediately lent a hand. The driver refused to let me pay my fare, insisting I was a guest in his country. A boy gave me his seat, since it was uncomfortable for me to stand, doubled over by the low roof. Another friendly passenger engaged me in enjoyable conversation.

The next day, in this land of startling contrasts, I went into Chiclayo to buy a back issue of a newspaper. People on the street were openly rude, calling me names and making fun of my height. Though I arrived during normal business hours, the newspaper office was closed without explanation. The bus to Reque was two hours late. My fellow passengers elbowed and shoved their way ahead of me, completely filling the bus and leaving me to wait for the next. Scheduled to meet a horseshoer at La Quinta, I had no more time to squander standing idly at bus stops. The alternative was a taxi, a luxury I could ill afford.

Upon arrival at La Quinta, the taxi driver tried to charge me double. He soon discovered a side of my personality last revealed to a certain secretary in Lima's Ministry of Agriculture. No pushover, the driver was slow to reduce the amount I owed, but I stood my ground.

My reward for rushing back to La Quinta was to wait the rest of the afternoon for a blacksmith who never showed up. After dark, I checked on the horses and found all three stall doors unlatched and ajar, thanks to unknown hands. Had my horses chosen, they could have made their way to the highway, where drivers guided their speeding cars through the twilight hours with only parking lights, risking their lives to save a little wear and tear on their batteries.

When things were going badly, I had a little ritual that provided a measure of relief. After carrying a sack of oats to the highway, I'd sit there, cleaning the grain and watching the inter-city buses pass. Peruvian bus lines used mostly vehicles that Greyhound had retired, and these still announced their old destinations behind the small window above the windshield. I didn't feel forever cut off from the world I knew and understood when I saw buses seemingly on their way to Green Bay, Houston, Chicago, even Reno.

As best I could, I continued to shepherd the processing of my export permit in far-away Lima. There was little I could do beyond being the squeaky wheel that called for grease, but I brought a notable persistence to that task. Periodically, I called the *Asociación* and gently reminded its bigwigs of my dilemma. At my prompting, the Ministry of Agriculture branch office in Chiclayo would regularly check with headquarters in Lima. I even convinced Jorge Baca's brother, a senator, to personally call the Minister of Agriculture in my behalf. In retrospect, I've often wondered if all my pushing had a negative effect. As far as I could tell, none of it did any good, beyond lowering my blood pressure.

One morning while young Pablo was watching me work with my horses, his father joined us.

"*Señor*," he said, "you are setting a very bad example for my son."

"In what way?" I asked, unsure if I should respond to the seriousness of his words or the twinkle in his eye.

"You're too serious," he answered, shaking his head. "You work all the time. You need to relax and enjoy yourself."

I laughed, misinterpreting his remark as a joke, and continued to work with the horses thirteen hours a day, feeding, brushing, riding, training, bathing, cleaning stalls, giving rub downs and more. The most time-consuming tasks of all were the special projects, such as shoeing. Though that could have been quickly and easily accomplished in the States, it took the best part of two weeks in Peru. The first six days were wasted making appointments with a shoer who kept none of them. The next three days were spent searching for another blacksmith, located only after Jorge Baca lent a hand.

The second shoer worked exclusively at the Chiclayo racetrack, and he had only lightweight nails, perfect for racehorses but inadequate for the trail. He swore that no other nails were available, but the resourceful Jorge Baca made him eat those words by obtaining exactly what my horses needed, from the local mounted police. As it turned out, my horses received their new shoes in the nick of time. The same day they were shod, there was a phone call from Lima. My papers were ready! On behalf of the *Asociación*, Carlos

Luna would fly to Chiclayo on Saturday to bring my export permit and see me off.

Jorge Baca had further unexpected news. He had arranged a farewell ceremony. The schedule called for me to ride to Chiclayo on Saturday. At the entrance to town, I would be joined by a group of horses and riders from the area's *haciendas*, and together we'd ride into the city. At the principal plaza, I'd join some of the town's leading citizens for a cocktail at an exclusive, private club. Then, just like that, after so many struggles, I would finally be on my way!

To get to the corral, they had to walk right through the police station (see page 88).

CHAPTER 5

The Bishop's Blessing

In all honesty, I admit there were days when I regretted having set out on my ride, but my last Friday at La Quinta wasn't among them. At long last, I was on the brink of my journey, and the future was filled with promise. Magic saturated the air, affecting others as much as it did me. One of those others was an elderly gentleman who lived near La Quinta. We hadn't met, but early that morning, he paid me a visit and ceremoniously handed me a sealed envelope.

"*Gringo*," he said, using an affectionate nickname as if we were long-time friends, "you must not open this until you arrive in Los Gatos."

He looked into my eyes for assurance that I would make and keep this promise. I returned a quick nod and a smile.

"There are three items inside," he continued. "The first is my prediction of your arrival date."

There was a long pause.

"When do you expect me to get to Los Gatos?" I asked, curious to know if he thought I'd be there in time for the Tevis Cup, in spite of the long delay.

"You'll find out after you get to California," he smiled mysteriously. "The second item is to help your journey be safe and successful. I can tell you only that it's the image of a saint."

Another long pause.

"The third item is a small gift," he teased. "I think you'll like it."

With that, he went on his way after warmly wishing me good luck. I was touched by his gesture and intrigued by the mysterious contents of the envelope. Promptly, I put it in the protective pouch that held my important papers. Soon after that, Jorge Baca took me aside to discuss the details of the next day's farewell ceremony. I soon realized that my send-off was going to be more elaborate than I'd been led to believe, and I made a comment to that effect.

"Of course," Jorge responded with a smile. "Invitations have been sent to all of Chiclayo's leading citizens. Most will be there."

"I thought this was going to be a small private ceremony," I said, a bit staggered.

"Why do you think Carlos Luna is coming all the way from Lima?" Jorge asked, his eyebrows eloquently raised. "We intend to properly inaugurate what we believe is an important event."

Of course, I was flattered but also embarrassed by the prospect of so much attention.

"When is all this going to happen?" I asked.

"Well," Jorge replied, "the television interview is this morning, and the parade will be tomorrow."

Television interview! Parade! I wasn't prepared for all this. Just when I was beginning to get used to the idea, there was a telephone call. It was from Jorge Baca's brother, the senator, who had arranged for the TV interview and was calling to advise that – in the time-honored tradition of Peru – it had fallen through. I received the news with mixed feelings. It would have served my purposes for the breed to appear on national television, but the interview would have taken time I didn't have. As it worked out, my ill-fated T.V. appearance was unexpectedly replaced by a magazine interview. A writer from *The Peruvian Times* arrived unannounced at La Quinta. *The Peruvian Times* was a respected, English-language newsmagazine distributed mostly among Peru's British and North American communities.

The writer, an elderly lady, remarkably tiny and withered, introduced herself only as "Miss Ward." She had a hooked nose and protruding chin, along with sunken eyes and cheeks that made her look very much like a witch. I soon discovered that her outer appearance didn't reveal what was within. She was kind, intelligent and admirable. Long before it was fashionable, she was a woman who lived her life exactly as she wished. To her considerable credit, she did this without a trace of abrasiveness.

Miss Ward needed to watch expenditures, something with which I could sympathize, and her appearance hadn't been enhanced by an all-night ride on the least-costly bus from Lima. I soon learned that she'd eaten only a piece of fruit for breakfast. In spite of that, she declined my offer of food.

Initially, I wished she had arrived on a less busy day, but the interview developed into a chat so pleasant that I would have been hard-pressed to think of a better way to spend my time. Temporarily forgetting all that I had to do, I relaxed. It was apparent that Miss Ward, too, was enjoying herself immensely. She was a British expatriate, a knowledgeable horsewoman and the first person I had met in Peru who truly appreciated the magnitude of the challenge before me. Most people dismissed my talk of difficulties with a cheery: "Don't worry about it. Everything will be fine." In contrast, Miss Ward expressed valid concerns about potential problems with food, water, climate, terrain and altitude. I assured her that such difficulties had been taken into consideration, and it was reassuring to hear her approval when I gave further details.

She also had a piece of good advice. Lucero had been off his feed following his experience with the cargo, the blindfold, the reservoir and the tree. Nothing I tried had corrected this. At Miss Ward's suggestion, I put all three horses in a single corral, where – comforted by the presence of his companions – Lucero quickly rediscovered his missing appetite. I had begun to suspect that Lucero might be too high-strung for the job he faced. Most people, however, regarded my black gelding as the most likely to reach Los Gatos. Miss Ward described him in her article as "… a horse I had wanted to buy when I rode him at the annual horse show in Lima two years before. I liked his sheep's face, also known as a Roman nose, a conformation which is supposed to denote stamina."

When she first saw Huascarán, Miss Ward abandoned her English reserve long enough to exclaim: "My goodness, he has the shoulders of a bull!"

That was the only comment she made at the time, but she obviously liked my gray gelding, a fact confirmed when her article described him as: "…a magnificent steed and a perfect ride, easily gaited, very light mouthed, his powerful muscles giving a sense of great force."

Miss Ward had been away from England long enough to have adopted Peru's relaxed lifestyle, and she would have been content to while away the day talking and looking at my horses. Unfortunately, minor emergencies were clamoring for my attention.

When the interview was over, I bade farewell to Miss Ward and took a bus to Lambayeque, the next city north of Chiclayo. Knowing Peruvians, I suspected that Jorge Baca's farewell celebration would undoubtedly last until late Saturday afternoon. As a consequence, I expected to arrive in Lambayeque after dark, and I thought it would be a good idea to arrange for accommodations in advance.

Once in Lambayeque, I went to see Augusto Carpena, a friend of Jorge Baca's. *Señor* Carpena invited me to stable my horses at his farm the following evening and insisted that I stay in his home. He also informed me that there was no horse feed whatever in the desert to the north and offered to send hay ahead to my five nightly stops between Lambayeque and Piura. *Señor* Carpena's generosity was typical of the exceptional treatment I would receive from horsemen throughout my journey.

That night I went to sleep in my bunk at La Quinta for the last time. I slept well, confident that my horses were, as Miss Ward had said (and later wrote): "… as fit as human hands could make them."

Saturday morning started with a flurry. Because of the previous day's demands on my time, I hadn't yet purchased oats for the journey ahead. By bus, I made a pre-dawn trip to Chiclayo. After buying oats, I took a second bus to Lambayeque. At *Señor* Carpena's farm, I divided the oats into five sacks and requested that he send these ahead with his hay. Next, I splurged on a taxi to take me back to La Quinta where I saddled up as speedily as possible. With two of Jorge Baca's hired hands, mounted on two of his best horses, I rode to Chiclayo. The ride was long enough to give me a preview of the problems I'd be having with my baggage. The packsaddle shifted here and there, and I had to stop repeatedly to make adjustments. Never having loaded the packsaddle with all two hundred pounds of cargo, I still had some important lessons to learn about balancing it. Soon I was pouring sweat because of equal doses of desert sun and frustration.

At the entrance to town, I was met by a *cabalgada* of twenty *Paso* horses and *chalanes* [4] from *haciendas* in the surrounding area. Almost immediately, we were joined by a police motorcycle escort and started our parade through the narrow streets of Chiclayo. At first, the spectators were mostly vendors who tended fruit and vegetable carts near the city's entrance. They watched in silence as the police cleared the way. Elsewhere in the world, the horses certainly would have been the center of attention. They carried themselves with aristocratic pride, as if leading a conquering army. Fleet and stylish, their four-beat gaits easily kept pace with the motorcycles. Each horse handled itself with lively vigor and was so smooth that the rider seemed to be floating through the air.

On this particular occasion, however, the animals attracted little attention, for Peruvians are accustomed to their National Horse. Most of the attention was focused on *me*. People recognized me – even if we'd never met – from newspaper articles and wished me well.

"*Que le vaya bien.*"

"*Buen viaje.*"

The further we went into town, the more spectators there were. Large groups of children tagged along with our procession shouting, "Pablito. *Gringo.*" It was embarrassing. I hadn't *done* anything yet. The recognition and honors were undeserved, given in anticipation of something I *hoped* to accomplish, but, nevertheless, as I neared the Central Plaza, ever-larger crowds filled the sidewalks, applauding and shouting encouragement. A small group of attractive young ladies was showing particular enthusiasm, and I tipped my hat.

"Thank you very much," I said, flirting.

"Why do *you* thank us?" one of them returned, eyes wickedly sparkling. "We were applauding the horses, not you!"

Everyone within earshot roared with laughter, and all eyes turned to me. Peruvians love word games, and people were anxious to see if I was any good at them. My mind went blank until I remembered that something very similar had happened to Alfredo Elias, a Peruvian friend of mine.

"I know, but my horses can't talk, and I'm answering for them," I took Alfredo's words for my own.

The crowd laughed, louder than before, and attention returned to the girls. They had no retort, fortunately for me! Scattered applause followed us all the way to the center of town. It swelled to a crescendo as our little parade entered the Central Plaza. I was smiling by then, surprised as I saw the plaza overflowing with people. In front of the city's most exclusive private club, I brought Huascarán to a stop. In a display of precision and skill, the other riders stopped their horses, half to my right and half to my left, in a perfectly straight line. I glanced behind myself and saw Lucero and Inka standing relaxed, unperturbed by the gathering of people around us. I dismounted. Someone took charge of my horses, and I was swept into a series of introductions that included the Mayor of Chiclayo, the Catholic Bishop, bank presidents, members of the press and prominent plantation owners. Finally, I said hello to Carlos Luna, who had just arrived from Lima.

After the introductions, we all entered the club's front door for shade, conversation, cocktails, hors d'oeuvres and Latin American ceremony. When the conversation lagged, Carlos Luna, true to form, made a long speech before presenting me with my horses' export permits. He also handed me a special parchment scroll from the *Asociación*. This I was to deliver to the American Association of Owners and Breeders of Peruvian Paso Horses. It was written in the exceedingly formal language of Cervantes and expressed gratitude for the promotion of the Peruvian *Paso* horse in North America.

The mayor followed with a shorter speech, during which he presented me with an official letter for the mayor of Los Gatos. There were others who had "a few words" to say, each followed by silence until someone else called for a toast and began speaking. This went on for some time, with each speaker expressing confidence that my journey would be crowned with success.

Toward the end, I scarcely heard the speeches. I was filled with the melancholy that comes over me whenever I leave a familiar place for an unknown destiny. I was also seized with fondness for Jorge Baca. I hadn't taken the time to really know him during my hectic days at La Quinta, but he had been consistently generous and patient with me. The busiest man I had ever met in Peru, he always found time to help with my many problems. Last but not least, he was single-handedly responsible for providing this elaborate send-off.

I became aware of a long silence in the room. All eyes were upon *me*. It was my turn to speak. In the best Spanish I could muster, I briefly stated that I had never known a city as friendly as Chiclayo and would never forget the people there. I singled out Jorge Baca as having been particularly helpful and thanked members of the *Asociación* for their support.

A resounding cheer followed my short remarks. Next came the raising of cocktail glasses all around the room. At long last, there was only one formality left, the Bishop's blessing. This was delivered with a profusion of Latin words sealed by the tracing of a cross in the air. With that, the ceremony came to an end, and we all proceeded outside. As I emerged into the plaza, I was surrounded by reporters who clamored for some final comment. I requested that they ask their readers to the north to please be generous with feed for my horses.

A few more people stepped forward to wish me *"buena suerte"* before my private parade continued amidst loud and prolonged cheering toward the northern exit from Chiclayo. At the city limits, I stopped my horses and turned to face the twenty riders who had escorted me. We were alone except for our police escort and a small group of curious street urchins. One by one, the *chalanes* rode their horses past me, shaking my hand and wishing me good luck. Their wishes were spoken quietly but with sincerity. More than the priests, the reporters or the bankers, they knew the magnitude of my task.

When all the farewells had been said, the motorcycles and police officers escorted the *chalanes* back to the city center. The *gringo* and his three horses turned to go alone in the opposite direction, north into the desert.

4 Peruvian *Paso* horse trainers.

CHAPTER 6

Onramp to the Royal Road

After leaving Chiclayo, I rode on the highway shoulder. One after another, northbound cars slowed as they came alongside, and several southbound cars made U-turns in order to do the same. In both cases, windows were quickly rolled down so the occupants could ask questions. Most wanted to know how I planned to find my way across thousands of miles of unfamiliar territory. My answer was disappointingly simple. I intended to follow the *Panamericana* or Pan-American Highway. I wouldn't always be right next to it, but as much as possible, I planned to keep it in sight.

The Pan American Highway was probably the most famous highway of the day. Hundreds of years earlier, Spain's King Charles I had envisioned building it, as a way to link his colonies in North, Central and South America. Before it was even started, it had acquired a name, *El Camino Real*, The Royal Road. Over a period of centuries, segments were built, but the Spanish were driven from their New World empire long before anything resembling an intercontinental highway finally took shape. Not until 1963 was a continuous road from Alaska to Argentina – minus Panama's impassible Darien Gap – completed. Three years later, I was ready to add my name to the short list of those who had followed this newly completed highway from South to North America.

I had heard and read a great deal about the *Panamericana*, but facts and figures had been of little use in helping me form an accurate mental picture. That was mostly because the word "highway" had misled me. Northern Peru's *Panamericana* was inferior to even the most remote back roads in California. There was rarely a centerline to separate the two opposing lanes. The roadway was often taken hostage by unsupervised livestock. Drifting sand routinely brought traffic to a stop while workers with shovels painstakingly cleared the way. Drivers had to dodge cavernous cracks and potholes. At both edges of the highway, the pavement ended abruptly, the only shoulder being desert sand, which might or might not provide traction for vehicles that pulled over. No signs, guard rails, banked curves, rest stops, emergency telephones, lighted intersections or other amenities graced the narrow, black ribbon of asphalt.

As bad as it was, the highway was no worse than most vehicles that used it. Many of Peru's cars and trucks qualified as antiques and routinely broke down. Typically, drivers made their own repairs, and these could take hours, sometimes even days. Without a shoulder for parking, repairs were made right in the traffic lanes, and other motorists were warned of this hazard by rocks, whitewashed and placed behind the disabled vehicle. When repairs were finished, these rocks were often left in the road, to be dodged by subsequent traffic.

Accidents were commonplace, and only the light traffic kept Peru's population from being decimated on its highways. Of course, it was also helpful that drivers had learned to anticipate the unpredictable from those who shared the road with them. Under most circumstances, Peruvians were extraordinarily courteous, but when they got behind a steering wheel, their personalities changed. The only rule of the road was "every man for himself." Evidently I was growing accustomed to Peru's motorized chaos. Along The Royal Road that first day, it seemed unremarkable when cars slowed to the speed of my horses, thereby obstructing the single northbound traffic lane.

Arriving at the outskirts of Lambayeque just after dusk, I proceeded to *Señor* Carpena's farm. There I cooled and brushed my horses, cleaned their nightly ration of oats, shoveled the leavings of previous occupants from their stalls, fed them, watered them, gave each a rubdown and cleaned the following morning's oats. Finally, I left the horses under the protection of the night watchman and made the long walk to the Carpena residence in town. Despite my late arrival, I was served a splendid meal and was joined by *Señor* and *Señora* Carpena. My apologies for delaying their meal were dismissed with the explanation that it's common to have a late dinner in the Peruvian culture. The food suited my North American taste buds better than any I'd eaten since leaving home. I had a generous cut of juicy steak with several servings of vegetables. There were even potatoes instead of the typical rice or yucca, which Peruvians appreciate a great deal more than I do.

After dinner, *Señor* Carpena presented me with a envelope full of newspaper clippings. I was surprised to see that my send-off in Chiclayo had been front-page news throughout the area. Disproving my impression that everything in Peru was done at a snail's pace, the various articles were illustrated with photos taken only hours earlier.

I was equally pleased by other news. My host had arranged for me to spend the following night at the *Hacienda* La Viña, famed for its splendid fighting bulls. At La Viña, of course, there would be plenty of feed for my horses, but *Señor* Carpena hastened to confirm that he still planned to send hay and grain to my other stopovers along the road to Piura. The perfect end to a perfect day was a clean, comfortable bed, where I had a wonderful sleep.

At 5:00 the next morning, *Señor* Carpena and I quietly slipped out of the house. Hardly able to sit still, I anticipated my first full day of travel while he drove me through the cool morning air. Soon after arriving at the Carpena farm, I noticed a young boy. He was near my horses' stalls, seated on a nice little *Paso* mare, and had eyes for no one and nothing else but me. After a while, he dismounted, tied his mare to a post and walked toward me.

"Pardon me, *señor*," he said in a hopeful, respectful voice. "If you want, I can show you a shortcut that will help you avoid traffic and save time."

An inner voice warned me that shortcuts often backfire and little boys can slow you down. When I didn't immediately respond to his offer, the boy excitedly babbled on. He had read about me the evening before in the newspaper and had managed to find out where my horses and I were staying. That morning, he'd gotten up early and ridden to the Carpena farm. By the time I arrived, he'd been waiting for almost an hour. It was touching to be the object of hero worship, even though it meant there was no longer any possibility of refusing his offer. My guide's face beamed when I told him I'd be grateful for his help. Together we rode to town and ate breakfast at the Carpena residence.

After thanking the Carpenas lavishly for their hospitality, I mounted up, and my young friend took charge, guiding me quickly to Lambayeque's northern exit. Before we parted company, he shyly handed me a wallet-sized photograph of himself, with a note and his signature scribbled on the back. Then he unfolded a newspaper clipping about my ride and asked me to autograph it. Self-consciously, I wrote a message in the margin and signed it.

"Thanks for your help," I said as I returned his clipping. "You saved me a lot of time."

He grinned, knowing as well as I did that it was true. Sadly, he turned his mare toward town. Over his shoulder, he expressed a wish similar to many I had already heard.

"I wish I were grown up," he said, "so I could go with you."

The outskirts of Lambayeque reminded me of something I'd observed the day before when leaving Chiclayo. Where the city ended, the desert began, without a transition. Greenery thrived where there was water but couldn't survive a millimeter beyond. In an instant, I was in the desert.

All along the way to Jayanca, people waved from their vehicles.

Some insisted on stopping to talk, and a few even visited with me on both legs of a round-trip. I had become a bit of a national hero, and almost everyone, it seemed, wanted to know how he might be of service. Later that morning, an Italian on a Vespa motor scooter pulled up next to me and matched his speed to mine so we could talk without stopping. Upon hearing my plans, he became so animated that his hands spent more time gesturing than steering.

"I, myself, am in the process of making the very same trip," he stated in heavily accented English, "using, as you can see, a motorbike instead of horses. It should take me four or five weeks to get to California."

"I'll probably get there about half a year after you do," I responded.

"I wish I had time for an adventure like yours," he said before bidding me a cheerful farewell, revving his engine and speeding out of sight. I never saw nor heard of him again.

That afternoon, near Jayanca, I noticed a rider coming from the opposite direction. When we were head-to-head, he stopped and introduced himself as Felipe. His friendly manner indicated that he knew me, though I couldn't remember having met him. Further conversation revealed that our roadside encounter was no coincidence. Felipe was a friend of Augusto Carpena's, and he was there to guide me to the *Hacienda* La Viña where, he explained, arrangements had been made for the horses and me to spend the night. Of course, I already knew that, but when I asked how Felipe knew, he grinned and claimed "special powers." I suspected that a telephone call from Augusto Carpena was a more likely explanation, but I never did find out for sure.

Before the two of us had ridden far, we were hailed by a couple in a passing car. They evidently knew Felipe and invited us to have lunch at their home just down the road. We were more than happy to accept and were served a sumptuous, home-cooked meal featuring a delicious vegetable omelet. I could have eaten several times the amount I was given, but I waited in vain to be offered more. Lunch had awakened my appetite without satisfying it. On the other hand, the meal wouldn't have been nearly as exquisite if the portions had been larger.

Peruvians consider it impolite to eat and run, and, therefore, Felipe and I talked with our hosts for a long while. By the time we continued toward La Viña, it was obvious we wouldn't get there until after dark.

I couldn't help noticing that my companion was a far more able rider than I. Though I had ridden thousands of miles as a boy, I was a novice with Peruvian *Pasos*. This isn't to say that I found them difficult to ride. Being a passenger on a Peruvian horse is the easiest thing in the world. Riding them properly, however, is another matter.

Felipe's gelding was gaiting superbly and had his head and neck collected into a beautiful position. My own horses weren't and didn't, circumstances I tried to quickly improve but couldn't. No doubt my companion could see my lack of expertise, and it suddenly seemed important that Felipe be made aware of my experience with long-distance riding. Relentlessly, I steered the conversation in a direction that allowed me to describe the many difficulties I was bound to encounter and prepared to overcome. While I was thus involved, my packhorse veered so that he passed a telephone pole on the opposite side from the horse I was riding. Of course the pole snagged the lead rope between, and all three of my horses became hopelessly entangled during the ensuing confusion.

Felipe watched in a calm, uncritical manner as I unsnarled the mess caused by my inattention. My predicament didn't elicit a single word of advice or even the hint of a smile. He was much too polite for that. Thoroughly discouraged, I gave up on trying to impress him, convinced that he was secretly planning to call Las Vegas and wager his life savings against the successful completion of my journey.

When we reached La Viña, it was twilight, and an unpleasant surprise waited. The huge *hacienda* was deserted!

One of my new horses was a half-brother to Hugo Bustamante's bullfighting horse (see page 16).

At the entrance to town, I was met by a *cabalgada* of twenty *Paso* horses (see page 49).

I was swept into a series of introductions that included the mayor, far right (see page 50).

A few more people stepped forward to wish me "Good luck" (see page 51).

Saying goodbye to Jorge Baca (see page 51).

After the farewell ceremony, I prepared to ride to the city limit and into the desert beyond (see page 51).

Alone, the *gringo* and his three horses went north into the desert (see page 51).

59

Chapter 7

The Phantom of La Viña

There wasn't a human being anywhere in sight and no sign that there recently had been. No lights shined; no machines were operating; and no dogs barked; nor were tire tracks visible on the dusty roads. The structures, including the house, must have been no less than one hundred and fifty years old and looked as if they'd had no maintenance since they were built. The architecture was typical of Peruvian *haciendas* with adobe walls, pillars and red tile roofs. We knocked on the front door of the main farmhouse, and no one answered. Felipe was as mystified as I. Together we set out to search the premises. It was a daunting prospect. Surrounding the main house was a complex of facilities that covered acres. From between cupped hands, Felipe repeatedly hailed someone, anyone, but there was no response. We rode among the shops and storage rooms and found only dirt roads as deserted as the streets of Dodge City just before a gunfight. It was quickly becoming dark, and still no lights burned anywhere.

A detour through the corrals and pens revealed that La Viña wasn't devoid of all life. There were mules and cows, but they hadn't been fed. Farther along, more substantial pens housed the mothers of the fighting bulls for which the *hacienda* was famous. These were calmly munching hay. Their having been fed was our first sign that someone was there. Felipe suggested that we check the worker housing, and our path took us near the farmhouse again. Watching Felipe ride through the darkness ahead, I suddenly saw someone materialize next to him. This unexpected event startled all three of my horses, not to mention their rider.

In the faint light of the hissing kerosene lantern he carried, I could make out a permanently stooped-over old man who introduced himself as the manager and with his eyes boring holes into Felipe, asked why we were there. Unnerved, Felipe stammered through a brief explanation.

He hadn't been told to expect a visitor, the old man explained curtly, and furthermore, there were no facilities or supplies that would permit him to host a guest, much less three horses. The whole area was suffering through a shortage of feed, which had obliged the *hacienda* to limit even its own animals to only one feeding per day. That last news was the worst. Positive that La Viña would supply feed and accommodations for my horses, *Señor* Carpena had sent neither hay nor grain.

Even Felipe had known I was supposed to spend the night at La Viña. How could the manager not know? Perhaps Augusto Carpena had advised me of the arrangements, intending – and somehow failing – to get through on Peru's notoriously unreliable rural phone system. Equally possible, La Viña's owner, who had left for Lima earlier that day, might have taken the call and afterward failed to tell anyone. What difference did it make? I had a serious problem!

Slowly and with elaborate politeness, Felipe spoke a second time, offering a thorough explanation of my circumstances. While listening, the old man turned his head and peered my way through the thick lenses of his eyeglasses. He raised his lantern and stood squinting, a shadowy apparition in the sputtering light. Apparently unable to see me clearly, he came closer. Abruptly, the old man's attitude underwent a startling transformation. Instantly, he became the very soul of hospitality. For some reason, it occurred to me that I must be the perfect fit for some diabolical plan he had in mind. Admittedly without justification, I was uneasy when Felipe rode off, leaving me alone with a ghostly figure who appeared no more than half my size and no less than four times my age. I decided I could handle him if he tried anything, unless he had special powers that didn't run in my family line.

The aged manager beckoned me to follow as he shuffled off, sliding his feet instead of taking steps. I followed on horseback, feeling guilty about riding while an elderly man walked. Quickly I considered and rejected the idea of dismounting. I had never led all three horses at once, and I didn't want to try it while they were skittish in unfamiliar surroundings. Presently, we reached pens surrounded by thick, high adobe walls. Inside I could hear animals snorting and moving about, and from time to time, I saw the silhouette of wicked-looking horns. We were within a few feet of mature fighting bulls, perhaps the most dangerous animals on the planet.

The old man reached through small openings in the walls and casually appropriated hay directly from the troughs where the bulls were eating. This he dropped, handful by handful, into a rusted, bent-up wheelbarrow with a misshapen iron wheel. Next he pointed to a nearby corral my horses would have to share with the milk cows already there. I didn't relish the idea of stabling Inka, Huascarán and Lucero with livestock that might provoke a quarrel or steal their feed. Seeing my hesitation, the old man apologized profusely. Over and over, he explained that he'd had no advance notice and at such a late hour, had no workers to prepare a corral where my horses could be by themselves. Like a ghost, he then disappeared after instructing me to meet him at the main house when I was finished.

While going over the geldings with brush, currycomb and flashlight, I noticed that Huascarán had developed a nasty swelling. Undoubtedly, the cinch on the packsaddle had caused it. Cursing myself, I vigorously massaged the area with liniment.

The transportation of my baggage was becoming a persistent problem. Because of my ineptness in balancing and tying them, the duffel bags rode poorly. To make matters worse, I couldn't trust the potentially explosive Lucero and was obliged to rotate the cargo between Inka and Huascarán, giving each of them cargo duty more often than I preferred.

After policing the corral to be sure it was hazard free, I tied my horses to the fence in the corner farthest from the cows. Immediately I brought the wheelbarrow, unloaded the hay into the feed trough and turned my horses loose. All three made a beeline for another corner. There they huddled, hungrily eating the few odd scraps of straw they found on the ground. Meanwhile, the cows, astounded by their good fortune, headed for my horses' abandoned hay. With a sigh, I chased the cows away and carried the hay over to my horses. There was no feed trough there, so I built three neat piles on the ground and watched the horses dig in as if near starvation. Small wonder that intelligence tests for horses have never become popular. People who love horses don't want to know!

At that point, it was so dark that I couldn't find my way without using the flashlight. Getting everything to the house took three trips, one with each duffel bag and one with my saddle and horse gear. The house had a wide selection of exterior doors, and I knocked on the one that gave access to the only lighted room. The old man answered. After asking me to leave the horse equipment on the porch, he swung the door wide open and indicated a spot inside where I could put my duffel bags. I entered and found myself in the biggest and most primitive kitchen I'd ever seen.

Next he ushered me to where he had laid out a wash basin, a pitcher of water, a bar of soap and a towel. After another elaborate apology – this one because the house had no running water – he invited me to wash. I thanked him and proceeded while he hovered and insisted on pouring water over my hands during washing and rinsing. As soon as I had dried my hands, he led me past a servant who was preparing my dinner on a wood-burning stove. The door to the stove's belly was open, and its fire provided most of the light in the dim room.

From outside, the house had appeared to have two stories, but once inside, I saw it was a single story with extremely high ceilings and nine-foot doors. After spending more time in rural Peru, I would learn that such grand scale is typical of old-style Peruvian farmhouses. At that moment, though, the oversized dimensions were a considerable mystery, especially considering that Peruvians had no need for that kind of headroom.

I was shown into a dark, cavernous dining room and invited to seat myself at an enormous table. Two candles flickered in the center of the table, their flames barely illuminating the area immediately around them. Sitting there, I could see that Edgar Allan Poe's gothic tales must have come easily in the days before electric lighting. The dark corners and moving shadows were conducive to macabre thoughts. Perhaps, I teased myself, La Viña's farmhouse – with its nine-foot doors and high ceilings – was a trap designed to lure tall North Americans to a terrible fate. My host's lavish politeness had brought to mind a story about a boarding house where the proprietor was a flawlessly courteous, elderly lady. Her hobby was taxidermy, and once someone moved into her house, it became a permanent arrangement!

Once the food was prepared, the old man dismissed the servant and insisted on serving my supper. Perhaps, I told myself, the cook had been dismissed in order to facilitate the addition of some special flavoring, bottled by a company with a skull and crossbones logo. That theory, however, was discredited when my meal proved much too small to contain a fatal dose of poison.

Unmindful of the fact that he was making me uncomfortable, the old man attended me hand and foot: refilling my tea cup whenever it was less than half full, sliding the salt closer even though it was within easy reach, not letting me do anything for myself, despite the fact that I repeatedly tried to stop him from going through so much trouble. All the while, he apologized for the inadequacy of his hospitality. His extravagant kindness bordered on servility. It took all the fun from my wild imaginings about my host's intentions, but it fed my growing desire to be free of him. I quickly finished my tiny supper and was shown to a room, which was little more than a cubicle with no door. A single light bulb hung from the ceiling by a frayed electrical cord. There was no furniture beyond two cots, without bedding. This prompted more apologies, but they were quite unnecessary. I already knew that it was uncommon to find comforts on Peru's *haciendas*, even though their owners were among the wealthiest men in the country. These owners usually had mansions elsewhere, most often in Lima, but lived a rustic life when at their farms.

The old man departed with his lantern, leaving me in pitch-darkness. Out of habit, I threw the light switch, but nothing happened. A noisy generator provided electricity between sunup and sundown, but it was shut down at night to save fuel and allow the residents to sleep in peace. Alone and starving, I fumbled around in the dark and unrolled my sleeping bag on one of the cots. Then, without further delay, I filled the howling vacancy in my stomach with fruit and candy bars from my saddlebags.

In the morning, I devised some padding so the cinch on the packsaddle wouldn't do to Inka what it had done to Huascarán. Anxious to be under way, I saddled up and said my "good-bye" and "thank-you" to the old man, who seemed gentle and harmless by daylight. Before I had gone far, my problems with the packsaddle were multiplied. I was riding Huascarán bareback to avoid having a cinch further aggravate the swelling on his underside. Inka, carrying the baggage, followed in second position. Single file and third in line came Lucero, carrying my empty riding saddle.

A large tumbleweed became entangled in Inka's tail. When it dragged behind him, he was startled and surged forward. Lucero, following behind and tied to the packsaddle, shied in the opposite direction. Unable to go in two directions at once, the packsaddle broke, and my duffel bags crashed to the ground. I managed a makeshift repair, but from that point on, forward progress would have to be made slowly and gingerly.

While passing through a small village, I heard the savage snarling and barking of a pack of ferocious dogs. I whirled in the saddle, expecting to see razor-sharp teeth snapping at my horses' heels, but there wasn't a dog in sight. After further investigation, I located the source of the barking on rooftops above. I had seen a similar practice in Lima, where houses are often built so close that they share a common wall with their neighbor on either side. Under those circumstances – with no front yard to speak of and only a postage-stamp-sized back yard – dogs are routinely relegated to rooftops. In a rural area, however, that same practice was hard to understand. To compound the mystery, roofs found in Peru's deserts are not usually substantial or waterproof.

In response to the alarm sounded by the dogs, men began coming out of the houses. Seeing me, they followed on foot. They knew who I was, thanks to the newspapers, and unlike their canines, they were full of encouragement and good wishes. Several followed me all the way to the northernmost extremity of town. Talking boisterously among themselves, they reached a decision to officially record the exact date and time I had passed through. It would, they assured one another, be information of great historical value once my ride was complete.

I might have been flattered were it not for the fact that every last man was roaring drunk!

Drifting sand routinely brought traffic to a standstill (see page 52).

CHAPTER 8

Beyond Olmos, Almost

Late that afternoon, the packsaddle broke again, this time irreparably. I had no choice but to fasten the duffel bags together and drape them across Inka's back as best I could. True to form, the little bay gelding calmly accepted his unfamiliar and uncomfortable burden. He proved to be a better sport than I. The unsecured baggage forced a maddeningly slow pace that soon brought extra color to my face. It was almost nightfall when we reached Motupe, and I studiously avoided eye contact with the numerous people who stopped to stare. Any of them, I was sure, would have been more than happy to engage me in conversation, but I was in no mood for that, being obsessed with finding accommodations and caring for my horses before darkness made those tasks all the more difficult.

One man, however, stepped in front of my horses, obliging me to stop.

"You must be the famous Pablito," he declared with a pleasant smile, explaining, "I recognize you from the newspapers."

"I don't know if I'm famous," I replied, working hard to respond to his smile with one of my own, "but I am called Pablito."

My forced smile must have announced my mood. The man got right to the point.

"If you plan to stay the night in Motupe, it would be my pleasure and my wife's to have you as a guest in our home. We have a spare room and a corral we can put at your disposal."

I'm sure my face brightened considerably. Without hesitation, I gratefully accepted, and my benefactor seemed tremendously pleased. On foot and talking every inch of the way, he guided me to his modest home. Soon I was unloading my gear with the assistance of the household's children. That accomplished, I gave the horses a good brushing and turned them loose in their corral.

Regretfully, I disappointed my host and his family by declining an invitation to dinner. The horses' work was done, but mine was just beginning. Putting first things first, I walked to the gas station where *Señor* Carpena had said he'd send that night's hay and grain. I found the place crowded with people who were standing around, talking. The attendant on duty was one of the few unfriendly Peruvians I have ever met. He looked me up and down, without replying, after I inquired about my feed. Evidently, he hadn't read about me in the papers, and his expression indicated that he thought it strange for me to be asking about horse feed at a gas station. He seemed to be wondering if I was aware that gas-powered transportation had replaced the hay-burning variety.

"I'm sorry, *señor*," he said, speaking after a long pause. "No hay was delivered here today."

"What about yesterday?"

"No, *señor*. Nor the day before."

Aloud, I speculated that the horses' feed might have been delivered to some other gas station by mistake. I was hoping for a suggestion or two. Instead of suggestions, I got insight into the way people in Motupe must have felt earlier when I had ignored their interest in my arrival. Without a word, the attendant busied himself with other tasks, uninterested in me, my problems or their solutions.

"There are other gas stations, *señor*, where your feed might have been delivered. It will be my pleasure to show you where they are. My name is Lucho."

Those words were spoken by a man standing nearby, with his hand extended for a handshake. He had overheard the details of my plight, and he guided me to every other gas station in town. Our search turned up nothing.

"Where can I buy some horse feed around here?" I asked Lucho.

"You can't," he replied. "There's nothing."

"There has to be," I said, stubbornly. "How do people around here feed their animals?"

"There's nothing. No one here raises hay or grain. You might just as well be seeking ..." he paused, having a hard time thinking of anything equally difficult to find, "the Seven Golden Cities of Cibola."

"I can't let my horses go without eating."

He sighed.

"Can you give me directions to a nearby farm?" I asked.

Lucho looked at me in disbelief before saying, "You have done everything you can. Why don't you relax and join me for a drink and some dinner."

I politely declined the invitation. Patience exhausted, Lucho went on his way. His parting words were meant to be reassuring but had the opposite effect.

"Stop worrying, *señor*. With time, things work themselves out. It will do no great harm if your horses go without feed for a few days."

I combed the area but only confirmed that the first person to buy horse feed in Motupe would deserve a place of honor in the Guinness Book of World Records. Lucho had known what he was talking about. If my horses were to eat that night, I needed to stop wasting time, take a bus to the nearest village and continue my search there.

Intercity buses picked up and delivered passengers at the gas station where I had first made inquiries. Returning there, I found a bus that had just come in from the south and would soon continue its northward journey. While waiting to board, I idled away the time, watching the driver. He was unloading the belongings – mostly packed in burlap bags – of passengers staying in Motupe. Even though any burlap bag looks much the same as any other, one seemed familiar. I strolled over to take a closer look and discovered one of the bags of oats I'd given to *Señor* Carpena. When I turned to claim it from the driver, he was unloading a large bale of hay. Better late than never, the horses' dinner had arrived!

My chance discovery saved me from wasting precious money along with additional hours of my time. It also resulted in my becoming the target of some good-natured razzing. Lucho had returned to the gas station and lightheartedly pointed out that I should have taken his advice. I couldn't argue. After all, if I had spent the past three hours eating, drinking and making merry, I would have been exactly as far along as I was after all my efforts. On top of that, I would have had some food in my stomach.

Later that night, I discovered that Huascarán had developed an ear problem. A check for ticks revealed nothing, but the inside of one ear was crusty and bleeding. I saturated a rag with cooking oil and gently rubbed it on the affected area. Then I hand fed each horse some salt to compensate for what they had sweat out during the day's intense heat.

Ten o'clock found me and my host's helpful children cleaning oats by lantern light on the kitchen table. Other horse-related chores followed, and midnight found us trying to plug a leak in the horses' water trough. We finally succeeded by using a stick to jam a pine-tar-soaked rag into the offending breach. Not wanting to further extend an already-full day, I thanked my hosts for their help and fell exhausted into bed. While I dropped off to sleep, I could hear the horses outside. The sound of their chewing was music to my ears.

Early the next day, I made my way to the gas station/bus depot and left my duffel bags to be sent on the next northbound bus.

Their destination was the National Guard Outpost in Olmos, where *Señor* Carpena had promised to send the coming night's hay and grain. After my experience of the previous evening, it was difficult to trust my irreplaceable supplies to one of Peru's buses. I'd have preferred to have the baggage under my control at all times, but the packsaddle was beyond repair, and the bus was the next-best option.

My lips had cracked painfully and were demanding attention. In response, I bought cocoa butter and – as I walked back to my hosts' home – repeatedly applied generous amounts until it ceased to be absorbed into my skin. Shortly thereafter, the excess added its flavor and greasy texture to my breakfast. Before breakfast was finished, a stranger knocked on the door. He turned out to be a newspaper reporter looking for an interview and photo session. My hosts were thrilled, especially when I asked the reporter to acknowledge their kindness in his article.

Sometimes I found these time-consuming interviews annoying. However, I put up with them because the resulting articles brought tangible benefits, such as invitations to home-cooked meals and the offer of accommodations for my horses and myself. Along the way, my hosts would include many warmhearted Latin Americans who read about my ride and then opened their doors and food cupboards for me. This hospitality was deeply appreciated, not only for the comfort and financial relief it provided, but because it helped overcome a negative perception of my fellow man, a perception that had been with me since my lonely childhood.

Once the reporter was gone, I saddled up, with my host, his family and what seemed like half the town looking on. When I was ready to go, the lady of the house handed me a paper sack full of sandwiches and fruit. I'd been eating little and infrequently and was delighted that the coming day would be different. I did my best to make sure the family knew that my gratitude was as much from the heart as their kindness had been. Full of conflicting emotions, I mounted Huascarán, waved goodbye and turned my big gray gelding in the direction of Olmos.

The early morning was cool, and the horses were fresh and energetic. Without urging, they left Motupe at a brisk pace. It was a welcome contrast to the previous evening when we had arrived in slow motion. Not far down the road, a bicycle overtook and began to pass us, its rider struggling mightily under the burden of a passenger on the handlebars. Responding to the challenge on their own, my three horses sped up, forcing the bicyclist to pump even harder before he was able to slowly inch ahead. When the bicycle had passed us, the passenger jumped off, introduced himself as a newspaper photographer and began taking pictures.

No sooner was the bicycle headed back to town than a soft drink delivery truck pulled over and stopped. The driver emerged and headed in my direction with an armload of soda pop and a bottle opener. While I was storing these in my saddlebags, a bus stopped. The door opened, and a passenger hopped out. Yet another photographer, he pointed a camera my way and rapidly snapped a roll of pictures. Before he was done, the bus began to move, and he had to literally jump aboard. The rapid succession of events was reminiscent of an old-fashioned silent movie. It was splendid entertainment, and I could hardly wait to see what would happen next. What happened next was that it got unbearably hot. As I proceeded northward, each day seemed hotter and drier. Water no longer flowed. Instead, it had to be painstakingly cranked up – bucketful by bucketful – from wells, and the sun was brutal. Ominously I'd been warned that this trend would continue all the way to Ecuador.

In the Peru of that era, air conditioning was nonexistent. Even in their vehicles, most people ventured into the desert only in the early morning or late evening. During the heat of the day, traffic dwindled to virtually nothing. Hours without seeing another human being was quite a contrast to the way my day had started. Alone and bored with the monotonous landscape, I soon found the blistering heat monopolizing my thoughts. Never had I felt anything like it.

What sustained me during the first part of that terrible day was the belief that everything would be fine as soon as the sun went down. That wasn't to be the case, however, and just before noon, I got my first clue. While getting ready to transfer from Huascarán to one of the other horses, I noticed that both Inka and Lucero were behaving strangely. It seemed to require considerable effort for Lucero to lift his right foreleg before striding forward. Concerned, I carefully checked his leg and hoof but found nothing out of the ordinary.

Inka was showing a different kind of distress. His ears were hanging almost perpendicular to the sides of his head, a sure sign he wasn't feeling well. I scrapped my plan to switch to one of the other horses at midday and continued riding Huascarán while keeping a close eye on his half-brothers. From time to time, Inka stopped, locked his legs and forced Huascarán to tow him a few steps before consenting to resume his lethargic movements.

Repeatedly I dismounted, picked up Lucero's leg and searched unsuccessfully for the source of his difficulty. Before long he was hobbling pitifully, unable to lift his right forehoof high enough to keep it from bumping against every ripple and rock in the desert sand. There was no alternative but to press on until we reached food, water and shelter. For hours we went at a pace that would have required an observer to line us up with a stationary object in order to determine if we were moving. I tried to distance myself from the discouragement I felt, but my thoughts wouldn't be controlled. I was as close as I had ever been to despair.

The blistering heat added to my discouragement. My metabolism is such that I'm comfortable wearing a short-sleeved shirt in near-freezing weather. People envy me in winter, but that's only because they don't realize the price I pay during hot weather. That day between Motupe and Olmos, I was in agony.

Chronically impatient, I was less anguished about my discomfort than I was about our sloth-like pace. Whenever we topped a rise, my eyes anxiously searched for a town. Time and again, there was nothing but another long stretch to be crossed before the next high ground would afford a fresh view. The worst moment came late during that interminable afternoon when we crested a hill. My eyes confirmed that there was nothing but desert stretching to a distant horizon. Knowing how long it would take Lucero and Inka to drag themselves to the next viewpoint, I suddenly felt trapped in an unending nightmare.

My only viable option was to mentally flog myself down the road and get through what was probably the worst day of my life. Finally, I reached the road that led from the highway to Olmos. A half-mile later, we were at the outskirts of town, a pathetic-looking caravan that had broken down after completing less than one percent of its intended journey.

Olmos was a typical desert settlement. By all appearances, it could have been an outpost in Arabia. It was hot, dry, gray and dirty. The human population was outnumbered by burros, goats, pigs, chickens and dogs that wandered through the streets taking little notice of my horses and me. At the first opportunity, I bought two family size bottles of soda pop and drank one right after the other while a crowd gathered to watch. I was still thirsty and could easily have downed a third, but by all rights, it was the horses' turn. I inquired as to where I would find the *Guardia Civil* Post and set out as instructed. It was necessary to ask several more times because peoples' directions consisted only of waving vaguely in a general direction. When I finally reached my goal, I received welcome news.

"Good afternoon, *señor*," greeted the sergeant, "My men and I have been expecting your visit. For the past couple of days things have been arriving here for you."

"That's good news," I said, much relieved. "I hope I haven't caused you any inconvenience."

"Not by any means," the sergeant assured me. "Your baggage got here a few hours ago, and some horse feed came last night. I had my men clean the corral and make up an extra bed in the barracks."

"Thank you very much," I responded, surprised that a sergeant in the *Guardia Civil* would take the trouble to anticipate and provide for my needs. "Your kindness is very much appreciated."

"One of my men will show you to the corral."

What the sergeant had called a "corral" was actually the prisoners' exercise yard. It was attached to the back of the jail and surrounded by ten-foot-high adobe walls. I was thankful the jail cells were empty, and I hoped there wouldn't be any prisoners needing exercise before the horses and I were on our way. The way my luck was going, a Peruvian convict – no, three of them! – would make a daring escape on horseback.

Perhaps because he foresaw the difficulties I might face, *Señor* Carpena had sent a full bale of hay to each overnight stop. These bales were several times what my horses could consume overnight, and most of the previous night's hay had gone to waste. I had a feeling that wouldn't be the case with the bale sent to Olmos. Our stay there was certain to exceed the single night I had originally planned.

When I turned the horses loose in the exercise yard, it was immediately apparent that Inka was far worse-off than I had thought. Most of the time, he stood stock-still, unmindful of anything around him. His tail – which usually launched into furious action whenever a fly came near – hung motionless, and he was soon covered with the hated insects. His ears continued to hang limply, and on the rare occasions when he moved, he looked ancient. Though he would drink, he had no interest in eating, not even when offered the choicest bits of hay and grain. He had no fever or other sign of infection, and all I could do was hope he'd feel better by morning.

For all intents and purposes, Lucero was a three-legged horse and looked as though he might stay that way a long time. I did what I could, including a forty-minute rubdown of his sore leg while it soaked in an oversized bucket of water. Even with me at his side – trying to keep him calm – my skittish, black gelding spilled the water three times, and three times I refilled it. After thoroughly soaking Lucero's leg, I found a sore spot on his fetlock. This I gently rubbed with liniment and wrapped with cotton and elastic bandages. Dutifully, I cleaned the next morning's ration of grain, and by the time I was free to look after myself, I lacked the energy. At midnight, without having eaten, I crawled into the spare bunk in the *Guardia* barracks. As tired as I was, I found it difficult to sleep. I was feeling sorry for myself and very angry.

I'd been raised to believe that effort is followed by success. However, that comfortable little formula didn't seem applicable in Peru. For weeks I'd neglected myself in favor of horses that were falling apart after four days and a mere hundred miles. Lucero might never take another sound step, and Inka might die from whatever he had! Fuming, I told myself that the *Guardia's* jail cells would probably see a few occupants come and go before the *Guardia's* exercise yard ceased to be a horse corral. The more I thought about it, the angrier I became. Finally, mercifully, I fell asleep.

The next morning, the sergeant of the *Guardia* seemed a good deal less friendly. I found out why when I asked if the horses and I could stay for a few days.

"On the condition that you supply the water for your horses from now on," he reprimanded in a firm, military tone. "Last night you used a three-day supply of our water. You were welcome to it, but we can't spare any more."

"I'm sorry," I said, and I meant it. "I'll be more than happy to replace what I used. Where can I find more?"

"You have to go to the wells and buy it," the sergeant explained and then briskly gave me a crash course on the intricacies of obtaining water in Olmos.

"If you use as much water every day as you did last night, you're in for a big expense and a lot of work. You can blame those," the sergeant said, pointing toward the distant Andes Mountains. "Those mountains prevent water from reaching us here on the coast."

The lofty Andes are all the more formidable because they actually consist of two or three parallel ranges, depending on the location. Said to be the backbone of Peru, they separate the country into east and west. They also stand between two of the most sharply contrasting climates on earth. Along the coast to the west are arid deserts in some of which rain has never been recorded. To the east is the Amazon basin, where torrential rains provide the Atlantic Ocean's largest single source of fresh water.

Practically every drop of Peru's rainfall comes to earth on the Andes' eastern slope. This rain feeds rivers, which, with few exceptions, flow in an easterly direction, away from the coast, where most of the population resides. The immense quantity of water in these rivers mocks the parched conditions to the west. The Amazon River is deep enough for ocean-going freighters and up to fifty miles wide. At its mouth, this extraordinary waterway spreads to an incredible hundred and fifty miles.

Olmos enjoys national attention whenever plans for diverting water there, from the Andean highlands, are discussed. This happens often because the area needs only water to become one of Peru's most productive agricultural regions. Its extraordinary fertility is demonstrated during those rare years when rains come. Soon afterward, the ground is covered with grass that reaches the bellies of mules. One year, I was told, the grass grew higher than a combined mule and rider.

However, diverting Andean water to Olmos would be a mammoth project, so expensive that it might never be realized. Even bringing water from the wells just outside Olmos was a significant chore, as I soon learned. A gallon of water weighs approximately eight pounds, and the daily requirements of Olmos were in the thousands of gallons, of which most had to be drawn by hand and transported on narrow dirt paths without the aid of motors. My own daily supply weighed in excess of two hundred pounds, more than I cared to tote by hand. I quickly decided to copy the locals, who used either mules or "tricycles." Choosing between the two was simple. In my state of mind, mules were out of the question. I was already spending enough of my time with uncooperative quadrupeds! I chose the tricycles.

Olmos abounded with three-wheeled, peddle-powered vehicles. These conveyances are in use throughout Peru and are called tricycles, though they bear little resemblance to the child's toy of the same name. Built with bicycle tires and a modified bicycle frame, they're meant for work. Unlike most three-wheeled cycles, these had two wheels in front. This made them tricky to steer, all the more so when burdened by cargo on the four-foot-square platform mounted between the front wheels.

Water was transported on these tricycles in large, square tins, which came to Olmos carrying lard, cooking oil or olive oil in bulk. Merchants would open the tins and sell the contents, little by little, to customers who brought their own containers. Once empty, the tins themselves would be sold. Like the tricycles, they were plentiful, and their principal purpose was to transport water.

The wells around Olmos were privately owned, and their water was sold by the gallon. Outside of business hours, metal covers were closed and secured with a padlock. The problem was that "business hours" could only be defined as: "times when the owner felt like doing business," which couldn't be predicted. As often as not, I found the wells closed and deserted after I had made the long walk from town.

Twice each day, I had to locate an open well, find someone who would rent me a tricycle and bring two or three tinsful of water back to the *Guardia's* exercise yard. In no time at all, I perfected several methods for arriving with less water than I'd had when I started. The tins were taller than they were wide and threatened to tip over at each bump and turn. Unfortunately, no one had yet devised a lid for them, a shortcoming I was unable to rectify with available material.

I made certain I got maximum benefit from every single drop of water. After my horses drank their fill, I used what was left to soak all four of Lucero's legs. If Lucero hadn't spilled it, I would then stand my other two horses in the same pail, one leg at a time. This routine did much to convince the good people of Olmos that riding under the desert sun is detrimental to the mental health of *gringos*. People listened skeptically whenever I explained that cool water is good therapy for a horse's legs, and they rolled their eyes when I described its beneficial effect on dried-out hooves.

If that's true, I'd hear them asking one another, *how come our mules are out working every day while this gringo is stuck here because two of his horses can't go on?*

CHAPTER 9

From the Frying Pan into the Fire

After a day in Olmos, Lucero's right front fetlock joint became hot to the touch. I was already massaging the leg and immersing it in cool water morning, noon and night, but this new symptom prompted me to set out in search of ice. I didn't really expect to find any in Olmos. Ice is hard to come by in rural Peru, where most food is fresh and people prefer beverages at room temperature.

A certain restaurant, I discovered, had a refrigerator that would have been an asset to a museum but produced the only ice in town. Twice a day, I bought its total production and used this to pack Lucero's leg. Unfortunately, there was no apparent benefit. Instead the leg worsened to the point where Lucero refused to lift it. The ground in the *Guardia Civil* exercise yard was soon crisscrossed by his drag marks. After two days of ice packs, the heat disappeared, and I began treating the leg with liniment.

Huascarán's ear problem vanished, but Inka's lack of improvement made me suspect that he'd picked up a bug. Inquiries around town led me to an unofficial doctor/veterinarian who wouldn't diagnose but if requested, would inject humans and livestock alike at reasonable rates. I vacillated between trusting the man and avoiding him like the plague. The scales tipped in his favor when he showed me his hypodermic syringes. Made of finely crafted metal and glass, they looked like works of art in their velvet-lined boxes, cradled in indentations that fit them perfectly. They were infinitely more impressive than their modern counterparts and filled me with confidence, despite the fact that their age qualified them as legitimate collectors' items.

The next problem was that this man's policy was B.Y.O.M. (Bring Your Own Medicine). I carried no antibiotics, since they require refrigeration, and hardly expected to find them in a place as primitive as Olmos. However, the town pharmacy, located in a small, dimly lit room with dirt floor and unplastered adobe walls, offered injectable penicillin and streptomycin. These came in an old-fashioned powdered form that I'd never before seen. The powder was hermetically sealed in single-dose glass containers called ampules and, of course, required no refrigeration to keep it from going bad. The effectiveness of such antibiotics was probably limited, but they seemed likely to have an effect, especially if I had Inka injected with both.

Its contents intended for human use, each container held only a fraction of what I needed, forcing me to buy every one in stock. I delivered these to the man I'd hired and, fascinated, watched him go through a procedure that was once state of the art but had survived only in primitive areas.

Each of the thin-walled ampules was three inches long, the diameter of a small test tube, and had a bullet-shaped head attached by a narrow neck. To open these, the neck was scored with a tiny blade, and the head was flicked with the forefinger, causing it to break off. With the syringe, distilled water was skillfully extracted from another ampule and squirted into the container with the powder. This was shaken, and when the powder dissolved, the resulting mixture was pulled into the syringe and injected into Inka's neck.

Following a series of massive injections over a period of two days, Inka's tail again began to chase flies. It was a sure sign he was feeling better. Soon thereafter, he regained his appetite and began curiously exploring the "corral." I never knew for sure what had been wrong with my bay gelding, but I suspected that he'd been suffering from sunstroke. Being from the highlands, he wasn't accustomed to the desert sun, of which even desert-bred horses can quickly get too much. I decided to consider traveling during night's cooler temperatures, *if* my horses and I ever traveled again.

Inka's appetite returned with a vengeance during our third day in Olmos, precisely when the horses' feed ran out. I responded by taking the bus to Ñaupe, my next scheduled overnight stop, and picking up most of the feed sent there by *Señor* Carpena. Thanks to the generous amounts provided, I could safely borrow from future supplies, and three days after my trip to Ñaupe, I traveled even farther north to a settlement known simply as Kilómetro 65 to retrieve most the feed delivered there. That particular excursion should have taken no more than a couple of hours, but unhappily it expanded to consume a long and tiring day.

A string of mishaps began when I missed the early-morning bus. It came through town half an hour ahead of schedule, contrary to Peru's most revered traditions. The next bus more than made up for this oversight. After two hours, I gave up on waiting and hiked out to the highway. Almost immediately, I caught a ride with a farmer in a pickup truck. A few hundred yards from where he picked me up, the man was obliged to pull over with a flat tire. After getting out and examining the tire, he sighed deeply and announced that he had no spare.

With more patience than I would have shown, the farmer pulled out a few rudimentary tools, took the wheel off the truck and began to laboriously remove the tire from the rim by hand. After a short while, he suggested that I try for another ride. There were few vehicles on the road at that time of day, and I thought it unlikely that another would pass before the tire was repaired. After all, patching a flat couldn't take more than a half-hour. Could it? Nearly an hour later, when I finally caught another ride, the farmer had succeeded only in removing the tire from the rim. I'll never know how much longer it took to patch the tube, reassemble the tire and inflate it with the worn-out hand pump he was carrying.

In Kilómetro 65, I claimed the majority of the feed waiting at the *Guardia Civil* outpost and spent several hours looking for a ride back to Olmos. When I finally found one, it was in the huge, empty, metal trailer of an ore truck. There was more than enough room for me and the dozen or so Indians who were sitting inside when I came aboard. Once under way, we passengers bounced around like rag dolls inside the stiffly sprung, dusty steel compartment. Metallic clanking drowned out all attempts at conversation, and the trailer was deep enough to block the view of passing scenery, even when I stood. The trip quickly became monotonous, and I began cleaning the oats I'd picked up in Kilómetro 65. The constant bouncing made it almost impossible to locate and pick out the smaller impurities. Necessity being the mother of invention, I hit upon the bright idea of using my straw hat as a sieve.

All the way around the top of its crown, my hat had a pattern, consisting of holes the ideal size for straining sand and miniscule bits of rock from the oats. This left only the larger contaminants to be individually removed. Though I suffered numerous bruises, I kept at my task for the balance of the return trip. In the process, I became the object of long, unblinking stares from my fellow passengers. I can only guess at the conclusions they reached about the giant *gringo*, absorbed in pouring oats into his hat and then … doing what? Finally they could stand it no longer and sent a representative to ask me the purpose of this mysterious ritual. My answer seemed to satisfy them until further inquiry revealed that all this was for the benefit of horses. That was the most puzzling news of all.

The truck dropped me off at the intersection where my trip had started, half a mile outside Olmos. There I borrowed one of those awkward three-wheeled cycles and loaded my hay and grain. After a quick round-trip, I hastily returned the tricycle to its owner. Next, carrying my three water tins, I jogged in the direction of the wells. It was twilight, and I feared the worst. Sure enough, the nearest well was padlocked. The same was true of the next.

At the third well, however, a kerosene lantern was lit, and customers were still being served, an extraordinary piece of luck that only half-solved my problem. I still had to find a tricycle to transport my water. At that late hour, there was only one to be found, and the owner would neither loan nor rent it to me. Instead, he insisted I hire him to deliver my three tins and their contents.

In pitch darkness, the going was slow. I could easily have walked faster than my deliveryman rode, but it would have been pointless. I needed what he was carrying to finish the day's tasks. Besides, I didn't know the man and wanted to be sure my water went to the right place. It was nearly midnight by the time my three thirsty horses got a drink. Afterward, with the remaining water, I soaked their legs, less thoroughly than usual except for Lucero's sore one. I felt guilty about slacking off, but even at that, it was 1:30 A.M. before I finally went to bed, once again without supper.

I missed a lot of meals in Olmos and not always because I was self-less. The staple diet there was goat meat, beans, rice and yucca, none of which appealed to my North American taste buds. The goat entrées were ten-percent meat (exceedingly tough) and ninety-percent bone, gristle, veins and cartilage. The yucca resembled a hard, stringy, dehydrated sweet potato, and rice was something I had never cared for. Beans I liked, but not the kind offered in Olmos. The result was that I ate a great deal of fruit and skipped a lot of meals.

While planning my ride, I had anticipated preparing my own food to save money. What I hadn't foreseen was that I'd lack the energy and often the time after a long, hard day. Neither had I realized how inexpensive it would be to buy meals. Even in Olmos – where the food was so bad – it made no sense for me to cook. After all, the ingredients I could have purchased were no different from those used in restaurants.

On the other hand, there was one time when I almost decided to cook for myself. It happened one afternoon when I was served a meal I wish I *had* skipped! Ever the optimist, I visited a small restaurant I hadn't previously tried. Looking around, I saw it was typical of Olmos. There was no glass in the windows. The floor was dirt, and a roof made of branches covered half the dining area and left the other half open to the sky.

Particularly hungry, I was the first to arrive for dinner. Even so, the waiter was slow to notice me. He was otherwise occupied, locked in close combat with legions of flies. Strapped to his back was an agricultural-type sprayer. Every once in a while, he would set the sprayer on the floor and pump it full of air, but most of the time he was dispensing poisonous mist with no regard for where it landed. Every horizontal surface was littered with dead flies and moist with fly spray. However, it shouldn't be assumed that no attention was paid to sanitation. A small boy with a filthy rag was methodically flicking the corpses from the oilcloth table covers. Miraculously, my appetite survived, albeit in a weakened state, and I seated myself. It would have made no sense to go elsewhere. All restaurants in Olmos were remarkably alike.

Among other things, that meant there was no point asking for a menu. On any given day, each restaurant prepared only a single meal, usually featuring goat and yucca. In the finest tradition of Madison Avenue, this offering was known as the "daily special." Without even asking what it was, I ordered it. Not until dinner was set before me, did I realize the magnitude of my mistake. On my plate was a goat's lower jaw! The only meat was the gums. Some teeth were right where they'd been when the goat was alive, but indentations in the jawbone showed where others were missing. It looked like the photos in those advertisements that dentists use to scare people into getting a check-up.

This second assault on my appetite was a complete success. I couldn't stand to look at my "food," let alone eat it. All in all, it was probably no worse than what's in most hot dogs, but at least a hot dog doesn't have teeth sticking out.

After four days in Olmos, Huascarán was bursting with excess energy and Inka was back to normal. To keep them fit, I decided to start exercising both on a daily basis. Ironically, I couldn't do so without taking them from the "exercise" yard, an operation that sounded deceptively simple. The way in had been unorthodox. Following the sergeant's suggestion, I had led the horses through the outpost's front door, into the office, past a desk, through a second door, down the walkway in front of empty jail cells and out the back door into the exercise yard. Four days later, two of the jail cells were occupied, and the sergeant felt that parading horses back and forth through the building wouldn't promote the proper respect for law and order.

The only other way out was a hazardous hundred-foot-long passageway between two high adobe walls. What made this narrow passageway dangerous was the concrete gutter that ran its entire length. About one-foot square, this channel was in the center of the walkway, and there were sharp corners where the sides of the gutter met the sidewalk. Worse yet, there was neither a grate nor any other protective covering. It was a trap capable of causing serious injury if a horse's leg found its way inside.

All went well when I led Huascarán into the passageway. He stood quietly while I shut the door behind him to keep the other horses where they belonged. While waiting, he calmly surveyed the situation, and when I led him forward, he carefully straddled the gutter, right legs on one ride and left on the other. After our ride, my big gray gelding was equally calm and cautious during his return to the exercise yard.

When I entered the same passageway with Inka, I received – but didn't recognize – advance notice of what was coming. If I'd been more quick-witted, I might have prevented it. Huascarán nickered. That should have been enough warning. He had always been aloof from his companions. They often called to him, but he never answered, and when he was separated from them, he didn't seem to mind. Nickering was not his normal behavior, and it signaled a deep concern about being left behind in a strange place.

Before I could shut the door, Huascarán abruptly charged into the passageway behind Inka. Immediately Lucero, who had a sheep's brain to go with his sheep's head, followed, creating a crowded and very dangerous situation. Quickly, I led Inka forward, hoping to relieve the congestion. Before I could decide what to do next, Lucero suffered a sudden panic attack. Blindly he reversed directions and bolted. In the process, he slipped into the gutter and fell hard, groaning as the bone in his legs came in contact with the sharp concrete edge. As Lucero scrambled to regain his feet, his thrashing unnerved Huascarán.

Although much bigger than Lucero, Huascarán did a better job of negotiating the tight confines he wanted to escape. He whirled around with the agility of a big cat and smoothly slid past the downed Lucero and into the exercise yard without missing a beat. Made clumsy by adrenaline, Lucero lurched to his feet and awkwardly fell once more, groaning again. After regaining his feet a second time, he followed Huascarán and disappeared around the corner. Gingerly I turned Inka and guided him back to the exercise yard. My concern for Lucero increased when I found him wild-eyed and panting, his sides working like a bellows. Worse yet, he was holding one trembling hind leg high off the ground, obviously in pain. Close examination revealed legitimate signs of superficial

81

injury but nothing that justified his extravagant reactions. Not for him to suffer in silence. He flinched and groaned in anticipation of my slightest touch. It was a disgusting performance from a horse chosen to demonstrate the toughness of his breed.

Each of the next few days, I exercised Inka and Huascarán under saddle. After resting Lucero for another day, I began to lead him, twice daily, through the streets of Olmos and into the surrounding countryside. It was the only way I knew to gauge the nature of his lameness. Some kinds improve with light exercise while others require a year or more of complete rest. If Lucero faced a long recuperation, I needed to stop wasting my time waiting for him to get better.

I never took Lucero far or fast, and in spite of his lameness, he obviously enjoyed getting out. Each of his excursions was followed by soaking all four legs in saltwater and rubbing them down. I concentrated mostly on his injured legs but didn't ignore the others. After all, an ounce of prevention is worth a pound of cure, and it is very common for a horse to strain a healthy leg while using it to spare an injured one.

Under this regimen, Lucero seemed to improve, but the signals were mixed. When his mind was on his woes, he hobbled along in obvious pain. When his mind was distracted, however, he walked with only a hint of a limp. Unavoidably, I began to suspect that his lameness might be more mental than physical.

On those leisurely walks with Lucero, I slowed down enough to really look at Olmos, and I discovered a friendly, peaceful and very happy town. No one ever seemed rushed or stressed and little wonder. People spent the heat of the day talking or daydreaming in the shade. When the evening brought cool breezes, they gathered in the central plaza to enjoy one another's company and listen to music from a loudspeaker. Watching this leisurely lifestyle, I suddenly became aware of the extent to which I was burned out. For the first time, I realized that pushing myself until I dropped wouldn't get me back on the road any sooner. I needed to limit my daily chores to eight hours at a reasonable pace. After that should come rest and enjoyment.

The instant I stopped rushing around, I started meeting people. The first were my age, and they laughingly scolded me, saying they had been waiting all week for me to slow down so they could approach me. By being so busy all the time, I had already missed two wonderful *fiestas*, but it was my good fortune that there was a birthday party scheduled for that very night.

Once it was dark, the guests assembled in front of the birthday girl's humble adobe dwelling. Next we announced our presence by setting off a series of homemade firecrackers, one for each year leading up to the birthday we had come to celebrate. According to custom, the door flew open, and we were invited inside for feasting and dancing.

It's a safe guess that Olmos hadn't seen many six-foot nine-inch North Americans. Once my pace slowed and my defenses went down, I attracted an audience whenever I was in public. People would follow me into restaurants and stores and stare while I ate or shopped. Complete strangers stopped me on the street and asked about the horses by name. The instant I stepped outside the *Guardia Civil* outpost, I'd be surrounded by children who had been waiting for me and loudly greeted their *Tío* (Uncle) Pablito.

One particular afternoon, I found myself being followed through town by a herd of children that would have made even the Pied Piper envious. With time on my hands, I stopped and turned to face my entourage. Immediately they gathered around, full of questions to which I provided answers for the best part of an hour. To my surprise, a large number of passing adults stopped and joined the impromptu interview. Suddenly, for no apparent reason, the children began to giggle, and before long the adults joined in. Everyone else's enjoyment was as complete as my own discomfort. I seemed to be the only one there who didn't know what was so funny, and, being human, I couldn't help but suspect that it must be something about me.

Or perhaps behind me? I turned and saw a tiny, stooped-over tailor. On tiptoe and beaming like a leprechaun, he was standing atop a wooden box he'd brought from inside his nearby shop. For my benefit he repeated his actions of the previous few minutes. First he went through the motions of trying to measure my height, and then he mimed a display of frustration when his measuring tape proved much too short. At this, the spectators laughed all over again.

To my considerable surprise, I also attracted a small covey of female admirers. In a town where everyone else was short and dark with brown eyes and black hair, I suspected that my drawing power was in my height, my blue eyes, my fair skin and my sandy hair. Confirmation of this came with compliments that were directed my way. Enormously flattering at first, the compliments soon became tiresome. At times I was more than ready to retreat to the seclusion of the *Guardia Civil* outpost. Even there, to my dismay, solitude and relaxation were hard to find. The Guardsmen, after all, expected their share of my attention, and as kind as they'd been, I could hardly withhold it. Even the prisoners managed to stake a claim to my time, since the only well-lit spot for cleaning grain was right in front of their cells.

I came to have a nodding acquaintance with the dogs, mules, goats, chickens and pigs that wandered the streets. It never ceased to amaze me that these animals spent the daylight hours unconfined. Those with financial value, at least, would have been sorely missed if they had meandered off or been hit by a vehicle. Theft also would have been a simple matter. Little expertise would have been required to alter the "brands" they wore. In the case of goats, for example, ownership was declared by simply threading and tying colored yarn through holes in their ears.

Most of the houses in town had attached corrals, and when night fell, owners would drive their livestock into these pens. At first light, however, the animals would invariably be released again, apparently to forage because the owners couldn't afford to feed them. To support this theory, I came up with three compelling pieces of evidence. One: Olmos was the only place where I had ever seen skinny pigs. Little more than skin and bones, they were perpetually hungry and constantly brawling over scraps of garbage. Two: the good people of Olmos routinely threw their household scraps into the streets. Three: those scraps never stayed long where they landed. Olmos had an uncommonly dedicated sanitation department.

Livestock wasn't the only animal life around Olmos. Lizards and vultures were also plentiful, as were snakes. While walking Lucero on the outskirts of town one afternoon, I saw an unusual specimen of the latter. Unconcerned by our approach, it slithered across the road, in no apparent hurry. This display of confidence told me to give that particular snake a wide berth, and I made sure Lucero did the same. Some youngsters, walking nearby, also saw the reptile and breathlessly announced that its species was poisonous and its bite sometimes responsible for the death of domesticated animals. I couldn't hold back the thought that if one of my horses had the bad luck to be bitten, it would undoubtedly be Lucero!

Later the *Guardia Civil* sergeant told me that it was common to find these snakes near livestock. According to him, this was because the serpents often sought refuge from the sun in the shadows cast by large animals. Biting such livestock was shortsighted on the part of the snake, I joked, especially considering the scarcity of shade. My attempt at humor went right over the sergeant's head. He apparently took poisonous reptiles very seriously.

"Even if you kill one," he warned, "handle it with extreme caution.

It should never be picked up by other than the neck."

If a snake can be said to have such a thing, I thought, keeping this latest attempt at humor to myself.

After eight days in Olmos, I had nearly run out of horse feed and was torn between alternatives. I could take the bus to Piura and buy an additional supply, or I could press on with my journey. At some point, I'd have to put Lucero to the test, and the more I thought about it, the more I could find no good reason to wait. I decided to push on to Ñaupe, asking Lucero to carry nothing but his own weight. If exercise didn't work out his remaining soreness, I had an expensive contingency plan. As a last resort, I'd send him from Ñaupe to Piura by truck and have him looked at by a veterinarian. One way or another, I'd get my three horses to Piura, regroup and send feed to our nightly stopovers as far as the border with Ecuador. If Lucero was no better after a few days and if the vet thought his recovery imminent, I'd send my black gelding by truck to the border. There, he could rest until I caught up. If he wasn't better by then, he would have to be left behind.

I asked the *Guardia* sergeant what he thought of resting by day and traveling at night, and he strongly advised against it, warning of two bandits working the area. *Bandidos*, including the pair active at that time, normally tended to strike under cover of darkness. Since the desert didn't become unbearable until midday, it was recommended that I start at dawn and quit around noon. That sounded like an acceptable compromise. If Lucero didn't slow us too much, my horses and I could be in Ñaupe by midday.

On the maps I carried, the area around Olmos was referred to as the Desert of Sechura, but I never once heard it called by that name. The locals without exception called it the *despoblado*, which translates as "wilderness," literally "unpopulated place." I'd soon learn the truth of this nickname. Were I to be assaulted, there would be absolutely no one to come to my aid. That was why bandits had sought victims there for centuries.

I was about to tackle what might well be the most dangerous part of my journey!

Chapter 10

Gambles that Failed

They say hope springs eternal, and throughout my ride, it did. Each time I felt myself sinking into a bottomless pit of despair, I was rescued by hope, exactly as promised by whoever "they" are. As the next leg of my journey drew near, I felt my optimism returning. I had been in a funk since Lucero's accident in the passageway, unable to reacquire my previous energy and dedication. In a way, my sudden interest in socializing had been a form of rebellion against my own self-discipline, a way of protesting against investing so much effort and having so little to show for it.

The price of this brief vacation was that I had plenty to do during my final evening in Olmos. Adding to my last-minute tasks, Lucero's rear leg swelled again. Stubbornly, I refused to postpone my departure; it was time to find out, once and for all, whether my black gelding could continue or not. However, just in case the swelling was a sign of infection, I again hired the man with the hypodermic syringes. He administered two injections of antibiotics; the first at 7:00 in the evening, and the second at 1:00 in the morning. At 2:00 A.M., I finished cleaning grain and caught an hour's sleep. At 3:00 A.M., I saddled up, mounted Huascarán and bid Olmos a silent good-bye. Slowly I rode through the dark, deserted streets and into the desert, hoping no *bandidos* were watching. For the first time, my Bowie knife hung from my belt.

I took what I regarded as an acceptable risk by starting earlier than the *Guardia* sergeant had recommended. With Lucero slowing our progress, the trip to Ñaupe might outlast the light of day. If so, being on the road after nightfall was more dangerous than being there just before dawn.

Though Lucero didn't improve with the miles, he didn't get worse either. The bad news was that he spared his sore limbs by virtue of a shuffle that slowed us more than I had anticipated. I'd hoped we might beat the sun's heat to our destination. Instead, the sun's heat beat on us long before we got there. Its rays had chased the overcast from the sky by 10:00 A.M., and by 11:00, my brain felt as if it had been thrown in a broiler. The temperature was oppressive, and there was neither relief nor escape. Heat radiated down from the sun and was reflected upwards by the sand. With no exertion on my part, sweat covered my entire body. Even the simple act of breathing was uncomfortable.

Everywhere I looked, the view was distorted by shimmering heat haze. Most of the time, the air was dead still. On the rare occasions when it moved, it felt like air from a blast furnace. I was reminded of a friend who had spent a few hours crossing a desert in an air-conditioned car and afterward wondered how deserts got their terrible reputation.

Let him be there from dawn to dusk on horseback, and he'll understand! I thought to myself.

It is well-known that desert heat produces physical discomfort. Less known is that it also attacks the mind. It saps the will, kills the appetite and imparts depression. It also produces the very thing I had hoped to escape in Peru, stupefying boredom. Even if I had slept more than an hour the night before, boredom would have provided a powerful incentive to sleep. For a while I stubbornly fought to stay awake, but it was a loosing battle. The gentle hissing of the horses' hooves in the sand and the steady motion beneath me were irresistible inducements to doze off, and soon my head was bobbing back and forth. I didn't sleep deeply, but it was enough to take me away from the almost-unbearable temperatures, though only for short periods.

Drifting between sleep and half-sleep, I somehow managed to stay upright and to keep us going in the right direction. I was repeatedly brought back to reality, several times by the clawing branches of thorny bushes that my mount passed too closely. Other times sleep's grip was broken by the buzzing of insects, so loud that it seemed amplified. Once I awoke amidst a group of startled buzzards. The large, evil-smelling birds had been picking at the carcass of a long-dead animal when the horses and I wandered through their midst. They boldly refused to give ground, and some took a step or two in our direction. None took their eyes from us until we were out of sight. I was reminded of the cartoon in which one buzzard is telling the other: "Patience, my ass! I'm gonna kill something!" Another time, in a state of semi-consciousness, I saw a desert fox watching us from the top of a sand dune. Constantly, I saw lizards wriggling across the sand after our approach chased them from wherever they had sought shade.

Knowing that the horses, too, were suffering, I shared the water in my canteen with them, but it was gone before doing any of us much good. I hadn't seriously considered having my horses carry water, feeling that the energy expended and discomfort suffered

87

would more than cancel the benefit. In sufficient amount for three horses, water would have been a heavy burden, and as I'd learned in Olmos, pound for pound there is no cargo more difficult to carry. Besides, I had always been able to find a way to quench the horses' thirst along the trail. There was never standing or running water, of course, but I had always been able to find a lonely shack where I could buy my horses a drink. Not in the *despoblado*, however. Where there are no people, there are no lonely shacks. Around mid-afternoon, I flagged down a large truck and paid a hefty price for a few gallons of water from a metal drum it carried. In spite of the water's temperature, my horses drank until every last drop was gone.

All in all, it took over fourteen hours to reach Naupe. It was near sundown when I finally arrived at the *Guardia Civil* outpost, where the horses and I were to spend the night. An invitation had been extended when I'd come ahead from Olmos to borrow half the feed sent by *Señor* Carpena. To my distress, the officer who had invited me wasn't on duty. Fortunately, his replacement was equally hospitable.

Once again, the horses' "corral" was attached to the *Guardia* outpost. This time, it was a courtyard, with no gate, accessible only from inside the building. One of the troopers and I temporarily rearranged the furniture and led my horses to their accommodations. Inka and Huascarán felt no immediate desire to eat, but Lucero – after traveling thirty-two miles with two sore legs – had a voracious appetite. From this, I gathered he was none the worst for wear. Huascarán, on the other hand, had diarrhea, and Inka – in the desert of all places! – had a cough.

After dinner, I doctored the horses and collapsed onto a bunk in the sleeping quarters. Lying there, I wondered how I'd manage to sleep. Naupe's *Guardia* outpost was built on the shoulder of the highway, and its function was to check the documentation of passing trucks. The endless parade of heavy vehicles made my bedroom a very noisy place. Evidently, Peru's truckers hadn't been notified when the muffler was invented. The unrestricted roar of heavy-duty engines was blended with the squealing of brakes, the grinding of gears and the sound of voices trying to make themselves heard above the din. Having seen very little traffic during the day, I was amazed at the change once the sun went down. Nearly all long-haul truck traffic moved at night because truck owners didn't want their tires and motors overheating during the day's intense temperatures. The activities of the two mule-riding bandits I'd heard about in Olmos hadn't caused them to alter that routine.

Even though they often plied their trade by night, the bandits weren't perceived as a threat by truckers. For one thing, these highwaymen preferred assaulting solitary travelers, and most long-haul trucks carried two drivers and at least one laborer. For another, mules were better-suited for assaults on those traveling by horse, mule or cycle. Favorite bandit targets also included people who stopped to sleep in their vehicles, which truckers seldom did because of the second driver. Another likely victim was anyone whose transportation broke down, but again, the trucks were more or less immune, owing to the number of people they carried.

Fearing I was going to be awake most of the night, I arranged myself as comfortably as possible on the small bed. Moments later, I was sleeping the sleep of the dead. The following morning, I awoke in the exact position I had assumed before falling asleep. Apparently, I hadn't moved during the entire night.

After feeding the horses, I took stock of my situation. It was unimproved since the night before. Huascarán's diarrhea continued, and he wasn't eating. Lucero was as lame as ever and discharging mucous from his nostrils. Inka's cough and appetite had worsened, and people kept telling me he was favoring a hind leg, though they disagreed on which one. I couldn't see anything wrong with him, but so many opinions to the contrary were hard to dismiss.

The horses' miseries added to the feeling of guilt that had plagued me throughout the day. Perhaps everything was my fault, because I asked too much of my horses. Well, maybe, but I had demanded even more from myself. The difference was that I saw purpose in the suffering and hard work while the horses saw only suffering and hard work.

It was no longer possible to doubt that Lucero's lameness was genuine. It would have been cruel to ask him to continue. However, shipping him to Piura and having him treated by a veterinarian would likely cost enough to doom my venture.

As sorry as I had felt for myself in Olmos, I'd also been filled with determination to solve my problems. That morning in Ñaupe, on the other hand, I couldn't see a good reason to keep getting up every time I was knocked down. For the first time, I entertained thoughts of quitting. I couldn't convince myself that success might be achieved if only I'd put forth another effort. The pattern was well-established. Even if I put forth a thousand efforts, fate would deliver a thousand and one blows to defeat me!

While unpacking supplies from my duffel bags, I came across the pouch containing my important papers. Inside was the sealed enve-lope from Jorge Baca's neighbor. The old man had told me that the contents included the image of a saint, to help me have a successful journey. *That* thought brought forth a bitter laugh. When the time came, I intended to make a mental note as to that particular saint's identity. Future supplications for help would be directed elsewhere!

Quite mysteriously, while eating breakfast at Ñaupe's only decent (a highly relative term in Ñaupe!) restaurant, I began to feel hope, eternally springing. I would find a way to accomplish my goal, even if it meant asking for help. The problem was: out there in the mid-dle of nowhere, who could I ask? I didn't know a single soul from Ñaupe to Ecuador. Nonetheless, there *was* a possibility. Admittedly it was a long shot, based on a man I hadn't met and whose name I couldn't remember. In fact, I knew nothing about him, except that he bred Peruvian *Paso* horses near Piura. Jorge Baca had suggested I visit him. Since his *hacienda* was out of my way, I had rejected the idea and promptly forgotten about him. Try as I might, I couldn't recall his name. I was still trying when a northbound pickup truck pulled off the highway and parked in front of the restaurant. The driver walked in, looked my way and nodded before sitting at the next table. When I stood to leave, he looked me over.

"You must be the famous Pablito," he declared with a friendly smile.

"I don't know if I'm famous," I responded, as usual, "but I am called Pablito."

"I saw your picture in the papers," he explained.

There was a brief silence and thinking the conversation was over, I started to walk away.

"The last I heard on the radio, you were delayed in Olmos," the man seemed determined to keep our conversation alive.

"And now I'm delayed in Ñaupe," I said, turning around.

"Do you have a moment to talk?" he asked, gesturing to one of the empty chairs at his table.

I had all the time in the world, and I sat down.

"How can I help you?" the man asked.

"Do you have a horse trailer or know a good veterinarian?"

"No," he responded. "I'm an agricultural engineer, but I don't really know much about horses."

"Do you know anyone near Piura who breeds Peruvian *Paso* horses?"

My question was a ridiculous long shot, considering that Piura was a fairly large city.

"You must be speaking of José Antonio Onrubia," came the answer.

I recognized the name. I *had* been speaking of José Antonio Onrubia! Yet another of my problems was solved when the man kindly offered to drive me to *Señor* Onrubia's *hacienda*. After asking the *Guardia* sergeant to keep an eye on my horses, I was on my way.

Looking back, I sometimes wonder what would have happened if I had known that *Señor* Onrubia was regarded to be the wealthiest man in Peru. *That* little piece of information would almost certainly have stopped me from going to see him, for in Peru, as elsewhere, wealthy men are usually intimidating and difficult to approach.

Although the drive took less than two hours, it seemed to drag on forever. Watching the desert go by, I speculated about what it would be like to cover the same ground again on horseback. I calculated that five minutes in the pickup translated to more than an hour in the saddle, if all went fairly well, which it hadn't yet done.

Upon reaching Piura, my benefactor took me to his home and offered me the opportunity to shave, shower and change clothes. I was served a simple lunch that seemed splendid compared with my other recent meals. After lunch, I was anxious to get started, but my host explained that it was too early. In those days, the *siesta* was still a part of Peruvian life. Businesses and offices would shut down for three hours, starting at noon. People went home for lunch and a nap, and at three in the afternoon, everyone went back to work until seven in the evening.

By the time we left for *Señor* Onrubia's *hacienda*, I was relaxed, confident and still ignorant of the fact that I was on my way to an audience with Peru's richest man. When I met him, nothing in his behavior, his demeanor or the way he lived made me suspect his lofty status. It must be rare for a man of such position and power to be as down-to-earth as the man I met that day.

I arrived at the *Hacienda* San Jacinto near the end of *siesta*, and *Señor* Onrubia postponed his return to the office in order to listen attentively to what I had to say. As we talked, he took me on a tour of his stable where he showed me his beautiful horses. I was especially thrilled to see *Piloto, a legendary sire that would re-enter my life years later and play the starring role in another adventure.

When I finished my tale of woe, *Señor* Onrubia offered to send his truck to Ñaupe. Lucero, he proposed, should be brought back to San Jacinto for rest, recuperation and examination by his vet, reputed to be the best lameness man in northern Peru. In the meantime, I could ride Inca and Huascarán as far as Piura and then be his guest for as long as necessary. Just like that, my venture was given new life.

"Please, make yourself at home," *Señor* Onrubia insisted as he prepared to leave for his office. "You can stay in my home tonight and go to Ñaupe with my truck and driver in the morning."

"I appreciate the offer," I replied, "but I need to get back this evening to take care of my horses."

"When someone is more concerned about his horses' well-being than his own," he observed with approval, "it's the unmistakable sign of a true horseman."

This was a satisfying compliment, especially in view of the doubts that had plagued me earlier. It was also the note upon which our first meeting ended. *Señor* Onrubia left for his office but not before asking San Jacinto's administrator to give me a bale of hay and drive me to the southern end of Piura. There, they both agreed, it should be a simple matter for me to find a ride to Ñaupe. It wasn't all that easy, though. Seeing that, *Señor* Onrubia's administrator kindly stayed with me and took charge of the frustrating search. For more than an hour, he drove from truck stop to truck stop, and as night fell, he finally found me – and my bale of hay – a ride with a convoy of cattle trucks.

That morning's ride to Piura had taken too long for my liking, but it took the slow-moving cattle trucks several times as long to make the same trip in reverse. This isn't to say the trucks made the trip in reverse gear. It only seemed that way. Twice, the convoy's sluggish pace halted because of mechanical difficulties affecting one of the trucks. Because many of Peru's trucks were so old that parts were no longer available, truckers had to be capable of making a carburetor out of a tin can, if need be. Ours were, and the necessary repairs were made on the spot.

A more worrisome delay occurred later when the trucks pulled over to the side of the road so the drivers could huddle together and chew coca leaves. Knowing coca to be the source of cocaine, I was unhappy over more than just the delay. Chewing coca leaves was widespread in the Peruvian *sierra* especially among *serranos*, mountain Indians who swore it provided relief from the effects of cold and altitude. Along the coast, it was less common but prevalent among truck drivers. They credited the leaves with helping them stay alert.

Years later, I learned that coca leaves don't have anything resembling the effect of their notorious derivative. In fact, I've since had coca tea when suffering from altitude sickness in Peru's Andes, and I can testify that it had no effect other than to provide relief. However, not yet knowing this and being a person who takes even an aspirin with hesitation, I was exceedingly troubled that night with the convoy.

Sitting next to what I fancied were impaired drivers, I watched the road with more care than if I myself had been driving. There wasn't much to see, aside from a roadside dotted with crosses and small shrines. These monuments marked spots where people had died in traffic accidents, undoubtedly caused by chewing coca leaves, according to my overactive imagination. Tired as I was, I remained wide-awake, busily hatching various schemes for converting Peru's truckers to an over-the-counter product for combating drowsiness. My eyes never left the road until I reached my destination, less than four hours before my next day would begin.

The next morning, I was up early in order to have Lucero ready at the appointed time. I also went through my duffel bags and separated everything, such as cold and rainy-weather gear, that I wouldn't need during the next few days. These items were carefully packed in one bag. This I planned to take to San Jacinto, when I rode back with Lucero, rather than send it by bus to my next two overnight stops.

While waiting for Lucero's transportation, I passed the time going over Inka and Huascarán. They seemed much improved. Only mildly interested in their hay the previous day, they had devoured every stalk and leaf of the meal I'd given them four hours earlier, upon my return from San Jacinto. In addition, they showed healthy appetites when I served breakfast.

By the time San Jacinto's truck and driver arrived, I'd had everything in readiness for three hours, hoping for a quick turnaround. Such a fantasy indicated that either I had forgotten I was in Peru or was suffering from a severe learning disability. The driver proceeded to the restaurant for a leisurely second breakfast while I fretted, knowing the delay would shorten my coming night's slumber. Due to be back in the saddle at 3:00 the following morning, I didn't relish another abbreviated sleep.

Finally the driver finished his meal and backed the truck up to an embankment so I could load Lucero. At that point, two facts became apparent. First: the driver was afraid of horses and knew nothing about them. Second: this truck was only slightly more appropriate for livestock than the one sent to take Hugo Bustamante's horses to the bullfight in Lima. It was in good condition and had no benches inside, but it wasn't properly appointed – by North American standards, anyway – for the transportation of horses.

I loaded and tied the skittish Lucero without mishap, but the instant I dismounted from the truck, he began to fidget. This continued until he took a hard fall, before his trip had even begun. The result was a nasty cut on his right foreleg. Never in my life had I seen such an unfortunate (and dare I say: stupid?) animal. Almost every morning, I found him newly wounded by some mishap that had occurred during the night. I climbed back inside the truck and doctored Lucero's leg. When this took longer than the driver liked, his sighs advised me that he was suddenly in a hurry.

"I can leave whenever you're ready," he finally said.

"I'm ready now," I said, just finishing. "Let's go."

"Are you coming, too?" His voice indicated surprise.

"I think it would be a good idea," I responded, not bothering to add that it would be more humane to shoot Lucero on the spot than to send him off alone in that truck.

"Don't worry about your horse. I can look after him for you," he offered.

Good manners dictated that I refrain from speculating aloud about Lucero's chances for survival while traveling with a driver who didn't know horses and would likely extend the same care and consideration he gave a load of cotton.

"He's a little difficult to handle," I said. "I think I should come along just in case."

"Your company will be welcome," the driver declared cheerfully, gesturing to the front passenger seat.

His enthusiasm made me ashamed of my unkind thoughts.

"I think I should ride back here to make sure nothing goes wrong," I announced, provoking a disappointed reaction.

It was a good thing I rode with my accident-prone gelding. In traffic and on rough stretches of road, I was able to help him stay on his feet more than once. On stretches of straight, smooth highway with no other vehicles in sight, however, I had difficulty staying on my own feet as I dozed, leaning against the railing.

We arrived at San Jacinto in the absence of *Señor* Onrubia. I was greeted by the trainer, a jovial man named Eusebio Rodriguez Baca. Full of good humor and wit, he helped me get Lucero comfortably situated and offered to look after my duffel bag. That done, he invited me into his home for a beverage. Located right next to the stable, the house was infested with flies.

"I haven't had time to spray," he apologized. "Please make yourself comfortable. This is a humble house, but it's cooler than outside."

I smiled.

"It's a very nice house, and I appreciate being invited in."

"Please sit down," he said, indicating the best chair in the room.

I sat, and that was the signal for hoards of flies to begin swarming around me. With an irritating persistence they landed on my arms, neck and face. I swatted and killed several, but the rest couldn't be discouraged. After Rodriguez whispered to his youngest daughter, she briefly left the room and returned with a towel. Taking up a position next to my chair, the tiny girl began swinging her towel at the flies, driving them away.

"That's not necessary," I said, as gently as possible.

If she had been peeling grapes and placing them directly in my mouth, I couldn't have felt more embarrassed.

"Please," Rodriguez replied. "You are our guest, and my daughter wants to do this for you."

After handing me a bottle of soda pop, Rodriguez removed the cap with an opener. It was his way of assuring me the contents were sanitary. Surprised to see how quickly I drained the small bottle, he brought another and another until I finally declined more even though I was still thirsty. Then he excused himself and left the room. I tried to start a conversation with his daughter, but she was so painfully shy that it seemed cruel to persist. Not one to sit idly, I took out a ball-point pen and a scrap of paper and started a list of the things I hoped to accomplish during the coming days. All the while, Rodriguez's daughter continued with her assignment. She was still at it when her father returned.

Rodriguez announced it was time for him to return to work. Before I stood up, I reached into my pocket and removed a coin, which I extended in the direction of the little girl. She looked at her father and made no move to accept my gift.

"It isn't necessary to pay her for being hospitable," Rodriguez assured me.

"Please," I said. "Your daughter did a very good job, and I would like the pleasure of rewarding her."

"Very well," Rodriguez relented. He lowered his eyes to his daughter's face and nodded his head up and down. Only then did the little girl break into a grin as she shyly stepped forward and took the coin.

"*Gracias*," she said in a whisper.

Her appreciation could be read on her beaming face.

"*De nada*," I responded. "You're welcome."

It was evening by the time I'd made my way to the south side of

Piura and found a ride to Ñaupe with a rancher. In contrast to the cattle convoy, the rancher's pickup truck negotiated the distance in less than two hours. To my surprise, Inka and Huascarán had polished off the feed brought from San Jacinto the previous evening. Fortunately, I'd brought more. After serving it, I slept until 3:00 A.M.

The next morning was the first time my journey was the equal of what I'd imagined when I started. At a vigorous pace, Huascarán easily carried me across a range of rugged hills that were enveloped in a cool, low-lying mist. It was invigorating and exciting, partly because of some rather anxious moments in traffic.

In those rocky hills, construction of the *Panamericana* had required considerable blasting and excavation. As a consequence, the roadway was narrow and had very little shoulder. Whenever oncoming trucks met, they would slow to a crawl before sliding past one another, each half on and half off the pavement. In compliance with Murphy's Law, whenever there were two trucks, they were traveling in opposite directions and would pass each other right next to us. At least, that's how it seemed. With the darkness, the mist and the glaring headlights, most drivers didn't see my horses and me. Repeatedly, we were pushed close to the edge of a cliff or pinned against a sheer wall.

Just as early morning had provided my ride's first sense of romance, the hours from 7:00 to 11:00 offered the first exhilaration. Prior to that, the horses hadn't moved beyond a walk for more than a few hundred yards at a time. But for four hours that morning, Huascarán and Inka were in a brisk *paso*, each, in his turn, asking for more rein so he could go even faster. To my delight, we arrived at Kilómetro 65 before noon, after making outstanding time.

At the entrance to town, there was a Highway Department repair station, little more than a small, fenced yard jammed full of material. As I rode by, the watchman waved me over and offered water for the horses. He refused payment, informed me that there wasn't an available corral within miles and proceeded to assemble a temporary corral, using four portable road barricades. Once my horses were unsaddled and cared for, I excused myself and walked up the highway toward the *Guardia Civil* outpost. My mission was to collect my horse feed, but I also looked forward to seeing a certain sergeant whose acquaintance I had made the day before when the truck carrying Lucero stopped for the required inspection. This particular sergeant and his fellow officers had reveled in poking fun at my predicament.

"I don't remember reading anything in the papers about plans to transport your famous horses in trucks," he had needled.

"Maybe you should sell your horses and buy two of ours," another had offered. "We ride through this country all the time, without all the complications you seem to be having."

It would have been pointless to downplay my problems. The sergeant was right up to the minute on every detail, thanks to his fellow officers at the outposts in Olmos and Ñaupe. Further comments revealed that the sergeant and his men, from poor families, considered *Paso* horses to be pampered playthings of the hated upper class. The sergeant's teasing made no pretense of being good-natured. He made it obvious that he was no more fond of North Americans than he was of the upper class in his own country.

Turnabout being fair play, a certain North American was joyously anticipating a small measure of revenge. Since my previous day's tormentors were federal police officers, there was a need for subtlety, of course, but I had no intention of completely restraining my desire to get back at them. In less than seven hours, Huascarán and Inka had covered thirty-two miles, most of it hard going in deep, loose sand. That was considerably faster than the *Guardia* made that same trip on their horses.

"You're here early. Did you ride all night?" the sergeant asked when I presented myself.

His tone of voice was pleasant enough to momentarily disarm me.

"No, I left Ñaupe at about 3:30," I answered. "The horses made good time."

"3:30! That *is* good time," he said graciously.

I knew that gloating would best be done later, but the opening was too perfect.

"How long does it usually take you?" I asked, innocently.

The sergeant looked up, without answering. His eyes bored holes in me. Thanks to his boasting of the previous day, I already knew the answer, and he knew that I knew!

My original plan had been to spend the night with the *Guardia* in Kilómetro 65 and go the rest of the way to San Jacinto the next day. However, I wasn't at ease with the prospect of tackling fifty miles in a single day. In order to shorten the coming day's ride, I elected to wait out the worst of the heat where I was and in the cool of evening to ride on to Kilómetro 50. That would shave nine miles off the next day's ride and spare me what was shaping up to be an uncomfortable night in the company of the *Guardia* in Kilómetro 65.

I passed the time cleaning grain and then sent that night's feed and my baggage to Kilómetro 50 with a passing truck. At 4:00 P.M., in preparation for getting under way, I walked down the road to my makeshift corral. From behind, I saw a man in a *Guardia* uniform standing there, quietly studying Huascarán. When I was closer, I realized it was the sergeant who had taken the lead during my previous day's hazing, the same man upon whom I'd taken my revenge a short while earlier. When he heard my approach, he turned his head.

"The gray horse is sick," he said without expression in his voice or on his face.

My heart plunged to the soles of my feet and kept right on going in the same direction. This couldn't be true, not on top of everything else! Could it?

❖❖❖

This is how he should have looked (see page 159)!

CHAPTER 11

The Worst Form of Unlucky

Huascarán hadn't eaten since being turned loose hours earlier. Neither had he passed any manure, which concerned me since I was pretty sure he hadn't done so on the trail that morning, either.

All was not well with my big, gray gelding, but he was standing proudly, breathing well and showing no other signs of distress. Constipation wouldn't have been a surprising aftermath of his recent diarrhea, and I elected to continue on to Kilómetro 50, riding Inka. I felt sure that a little exercise would loosen Huascarán's bowels. I only wish this guess hadn't been quite so accurate! No sooner were we out of sight than Huascarán began to have frequent bowel movements, which became progressively looser until he was passing green liquid. To make matters worse, I didn't like the way Inka was moving. Though there was no definite evidence of his being footsore, he seemed to be walking on eggs. As a precaution, I dismounted and led Inka with Huascarán tethered to the saddle in such a way that we proceeded single file.

At first, I selected a route far from the highway, too proud to be seen in my current circumstances. Soon, however, the horses' hooves were sinking out of sight in the loose sand. This forced them to work harder than necessary at the same time I was walking in order to spare them. Practical considerations took precedence over pride, and we returned to firmer footing next to the highway. Curious motorists immediately asked the inevitable questions. Over and over, I answered these by saying: "No, nothing's wrong. I'm just stretching my legs."

Just before dark, a bus passed. Every passenger was crowded against the windows on the side nearest me. All were smiling, and they had their hands in front of the windows so I could see, if not hear, their applause. They knew things had been difficult, but they'd never know how much their gesture picked up my spirits, at a time when I desperately needed it.

By the time we reached Kilómetro 50, Huascarán's head hung low, and his hindlegs and tail were caked with dried diarrhea. It was a heartbreaking sight. I thought back to the look in his eyes after he had bested me at Jorge Baca's farm, having broken every rope I had. When I compared that with what I saw before me, I was painfully aware of how badly things had gone wrong. Before I did anything else, I washed him off as best I could in view of water's scarcity. When I finished, the coating of manure was gone, but his tail and hindquarters were still stained green.

Kilómetro 50 was the smallest, most humble settlement I'd yet seen. It was located astride the highway, exactly thirty miles from Piura. Referred to as a *caserío*, the tiny hamlet was nothing more than a few restaurants, huts really, their walls made by planting sticks upright in the ground, side by side. Without exception, these huts were restaurants catering to truckers. Other roadside merchants were too poor to erect even such simple structures. They sold meals from carts next to their open cooking fires. Other vendors offered cigarettes and candy displayed in trays made from cardboard boxes. Even they weren't at the bottom of the totem pole. One withered Indian lady was pulling at the udder of her burro, laboriously extracting milk, a "refreshment" she was offering for sale.

Even in a place where people had so little, hospitality was generously extended to the "famous Pablito" and his horses. The horses slept in a small, fenced storage yard that was nearly filled with what can only be described as junk, and I dozed fitfully in the back room of a little ramshackle restaurant.

Having gotten precious little sleep, I checked the horses at 3:00 the next morning. Alternating between diarrhea and constipation, Huascarán hadn't passed any manure, consistent with the fact that he hadn't eaten. He looked terrible. I considered resting him for a day, but he was dehydrated to the point where drinking wouldn't have easily solved the problem even if he'd shown the inclination to drink. I figured it would be best to press on and get him to a vet in Piura. Inka still acted as if he might be footsore, and rather than risk making him worse, I led both horses as I had the previous afternoon. Once we were moving, Huascarán's bowels began to do the same. He was still producing thick, green liquid.

At about 10:00 that morning, a man on a spotted mule ventured out from the roadside brush and onto the pavement ahead. He stopped in the middle of the highway and sat there, giving the horses and I a very thorough looking-over as we approached. I was busy making observations of my own and regretfully took note of the fact that the man was packing a pistol! The appearance of oncoming cars seemed to make him uneasy, and he divided his attention equally between the approaching vehicles and me. Was he unhappy about the impending arrival of potential witnesses, or were such thoughts simply the product of an over-active imagination? Doing my best to look as poverty-stricken – and large! – as possible, I cheerfully greeted the man as the horses and I passed by.

"*Buenos días*," he greeted in return, and then he asked, rather boldly, "Where are you heading?"

"North," was my intentionally vague reply.

The man nodded and hastily rode into the tall roadside brush, where he disappeared just as a line of cars passed at high speed. It was the first time, I had wished that passing motorists would stop for a nice, long chat. As Inka, Huascarán and I continued on our way, I tried to determine which way the lone rider had gone, but the thick brush prevented that.

A short while later, I noticed that I was being followed at a distance by a mule and rider. I tried desperately to increase that distance, but Huascarán refused to cooperate. Whenever I stepped up the pace, he planted his feet and stiffened his legs, stopping Inka dead in his tracks because of the rope between them. When I started Inka forward again, my gray gelding would follow only so long as I didn't try to go faster than he wished. There wasn't much choice but to continue as best I could while the man behind me drew steadily closer.

More cars were approaching, and I hoped their presence would have the same effect as those that had passed before. Sure enough, the rider steered his mule into the roadside brush and stayed out of sight until the vehicles had passed. I couldn't be certain if this exit from the roadway had left him visible from passing cars or if he had hidden. That information would have gone a long way toward revealing his motives. After all, mules are notoriously unpredictable. He might be doing no more than keeping a prudent distance from traffic.

The next time a car approached, I took advantage of the situation by stopping to adjust my saddle and snug up the cinch, just in case I later needed to make a quick getaway. I wasn't sure how I was going to convince Huascarán to do *anything* quickly, but first things first. Until I adjusted the saddle, I wouldn't be able to ride Inka at all, fast or slow. Huascarán's sudden stops had pulled the saddle far behind its correct position, and there was daylight between the cinch and Inka's belly.

The rider on the mule continued along the highway shoulder rather than duck into the brush while this latest car passed. By doing so, he deprived me of the amount of time I expected to have and caught up just as I was finishing with the saddle. When abreast of me, he slowed his mount and meandered past. We both said "*buenos días*" and exchanged what passed for friendly nods, all the while sub-jecting one another to a thorough scrutinizing. This was not the same man I had previously seen, but there was one ominous simi-larity. On his saddle this second man carried a rifle. Aside from the first man's pistol, it was the only firearm I'd seen in the possession of a Peruvian civilian. Fortunately, another car was drawing near, and the man reacted by silently disappearing into the brush on the opposite side of the highway.

Instantly, I untied Huascarán and swung into the saddle without touching the stirrups. With all our combined strength, Inka and I hauled Huascarán pell-mell down the road. After about a mile, the roadside brush thinned out, and after two more miles, I dismount-ed and assumed a more sedate pace. I was feeling slightly silly for having allowed myself to be stampeded, but I also felt much safer where I could see for miles in any direction.

At the time I had my doubts, but in retrospect I'm certain I had the pleasure of meeting the two celebrities against whom the sergeant of the *Guardia* in Olmos had warned me. Who else would suddenly appear in the middle of the desert, carrying firearms, rid-ing mules and investigating me with such care? Fortunately, I must have looked too big and too poor to be worth their trouble, or maybe they'd heard about my luck and feared it might be contagious!

Such is human nature that one minute I was anxiously fleeing potential danger, and the next I was trudging along, boredom hav-ing replaced apprehension. One minute, I was constantly scanning the countryside, looking in all directions for men on mules. The next, my stare was unmoving, focused on the horizon ahead, search-ing only for the oasis called Piura.

After passing through an area where the brush was high enough to hide a mule and rider, we emerged where there was only sparse, stunt-ed growth. Yet farther along, spectacular sand dunes dominated the landscape, looking as if they were ocean waves rolling toward the highway. At first fascinating, the dunes attracted my gaze so often that they lost their appeal. After that, my eyes were again fixed straight ahead, seeking Piura and relief from a long walk in a hot desert.

At Piura's southern edge, there was a landmark I hadn't heeded when I'd passed it in trucks. I noticed it immediately, though, when I was on foot, followed by thirsty horses. The Piura River flowed beneath the highway bridge at the entrance to town. I took a wel-come detour down to the riverbank so my horses could drink. When they'd both had their fill, I removed my boots, unsaddled and led them into the river. Almost halfway across, the water was little more than two feet deep. Being shallow and slow moving, it was disappointingly warm. Knowing that a crowd would soon gather, I quickly prepared Inka and Huascarán to appear before an audience. Step one was to wash the caked diarrhea from Huascarán's hindlegs and tail. After a thorough scrubbing, the green stains remained. I frantically tried to purge them, but with only hand soap at my disposal, the results were mediocre.

Next I thoroughly rinsed both horses, using one of my canvas feed bags as a bucket. It must have felt good because neither moved a muscle, even though mild protest had been their unfailing reaction whenever I had bathed them in the past. I finished the horses' bath at a leisurely pace, cooling them – and myself – at great length. It was still a long way to San Jacinto, and we needed time to gather the strength to continue.

All the while, onlookers gathered, and finally, a camera-wielding newspaperman descended on us. Evidently he was more reporter than photographer. Long before he took a single photo, he was excitedly asking questions and taking notes. However, he was anything but inept with his camera. During the time we were together, he pressed his shutter release only twice and produced two splendid photographs, both of which would appear the next day in northern Peru's most important newspaper. His camera clicked as I poured water over the horses, the three of us standing knee-deep in the middle of the river (caption: *Pablito's Horses Bathe in the Río Piura.*). Again it clicked after I had resaddled Inka and was riding across the bridge above the river (caption: *Yesterday Pablito Arrived in Piura!*).

A certain *Guardia Civil* sergeant would have been delighted to debunk the notion that my horses were conquering heroes, but as I rode into town, I did everything I could to promote it. I would have preferred to completely avoid spectators, but the road to San Jacinto passed through Piura. The best I could do was to choose a course down quiet residential streets, as far as possible from main thoroughfares, commercial areas and crowds. Obliged to have an audience no matter what route I chose, I was too proud to let people see my true situation. I sat straight and smiling in the saddle and from time to time, squeezed Inka with my legs to perk him up. There wasn't much I could do about Huascarán except try to deflect attention from him and act as if our tortoise-like speed was my idea.

I had crossed Piura in motor vehicles on four occasions, but this was the first time I took note of my surroundings. I liked what I saw.

In the coming days, I would get to know the city well and would find it absolutely charming.

Piura was founded in 1532, three years before Lima, by Pizarro's *conquistadores*. A statue of the man who conquered the Inca empire is found in the appropriately named *Parque Pizarro*, and not too far away, is the church where the city's independence from Spain was declared in 1821. On my maps, Piura appeared to be one of Peru's more important cities, and in terms of population, it was. But its character and atmosphere were those of a small, old-fashioned community sustained mostly by the agriculture that surrounded it. As in farming communities the world over, things moved slowly in Piura, and in the coming days, I'd learn to enjoy its relaxed pace and friendliness.

Of course, my cheerful passage through Piura was not indicative of the facts, and sooner or later, truth usually makes itself known. Within the next few days, my difficulties would become common knowledge, spoiling any chance that the town might erect a statue of me in some plaza named *Parque Pablito*.

As I exited the west side of the city, I was famished and parched, and with good reason. After delivering Lucero to San Jacinto, two days earlier, I had rushed into town to cash a traveler's check. Unfortunately, Piura's banks had closed early that day, and I had returned to Ñaupe with only five *soles* (the equivalent of twenty cents) in Peruvian money. I was also carrying hundreds of dollars in traveler's checks, but there was no hope of cashing these outside major cities. By the time Huascarán, Inka and I reached Piura, my twenty cents were gone, spent on four bananas, two soft drinks and several cups of tea, not much to live on during two days in the desert.

Once I was alone on the road to San Jacinto, I stepped from the saddle and walked, as I'd done all day except for the getaway from the "bandits" and the time spent inside Piura's city limits. Almost immediately, Inka came to life, bubbling over with pep and mischief. No further inducement needed, I climbed back into the saddle. The rest of the way to San Jacinto, Inka frisked and asked for more rein so he could increase the pace. I had walked thirty miles that day and nine the day before because it had seemed he was footsore and tired. He was neither, and we approached our destination with him shying and snorting at everything in sight. He showed no signs of having traveled nearly eighty miles in two days, towing Huascarán the best part of the way. I'd never seen him feeling better.

Lucero, on the other hand, had gone downhill by the time we rejoined him. Evidently upset at being in a strange place without his companions, he had eaten little and drunk less during the preceding two days. More importantly, his bad legs were as touchy as ever. When the vet examined him the next day, the prescribed treatment was to stand him in shoulder-deep water for two hours a day.

"How long do you think I'll have to do that?" I asked.

"Probably no more than two or three weeks," he responded cheerfully, as if that were good news.

As much as three more weeks of delay! It was a ghastly prospect, made worse by my nagging suspicion that Lucero would actually need *much* longer than that to heal sufficiently for my purposes.

The vet diagnosed Huascarán's condition as food poisoning. The big gray remained lifeless and would neither eat nor move around. He ceased lying down at night, though that had been his unfailing custom, apparently to avoid the effort of climbing back to his feet. His exhaustion was so complete that he seldom opened his eyes. When he did, it was barely wide enough to see between the lids. When I led Huascarán to the watering trough, he would open his eyes just long and wide enough to get there, then shut them while he drank. In the pitiless heat, the other horses gulped their water, but he drank without gusto. The swallows of water could be seen traveling down his throat with the frequency of a dying man's pulse. Never in my life had I seen a horse in such a bad state.

The situation was grim. My faith in the beneficial effects of hard work was gone, and I knew I wouldn't be able to restore it until I was in a better state of mind. I needed a brief vacation from worries and responsibilities, and by coincidence, I had arrived just in time for the "Week of Piura," an agricultural exhibition along the lines of a state fair. The festivities were to include the Northern Peruvian Tournament of *Paso* Horses.

José Antonio Onrubia took me into his home and under his wing. He had the entire week set aside for the horse show and related social events, and wherever he went, he took me. There was a seemingly endless series of banquets, and I took full advantage of the opportunity to regain some of the weight I had lost. In the process, I quickly acquired a reputation that spread far and wide. Whenever I met someone for the first time, that person was almost certain to exclaim, in so many words: "Oh, *you're* the one who eats three double *ceviches* and drinks nine Cokes before dinner!" Few acknowledged me as the fellow making a horseback ride to North America. Almost everyone seemed to consider my consumption of food and drink (the non-alcoholic variety) more spectacular than my stalled horseback trip. The advantage of this was that everybody was anxious to introduce me to a favorite dish, most of which were fit for a king. While in Piura, I tried a number of Peruvian delicacies that still remain among my favorite things to eat.

The best was a fish salad known as *ceviche*. Despite being a confirmed fish-hater with a meat-and-potatoes palate, I went wild over it. *Ceviche* is usually made from sea bass or sole. The meat is diced and cooked only by being immersed in a particularly acidic lime juice. Mix this marinated fish with mild, tasty onion, corn on the cob and chunks of sweet potato, and you have *ceviche*. Other well-remembered treats included several varieties of avocado, all superior to any I knew, an otherwise normal-looking banana with pink flesh, another banana with a taste that resembled an apple, yet another that tasted like a pear and some theretofore unknown varieties of potato, including a yellow one with an absolutely magnificent flavor.

When we weren't eating or I wasn't standing Lucero in a deep pond at San Jacinto, *Señor* Onrubia and I spent our time at Piura's week-long *Paso* Horse Tournament. I eagerly looked forward to each day and wasn't once disappointed. Peruvian horses fascinated me in a way nothing else ever had or would.

After the show's first day, I couldn't help fantasizing about entering one of my horses in the upcoming gelding class. Under normal circumstances, Huascarán might have been a strong contender, but in his condition, he could hardly be shown. Lucero, even at his best, was no show horse. That left only Inka, a horse I had almost traded because he was half-blind. My opinion of Inka had gone sky-high. The only survivor of our trials in the desert, he was gaining weight, despite the fact that I rode him hard in the early mornings at San Jacinto, to keep him in shape. I didn't really believe he was a show horse, but I was sorely tempted to enter him, just to see what the judges thought. I casually mentioned this, and José Antonio [5] immediately took charge of making the last-minute entry, transporting Inka to the showgrounds and arranging for a good rider to present him.

Thanks to his new rider's expertise, Inka entered the arena looking better than I had ever seen him. Two breeders standing nearby were kind enough to congratulate me, and one enthusiastically speculated that my bay gelding was in the running for one of the top places. I suddenly found myself richly entertained by fantasies of arriving in Los Gatos atop Northern Peru's 1966 Champion Gelding.

After all was said and done, Inka placed sixth, but there was a silver lining in the cloud that briefly descended over me afterward.

Juan Miguel Rossel had come to Piura as one of the judges, and like the true gentleman he was, he refunded half of Inka's purchase price after confirming that the horse was indeed half-blind. The refund was a godsend. After the unexpected delays and expenses, I desperately needed the money. From that point of view, it was fortunate that Inka hadn't placed higher. After all, a championship certainly would have dampened *Señor* Rossel's generosity and might have negated it altogether.

My only sad moments came when I begrudgingly acknowledged that this wonderful, carefree week would have to end. When it did, I'd be faced with somehow jump-starting my ride. I dreaded that task as none I'd ever faced but tried to console myself that the trail ahead was unlikely to be as difficult as what I had already done. My three horses and I had crossed two hundred miles of killer desert, a place littered with sun-bleached bones and patrolled by flocks of circling vultures. It was no small achievement.

The great Amie Tschiffely had declared northern Peru's deserts to be among his greatest challenges during an incredible ten-thousand-mile, two-and a half-year ride from Buenos Aires to Washington, D.C. In the early 1930's, Tschiffely rode two Argentine *Criollo* horses named Mancha and Gato on one of the epic horseback journeys of all time. No traveler – including Marco Polo himself – had ever made a more difficult journey. Nonetheless, Tschiffely singled out Peru's deserts as having been particularly arduous, and of them he wrote:

> "Dante's inferno is a creation of stupendous imagination, but the Peruvian deserts are real, very real."

In spite of this forbidding desert and a run of unusually bad luck, I had reached Piura, and nothing would stop me from going on to Los Gatos. I'd nurse the horses back to health. Then we'd cross the next stretch of desert and in Ecuador, climb up into the moderate temperatures and green valleys of the Andes. My horses would certainly do better there, for the high *sierra* was their natural environment. Right? For cryin' out loud! Who did I think I was kidding? How well I knew that the prospects for my naive little scenario were nonexistent. I had failed and just didn't know it yet! It was time to come to grips with some serious decisions. How and whether I would continue my journey were the main questions in the balance.

If I was to go on, I had to put sentiment aside and consider some hard, cruel facts. No matter what the veterinarian said, Lucero wouldn't be sound for months, if then. His hind leg was much improved, but his foreleg was no better at all. Deep down I knew it was time to bid him good-bye.

Huascarán had gone eight days without eating and was being fed intravenously. Instead of *brío* and *resistencia*, he displayed a needle in his neck, which conveyed liquid nourishment from a bottle suspended above. He was prone to severe intestinal disorders, evidently provoked by changes in feed, water and bacteria. Such changes would be more frequent and harsher as we went farther north. Even if he recovered from his current difficulties, Huascarán would likely come to grief again on the trail ahead. The inescapable truth was that he, too, should be left behind.

Even if I went back to my original plan and used only two horses, I needed a new one to go with Inka. Since I couldn't possibly afford one, my journey, for all intents and purposes, was over. As one will do at such times, I went back over the decisions I'd made and the ones I hadn't. With a clear conscience, I concluded that there were no regrets. I had given it my very best shot and failed. There was no one and nothing to blame except wretched luck. It was all very logical, but emotionally I couldn't finalize a decision to quit. I was looking failure straight in the eye, but I was too stubborn to blink first. There had to be a way to turn things around.

The final day of the *Paso* Tournament brought an unexpected ray of hope. Aníbal Vasquez, a prominent breeder from Paiján, magnanimously offered to trade mares for my geldings, straight across, so my ride could continue. I was certain I had misunderstood, and I asked him to please repeat himself. He did so, leaving no doubt that I'd heard correctly. Delirious with happiness, I blurted out a long and rambling thank you. Life seldom offers second chances, and I was thrilled to have one. In the back of my mind, I also had some nagging doubts, but for the time being, I kept them to myself.

Later that day, I privately sought guidance from one of the Tournament's most distinguished visitors. Dr. Horst Seifert oversaw Peru's largest horse-breeding operation at the *Hacienda* Casa Grande. German-born and brilliant, he was generally considered the finest veterinarian in the country, and his advice would be all the more valuable because he was Aníbal Vasquez's neighbor.

"Consider yourself very lucky," he said. "You couldn't do better than Aníbal's horses. They should be ideal for what you have in mind."

"I was told in Lima that mares probably won't be up to the job," I said, getting down to what was troubling me.

"I certainly don't agree with that. Mares should do just fine if you prepare them properly." Dr. Seifert, as usual, was direct and to the point. "Besides, Aníbal has a good business selling geldings. He won't likely have three available, and if he does, he'll prefer to sell rather than trade them. Mares are a different matter because he has hundreds, and there's very little market for them. It's in his interest to trade for your geldings; he can easily sell them for good prices once they're in better shape."

"Do you think horses from the desert can handle conditions in the Andes?"

"At Casa Grande," he answered, "we raise livestock, including horses, in the *sierra* as well as on the coast. The animals raised on the coast are bigger, healthier and stronger, mostly because the feeds grown there are more nutritious."

Busy digesting this information, I said nothing.

"Look," he continued, squatting down and tracing a map of my intended route in the sand, "the majority of your trip will take you through deserts and tropics, hot places. Desert-bred horses are probably your best bet."

"Do you think I should trade all three of my geldings or keep the one you saw in the show today?" With those words, I revealed the last of my uncertainties.

"That's up to you. I can only point out that mares bring better prices in the States."

Earlier that day I had appreciated Aníbal's offer because there was no alternative, but now I was wildly enthusiastic. I was back in business, rescued from certain failure. In some respects I'd soon be even better off than when I had left Chiclayo. It was too good to be true.

The replacement of my horses would significantly delay me. I'd be faced with getting another export permit and preparing new animals for the trail. It pained me to have worked so hard and spent so much, only to start all over again, but these new problems were miniscule compared to the ones they replaced. Anxious to get started, I made arrangements to visit Paiján and see Aníbal's mares. Since he'd be driving home from Piura after the show, Aníbal invited me to travel with him.

On the Tournament's final evening, the participants were treated to an elaborate *pachamanca*, a Peruvian-style barbecue. Held in the middle of a grassy field, the event was very much out of the ordinary.

Smoking torches kept insects at bay. Gaily colored lanterns hung above the dining tables, and black, wrought-iron birdcages, occupied by sherbet-colored canaries, hung among the lanterns. A whole suckling pig had been buried underground and cooked overnight, in a way that produced the most succulent and tasty pork I had ever eaten. The trimmings were equally delicious. Giant serving tables were covered with colorful Peruvian delicacies. Dishes filled with saffron-yellow rice sat next to purple plum pudding, yellow potatoes and chocolate-colored beans. The remaining vegetables, fruits and tropical punches also came in a wide array of hues. Even to me, it didn't seemed possible that so much food would be necessary, but when the dinner bell sounded, the guests piled their plates high, leaving the serving platters clean. Before long, the plates matched the serving platters. The food had been sensational. If there had been more, I'm sure everyone would have gone back for seconds. To make the occasion complete, Aníbal Vasquez reaffirmed his offer to trade mares for my geldings. It was the perfect end to a perfect day.

The following morning, I was out of bed before sunrise, dutifully standing Lucero in water for the recommended two hours. Afterward I ate an early breakfast and took a bus to the Plaza de Armas in downtown Piura. There Aníbal was to pick me up "between 9:00 A.M. and noon."

Knowing Peru, I was pretty sure our appointment wouldn't be kept until at least 1:00 in the afternoon, but I didn't want to take even the slightest risk of delaying Aníbal. Better I should wait than he. Not only that, but far better I should wait than he should leave without me!

There can't be many on this earth who are more poorly constituted for waiting than I. On that of all mornings, I was dying to get started. Biding my time was pure, unadulterated torture. I paced back and forth, struck up conversations with strangers and otherwise sought to while away the hours. Fearful of giving Aníbal an excuse to leave without me, I didn't dare step away from the plaza to buy a magazine, a beverage or even, when the time came, lunch.

By early afternoon, the combination of heat and boredom were taking their toll. Drowsy, I found myself listening to a little voice that proposed a nap as the fastest and most painless way to pass time. The idea was highly appealing, but I decided against relaxing my vigil. After resisting sleep until well after 2:00, however, I stretched out on a bench. Moments later, I was awakened by a policeman who tapped his nightstick across the soles of my boots.

"Sleeping is not permitted in the plaza," he said firmly when I opened my eyes and looked up at him.

I rubbed my eyes and sat up. For the best part of two hours I fought to stay awake, rewarded for my success each time the policeman's rounds brought him back to the plaza. When an elderly gentleman sat down next to me, I remembered him from a conversation we'd had earlier in the day.

"Your friend still hasn't come to pick you up?" was how he opened our second conversation, though the answer seemed obvious.

"No," I answered. "He's late."

"Maybe he isn't coming."

"Oh, he'll be here," I said confidently.

"Don't be too sure," he said gravely. "You seem to always have bad luck. To tell the truth, I fear you may be a *salado*."

"A *salado*!" I laughed. "I hope not. Anything would be better than that."

The best possible definition of the word *salado* can be found in the opening lines of Ernest Hemingway's masterpiece, *The Old Man and the Sea*:

> "He was an old man who fished alone in a skiff in the Gulf Stream and he had gone eighty-four days now without taking a fish. In the first forty days a boy had been with him. But after forty days without a fish the boy's parents had told him that the old man was now definitely and finally *salado*, [6] which is the worst form of unlucky..."

I was still waiting at 4:00, when Juan Luis Ruesta drove by. Juan Luis bred *Paso* horses near Piura, and we had met at the Tournament. Seeing me, he stopped his car at the curb and motioned me over.

"Are you waiting for Aníbal?" he asked.

I answered in the affirmative, once again amazed at the way everyone in Piura seemed to know everyone else's business.

"I just left him at the fairgrounds," Juan Luis said. "Why don't I take you there? That way you won't have to wait any longer, and he won't have to drive all the way over here."

Sick and tired of waiting, I was sorely tempted but didn't think I should leave the plaza for fear Aníbal would show up while I was gone. Juan Luis convinced me otherwise, pointing out that there was only one road to the fairgrounds and that we'd see Aníbal if he drove toward Piura.

We found Aníbal at the fairgrounds. Worried that he might have already left for home, I greeted him enthusiastically. He didn't seem equally happy to see me. Quickly, he took me aside, away from Juan Luis, his normally booming voice reduced to confidential tones. Quietly, without looking at me, he advised that something had come up and he wouldn't be going directly to Paiján, after all. He suggested I meet him at his *hacienda* in a couple of weeks, more or less.

As soon as we were back in his car, the insightful Juan Luis turned to me and translated my worst fears into words.

"Aníbal has changed his mind about trading horses with you, Pablito. You know that, don't you?" As he spoke, Juan Luis sliced a finger across his throat.

It was no coincidence that Juan Luis' path had crossed mine at the plaza. He had gone there looking for me after speaking with Aníbal and sensing the man's second thoughts. Aníbal's generous offer had been made after the consumption of several beers and in the presence of prominent and influential people. The gesture had resulted in embracing, slapping of backs and cries of *Bravo!* Later, when his admirers were gone and he was no longer the center of attention, Aníbal had decided it didn't make sense to trade three good mares for a sick gelding, a lame gelding and a half-blind gelding. Looking at his best interests, he'd come to very different conclusions from those reached the day before by Dr. Seifert.

Juan Luis drove me back to San Jacinto. Neither of us spoke until we came to a stop in front of *Señor* Onrubia's house, where Juan Luis gave me an empathetic pat on the shoulder.

"You have problems, don't you, Pablito?"

I nodded my head, feeling as if my picture belonged in the Spanish dictionary right next to the word *salado*, "which is the worst form of unlucky…"

---

5 In Spanish-speaking countries, as in the southern United States, it is common to address and refer to some people by both their first and middle names.

6 In his book, Hemingway used the Portuguese spelling, instead of the Spanish spelling used here.

CHAPTER 12

Honest Juan's Slightly Used Horses

"Do you like her, Pablito? She was mine once."

On two different occasions, Juan Luis Ruesta spoke those words when he caught me admiring an attractive girl. Not much older than I, Juan Luis was handsome, charming and much sought after by the ladies. He should have been footloose and fancy-free, roaming the world and getting the wanderlust out of his system. Instead, he had his nose to the grindstone, preparing to fill his aging father's shoes as head of the family *hacienda*. The more I came to know him, the more I realized that Juan Luis was not doing what he wanted with his life. Later on, he'd probably enjoy running the family business, but that wasn't yet the case. He had the soul of an adventurer, something that became obvious from the way he empathized with what I was doing.

"If I weren't tied down," he frequently told me, "I'd ask your permission to go along with you."

"Your company would be more than welcome," I responded each time.

I never bothered to mention that others had expressed similar sentiments. If I had, I would also have told him that he was the only one I believed and the only one I would have been glad to have along.

The first time Juan Luis expressed his desire to do what I was doing, I had no idea he really meant it. The reason was that I didn't yet know him. At the time, we were sitting in his car in front of José Antonio Onrubia's home, in the immediate aftermath of my cancelled trip with Aníbal Vasquez. He followed that first declaration with another, equally improbable.

"I'm going to help you."

I smiled to mask my feelings. During the *Week of Piura*, many had said, "I'm going to help you." Some – such as Aníbal Vasquez – had even proposed specific ways in which they intended to help. But nothing further had happened, and nothing would. That's how things went in Peru. Apparently these thoughts could be seen in the look on my face.

"I'm not like the others," Juan Luis said softly. "I *really* want to help you. Would it be enough if I sold two of your horses and had my father buy the other?"

His tone of voice made it very difficult to doubt his sincerity.

"That," I replied, "would be the greatest favor anyone could possibly do for me, but who'd buy horses that are in such sorry condition?"

"Don't worry. Come to my office in the morning so we can get started," Juan Luis said with a smile. It was the beginning of a beautiful friendship.

That night, I lay awake for hours, adjusting and readjusting my plans. If Juan Luis could sell my geldings for enough money, I could buy replacements and resume my journey. Though I had my doubts that all this would actually come to pass, I made some decisions, just in case it did. Number one: I'd continue my ride on breeding animals. If I was to put this much effort into importing horses, I wanted them to contribute to our North American bloodlines and to have the immortality that offspring would bring. Given the intimate stabling arrangements I'd find along the trail, I obviously couldn't use stallions, so I revived my original plan to use mares. Number two: if possible, those mares would come from the *Hacienda* Casa Grande. I had always regarded Casa Grande's horses to be particularly durable, and under the watchful eye of Dr. Horst Seifert, they were among the best cared-for animals in Peru. Number three: I would sell Inka. This was the most difficult decision of all, but it would have been foolishly sentimental to do otherwise. After all, a one-eyed gelding wouldn't be worth a whole lot in the States.

The next morning, with the help of Juan Luis Ruesta, I embarked on a two-day, non-stop horse-sellathon. Perhaps it's misleading to say that I had Juan Luis' help because that infers that he had mine when, in truth, I was a mere observer. Blind luck and the law of supply and demand played a role in our venture, but Juan Luis' salesmanship made the biggest contribution. It turned out there was a desperate need for geldings in Piura, and my three were the only ones for sale. It was a classic seller's market, and Juan Luis knew exactly how to exploit it.

Even though we called attention to his blind eye, Inka miraculously sold for three times his original purchase price, of which half had been refunded. The buyer was Piura's most infamous tightwad, and he was in a hurry to close the deal until he heard how much we were asking. Craftily, he stalled, with the objective of reducing the price. I would have been perfectly happy with less, but Juan Luis wouldn't hear of it. Showing why he'd been chosen to take over the family business, he succeeded in jacking up the price even higher. This he did by offering Inka to a second buyer and letting the two parties bid against one another until the tightwad finally won.

Feeling better and eating again, but terribly underweight, Huascarán also brought a hefty price. A young farmer wanted him and signaled strong interest by doing a very un-Peruvian thing. He agreed to the first price quoted. That was when the fun started. The young man's grandfather held the purse strings and refused to pay the amount agreed upon. In Peruvian *soles*, the price seemed exorbitant, but despite my private urgings to lower it, Juan Luis insisted it was firm. The deadlock was broken the following day thanks to an ingenious solution proposed by – who else? – Juan Luis. When all was said and done, the grandson paid me a considerable sum on the sly before taking me to his grandfather's house where I accepted the old man's offer and collected the remainder of the asking price.

Having lost out on Inka, a horse he'd honestly hoped his father would buy, Juan Luis offered me a handsome price for Lucero. He had already done so much that I couldn't accept this further generosity. Lucero was still lame in the foreleg, and his future was uncertain. I insisted that no one else would consider him at more than a third of what he had offered, and we settled on that amount.

My three horses – two in far worse condition than when I bought them – had brought several hundred dollars more than I had paid. Not only would I be able to afford new horses, but I should have a few *soles* left over to help cover the considerable cost of my latest setback.

With spending money in my wallet, I caught a ride with a southbound cattle truck, arriving at the truck's destination in Lambayeque at midnight. Next I caught a ride with a banana truck, continuing south for the rest of the night. In the morning, I was dropped off in Chocope, and from there, I took a bus to nearby Casa Grande. I was primed to buy three mares and get them back to Piura as quickly as possible. Such was my sense of urgency that I hadn't budgeted a single second for a look at one of the world's most extraordinary agro-industrial empires.

Casa Grande was established by a German immigrant named Juan Guildermeister. When Guildermeister turned his attention to the Chicama Valley, the area was home to twenty-five large plantations and five thousand small farms. Thanks to abundant sunshine and water from the Chicama River, a wide variety of crops made the valley a year-round patchwork quilt of contrasting greens. Fifty years later, all had been combined into a single entity, a quarter the size of Switzerland. Thanks to Guildermeister and his descendants, the entire valley was converted into an unending sea of sugar cane, making Casa Grande the largest privately owned sugar plantation on earth.

Practically self-contained, Casa Grande produced enormous quantities of cane. This it harvested with its armies of workers, transported in its own trains or on its own highways, processed in its own mills, sold through its own world-wide organization and shipped from its own seaport. Within Casa Grande's borders were entire communities of workers who lived in company housing and could satisfy most of their needs without leaving the *hacienda*. If anyone had bothered to research the issue, Casa Grande's company stores would probably have been among Peru's larger retail chains.

Casa Grande stretched from the Pacific Ocean to the Andes and beyond to the jungles of the Amazon Basin. With twenty-five thousand head of sheep, twelve thousand head of cattle and five hundred head of horses, it was where I should have gone in the first place. Better late than never, I arrived before working hours and went directly to Dr. Seifert's home. Over breakfast, he strongly seconded my decision to replace my geldings with animals from the coast. Warming to this theme, he informed me that, by the time they're six, animals raised on Peru's coast were two years more developed than their cousins raised in the *sierra*. Furthermore, his analysis of feed grown in the *sierra* showed it was lower in nutrition than coastal crops from the same seed.

"That probably explains the poor performance of your geldings," he concluded, as we finished breakfast.

I spent the morning looking through vast fields of mares, accompanied by one of Dr. Seifert's assistants. My mission was to write down the number branded on each animal I wanted to try under saddle. Casa Grande's horses were branded, just above the gaskin (thigh), with the letters *CG* and a number. These large brands were easily read from a distance, which was as close as I could get since some of the mares were half-wild and all were wary of strangers.

With nearly three hundred mares wearing that brand, I expected to compile a sizeable list, but my options were surprisingly limited. To start with, I was advised not to waste my time in the field containing what was by far the largest herd of mares. The horses there were "select" and either not for sale or priced beyond my means. Another limiting factor was my requirement for mares that weren't pregnant, which eliminated most adult females. Among the few mares not yet ruled out, I had to overlook those nursing young foals, those too old or too young and those that had never been ridden. All in all, I could find only four potential candidates.

When I presented him with my list, Dr. Seifert compared the

numbers I'd copied with information in Casa Grande's records. The first mare didn't yet show, but her pregnancy had recently been confirmed. The second didn't belong in the field where I'd seen her. She was the result of a mating selected to produce a prizewinner at the National Tournament, and so far, she was living up to expectations. The third mare was much older than she appeared. The fourth – it just so happened – was a mare Dr. Seifert had intended to recommend. Her name was Hamaca, [7] and she seemed fitted to my needs in all respects, including that her last pregnancy test had been negative. Solid black, without a single hair of another color, she was one of the prettier of Casa Grande's mares. Though not tall, she was particularly well-built, with straight well-muscled legs and short, well set-up pasterns. If she performed under saddle, I'd be delighted to have her.

Hamaca was in a large field where she lived free from contact with man, except when it was time to administer veterinary care, tune up her training or introduce her to one of the stallions. She wasn't tame enough that it was possible to walk up to her, and Dr. Seifert sent men with lariats to bring her in. I went along to see the show. During round one, the men trapped the horses in a corner where they milled around in mass confusion. It was amazing how quickly Hamaca realized that she was the target and how cleverly she denied the ropers a shot at her.

During round two, the ropers drove the horses to a smaller field. There, they forced the herd to circle, all in the same direction, at a gallop. Patiently the men waited for the object of their hunt to come clear of the others. By and by, she did, revealing that the "ropers" weren't ropers. They were field hands who had little experience with a lasso. Loop after loop sailed through the air and missed its target. When a noose finally settled around her neck, Hamaca stopped dead in her tracks. She had obviously been roped before and knew how unpleasant further resistance could be.

Once she was saddled, I took Hamaca for a test ride along one of the dirt roads that cut through the cane fields. The scenery was monotonous, but I was hardly bored. I had a horse to evaluate and a decision to make. Hours and miles passed in what seemed like the blink of an eye. Hamaca seemed rugged, willing and energetic. All things considered, I liked her and agreed to buy her. One down and two to go. To see if I'd overlooked any other likely candidate(s), it was agreed that Dr. Seifert and I would go through the herd together the following morning.

That evening Dr. Seifert invited me to dinner at his home. He also invited several of the *hacienda*'s administrators and their wives, all born and raised in Germany. For my benefit, all conversations, including those in which I was not participating, were in English. To someone from the United States, it was an impressive display of linguistic ability. Each guest's English was more than adequate for in-depth discussions of any subject that came up, without resorting to hand gestures or pantomime. I was impressed and said so. In response, I was informed that everyone in the room also spoke Spanish and at least two other languages, besides German. It was the first time I had realized how limited we Americans are when it comes to languages.

There was one otherwise-pleasant gentleman whose favorite subject was that people from the States were highly unpopular in Peru. During an evening that was delightful in all other respects, he repeatedly forced his pet subject into the conversation. My experience didn't confirm his claim, and I told him so whenever he brought the matter up. Each time, to my naive surprise, Dr. Seifert and the other guests readily sided with their countryman.

"Peruvians are too polite to tell you to your face," they insisted, each in his or her own words.

I knew we Yanks had our Peruvian critics, and I'd seen graffiti saying "*Fuera Yanquis!*" (Get out, Yankees!) and "*Cuba, Sí! Yanquis, No!*" (Cuba, Yes! Yankees, No!), but I felt sure that my good hosts were exaggerating. Many Peruvians I knew approved of at least as much U.S. foreign policy as I. In addition, most had a rather sophisticated way of making distinctions and would have been able to disagree with official U.S. policy without disliking individual American citizens. As for the one gentleman's relentless pursuit of this topic, I can only guess it pained him to hear criticism of his own country and that misery loves company.

The next morning brought some sort of emergency, and Dr. Seifert was unavailable to go through the mare herds with me. He left word that he had arranged for a private guided tour of the sugar mill in his absence. I would have preferred not to indulge in tourism while my mind was filled with other thoughts, but I felt obligated because the arrangements were already made.

As was the case with everything else at Casa Grande, the mill operated on a gargantuan scale. It turned out hundred-pound bags of sugar at such a rate that a long string of freight cars was parked on a nearby railway spur to receive them. The waiting cars were filled and replaced at least once during my hour-long tour, all the more impressive when one considers that the mill was in operation twenty-four hours a day, three hundred sixty-five days a year.

That afternoon's search with Dr. Seifert produced no additional candidates for my ride. In fact, we found no prospect promising enough to even merit a tryout. Even with so many mares to choose from, I was about to leave Casa Grande without the three I sought. It was a plight that showed why Fernando Graña had steered me toward geldings when I first arrived in Lima.

The following day, from sunup to sundown, I searched nearby *haciendas*, none of which could show me a mare – in my price range and not pregnant – that merited consideration. At Dr. Seifert's suggestion, I next visited breeders in nearby Trujillo, Peru's second-largest city, with the same results.

At that point, there was only one major breeder left in the region. It was obviously in my best interests to leave no stone unturned, so I swallowed my pride, picked up the telephone and placed a call to Aníbal Vasquez. I intended to tell him that I had sold my geldings and was in the market for mares, as if the decision not to trade was mine rather than his, but I never got the chance. Instead, every time I called I got a runaround that ended without my having spoken to Aníbal. It didn't take much of that before my pride asserted itself. It was time to continue my search elsewhere, and I made up my mind to try Chiclayo, halfway between Casa Grande and Piura. First, however, I wanted to deliver Hamaca to San Jacinto for safekeeping. Luckily, I found a cattle truck deadheading north, and the price was so low that I suspect the driver pocketed my money without reporting it to his employer.

The truck pulled out of Casa Grande in the late afternoon with me in the back, alongside my newly acquired mare. We were no further than the nearby town of Chocope when a floorboard broke beneath Hamaca's hindquarter. She fell to the floor like a stone, with one of her hindlegs protruding beneath the bed of the truck. Momentarily she looked confused, unable to figure out what had happened. Both forelegs were fully extended at crazy angles, making her look like she'd been dropped from a thirty-story building.

When she began struggling to regain her feet, I saw that Hamaca's dangling hind leg was only inches from one of the wheels. Through the hole in the floor, I could see the tire rotating like a huge, malevolent saw blade. If Hamaca's frantic thrashing brought her leg in contact with that tire, skin and flesh would be peeled away, right down to the bone. Frantically I signaled the driver to stop. It took a while to get his attention, and even then, he wasn't easily convinced.

When we were no longer moving, I squatted near Hamaca's head and did my best to keep her calm. The immediate danger – now that the tires had ceased turning – came from the jagged edges of the broken floorboard. They threatened Hamaca's leg from ahead and behind. At my request, the driver brought a crowbar and broke off the lance-like splinters. Then he and his helper locked arms behind Hamaca's rump, while I took a firm grip on her tail. At a pre-arranged signal – with very little help from her – we lifted my frightened mare to her feet. She was undamaged, except for a slightly skinned hock (rear knee).

It turned out that I was the more seriously injured. During Hamaca's struggles, she had flung her bedding – dry, pulverized sugar cane – in every direction. A small piece had lodged painfully beneath my eyelid. Immediately, I felt the jagged speck being dragged across the surface of my cornea whenever I blinked. In self-defense, I closed the eye and kept it that way throughout the process of extracting Hamaca's leg from its dangerous predicament. As soon as I confirmed that Hamaca was uninjured, my production of adrenaline trailed off, and I became aware of the severe pain in my eye. I couldn't even open the lid long enough to attempt removal of the offending material. Tears flowed freely but were unsuccessful in flushing out the irritating splinter. Evidently it was snagged in the flesh on the underside of my eyelid.

It was my unbelievably good fortune that we had stopped directly in front of the Chocope Hospital. When no one could budge the stubborn splinter, I made my way inside, accompanied by the driver. It was a strange sensation to enter a hospital emergency room and find it without patients, hospital personnel or any system for summoning help. Feeling that my problem was more uncomfortable than threatening, I sat down, confident that someone would appear at any moment. But nobody came.

It became necessary to verbally restrain the driver. He had worked himself up to where he was ready to comb the entire hospital and drag someone to my aid. Finally, enough was enough! The driver and I wandered into a deserted hallway, down two straightaways and around two corners before finding an orderly. He scolded us and commanded that we return to the emergency room. We agreed after he swore he'd send someone to attend us. Despite this promise, another long wait ensued. Finally, a nurse sauntered in, and when she couldn't remove the speck from my eyelid, she set out in search of a doctor. Not five minutes later, a doctor succeeded where the rest of us had failed.

We drove through the long night without further incident and arrived at San Jacinto the following morning. Not having slept all night, I felt exhausted. Quickly, I unloaded Hamaca and made her comfortable in one of the corrals. The stable area was empty. I moved quickly, hoping to make it to my bed before anyone engaged me in conversation, but a small group of men, including José Antonio Onrubia, suddenly materialized out of nowhere. Once everyone got over his surprise at seeing that I had returned with only one horse, the men got down to the business of evaluating my new mare. It was soon obvious that they approved. Eusebio Rodriguez, the trainer whose daughter had defended me against the hordes of flies, seemed to take a special liking to my new mare. He stayed after everyone else had gone, and the two of us leaned against the railing of Hamaca's corral studying her and enjoying one another's company. The horse talk had energized me; sleep could wait.

When sleep came, however, it held me in its grip most of the day. The few times I woke up, I went out to check on Hamaca. Each time I lingered, admiring my new acquisition with satisfaction. The day's final visit to Hamaca's corral took place after dark, as Rodriguez returned from hunting birds.

"There are lovers who take less interest in one another than you take in that mare," he teased me, his good-natured laugh punctuating the end of his sentence.

He stopped and leaned his shotgun against the corral. For a while, the two of us stood there, discussing how to best prepare Hamaca for her upcoming task. Suddenly, I noticed a fox, barely thirty yards away. I quietly informed Rodriguez, and he stealthily picked up his shotgun and blasted away. A geyser of dust erupted next to the fox, and a startled Hamaca bounded across her corral. Unscathed, the fox ran off.

"Maybe it's an omen," Rodriguez decided.

"What kind?" I wanted to know.

Rodriguez giggled in his usual gleeful manner and left the question unanswered.

At sunrise, I set out again through the desert I had crossed so many times. From the cab of yet another truck, the scenery was monotonous as ever. Hour after hour, desert assaulted my eyes.

Variety was rare and found mostly where rivers made their way from the Andes to the Pacific Ocean. There, irrigated ground sprouted green crops.

Late October marked the change of seasons. The worst of the summer's heat had passed, and travelers left each oasis with less hesitation and looked forward to the next with less urgency. My destination was Chiclayo, where my ride had begun, and once I arrived, I went to see Jorge Baca at La Quinta. Understandably surprised to see me, he was as gracious and helpful as ever. We spent a short while looking at his mares. He wasn't willing to part with any that fit my criteria.

The next morning, I went to yet another of Peru's giant sugar plantations. The *Hacienda* Cayaltí had once produced horses that earned it a permanent and glorious chapter in the history of the Peruvian breed. Unfortunately for me, those once-extensive herds were in the past. The few horses that remained fell into four categories: those that were pregnant, those that were too young or too old, those they didn't want to sell and those I didn't want to buy.

I spent the afternoon in the outskirts of Cayaltí looking at horses owned by *campesinos*. The area's peasants had horses descended from some of Cayaltí's best lines, and it seemed worthwhile to have a look at them. While doing so, I encountered a brand-new phenomenon, Peruvians who were anxious to sell horses. The *campesinos* bowed, scraped and succeeded only in making me feel uncomfortable. To flatter me, they constantly referred to me as *mister*, which they pronounced *meestair*. One by one, I visited every horse owner within miles. Each offered to sell me horses, which came down in price every time I declined to buy them. This continued until some were unbelievable bargains, if such can be said of something one has no interest in buying.

After two days of combing the Chiclayo area, I realized that bad luck wasn't at fault for my failure to find what I sought. Peru's economy was in transition. Management of the *haciendas* had passed from the hands of people who were willing to spend money on horses. The new managers were modern capitalists looking to cut costs wherever possible. They didn't see profits as something from which even a very small percentage might be used for breeding horses. Horses, to them, were relics of the past, and *haciendas* weren't museums.

Long after the same had happened in the rest of the world, machines were replacing horses in Peruvian agriculture. Stalls were being converted into storage rooms. Cash crops were being planted in fields where horses once grazed. Trainers and stable boys were being reassigned to more profitable work. Trained, well-cared-for horses were increasingly rare and if for sale, were expected to fetch good prices. Those for sale at old-time prices weren't worth buying.

Finding good mares was going to challenge even *my* considerable determination!

[7] Spanish for "hammock."

Sparks flew as horseshoes hit slate (see page 152).

CHAPTER 13

Two for the Road

As a last resort, I visited the *Hacienda* Pucalá, a leading breeder of prize-winning Peruvian *Paso* horses. Seeing a potential foreign market for their horses, Pucalá's owners had increased, rather than diminished, their supply. They had as many good animals as anyone, and more than most, but I went there only because no alternative remained. After all, I knew Pucalá's prices to be far beyond my means, and I considered their horses too stylish for my purposes. On the other hand, I needed a miracle and couldn't afford to be fussy about where I might find it.

The miracle I sought was at least the thirtieth horse they showed me. Named Ima Sumac, after a world-famous Peruvian singer, she was black except for a small white star on her forehead. Ima Sumac was – as the trainer enthusiastically recited – sired by Chalpon, who was by a famous sire named Carnaval, son of Limeñito, brother of Principe and father of Minerva and Cleopatra. Her dam was Flor de Caña, also the mother of Campesina and Madreselva, two young fillies that had placed very well at the National Tournament. In the interest of negotiating a good price, I feigned inability to appreciate even such an impressive pedigree.

"What else do you have?" I asked, turning my back disdainfully on the first mare since Hamaca to meet my requirements.

Actually, Ima met only *some* of my requirements, but I saw an advantage in that. I needed a club to beat down her price, and I had two. She was young, only four years of age, and she wasn't yet trained under saddle. That was where I steered the conversation when the haggling began. After a half-day of spirited, on-and-off bargaining – spanning two meals at the administrator's home – I bought Ima at the best price imaginable. Even at that, it was a difficult decision. For one thing, she cost as much as I had been planning to spend for two horses. I could no longer afford a third, and in North America's still unsophisticated market, two mares would sell for only two-thirds the price of three.

In a way, I didn't feel right dwelling on financial considerations. The original idea had been to make my ride for the benefit of the breed and the love of adventure. Not too surprisingly, though, hardships and difficulties had altered my outlook. My investment would include every dime I owned and nearly a year of my life. I wanted something to show for it besides memories of long walks in the desert.

The next day I hired a pick-up truck to carry Ima and me to Piura. As was my habit, I rode in the back with my horse, and thank goodness for that! The driver was interested only in making time, and he gave us a roller coaster ride, in spite of my pleadings whenever we stopped. At times, I had to brace Ima, and frequently, I prevented her from falling. Once, however, I failed. The driver slammed on his brakes and dumped her hard. As a result, Ima's knees were mildly swollen by the time we reached Ñaupe. Between Ñaupe and Piura, the landscape was much too familiar. In less than three weeks, I had traveled it nine times, in one direction or the other and by one means or another, and I sincerely hoped this would be the last, at least for a long while.

To introduce them, I put Hamaca and Ima in adjoining corrals. They looked like sisters and perhaps for that reason, took an instant liking to one another. True black horses being uncommon, it was amazing that, without trying, I had wound up with a matched pair of them. The only notable difference was Hamaca's missing forelock, clipped off, as was the practice with Peru's mares in those days.

The first thing I did the following morning was to find Juan Luis Ruesta, bring him to San Jacinto and show him what he'd made possible. He seemed to like Hamaca as much as I did, but ever-so-politely he questioned the purchase of Ima. Later, it was disturbing to find that my other friends in Piura felt the same. Unanimously, they gently suggested that Ima lacked strength. As I saw it, Ima's hooves were badly shaped, the toes much too long and the heels much too short. Because of that, her pasterns, the bones that connect the hooves with the first joint above, were at an angle that encouraged her to carry too much weight on her heels. The result was that she appeared to lack strength.

Ima's problem could be solved I hoped – and believed! – with corrective trimming and proper shoeing. Her toes could be shortened and her heels, protected by shoes, would grow to the correct length. When I described this theory to the Peruvians, they politely refrained from looking me in the eye, lest I sense what they thought of my strange ideas. In defense of my theory, I told myself that since Peruvians didn't shoe their horses, they had no experience with the wonders that shoeing can accomplish.

The first order of business, even before training and conditioning, was to apply for export permits. The frustrations of that process were fresh in my mind, and I feared the paperwork would prove even slower and more troublesome the third time around. In Piura, I was farther away from civilization than I'd been in Chiclayo. Communication with the Ministry of Agriculture in Lima would be difficult. It would also be a problem to find the required vaccines, not to mention the officials and professionals whose services I would need. To motivate myself under these difficult circumstances, I created a convenient fiction: the processing of the permits would go more quickly now that I was familiar with the procedure. In the jargon of modern psychology, this is called denial. I was ignoring *The Peruvian Factor*, a phenomenon too terrible for me to openly acknowledge.

The Peruvian Factor is a corollary to Murphy's Law, or perhaps it's the other way around. It really doesn't matter. All one needs to know is that *The Peruvian Factor* proves Murphy to have been an incurable optimist! A theoretical example of its effect will best define *The Peruvian Factor*:

Earthquakes frequently occur along faults near Peru's coast, and from time to time, geologists dutifully warn of the impending "big one." This as-yet-mythical quake will, they say, cause a sizeable portion of Peru's coast to sheer away and tumble into the Pacific Ocean. I'm sure these geologists have a thorough knowledge of their science, but their predictions demonstrate a lamentable ignorance in other areas. Because of *The Peruvian Factor*, the big one, of course, will actually cause everything *east* of the fault, including Brazil, to fall into the Atlantic Ocean!

The effects of *The Peruvian Factor* on my efforts to get export permits were devastating It first reared its ugly head when I arranged for the government veterinarian to examine my mares and administer the required inoculations. On schedule, the vet came to San Jacinto and performed the examinations, but he mysteriously postponed the injections until the following day at noon. The next day, noon came and went without any sign of the vet, so at 3:00 P.M. I phoned him. He said he hadn't been able to find the necessary vaccines, and he promised to check further and call me right back. At 5:00 I called again, and the vet advised me that a local supplier had encephalomyelitis vaccine but would have to order the one for *adenitus equinus* from Chiclayo. Acting on a hunch, I visited this supplier and found that he hadn't ordered *adenitus equinus* vaccine and had no way of doing so.

José Antonio Onrubia had an office in Chiclayo, and I asked him if someone there could purchase the vaccine and send it to me. He called Chiclayo and was promised delivery the next day. The following day, no vaccine arrived. I phoned Chiclayo. The voice at the other end of the line said *"mañana."* *Mañana* came and went and no vaccine. More *mañanas* passed before the vaccine finally came. Several days after its arrival, the vet still hadn't gotten around to injecting it.

Professionally taken "passport" photos of each horse were also required. I located a photographer and made an appointment he didn't keep. The next morning, bright and early, I went to his office. He promised to be at San Jacinto by noon. At 4:00 P.M. I went to his office again. He was apologetic and promised to be at San Jacinto by 9:00 the following morning. At noon the next day, the photographer finally arrived and took the pictures. To compensate me for the many delays, he promised they would be ready at 4:00 that same afternoon. At 4:00, I dropped by his office to pick them up. He was out, and no one knew where my photos were. The secretary promised to have them ready for me by 11:00 the following morning. At the appointed time, I went all the way into town only to be told that a messenger had the photos and was delivering them to San Jacinto at that very moment. After returning to San Jacinto, I waited the rest of the day. No messenger – and, of course, no photos – came. The next day I was told that the pictures were no good and would have to be taken again.

I consoled myself that I could utilize the delays for training and conditioning my mares, but before I could work my new horses, they needed to be shod. That meant dealing with a Peruvian blacksmith, an experience I'd already had in Chiclayo!

Horseshoers, in general, are a breed more than members of a profession. Anywhere I've ever been, including the United States, most seem to be unreliable. I dreaded dealing again with the Peruvian variety, but there was no alternative. Piura's sand was abrasive. It would rapidly wear away unprotected hooves, and Ima's heels were already too low. Wearing them further would have been unforgivable, especially since the heel is the slowest-growing part of the hoof.

I made an appointment with a blacksmith and – miracle of all miracles! – he came to San Jacinto exactly as promised. I greeted him with a huge smile, mentally scheduling a workout for my new horses the following morning. The blacksmith wiped the smile from my face with his first words.

"I have come only to measure your horses' hooves. The rest of the job can't be done for several days."

"What?"

That was a new one. In the States, a blacksmith arrives carrying an assortment of shoes, ready to immediately do his job.

127

"There are no ready-made horseshoes in Piura. I myself must take a bar of iron and custom-make a set of shoes from scratch, one to precisely fit each hoof of each horse," the blacksmith proudly announced. "The first step is to measure the hooves."

He *measured* only with his eyes, quickly glancing at the mares without going inside their corrals or picking up their feet.

"Can you at least trim them today, so they'll be standing at the proper angle?" I asked, trying to push without seeming pushy.

"That wouldn't be a good idea," he returned, the tone of voice indicating that his answer was final.

I wasn't able to speak with the blacksmith again for days, though not for lack of trying. Late one evening I finally went to his home, and he promised to do the job the following morning. He didn't come, and typical of these kinds of experiences, I couldn't reach him again for days.

Of course, I didn't string my various tasks end-to-end. I tried to accomplish them simultaneously, which meant that these frustrations came in bunches, one right on the heels of the last. The cumulative effect was devastating! Eventually things worked out, however, mainly because of *Señor* Onrubia's car. He loaned it to me one day, and I went from place to place, cornering my tormentors and popping them into the car. I drove each one wherever he had to go to do whatever he had to do to finish his job. I begged, badgered and bullied, and by nightfall, I had my mares shot, shod, photographed, wormed, examined and certified.

As I drove José Antonio's car back to San Jacinto that evening, desert foxes darted across deserted streets on the outskirts of Piura, briefly illuminated by the headlights. Lending charm to the twilight, the small foxes reinforced my feeling that I was indeed in an exotic land, living an adventure. My mood couldn't have been better. Of course, it helped that I had just finished wrapping up all those loose ends.

Before calling it a day, I phoned Tuco Roca Rey at the *Asociación* in Lima. Unaware of my problems with the geldings, he was sympathetic and offered his assistance with the new export permits. I told him I had prepared a package containing everything needed to apply, and he suggested I send it by bus so he'd receive it at the earliest possible time. I borrowed *Señor* Onrubia's car the instant I hung up and drove to town in order to put my package on that very evening's bus. Perhaps if they saw how anxious I was to save time, the people at the *Asociación* would make every possible effort to speed things up.

Once shod, the mares began their conditioning program. Their workouts were strenuous. Piura's deep, loose sand made for hard going, and all the more so because it was often covered by a deep layer of fine powder-like dust. Whenever I walked in this peculiar material, it swallowed my boots to a surprising depth. With smaller feet that carried more weight, the horses found the going even harder than I did. For this and other reasons, I began my mares' conditioning program by leading them. This made it possible to put in more miles and hours than would have been prudent if they'd been carrying my weight. A side benefit was that I slept marvelously well, despite my lengthy list of worries!

In the evenings, after our long walks in the desert, I introduced Ima to the saddle and rode her for short periods in San Jacinto's stable area. Tired as she was after her day's activities, she willingly went along with the program. That was a godsend because, following a day of hard exercise, I was anything but ready for a struggle.

Compared to their predecessors, I found Hamaca and Ima more sensible and better able to handle the heat. In addition, they seemed more adaptable at mealtime. Before I'd left Casa Grande, Dr. Seifert had given me several bags of a special livestock supplement he'd formulated, based on the best ingredients Peru had to offer. It contained milled *algarrobo*, cottonseed meal, milled corn and fishmeal. I added mineral salts and fed it daily. It quickly improved both mares' appearance, but in time, I realized I was making a mistake.

The problem was that few of the ingredients in Dr. Seifert's mixture would be available where I was going. I needed to get my horses used to what I'd be able to give them along the trail, so I supplemented the supplement with small amounts of plain barley in the morning and corn at night. Unlike my geldings, the mares quickly developed a taste for both. It was a good sign and only one among many.

The feed bags I had made at La Quinta were marked with initials – an "H," an "I" and an "L" – which identified their former owners. Lucero's bag was retired, but the one with the "H" fit Hamaca perfectly and the "I" bag seemed custom-made for Ima. It was uncanny how closely Hamaca and Ima resembled the feed bags' former owners.

Ima was another Inkie, sweet, friendly, quiet and matter-of-fact. Dust made her sneeze exactly as it had with him, and she had his baby face, though with two perfectly good eyes. Built along similar lines and with much the same gait, but smoother, she had a free-swinging walk that allowed her to keep up with other horses' slow *paso* without breaking into her own. After a hoof trim aligned her feet and legs, I felt vindicated in my original high opinion of her.

Hamaca was Huascarán all over again. She wasn't nearly as tall but had his short, straight legs, deep body and handsome head. Her gait was a bit more economical. She just barely picked up her feet and stepped along quickly, without wasted motion. Her most serious fault was the one I'd noticed the first time I rode her: she didn't take a long-enough stride. Like Huascarán, Hamaca was inclined to pull back when tied, and she showed the same bug-eyed frustration when I put the heart rope on her. She did not, however, have Huascarán's determination or his conceit, and unlike him, she was anxious to please.

Ima soon developed Inka's habit of sticking her head over the fence, after she'd finished her grain, to advise that she wanted her feed bag removed. Hamaca, true to Huascarán's tradition, figured out how to remove the bag by herself.

A week after sending my application to Lima, I began to consider leaving Piura before the arrival of the horses' export permits. I was fed-up with leading Hamaca and Ima in giant circles that began and ended at San Jacinto when the same effort could have brought me closer to Los Gatos. Already I'd lost too much time. With the health certificates I had used to bring Hamaca and Ima to San Jacinto, I could go as far as Ecuador. The *Asociación* in Lima could send my export permits to the border station as soon as they were ready, and I could pick them up there.

Of course, I'd be running the risk that *The Peruvian Factor* would delay the processing of my export permits, as it had when I was at La Quinta. If this happened, it would be much more difficult to set things straight from a tiny border settlement than from Piura. But the opportunity to gain a week was powerful incentive, and I finally decided to leave for La Tina, on the Ecuadorian border, with the hope that the mares' international papers would get there by the time I did.

Joyously, I threw myself into my preparations. With the help of Juan Luis Ruesta's father, I selected my overnight stops between Piura and Ecuador. Rations of hay and grain were sent ahead by bus. Equipment not immediately needed was packed into a duffel bag and sent to the *Guardia Civil* post in La Tina. I sewed torn clothes and put my horse gear in the best possible shape.

Thanks to the stress and strain involved in training new horses, a buckle and strap on my saddle needed replacing. This seemed a simple matter until I found there was no saddlemaker in Piura. The repairs were more than I could manage myself, and my search led to the discovery that there was a good saddlemaker in the nearby village of Catacaos, a small town with an international reputation for its artisans. Home to some of the finest craftsmen in South America, Catacaos boasted outstanding gold and silversmiths along with hatmakers said to produce the finest hand-woven straw hats in the world. It was a place worth seeing, entirely aside from my need for the services of its saddlemaker.

For my trip to Catacaos, *Señor* Onrubia again offered his automobile. I had driven in Peru only once, the day he had first loaned me his car, and for a number of reasons, I wasn't sure if I wanted to do it again. To start with, I was unfamiliar with Peru's traffic laws. Of even more concern, I wouldn't necessarily have to break one of those laws in order to be pulled over. It was common practice for Peruvian policemen to stop drivers for the sole purpose of extracting a bribe. If the motorist paid, it would fend off a ticket he didn't deserve. If he didn't, he'd be taken straight to jail and held for trial. The police were known to concentrate on tourists in the belief that they always carried plenty of money. I felt particularly vulnerable because I had no international driver's license and wasn't reassured when people told me they were "pretty sure" a tourist could legally drive in Peru with a valid license from back home.

On the other hand, the drive back and forth to Catacaos was less than two hours, compared to spending the best part of a day on the same trip by bus. My decision was made easier when Rodriguez recommended a shortcut on dirt roads across private property. This, he assured, would make it possible to avoid driving more than a few hundred yards on public roads. Rodriguez further assured me that his shortcut was much shorter than the circuitous route followed by the highway. This analysis was accurate, but it ignored the fact that the shortcut was more cattle trail than road, and several times José Antonio's car nearly bogged down in soft pockets of sand and powder.

After a while, the road led to the edge of a river and disappeared beneath the water's surface. Not positive that the road actually crossed the river, I glanced at the opposite bank where it reappeared. Here was irony at its very finest! While planning my ride, I had anticipated fording many rivers on my horses. Now that the time had come for my first such experience, I was in a borrowed car. Uncertain of how to proceed, I brought the car to a stop and waited for the dust to settle before opening the door and stepping out. The water was muddy, and that was bad news. To evaluate the depth and composition of the bottom, I'd have to wade in.

It's my nature that I hate to invest time in something and abandon it. Furthermore, I wanted to avoid the highway, where my lack of an international driver's license might cause problems. Brimming with determination, I put one foot up on the bumper, in preparation for removing my shoes and socks. As I was untying the laces, an elderly Indian gentleman arrived at the opposite bank of the river. He was riding a scrubby little horse and leading a string of three pack mules. Without hesitation, he and his pack train entered the river and made their way toward me. I was encouraged to see that the water wasn't quite knee-deep on the old gentleman's stubby horse.

As his mount emerged from the river, the old Indian nodded and touched the brim of his hat in greeting. Next he swept his hand back toward the river in a gesture that ended with his arm fully extended in the direction from which he had come. Apparently, he was indicating that it was safe to cross, and for the first time, I saw the fresh tire tracks emerging from the water on the opposite bank. When I hesitated, the old gentleman dismounted and handed his reins to an assistant who was following on foot.

"Please follow me, *señor*," he said. "I can show you the best way across."

While I got back inside the car, the old man rolled up his pant legs, waded into the water and turned to motion me forward. As the car entered the water, I instinctively looked at the floor, ready to throw the car into reverse if water started pouring in. It was an unnecessary precaution. The only real danger was that I might get stuck, but fortunately the old mule skinner kept me on firm ground all the way across.

Catacaos wasn't the sort of town that would have housed a colony of famous artisans in other parts of the world. It had dirt streets and no running water or electricity. The adobe houses and shops were as rundown as those in the poorest section of any Peruvian city. Nothing hinted at the craftsmen inside, working their magic with precious metals and other fine materials. A few advertisements were posted on walls, but these ignored the local artisans in favor of products such as Coca Cola, Inka Kola and laundry soap. There were not even signs to distinguish stores from homes. In response to my inquiries, I was sent to three different locations before I found the saddlemaker. Even when I finally arrived at the right block on the right street, I had trouble finding him.

"Why don't the businesses here have signs?" I asked in frustration when I was finally face-to-face with the man I sought.

He looked at me for a long time.

"What for? Everyone knows where we are."

"What about people from out-of-town?"

"Hardly anyone comes here."

"In that case, who buys your merchandise?"

"Our merchandise goes to shops in big cities."

Meaning that middlemen profit from your talents more than you do, I thought.

While killing time, waiting for my saddle, I strolled through town and discovered that the tiny adobe hovels contained extraordinary treasures. Most had display cases filled with stunning silver jewelry most of which, upon request, could be duplicated in gold. I found myself especially impressed with the intricate filigree work. Reputedly, the local silversmiths produced some of the world's finest, in which yards and yards of fine silver wire were tightly rolled and gracefully twisted into exquisite figures. The finished pieces represented everything from fighting cocks to pianos, with endless strands of fine silver wire providing their form and dimension.

Two hours later, I was steering around potholes, crossing Catacaos with my newly repaired saddle in the trunk. Near the center of town, I made a right turn and pulled into traffic on the main street. *Traffic* in this case was a Land Rover equipped with four large loud speakers, one pointing outward from each corner of the roof. I had seen it all over Piura the week before, serving as a campaign tool for political candidates, and lost in my thoughts, I paid it no attention until I noticed something peculiar.

Listening more closely, I distinctly heard the word "poverty." Curious as to why English was being used where few, if any, understood it, I listened carefully. What I heard was as unexpected as *anything* possibly could have been! I turned my head and looked behind me to find the occupants of the jeep grinning and waving. I didn't recognize them, but they obviously knew me because the van's loudspeakers were blaring, in a highly accented version of my native tongue: "Vote for Pablito! He is the only man who can end this terrible poverty! Pablito for Mayor!"

They followed me all the way to the outskirts of Catacaos, plugging my *candidacy* every inch of the way. I've often wondered if I got any votes ....

CHAPTER 14

Borderline

Shortly before leaving Piura, I revised my travel plan, converting it into an extension of the conditioning program already under way. Under the new program, I intended to walk, leading the horses, for the first few hundred miles. There were several reasons for this. I didn't want to lose any more time conditioning my mares, yet they were far from ready for hard labor under saddle. Ima was barely more than a filly, and Hamaca, too, had never known toil. Both needed to be slowly introduced to hard work, especially considering that they would also be adjusting to changes in feed, climate, surroundings and altitude. With me walking instead of riding, they could get in shape and make the other adjustments without undue stress.

During my last night at San Jacinto, Juan Luis Ruesta brought three friends to see my mares. To facilitate this, I led Hamaca and Ima, one by one, from their dark corrals to an area illuminated by a floodlight. Having no halter handy, I did something unhorseman-like: I led each mare with my belt around her neck. Hamaca behaved perfectly, and so did Ima, until Juan Luis unexpectedly slapped her on the rump, hoping to see a display of elegant *brío*. He saw *brío* all right, but it wasn't all that elegant.

Startled by the slap, Ima bolted. I held on but couldn't turn her, and she steadily gained speed until I could no longer keep up. The situation would have been easily controlled if she'd been wearing a halter, but with only my belt around her neck, I had to let go. The moment I freed her, Ima scampered back to the security of her corral. There she stood, blowing bursts of air through her nostrils, as horses do when well-fed and excited. I reclaimed my belt, chuckling at the comical look on Ima's expressive face. It tickled me to see such an eloquent reminder of her youth and inexperience.

Threading my belt back through the loops in my jeans, I walked toward Juan Luis and his friends, limping every step of the way. During her mad dash, Ima had inadvertently slammed a hoof down on the inside of my right ankle. Already it was swelling, and this continued until there was a protrusion the size of a half-grapefruit. The painful throbbing increased proportionately. All in all, it wasn't something I welcomed the night before I resumed my trip … on foot.

Later that evening, I thanked José Antonio Onrubia for his help and hospitality. I had come to feel a great affection for *don* José

Antonio. His assistance had saved my enterprise from certain failure, and I thanked him at great length. In addition, I told him how much I had learned from him. He was the first *aficionado* who'd taken the time to teach me about the Peruvian breed. I had also learned important lessons about life from him. As a young man, I found it difficult to speak about such matters, and regrettably, I left much unsaid.

I'd be gone long before anyone else was awake the following morning, and before retiring for the night, I said my good-byes to *Señora* Onrubia and the children. That done, I went to get some sleep before resuming my adventure.

******

Since Chiclayo, the Peruvians had been describing their deserts by saying: "There is nothing there, except sand." That description had always been bleaker than the reality I found. At worst, there had been sparse vegetation and a few assorted desert creatures. Between Piura and Sullana, however, there were places where the land lived up to its advance billing. With the exception of an occasional, dried-out bush, there truly was nothing except sand, if one overlooked sun, highway and roadside crosses. The crosses – sometimes in clusters – marked locations where people had died in accidents. On a couple of occasions, they even identified a roadside grave. Meaning no disrespect, I couldn't help wondering if any of the graves contained fools who had tried to cross this particular desert on foot.

During that first day, my ankle throbbed with pain, steadily worsening until I was groaning with even the slightest misstep. While I walked, my ankle sent lightning bolts of misery shooting in all directions. Whenever I stopped, I had to alternately lift one foot and the other because the soles of my boots conducted the sand's searing heat. That heat was unpleasant even when I was moving, but when I stopped, it became unbearable. In spite of the recent change of season, I had little doubt that day's temperature was the hottest I'd ever experienced. If so, I was well-acclimated, for my discomfort had been even more intense on other days, except for my feet.

Following the recommendation of Juan Luis Ruesta's father, I made my way to a picturesque cavalry fort on the outskirts of Sullana. It was typical of nineteenth-century military fortifications, but in the twentieth century, it looked out of place, suggesting, perhaps, a Latin American stronghold of the French Foreign Legion. A tall, thick adobe wall surrounded the entire installation. Inside were rustic facilities (for the conscripts) and others that were rather luxurious (for the officers). The entire complex was immaculate and well kept, with freshly whitewashed walls, a few carefully manicured gardens and paths lined on either side by uniform rows of stones. There wasn't much grass, but every inch of dirt was neatly swept.

At the mention of *Señor* Ruesta's name, the commander invited my mares and me to spend the night. Hamaca and Ima were assigned to comfortable stalls in a barn they entered by passing beneath a stone archway that bore a sign proclaiming: "Peruvian Cavalry." In Peru, cavalry didn't use tanks, as in the States. They still used horses. Aside from being colorful, this was providential, for it meant there was a veterinarian and a blacksmith, trades for which there would have been no need in an armored corps. Not long after I arrived, both of these specialists came to offer their services.

The vet took one look at Hamaca and proclaimed that she was pregnant. If so, it was very bad news! I had declined to purchase numerous otherwise-suitable mares because they were in foal. Carrying a foal was an avoidable burden with potentially grave consequences.

"How can you be so sure?" I asked, apparently with a dubious tone in my voice.

"I'm a veterinarian," he responded in a tone that suggested his authority ought not be questioned. "I know a pregnant mare when I see one!"

The vet thoroughly examined both mares and pronounced them in excellent condition. His diagnosis of Hamaca's pregnancy was repeated after the examination, despite the fact that he hadn't done anything to confirm it. The man's insistence notwithstanding, I doubted his assessment. Hamaca's pregnancy test at Casa Grande had been negative, and she had come in heat right on schedule at San Jacinto. However, neither of these was proof positive. Something else *was* positive, though. One of Hamaca's rear shoes had worked itself loose, and we'd soon be in terrain where it would be sorely missed if lost. The fort's blacksmith was kind enough to renail it.

I spent a miserable night in Sullana. My ankle hurt and wouldn't stop no matter what I tried. I wrapped it, elevated it and took aspirin, all without finding relief. To add to my discomfort, I seemed to have picked up some sort of bug. Aspirin or no aspirin, it wasn't long before I became feverish.

By morning, I had recovered enough to set out for the *Hacienda* Chilaco, my second overnight stop on the road to Ecuador. Not far from Sullana, the road began gaining altitude, and stark desert terrain gave way to increasing greenery. Hamaca took advantage of this by sidling over to roadside bushes and pressing against them, currying herself while walking past. I quickly put a stop to that. It was gouging the leather on my saddle.

This scratching was right in character for Hamaca. She seemed to have a perpetual itch. Whenever I turned her loose after a bath, she'd roll and roll – a horse's equivalent of scratching its back – until she was coated with dust. If I gave her a thorough brushing afterward, she would roll again the instant she was turned loose. This little war was never-ending. I wanted her to look clean and well cared for, and she wasn't comfortable without a covering of dust. It was her talcum powder and apparently very effective at soothing her itches.

Thus afflicted, Hamaca had mixed feelings about her morning brushing. While it was in progress, she showed pleasure by flexing her upper lip until it extended farther forward than the lower. Afterward, though, she longed for the dirt I had swept from her. As we set out on each day's travels, she would lower her nose to the ground, looking for a spot to roll, and had to be denied the opportunity to do so.

That day's journey couldn't have ended soon enough for me. My feet hurt even more severely than the day before, and my fever of the previous night was now accompanied by all the other symptoms of dysentery. It was with considerable relief that I finally sighted the *Hacienda* Chilaco. My arrival was "déjà vu all over again," reminiscent of my arrival at La Viña. Chilaco seemed deserted when I got there, and a long search finally turned up an old man who was in charge and wasn't expecting me. Fortunately, that was where the similarity ended.

The old man had received the feed I'd sent and showed me its location in a shed next to an empty corral where he invited me to put my mares. When I began caring for Hamaca and Ima, he told me to make myself at home – pointing to the main house to indicate where I should do this – and walked away. When I was finished with the horses, I made my way to the main house, expecting to find my host there. No one answered my repeated knocking, and after a half-hour, I went inside, searching and calling out until it was well confirmed that no one was there.

I spent the rest of the night as the lone resident of a large, very old and primitive house with little furniture and no electricity or running water. Chunks of plaster had fallen from the walls, and other signs of disrepair were everywhere. In spite of this, I found my lodgings charming and picturesque.

Chilaco's main house, in spite of everything wrong with it, had a certain elegance. This was mostly provided by its location atop a small hill overlooking irrigated, green fields. In Peru, it was typical for farmhouses to be built on high ground in order to command a view of the surrounding acreage. In the absence of natural high ground, a towering building pad would be raised by piling and compacting dirt until the desired vantage point had been created.

As sick as I was, I had no desire to eat, but I came up with another way to indulge myself. I carried bucket after bucket of water from the outside tank where I had earlier watered my horses. These I poured into an ornate tub in the main bathroom. The tub was old and deep, standing on four ornate feet, and had been installed long after the house was built. When the old-fashioned plug was pulled, the water emptied onto the floor, which sloped to a drain. The tub's porcelain was chipped and pitted, revealing rusty cast iron beneath, but in its day it must have been a considerable luxury out there in the middle of nowhere. That night, it briefly regained its former glorious status.

For well over an hour, I soaked my feverish body in the cold water. It was long after dark when I'd finally had enough. By then, my toes and fingers were shriveled, and my teeth were chattering, but I felt wonderful! It was the first time in two days that I hadn't felt drastically overheated.

After checking my horses to make sure they were eating and comfortable, I made my way to one of the bedrooms and by moonlight, unrolled my sleeping bag on a bed with sagging, creaky, bare springs. Then I stretched out on top, hoping to prolong the marvelous sensation of coolness until morning.

Since arriving at Chilaco, I'd seen no one except for the old man who'd welcomed me and disappeared. He must have been the administrator. In the owner's absence, he had apparently chosen to escape the heavy burden that Peruvian hosts impose upon themselves. If such was the case, I didn't mind since I was equally happy to escape the burden of being someone's guest. With my various ailments, it was a relief not to have to make polite conversation and a pleasure to be able to do what I wanted when I wanted.

My only discomfort came from the prospect of sleeping in a house that wasn't locked. Following the habits of a lifetime spent in cities, I had already checked the exterior doors and discovered ancient locks that couldn't be engaged without a key. Since the house had been standing unlocked, it seemed pointless to search for the key. It probably hadn't been seen for decades.

In the morning, I still had no appetite, and freed from the need to prepare and eat breakfast, I got an early start toward my next stop, the town of Las Lomas. When I left Chilaco, there was no sign of life and no one to thank for the hospitality. All I could do was leave a note, in Spanish, on the kitchen table.

All day, the mares and I continued to gain altitude, and the countryside continued its change from desert to what would have been semitropical if there had been sufficient water. The land was eager to bring forth lush, green vegetation, and wherever water was found, there were shrubs, trees, blooming flowers and even flocks of parrots.

In Las Lomas no one stepped forward to volunteer horse accommodations, and for the first time, I had to offer to rent a corral. The next morning, to my surprise, the corral owner, instead of refusing payment, demanded a very healthy fee. A little reflection reminded me that his eyes had narrowed considerably when he saw me giving my horses hay and grain the previous evening.

"Where did you get such excellent feed?" he asked, amazement in his voice.

"I shipped it here by bus," was my matter-of-fact reply.

There was an instant and none-too-subtle change in the man's attitude. His treatment of me became formal and overly respectful. Apparently he had concluded that I must be wealthy beyond his wildest imaginings. Only an incredibly rich man, after all, would ship hay and grain for mere horses, and needless to say, such men didn't need favors from the less fortunate.

My own lodging in Las Lomas was free. Once again, I was a guest of the *Guardia Civil*, which had a small outpost in the center of town. I tossed and turned in my bunk a good part of the night, kept awake by a particularly annoying mosquito. It's the stealthy female mosquitoes, I'm told, that leave the itching bites behind but make no sound while in flight. If that's true, it was a male that loudly buzzed past my ears all night, needing a muffler as badly as the trucks that stopped outside for the mandatory document check

The mares and I were up at 3:00 A.M. and off to cover the thirty miles to our next stopover, in the town of Suyo. Every step still hurt, but less than before, and I was able to force this reduced pain from my consciousness.

A person of sound mind seldom pays attention to telephone poles, but those along the highway to Suyo were difficult to ignore. Each was a unique original that looked like a reflection from a funhouse mirror. They were only inches in diameter, bent, twisted, crooked and short enough that, from horseback, I could have reached the single wire they supported. Amazingly, that lone, thin wire was Suyo's only means of communicating with the outside world.

Suyo itself was quaint. From a distance, my impression was that I approached a village in Spain, owing, I suppose, to the gorgeous red tile roofs. As I drew closer, however, more detail was revealed, and I could see the shabby hovels beneath those picturesque, handmade tiles. The contrast was jarring. The roofs would have graced even the most elegant homes in the United States, yet the houses beneath them wouldn't have been considered suitable quarters for pets.

These tile roofs were yet another sign of how quickly my world was changing. I had come from an area where roofs were only sunshades and often consisted of nothing more than branches laid side by side. In the foothills, however, rain was apt to fall, and tile was the only way to make the roofs watertight.

The countryside around Suyo was covered by tinder-dry scrub brush where yet another startling contrast could be observed. The scorched, gray twigs and branches bore few leafs but were home to beautifully colored birds. Here and there, living patches of scarlet, brilliant green or yellow darted about. Equally amazing were the solitary but unbelievably lovely blossoms that occasionally added further color.

After an uneventful day, the mares and I spent the night at a small cavalry outpost in Suyo. There was only one stall available, meaning that Hamaca and Ima had to be quartered together. They didn't like being separated, and to their mutual delight, sharing a stall or tiny corral would be common in days to come.

Noticing Hamaca's and Ima's well-worn shoes, the post blacksmith graciously offered his services without charge. While he replaced all eight horseshoes, I held the mares, and a group of gregarious troopers gathered, anxious to offer me advice. Listening to them gave me further insight into how much my surroundings had changed in only three days. The hazards of the desert were behind me, but others had replaced them. To start with, there were mosquito-borne diseases that would almost certainly be transmitted to my horses if I didn't take precautions. I also needed to carefully disinfect all wounds the horses might get – no matter how insignificant

– because of a germ that could enter a horse's body through cuts or abrasions, with disastrous results. That particular germ was said to initially cause the loss of all hair around the infection. During the next stage, the flesh in the affected area would slowly rot, producing an ache so terrible that horses often sought relief by biting off chunks of their own decaying flesh.

When the new shoes were in place, the soldiers hung around to watch as I went through my nightly horse-care routine. Afterward, they advised me that I'd forgotten a very important precaution, and they proceeded to hang *sabila* near the stall's external openings. *Sabila* is a native plant, which, I was told, would repel bloodsucking vampire bats. Vampire bats! To me that sounded like one drastic warning too many. I suspected a test of my gullibility. Sensing my skepticism, the troopers showed me several horses that had suffered nocturnal visits from vampire bats. Because these winged creatures are notoriously filthy, most of the bites were hideously infected, and the sight of those festering wounds was enough to dispel all doubt. Until I was beyond vampire country, I would carry and use *sabila*. Beyond that, I would apply strong insect repellent to my mares three times a day, in the hope this combination would force bloodsuckers of all sizes and descriptions to keep their distance.

On his famous ride, Amie Tschiffely ran afoul of vampire bats more than once, and his following musings, taken from his book, are of interest:

> "I was puzzled how a horse or mule could let so big an animal bite him, when a mosquito or a fly will make him defend himself. At a later period I had the chance to observe how these bats attack, and I feel inclined to believe in the theory of some mountain people.

> "Bats have a peculiar way of flying around the horse in circles until he becomes drowsy and half dazed. These bloodsuckers usually exist in deep quebradas, as the rugged valleys are called, and owing to the hot and damp atmosphere the horses perspire even during the nights. Gradually the bats circle closer and closer around the now sleepy horse, and

141

presently they hover near the spot where they intend to bite, all the time fanning air against the victim. Once the horse gets used to the pleasant sensation of feeling cool the vampire gently settles down and bites through the hide with his sharp little teeth, keeping up the fanning with his wings."

The following day at noon, I arrived at my ride's first milestone, the border town of La Tina. It was a miniscule accomplishment, compared to what I hoped to do, but it was a start. In spite of everything, I had successfully made it to where Peru ended and Ecuador began, the first of ten borders between Chiclayo and Los Gatos.

My new horses had traveled two hundred miles and had come through with flying colors. That was a much more important accomplishment than it might seem. After all, the early miles are often the most difficult, as my geldings had discovered.

Myself, I had come four hundred miles since my send-off in Chiclayo, not including the six hundred or so miles covered while conditioning two different sets of horses. It was a time to take pleasure in small victories and to rededicate myself to greater things in the weeks and months to come.

CHAPTER 15

The Smuggler in the Mirror

Good news awaited! Despite my premonitions to the contrary, the horses' international travel permits were waiting at the *Guardia Civil* post in La Tina. For some reason, the papers weren't valid until the following day, but that was no problem. I'd be busy all afternoon, anyhow, with a problem that had to be solved before I took my horses into Ecuador

After stationing the horses in a rented corral at a small farm, I checked into an inexpensive hotel room. My appetite had returned with a vengeance, and I ate a substantial lunch before taking a long, leisurely shower. I'd always found the shower an excellent place for thinking, and before long, I was considering the pros and cons of a little extracurricular incursion across the border with illegal contraband. The more I thought about it, the more the idea appealed.

According to the best information available, there wouldn't be any animal forage available until I was two or more days inside Ecuador. I had prepared for that by sending extra hay to La Tina, intending to take it across the border. However, one of the officers of the *Guardia Civil* in Las Lomas had pointed out the flaw in my plan.

"I can assure you," he'd said, "that you won't be permitted to cross into Ecuador with Peruvian hay. It will definitely be confiscated."

To complicate things further, it was a very long journey from the border to the first overnight stop where horses could be accommodated. The road we'd travel climbed steeply into the Andes mountains and would sap our energy, challenging us to reach our destination by nightfall. This road was also narrow and passed through terrain so steep that the only way to travel would be on the road itself. None of this was good news to someone whose horses were unaccustomed to being in close quarters with traffic.

In bright sunlight, that first day in Ecuador would be dangerous. By moonlight, the risks would be multiplied tenfold. For that reason I needed to be under way at first light, and, to save time, I desperately wanted to start into the Andes the very next morning. To my dismay, though, that didn't seem to be in the cards because, in the event my horse feed was confiscated, it would take a full day to go ahead by bus, find more and bring it back to Macara. Worse yet, if no cured hay was available, I'd only be able to bring back enough freshly cut forage for one day. Even if allowed to take my provisions into Ecuador, I wouldn't dare continue on by the time I'd planned my itinerary and shipped the feed and baggage ahead. No matter how I sliced it, I stood to lose no less than a full day in Macara, the town on the opposite side of the border from La Tina.

As I emerged from my shower, I still had most of the afternoon ahead of me. I also had a plan to make good use of it. The seeds were planted by the *Guardia Civil* officer who had told me that my hay wouldn't be allowed into Ecuador.

"Put the hay on your horses and take it across the river someplace where no one will see you," he had suggested.

It was a strange recommendation from a man charged with enforcing the law. If I got caught, I could just imagine trying to defend my actions to the Ecuadorian authorities.

"I didn't think it would be a problem because an officer in the Peruvian *Guardia Civil* gave me the idea."

I could easily predict the prospects for that particular defense, especially since Peru and Ecuador were near a shooting war, due to a territorial dispute. Clearly, though, I could save time, money, effort and wear and tear on my horses by making an unauthorized logistical incursion, without officially leaving Peru or entering Ecuador. With any luck, I should be able to take my hay and excess baggage to Macara and get reliable information about the road ahead. With that, I could choose destinations for my feed and baggage and ship them. Boldly, I resolved to do this, and immediately thereafter, I had second thoughts. What if I got arrested as a smuggler? Perhaps I should cross into Ecuador legally and have a look around. At the very least I could ship my baggage ahead and try to find a way to provide feed for my animals without smuggling it. Unfortunately, that plan presented its own set of problems.

I had a visa for Ecuador, freshly stamped in my passport on my last day in Piura. However, once I used it, a new visa would be required to return to Peru and yet another to re-enter Ecuador the following morning. The problem was that visas for either country weren't available at the border.

When I went down to the hotel lobby, there was a man sitting there. I thought he might be a trucker and, therefore, a source of reliable information. There was one way to find out.

"Are you a trucker?" I asked.

"*Sí, señor.*"

"Do you know where I can get a visa for Ecuador?"

"The nearest place is probably Piura," he answered. "You should have gotten a visa before you came here."

"I already have one," I answered, "but I need another so I can go back and forth this afternoon and then enter Ecuador again in the morning."

"Go up the river a ways and walk across," he advised.

"And what happens if the authorities catch me?"

"They don't pay any attention to that kind of thing. Do you think people in La Tina get a visa every time they want to visit their friends on the other side of the river?" He answered.

"I'm planning to cross the border tomorrow with several bales of hay …"

"They won't let you, *señor*."

"Surely there must be some way to …"

"The only way would be to take your hay across the river as contraband."

"What will happen if I first try to cross the legal way?"

"You'll lose your hay. I regularly bring cattle from Ecuador, and I don't even dream of bringing hay across the border, not in either direction. The border guards on both sides confiscated my hay every single time I tried. Bastards! They sold it every time, after I was gone."

"Is it true there's no animal feed within the first hundred kilometers to the north?"

"More than that, probably, but it's no problem," the trucker answered. "Horses can go for days without eating. Don't worry. They won't die."

That was the last straw. I went back to Plan A. Anyone (of my temperament!) who had already endured as many sick horses and as much bureaucracy would have gladly made the same decision and assumed the same risks. I was convinced that local residents knew how to cross into Ecuador, out of sight of the border station and without going through any formalities. Furthermore, there were plenty of mules around, and I theorized that a few coins would rent as many as I needed, along with their owner's services as guide.

Both assumptions were correct, and mid-afternoon found me fording a knee-deep (my knees - not my guide's!) river behind four tiny mules loaded with my hay, grain and baggage. No doubt it was a risky move, but if anything went wrong, I had a visa to show I was entitled to enter Ecuador. I planned to say that I had inadvertently failed to pass through immigration because I'd come cross-country. Once inside Ecuador, I intended to make my way directly to the local military outpost. When he heard this, the man in charge of the mules raised his eyebrows and refused to accompany me to my first destination. He showed me a spot along the river and instructed me to meet him there after I was finished consorting with the Ecuadorian army. Not knowing much about him, I was uncomfortable with the prospect of leaving this man with most of my worldly possessions. Casually, I let it slip that I was friendly with the officers of the *Guardia Civil* in La Tina and could count on their help whenever I needed it.

At Macara's military post, I introduced myself and asked for information. No one asked for my documents. Instead, the *comandante* himself graciously welcomed me, giving the impression that my arrival was a welcome break in an otherwise dull day. He cheerfully offered to help plan my itinerary and led me to his desk where he spread out a couple of maps. The *comandante* didn't know the area well, but the things he said confirmed what I had heard elsewhere. Feed was unavailable for several days' ride, and there was a considerable distance between Macara and the next settlement to the north. It took us no more than thirty minutes – punctuated with much polite conversation – to select my next six overnight destinations. Except for the long first day, my scheduled stops were a convenient twenty to thirty miles apart. Armed with this information, I proceeded back to the riverbank where I was relieved to find hay, baggage, guide and mules.

My bales of hay weren't sufficient to feed two horses for six days. I divided them into six unequal bundles, which I packed in gunnysacks. Three were large enough to cover nights when other feed wouldn't be available. The others were smaller but would provide familiar feed to supplement whatever was available as we worked our way deeper into Ecuador.

Again in the company of my mule train, I set out for the bus station. There the six gunnysacks and my duffel bag were dispatched to my overnight stops, each tagged with instructions to hold it until I arrived. I also needed to do some shopping in Macara's commercial district, which was many times as large as its Peruvian counterpart across the border. My guide refused to wait while I did this. His mission accomplished, he insisted I pay his fee so he could return home. I sent him on his way with misgivings, hoping I'd have no trouble finding my way back across the river in the dark.

One striking difference from Peru was immediately apparent in downtown Macara. In La Tina, just as in the rest of Peru, most building and houses were adobe. Just a few hundred yards away, across an imaginary line, most of Ecuador's structures were wooden.

In a day filled with many lasting impressions, the most memorable came as darkness fell. Macara's business district was suddenly invaded by swarms of flying beetles, apparently attracted by the lights. I was the only person in town who seemed to think the event was noteworthy. Seeing my astonishment, one passerby volunteered that the beetles were "right on schedule." A plague of biblical proportions, this phenomenon, I was told, was a nightly event. Canister-type sprayers, filled with the appropriate mixture of chemicals and water, were removed from storage places. Without a word having been spoken, employees from every establishment on either side of the street calmly began spraying insecticide with well-practiced movements. The beetles responded by dying in droves until their corpses blanketed the sidewalks. Putting down their sprayers, the army of waiters and clerks proceeded to sweep the carcasses into large mounds.

Apparently, the insecticide posed no threat to human beings, or at least no one thought so. Even in the restaurants, people seemed unconcerned, and no one restrained the dogs that suddenly appeared and began dining on the piles of dead beetles. Macara was the first South American town I'd seen where the dogs weren't walking skeletons, proving, I suppose, that even a cloud of beetles has a silver lining.

It was after nightfall when I hired two boys to guide me back to the river, and from there, I found my way without difficulty. When I arrived in La Tina, I discovered that someone had turned hungry cows into the corral with my horses. The bovines had eaten every stalk, leaf and kernel of the mares' hay and grain.

Before leaving for Macara, I had given Hamaca and Ima an exceptionally large feeding, intending for them to eat by free choice until morning. I couldn't be sure how much, if any, lunch they'd eaten, but obviously they'd had no dinner and would have no breakfast unless I took action. After shooing the cows out and wiring the gate shut, I woke a shopkeeper and bought cooking oats, there being no hope of finding the much-cheaper variety I'd been feeding. Then I made my way to the riverbank with a borrowed lantern and machete. There, I cut two bundles of elephant grass, the only local forage available. Finally, I sat down to a restaurant meal at 10:00. By that time, my blistered feet were killing me. Worse yet, they faced a forty-mile, uphill hike the next day. At least my dysentery had subsided, and, all in all, I was feeling the best I had for days, in spite of having lost enough weight to require punching new holes in my belt.

The next morning I was first in line when the border opened. I had arrived an hour early to assure that position because I was expecting a prolonged ordeal. In South America, border officials check the documents of those who exit their countries as well as those who enter, meaning that I had two sets of officials to satisfy. With two horses to declare, I anticipated a hassle, first from Peruvian authorities and then from those in Ecuador. However, the crossing was quick and uncomplicated. No one on either side asked to see the horses' papers or inspected my baggage. On the Peruvian side, it was noted that I had gotten an extension of my Peruvian visa in Piura, and I was asked why, since I was leaving the country on the final day of my original visa. I explained the uncertainties of travel by horseback, and an exit stamp was promptly placed in my passport right next to the stamp that had officialized my entry, ninety days earlier.

"Good luck, *señor*," I was told in a tone of voice that seemed to indicate I'd been recognized.

On the Ecuadorian side, an official asked what I'd been doing in Peru, stamped my passport and welcomed me to his country.

The capacity of the human body for recuperation can be astounding. The evening before, my aches and pains had me dreading the upcoming forty-mile hike, but after crossing the border, I was actually looking forward to the challenge. I was determined to be at my destination before dark, and I wasted no time passing through Macara and starting up into the Andes. Before long, the steady climb had me wondering if I was physically capable of maintaining the necessary pace. There was also psychological stress. I wasn't at all comfortable with my first look at Ecuador's mountain Indians, popularly known as *serranos*. I'd seen them only from a distance, but they struck me as being aggressive and much less friendly than the Peruvians.

Late that morning – well into the mountains – I was suddenly confronted by a large group of *serranos* walking single file along the side of the road. Carrying machetes, they were headed in the opposite direction, bringing us closer together with every step. I knew the men were workers who used their machetes for legitimate purposes, but that provided scant comfort. The long, sharp blades looked formidable, and the men who carried them looked sullen. They observed me with what can only have been suspicion as we drew closer. When we came abreast of one another, the first man in line greeted me with a nod of his head and a *"Buen día,"* to which I responded in kind. The second man did the same, and so did I. One after the other, every man in the long line said *"Buen día,"* and I was only too happy to answer each of them by parroting the same two words.

This was a process that was repeated frequently during the next few hours. Andean courtesy, it seemed, demanded that each person I pass greet me with none other than the words *"Buen día"* and that I answer them in the same fashion. That was fine with me. If people carrying machetes wanted to be sociable, who was I to disappoint them? As the day wore on, however, the appearance of machete-carrying *serranos* became less alarming, and I began to find the endless exchanges of greetings tiresome. If only each group would name a spokesman to handle the social amenities or, better yet, simply dispense with them. When I got my wish, it was chilling!

Toward late afternoon I passed a small group from which no one greeted me. Worse yet, no one acknowledged *my* greetings, which ceased after the first few men. Not one of them even turned his sullen gaze in my direction. I knew there were *serranos* in the Andes who still spoke only their ancient tongues, and I fervently hoped that language and not something sinister was the explanation. Whatever the reason, this same procedure was repeated with two more groups. It was unsettling, and both times after we'd passed, I could hear the grim-faced men exchanging staccato phrases in a language I didn't understand. Trying to seem casual, I looked back over my shoulder each time the chill between my shoulder blades became unbearable.

In Peru, I always had my *public*, people who knew me as someone who was promoting their national horse. In Ecuador, no one knew or cared who I was. Even those who were outwardly friendly seemed to regard me with suspicion. At best, I was an oddball leading two perfectly healthy horses that should have been carrying him.

It was beginning to look as if the road behind had been more hospitable than the one ahead.

CHAPTER 16

The Andes

Initially, I had strong misgivings about Ecuador's people, but as it turned out, the environment was the more inhospitable. My travels in the Andes weren't as uncomfortable as those in the Peruvian desert, but they were more dangerous. Humans and nature were locked in conflict in those towering mountains, and nature held the upper hand. Ever-aggressive, it even sometimes turned upon itself.

During that first afternoon beyond the border, I saw an entire forest under attack by parasitic plants. Leech-like growths with the appearance of thistles had fastened themselves to tree branches and were sucking nourishment. These thistles grew to a considerable size, and the bigger, healthier and more numerous they were, the more sickly was the tree that fed them. As with other parasites, death was inevitable once they had grown big enough and numerous enough to kill their hosts. By that time, unfortunately, they had reproduced themselves on the branches of neighboring victims. I was told that this plague had killed a significant portion of the trees for the next forty miles. Worse yet, nothing was being done, or even planned, to stop this destruction. I continued to see decimated expanses of trees until the road turned away from the valley where they had once flourished.

That particular forest was home to flocks of small, brightly colored parrots. I had been surprised to see parrots in Peru being hunted for their meat, and on my first day in Ecuador, I again felt outrage each time I saw a peasant pull a shotgun to his shoulder and drop a beautiful parrot from the sky. My reaction was undeniably hypocritical. In my own life, I had hunted game birds and couldn't justify this by saying I had needed the meat, as Ecuador's peasants unquestionably did.

After I left the forest, there were very few people along the road, and it was hard to imagine where even so few were living. The mountains quickly became barren, and I saw no signs of housing or food production. Making a mental comparison to mountain areas in the States, I couldn't help but notice the absence of secondary roads and driveways. Looking hard for signs of life, I noticed barely distinguishable footpaths intersecting the highway at long intervals. These, I realized, were the *driveways* of the locals. If I followed one, I would almost certainly find huts and people, although I might have to go a considerable distance.

As the afternoon waned, I became aware of small flashes glimmering here and there in the shrubs, becoming more visible as daylight faded. It took a while to realize what they were. Recognition was followed by astonishment at the staggering number. Large fireflies were everywhere I looked, blinking on and off with an eerie regularity.

My destination that evening was a settlement named Empalme. The *comandante* back in Macara had warned me that Empalme wasn't much more than a collection of small kiosks, but as night approached, even such a desolate place sounded good. With darkness slowly falling, my eyes swept the canyons ahead, looking for huts, lights, planted or plowed fields, anything to show that people lived there. After eleven hours of steady climbing, we reached Empalme, just as darkness became total. Empalme was as the *comandante* had described. The only flat ground was where the roadbed had been carved and blasted from the mountainside. For one of a few times since Macara, the *Panamericana* was wide enough to easily accommodate two lanes of traffic. There was even something of a shoulder where the kiosks sold food and beverages.

The two soldiers at the military checkpoint received me with a stiffness that relaxed when I presented a letter from the *comandante* in Macara. The tiny outpost was a traffic checkpoint with a function similar to that of the *Guardia Civil* posts along Peru's highways. The officer in charge promised me a place to sleep and pointed toward a corral where the horses could spend the night. My guess was that this particular corral served as a holding pen for animals impounded from passing trucks. It didn't seem to have been used for a long time. Built on the side of a steep slope covered with slate-like rock, it was far enough below the road to make access difficult by day and treacherous in the dark.

Realizing how terribly difficult it would be to carry anything on such a steep grade, I decided to water the mares beforehand. Giving them a drink, however, was not easily done. After four hundred miles of desert travel, I experienced my greatest difficulty yet in finding water. No one could spare much, even when I offered to pay handsomely. I finally resorted to buying a pitcher here and a pitcher there, until I had patronized everyone in Empalme.

Once the horses had quenched their thirst, I hired a boy to hold Ima while I led Hamaca down the narrow, well-worn path to the corral. As the distance between them grew, both mares became anxious

151

over being separated for the first time since Ima's arrival at San Jacinto. They fretted nervously and incessantly called to one another. Though she was struggling to stay on her feet, Hamaca's mind was elsewhere, and she paid the price. Looking back toward Ima, she lost her balance, slipped off the path and began sliding downhill. As Hamaca scrambled for a foothold, her frantic struggles dislodged large slabs of loose rock. These clicked together with crisp sounds as they slid in the same direction she was headed. Only my hold on her leadline kept the situation from deteriorating further, and there was no way I could maintain that grip for long.

Not knowing how to handle such a crisis after a lifetime on the flat deserts of Peru, Hamaca panicked and redoubled her efforts. Sparks flew every which way as her horseshoes ricocheted off the flinty slabs of rock. Despite her lack of mountaineering skills, she made her way back to safety through sheer force of will. The rest of the way to the corral, she watched where she was going, having gained a new respect for the perils of the Andes. The path ended at a gate that provided access through the corral's upper fence. About twenty feet square, the interior was as sharply sloped as the hillside around it. A narrow shelf of rocks and dirt had collected inside the lower fence, forming the only place where a horse would be able to comfortably stand and eat.

Unfortunately, there were no stairs to assist those whose destination was the narrow shelf next to the lower fence. The descent was too steep for me to negotiate in a standing position. I had to sit, carefully slide a few feet, stop myself, stand up, bring Hamaca forward and then repeat the whole procedure, over and over, until we reached our destination. It took three more trips to bring Ima, the hay and the grain. On my last trip back up the hill, I fastened the corral gate shut with my belt, in the absence of a latch or chain. As for tending to my own needs, I ate several bananas and spent the rest of the night trying to make myself less uncomfortable on the small, hard, wooden bench where I slept inside the one-room military checkpoint.

In the morning, I was famished and ready to give up my whole adventure in exchange for a meal at a Texas steakhouse. I went from kiosk to kiosk with my appetite diminishing each time I saw the lack of hygiene. Even after having had my standards lowered considerably in Peru, I was appalled. I couldn't afford to be sick and habitually reminded myself of that when it came time to eat or drink. As I traveled farther from large metropolitan areas, however, sanitation was becoming almost nonexistent. In response, I formulated two simple guidelines to protect myself. Number one: whenever possible, eat food that came in cans, bottles, peels or shells. Number two: when these were unavailable, insist that my meals be overcooked – preferably boiled – to the point where even the heartiest germ had no prospects for survival. In accordance with these rules, I had six fried eggs, cooked to a rubbery consistency, and four large, over-baked rolls, fresh from a brick oven. It wasn't a delicious meal, but it was as welcome as any I've ever eaten.

From Macara on, I carried my canteen, filled with water. Up until then, I had been hesitant to trust my chlorine tablets and worried about the effect they might have on my stomach. Logic, though, convinced me that water, once chlorinated, would do me less damage than the amount of soda pop required to satisfy my raging thirst.

When I retrieved Hamaca and Ima from their hillside corral, I found that my belt had been stolen and the gate was standing open. There had been no immediate consequences since neither mare had been tempted to leave the lower edge of their enclosure. In fact, Ima had made herself supremely comfortable there after aiming her hindquarter straight uphill, folding her rear legs beneath herself and sitting, much as dogs do. She looked quite relaxed and pleased with herself.

That day's journey took us to the village of Las Playas. Upon arrival, I found that my hay and grain had been delivered in error to a schoolhouse far from the highway. I wasn't surprised by such a minor piece of disorientation in a mountain village, far from any noteworthy body of water, with a name meaning "The Beaches."

Tired after a hard day, I gave in to a temptation that had long beckoned. From the boys that collected around me – as they always did – I asked the biggest and strongest how much they would charge to help with my chores. They asked for only a few pennies, and their faces showed that they'd be thrilled to get that much. I gladly paid one lad about ten cents to take his family's mule and bring my feed from the schoolhouse to the corral I had been offered. Another couple of boys stood Hamaca and Ima in the river for a half-hour. Later, while policing that night's corral for dangerous contents, I discovered the need for extensive cleaning and repairs. Looking up, I saw a couple of youngsters still spectating. Once I'd verified that my pocket contained enough change, I decided that if they were watching, they might as well be helping. They turned out to be good workers.

During my ride, Lima was the farthest I ever got from Los Gatos. While there, I heard from no one who didn't think my journey would come to a successful conclusion. Ironically, the more I traveled northward – closer to Los Gatos – the more I heard from people who proclaimed doubts. In the Andes, starting with Las Playas, the local gentry would click their tongues and predict the worst: the horses would break down, take sick or die before I got to California; I'd be assaulted by bandits or felled by disease; my journey would end where terrain was impassible, food was unavailable or people were hostile to North Americans; and so on.

These dismal forecasts reflected the limited use people in the Andes got from their own animals, no surprise considering the care those animals received or, more accurately, didn't receive. In view of the harsh lives they themselves led, I could see why peasants in Peru and Ecuador were largely unconcerned with the welfare of animals. Unfortunately, they didn't simply lack empathy. Raised in a society that condoned bullfights and cockfights, they were inclined toward cruelty.

On the road to Las Playas, my mares and I had been passed by a rider on a stunted and undernourished horse with a hideously malformed leg. A birth defect had caused one rear pastern to grow sideways in such a way that the hoof didn't touch the ground. The unfortunate beast was hobbling along at a speed that was remarkable in view of his handicap, but it wasn't enough for his rider who incessantly whipped him, demanding more. That same day I saw a man, a woman and two children, all four mounted on one skinny little burro. Under their considerable load, the burro's pasterns nearly touched the ground, but the brave little animal was stepping along at a lively pace. Despite these extraordinary efforts, the man was briskly smacking the burro's side every few steps with the flat side of a machete.

My philosophy on how to get the most from my own horses was based on sowing first and reaping afterward. The peasants I met in Ecuador regarded this brand of horsemanship as a bad investment of time and money. At least that's what they quietly told one another when they saw me going through my routine, immediately after arriving in their towns. However, attitudes almost always underwent a dramatic change by morning. Perhaps people needed time to think about practices that were so completely foreign to them.

In the morning, someone would usually walk up, pat me on the shoulder and say something like: "Your horses live better than a *cristiano*. [8] With the care they receive, they should easily get to the *Estados Unidos*." For some reason, these comments were reassuring, never mind that they came from people who knew next to nothing about the subject they were discussing!

Night after night, I was approached by people who said that they had never seen such beautiful horses. While such compliments were very nice to hear, I had to remember that most people in that part of the world had never seen a well-fed, well-cared-for horse. In fact, it seemed they'd seen few horses of any sort. Ecuador's peasants used mules, and many didn't even seem to know the word *caballo* (horse). It was common for them to refer to Hamaca and Ima as *mulas*, a reference that seemed downright insulting the first few times I heard it.

[8] Throughout the Andes, peasants rarely used the words "human beings" or "people," preferring to use instead the word *cristiano* (Christian).

I thoroughly rinsed both horses, preparing them to appear before an audience (see page 103).

That morning in Motupe, a crowd gathered to observe my morning ritual (see page 69).

Hamaca being prepared for her "test ride" (see page 117).

On the outskirts of Olmos (see page 71).

To make sure I had not overlooked anything, Dr. Seifert went through the herd with me the next day (see page 119).

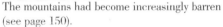

They looked like long-lost sisters (see page 125).

The mountains had become increasingly barren (see page 150).

CHAPTER 17

My Friend the Witch Doctor

Hamaca wasn't well that evening in Las Playas. Her ears were cold, a symptom of congestive illness, and more than twelve hours after her last meal, she had no appetite. The locals were full of suggestions as to what I should do, and fearing another round of horse problems, I was more than willing to listen. One dignified man casually mentioned that he had seen many mules with the same symptoms. He went on to tell me about a local doctor who could cure Hamaca and wouldn't charge anything. A doctor who doesn't charge was enough of a novelty that I wanted to meet him, whether he could produce results or not.

The doctor arrived with an entourage of spectators who obviously held him in very high esteem. He was a *mestizo*, combining Indian and European ancestry, and in that respect, was stereotypical of people in Las Playas. Wearing a suit and a fedora hat, he looked like a fugitive from a Humphrey Bogart movie. In this choice of clothes, he also was typical of the people among whom he lived. What set him apart was his demeanor. His carriage was dignified and his manner composed. Every movement exuded the confidence of those who are accustomed to taking charge.

I was holding Hamaca by her halter so the doctor could take a close look, but he conducted no examination beyond glancing in her direction.

"Do you know her birth date?" he asked.

"She's six years old," I answered.

"And the exact date of her birth?"

"I don't remember. It's on her registration papers, but they're packed away."

He continued to quiz me, requesting information that, as far as I could see, had nothing to do with the task he'd come to perform. His questions led me to doubt his competence, and I soon resolved to decline if he offered treatment. Suddenly, the *mestizo* removed his coat and called for his machete, a strong signal that things were about to go in a direction I wouldn't like. Someone brought him a long, shiny, wide-bladed machete, which, to my worried mind, seemed the size of a Crusader's broadsword. I inserted myself between him and Hamaca. Before I could gather my wits, the doctor calmly stepped around me. Had his manner been less relaxed, I don't think he'd have gotten past me. I had firmly resolved not to let him close to Hamaca, but he moved with a serenity that disarmed me.

"What are you going to do?" I asked.

"I'm going to cure your mare," he said calmly.

"How do you intend to cure her?" I persisted.

"You can watch everything," he said. "Take a short grip on her rope, please."

He touched the flat of the cold steel blade to Hamaca's underside just behind the foreleg and slowly slid it toward her flank. When the machete was past her ribs, he tapped gently, several times. After numerous repetitions, he placed the blade on her back near the withers and slid it toward her hindquarter, passing it across the top of the rib cage. When he was near her loin, he tapped, as he'd done below. This, too, was repeated numerous times. Then he walked to her other side and duplicated the procedure, using the same strokes and taps in the same sequence. So far, this treatment made sense. The massage and the coolness of the steel could easily relieve certain kinds of distress. Moreover, Hamaca's reaction showed the massage to be soothing. With half-closed eyes, she sighed deeply and lowered her head. Unfortunately, this moment of repose was short-lived. Hamaca was terrified by what happened next, and so was I!

With the machete, the *mestizo* went into a frenzy, violently slashing the air above Hamaca's back, all the while chanting in a harsh cadence. He moved in frantic bursts, swinging the blade in a manner that made my hair stand on end. It was then that the truth dawned on me. Hamaca was being cured by witchcraft! Her "doctor" was drawing mystic signs in the air. I breathed easier when the gyrations stopped and the machete was returned to its owner. Complete relaxation, came shortly thereafter when the doctor left without making any mention of payment.

A few hours later, at 2:00 A.M., I crawled out of my sleeping bag and checked on Hamaca for the third time since going to bed. She was devouring hay and grain, an unmistakable sign that she felt better. I couldn't resist thinking that my geldings might have benefited from a little witch-doctoring!

In the morning, Hamaca showed no trace of the previous night's distress. There being only twelve miles scheduled that day, I decided to press on, and Hamaca handled the trip without difficulty or complaint. She seemed strong and full of vitality even though most of the twelve miles were uphill. I, on the other hand, must have appeared to need help, for I had two offers from passing truckers willing to take my mares and me as far as Quito, free of charge. I was briefly tempted. After all, free rides might not always be available, and I'd be obliged do a lot of traveling by vehicle if I was to reach California by my deadline. However, I preferred to do my motorized traveling in monotonous surroundings, such as the deserts of Mexico. With its towering mountains and witch doctors, Ecuador was an experience far too interesting to be rushed.

We were the center of attention as we arrived in Catacocha, the largest Ecuadorian city we had yet seen. Everyone in sight stopped to stare. They saw a slightly lame, emaciated *gringo* giant who, after the theft of his belt, kept his pants up by tying the two front belt loops together with a handkerchief. Following along behind were two plump, sassy, black mares.

At a relatively level, narrow plaza alongside the highway, it was my turn to stare … at a long line of people who stood patiently waiting their turns. Seeing Latin Americans in an orderly line was rare. While standing there, some were holding mules or bicycles laden with containers of every size and description. Others carried their own pots, pans, pitchers, tins or whatever. The goal of all was a concrete structure with several protruding pipes that gushed water for the benefit of Catacocha's less-affluent citizens. It was as good a place as any to water Hamaca and Ima, and I stepped up to the end of the line.

Though I steadily moved forward, the length of the line didn't diminish. For each person who left with his or her containers full of water, another stepped up behind the last person in line. It amazed me that no one seemed impatient or resentful of the need to invest so much time in order to accomplish so little. In fact, I was repeatedly waved to the head of the line by smiling people standing ahead of me. Each time I thanked them but continued to wait my turn.

Once the mares were watered and I focused attention on my surroundings, I saw that Catacocha was out of the ordinary. It was built on a series of steep mountainsides. Streets, as well as buildings, conformed to the contours of the land. No architect or engineer had laid the town out on paper. It had been built without regard for overall aesthetics and without planning for problems until they actually presented themselves. Strangely enough, the outcome had considerable charm.

After I struck a bargain with the owner, Hamaca and Ima were turned loose in a large storage yard surrounded by an adobe wall. They shared this accommodation with broken-down cars, buses and trucks parked in rows and waiting to be repaired. More interested in exploring than eating, my mares ignored their hay, even after I moved it three times in the hope of provoking their appetites. Having decided

I was hungrier than they, I left my wandering mares and went for lunch.

I had rented a room for myself and a night's lodging for Hamaca and Ima from a man who owned a mechanic shop. My bedroom window overlooked the enclosure where the mares were quartered, and from that angle, they were a comical sight. Never straying far from one another, Hamaca and Ima were constantly on the go. Tirelessly moving along paths between rows of parked vehicles, they looked like two black mice in a maze. I was impressed that they felt like exploring on their own after seven days of hard travel.

Now that I was no longer in Peru, my days as a national hero were over, and so was the sense that I was involved with the local people in a joint project. I had seldom found Peruvians willing to accept money for their hospitality. Ecuadorians, on the other hand, seemed to expect a little something and weren't shy about asking for it. That night in Catacocha, for example, my host invited me to a home-cooked dinner with his family. Later when he presented my bill for lodging, a charge for the meal was included.

The *comandante* in Macara, consulting his maps, had calculated twenty-four miles from Catacocha to La Toma, and I had sent the horses' feed accordingly. Unfortunately, this estimate was of the *as-the-crow-flies* variety. It didn't take into account the mileage added by the meandering road's curves and switchbacks. The truth came to light in a conversation with a trucker in Las Playas who had taken an interest in my itinerary.

"Surely you plan to spend a night somewhere between Catacocha and La Toma!" he had exclaimed, instantly spotting the problem I didn't know I had.

"No," I had responded. "It's only about twenty-four miles. I've gone farther than that."

"Twenty-four miles!" he exclaimed. "Who told you that?"

"The army *comandante* in Macara."

"That explains why Ecuador has never won a war!" he said with a grimace. "The actual distance is two and a half times that far."

At first, I clung to the hope that the trucker was mistaken, but his estimate was confirmed by everyone I asked. I kept asking until it was obviously wishful thinking to doubt my predicament. Estimates of the distance varied, but they never went below sixty miles, and I was pretty much obligated to make the entire march in a single day. After all, there was no way to feed my horses between the two cities, short of making efforts and expenditures I could ill afford.

While in college, I had placed second in a fifty-mile walking race. It

161

took me a little over eleven hours, and tested me as nothing before or since. Only two of sixty-three starters finished. The winner beat me by minutes and spent two weeks in the hospital. I myself spent several days in utter agony, swearing I'd never again do anything so stupid. Now I was scheduled to relive that torture plus ten additional miles, in the Andes rather than gently rolling countryside, wearing boots instead of athletic shoes and hampered by the need to lead and care for horses. The prospect was intimidating.

The next morning, I set out from Catacocha filled with determination and energy. After a few miles, I understood how the *comandante* in Macara – measuring distances on a map with a ruler – had made his mistake. The road meandered like no other I had ever seen, with no regard for the fact that the shortest distance between two points is a straight line. This wandering was absolutely necessary so that the *Panamericana* could maintain a reasonable grade. It couldn't simply drop straight down into a precipitous canyon and climb straight up the other side. If it did, no vehicle on earth could have used it. The Pan-American Highway had to do what most highways do in mountainous terrain; it had to follow the contours of the land.

However, the *Panamericana* did this to an unbelievable extreme, for basically two reasons. One: the road was built completely without cutting and filling or bridges, which keep U.S. highways from similar meandering. Two: the designers had taken into account the combined effects of: altitude, dirt or gravel road surfaces which were often wet and slick, and the subpar vehicles that had to be accommodated. Therefore, the maximum acceptable grade was quite a bit less than in, for example, California.

To get from one side of a canyon to the other, the road would skirt the near wall until it reached the head of the canyon. There it would finally cross to the opposite wall and work its way back. In networks of intersecting canyons, the route could be unbelievably roundabout. I had been walking at top speed for over two hours when I saw Catacocha across a canyon, so close that it seemed I could have thrown a rock into the central plaza. It was depressingly little progress compared to the effort expended.

By 2:00 in the afternoon, we had covered twenty-four miles, not even half the distance we had to go. As if I didn't have enough headaches, work crews were preparing to re-gravel the upcoming section of road. In the absence of a shoulder, crushed rock had been dumped in a continuous pile along one traffic lane. This reduced the already-narrow road to half its normal width, bordered on one side by a sheer drop-off and on the other by a continuous wall of crushed rock. This new hazard slowed our progress and added to its danger, mainly because Ima picked that very moment to rebel against staying out of the roadway.

In order to travel single file and present a narrow obstacle to passing traffic, I was leading Hamaca and had Ima tied to Hamaca's saddle. This placed Ima far enough from me that I had difficulty obliging her to muck along the edge of the road when the going was so much easier a few feet away. Repeatedly she strolled into the traffic lane, and I had to shoo her back where she belonged. She survived mainly because the terrible condition of the road held traffic to a snail-like pace.

Ima quickly figured out that I wouldn't start a fight when traffic was passing. Consequently she stayed where I wanted her until a vehicle approached and then wandered into the road, where she would stubbornly challenge car, bus or truck for the right-of-way. If a vehicle came at her head-on, she broke into an excited *paso*, bowed her neck and dared the driver to just try and knock her down! When vehicles came at her from behind, she refused to give ground, instead increasing her speed until she broke into her *paso*. Simultaneously she lowered her head and started swishing her tail as though a ten-ton truck could be dismissed as easily as a fly!

A confirmed tail swisher, Ima seemed to figure that was the answer to any and all problems. If there was a fly within a hundred yards, her tail would start cutting through the air. If I was working around her and she didn't like what I was doing, that same tail would come out of nowhere to lash me. And on the way to La Toma, she fell back on that same time-honored formula whenever motor vehicles came closer than she liked. In retrospect, Ima's behavior that day seems funny and even charming. At the time, it was anything but! Despite my best efforts, she was involved in a couple of near-misses.

Late in the afternoon, a roaring wind came up, making it impossible for me to hear approaching vehicles until they were almost upon us. At that point, my situation became critical. We obviously wouldn't reach La Toma until long after sundown, and I became frantic with worry about what might happen when darkness overtook me on that road with two black horses.

There was a relatively simple way to improve my situation, but I was slow to think of it. Finally, I realized that I could move the saddle and cargo to Ima and ride Hamaca. That would place me closer to Ima and make her easier to control. I'd be obliged to ride Hamaca bareback because I hadn't yet bought a new packsaddle, but that was preferable to having Ima hit by a truck.

While I was looking for a place where I could safely transfer the saddle and cargo to Ima, another truck came up behind us. On cue, Ima launched into her well-established ritual, and after I moved her out of the way, the truck driver pulled abreast and started gesturing. Pretty sure he was upset, I extended both hands out from my sides, palms up, and shrugged. At that, the trucker rolled down his window and stuck his head out. I thought I was about to be scolded. Instead the man looked down at me and smiled.

"I'm on my way to pick up some cargo in Quito," he said. "If you want, I can take you and your horses there … free."

"I don't want to go all the way to Quito," I told him, returning his smile, "but I'd be very grateful if you could take us as far as La Toma."

"A little further up the road, there's a pile of dirt and stones," he informed me, after sweeping the area with his eyes. "We can load your horses there."

With that, the kindly trucker drove ahead, and by the time I caught up, he had his truck backed up to a pile of debris with the tailgate open. I didn't like the looks of the loading ramp, but I preferred it to that damnable road, and I studied the situation looking for the safest way to load my horses. In order to board, the mares would have to climb the rickety pile and then step into the truck's cargo area, two feet higher. While pulling themselves up into the truck, they were also required to duck under a low crossbeam. I wasn't so sure they'd buy into the idea, but Hamaca went in with little hesitation, moving like a big, graceful cat. Left behind, Ima was anxious to follow but found it difficult to claw her way to the top of the shaky pile. Finally, she got close enough to place both forehooves in the bed of the truck. As she scrambled to pull herself the rest of the way to her goal, she planted one foot heavily atop my own. Ouch!

Most truckers in Latin America christen their vehicles with names that are painted on the wooden rack enclosing the cargo area. These names are akin to the CB "handles" of truckers in the States and consist of words or phrases. Many lament unrequited love, proclaiming, for example: "You Look At Me, But You Don't See Me" or "I Sigh When You Look My Way." Others boast of desirable attributes such as: "Swift and Agile" or "The Lion of the North." Still others have religious themes, and the truck that saved my day was of that variety. Appropriately enough, its name declared: "I Am Your Salvation." Amen!

Within a few miles, the pile of crushed rock ended, restoring use of the entire road to traffic. In spite of that improvement, I felt fortunate my horses and I wouldn't be there after dark.

In La Toma, I was relieved to find the horses' feed waiting exactly where it was supposed to be. Thus far, it had been delivered at more or less the right spot in each town since Macara. It was a good thing, too, for in Empalme, Las Playas and Catacocha, the horses would have gone without eating, were it not for the feed I had sent. In La Toma, however, I was able to purchase freshly cut fodder to supplement my alfalfa. It was after nightfall by the time I rented a corral, bathed and fed the mares and ordered dinner at a restaurant. My meal turned out to be tasty (potatoes instead of rice for once), and while eating, I relaxed for the first time all day. In the midst of this welcome moment, a very excited young boy suddenly burst into the restaurant. He looked around and then ran toward my table.

"*Señor! Señor! Señor!*" In his agitated state, that was all he could manage.

"What's wrong?" I asked, not certain I was the *señor* in question.

"The horses! The horses!" he answered, eyes wide.

That confirmed it; I *was* the *señor* in question.

"What about the horses?" I asked, concerned.

"*Your* horses!" he explained breathlessly, by this time impatient with my obvious stupidity.

The lad hastily rattled off a string of words, but I didn't get their meaning. I tried to calm him, but words directed his way weren't reaching their objective. Based on his extreme agitation, it seemed like a good idea to check on Hamaca and Ima, and I stood up, which pleased my young informant. It also jarred loose the first useful information he'd yet given me.

"Your horses are loose in the streets! Follow me! I can show you where they are!"

I dashed off leaving my dinner half-eaten. My stomach churning and my adrenal glands pumping, I did my best not to lose sight of the fast-moving youngster who had suddenly assumed a position of great importance in my life. Before too long, we found Hamaca and Ima cornered by a group of townspeople, a police officer among them. Soon I had my mares in hand. After some stern inquiries by the policeman, I was informed that a street urchin had entered the horses' corral and left the gate open "just a little bit." Subsequently, my mares had slipped out to tour the town.

At the suggestion of the officer, I found a more substantial corral, this one with a chain and padlock, and I moved mares, hay, grain and water. That done, I returned to the restaurant to find my half-eaten dinner gone. The owner insisted on serving me a freshly cooked meal to make up for what he called the "discourtesy" of his town.

I needed to rein in my expenditures, and that night, I planned to sleep in an abandoned shed next to the mares' corral. This accommodation was chosen of my own free will, but I wasn't enthusiastic about it. I was in need of a better rest than I figured to get in such a cold and uncomfortable location, and fortunately, my prospects for a good sleep were improved by a visit from the policeman who had helped me earlier. He came to check on the mares and – seeing my intentions – insisted that I should spend the night in one of the empty cells at the police station. My acceptance of this kind invitation was immediate and, of course, voluntary!

The next day, the road climbed over a 9,400-foot pass before descending to Loja. That was almost as high as the mares and I would be able to go without risking altitude sickness, an affliction about which I was beginning to be deeply concerned. According to my maps, we'd soon ascend to 14,500 feet, equal to the highest point in the continental United States, and I wasn't sure how any of us would react. Having been at such heights and more during the jeep trip with LuBette and Hillary, I knew I wasn't immune to altitude sickness. Although riding in a vehicle and exercising little, I had suffered through an extremely unpleasant attack of the altitude sickness known as *suroche*. It wasn't something I wanted to experience again.

******

In Loja, we were accommodated at a military fort, thanks to a letter from the *comandante* in Macara. There we had our first day of rest since Piura. At least it was a day of rest for the mares. I had a great deal to do and was up at the crack of dawn. My day began with an outdoor shower, trooper style, which – at 7,000 feet – meant icy water and freezing-cold predawn air. For days, I'd been undressing in the dark of night and dressing again before dawn. Lights being a rare luxury, I hadn't seen my bare feet for a while and the huge, bloody blisters were a bit of a shock. They were everywhere, between my toes and on my heels and soles. As much as my feet had been hurting, I wasn't surprised.

I was in the process of developing a theory on pain and had concluded that it's impossible to recall the sensation once pain has passed. One will remember that something hurt but have no memory of exactly how it felt. This must be nature's way of protecting us from our own cowardice. I'm not sure I could have forced myself to start out each morning with a clear recollection of how I'd felt the previous night.

After breakfast, I was allowed to use one of the post's ancient, mechanical typewriters, and I spent several hours writing letters and the first installment of my series of articles for *The Peruvian Times*. Later, I mailed my letters, took my clothes for laundering and dropped my saddle off to have a cinch strap replaced. For the second time, Ima had put too much strain on the saddle while tied to it. A natural-born comedienne, she was quite a sight when it suddenly jumped off Hamaca's back, apparently coming after her! She took off running with the saddle in hot pursuit. After a hundred yards, she stopped and whirled around to face her assailant, tail swishing angrily. When her pursuer came to a simultaneous stop, Ima looked at me as if to say, "I guess I showed that thing!" As a precaution, however, she didn't stop swirling her tail until I untied her from the saddle.

In Loja – which was surprisingly up to date – I was able to buy a prepared mixture of grain and molasses, at a very reasonable price. Never before having seen such a product in Latin America, I was overjoyed to find it. For a while, at least, I wouldn't have to clean and mix the horses' grain by hand.

I looked long and hard for cured hay to send ahead with the grain, but the only hay to be found was freshly cut. Sending it ahead would have been a waste of money since the moisture content would have immediately begun turning each bundle into a steaming pile of compost.

Before dozing off that night, I took time to reflect on how well things were going. My mares had a long way to go, but they couldn't have done better so far. I'd already covered more ground with Hamaca and Ima than I had with the geldings. Both were holding their weight and adjusting well to changes in water, feed, climate and altitude. Before much longer, they should be ready to carry me.

It may seem strange that I praised my mares for doing little more than I myself was doing, but the praise was well-deserved. Horses, after all, are not nearly as well constituted as humans for traveling. Before they domesticated horses, North American Indians found that, on foot, they could exhaust and capture wild mustangs. The secret was to interrupt the mustangs' routines, especially those related to eating, drinking and sleeping. It took only that – done for a long-enough period – to weaken even those remarkably hardy horses.

Hamaca and Ima had also shown splendid attitudes. In the mornings, they'd walk right up to me, obviously anxious to continue our travels. At the end of a long, hard day, they were immediately comfortable in whatever accommodations. After a quick look around, they'd eat their fill, lie down and go to sleep, as calmly as you please. Best of all, they were willing to try whatever I fed them and most often found it to their liking. Both had held their weight while tolerating an assortment of feeds, including *algarrobo*, Sudan grass, cottonseed meal, fish meal, green and dried alfalfa, elephant grass, *Chilean straw*, wild reed grass, oats and barley.

If that wasn't a demonstration of *resistencia*, I don't know what would be, and that night in Loja, I reaffirmed my faith in the wonderful attributes of the Peruvian *Paso* breed.

Looking for new horses (see page 116).

CHAPTER 18

Turkey Day

As horses work their way into better condition, they produce more energy, and by the time we reached Loja, Hamaca and Ima were bursting with vitality even after a long, hard day. At first I welcomed this evidence that my efforts were producing results. However, my initial enthusiasm waned after two day's rest in Loja during which the mares' energy increased tenfold.

Once we were again under way, I found myself handling the equivalent of hyperactive children. The mares found it impossible to simply walk down the road. Instead they danced, pranced and threw in some pirouettes for good measure. Twice, Ima wrapped herself in the lead rope tied between them and had a fit over the unwanted confinement. An equal number of times, Hamaca got the rope under her tail and – as horses will do under that circumstance – went on a kicking spree. She had no target in mind and was only protesting the discomfort. Nonetheless, it was a matter for concern. She repeatedly fired both back legs with enough force to do harm if anyone accidentally wound up on the receiving end.

Both times, I had to work my way around to Hamaca's hindquarter and remove the rope from beneath her tightly clamped tail. It was a challenge to move fast enough while looking out for myself and keeping her positioned so the kicks didn't connect with Ima, who, of course, was tied to the saddle.

Ironically, I resented this excess energy while at the same time worrying about how I'd continue to provide the raw material that produced it. From Loja, onward, feeding my mares was going to be a problem. I knew I'd have the grain supplement I'd sent ahead, but each night Hamaca and Ima would be dependent on locally grown hay. I had no idea what I'd find, how much would be available, whether my mares would eat it, or if it would have any food value. While dealing with the mares' misbehavior, however, I became less worried about these problems. To tell the truth, I was beginning to see advantages in the time-honored tactic of starving the enemy into submission!

The trip from Loja to San Lucas became pleasant once the mares settled down. The climbs were gentle. Most of the day, the road paralleled a river at the bottom of a deep, rocky, rugged canyon. The scenery was spectacular, especially the barren rock formations.

But I had new concerns to keep me occupied. Poisonous plants were native to the region, and I had been told repeatedly that they were very attractive to equines. This produced an incongruous situation wherein I worried one moment about whether Hamaca and Ima would eat and the next that they would eat when I wasn't looking. Time would show ample justification for both worries!

I had no idea what these toxic plants looked like. This meant that I had to prevent my mares from sampling anything along the trail. Before long, like a good North American, I was wishing that someone had identified the plants in question with a sign bearing the appropriate skull and crossbones.

In the States, we try to eliminate dangerous situations or to mark them with a warning sign. Thanks to this, we're largely spared much of the need to look out for ourselves. In South America's Andes, the approach is quite different. Unmarked, dangerous situations abound, and those who get hurt are asked why they weren't more careful.

Admittedly, a sign warning of poisonous herbs was a whimsical thought, but later in the day that didn't stop me from wishing for yet another, one that said: "Falling Rocks." It would have required a truckload of signs to mark all such hazards in the steep-walled canyon we traveled. The entire area was unstable, and the resulting rockslides weren't conveniently confined to certain areas. Constant vigilance was required, and my hearing was the first line of defense. Constantly, I heard rocks tumbling down the precipitous slopes around me.

When I caught sight of the boulders that produced those sounds, their size was cause for concern. The largest I saw were the size of watermelons, and they reached the road with enough momentum to bounce all the way across without slowing down. On the downhill side of the road I saw massive chunks of rock, up to six feet in diameter, which had cartwheeled down to their resting-places from the slopes above.

Twice, I detected slides directly above us. Each time I was able to quickly determine where they would cross the road. In the first case, I retreated. The second time, I escaped by speeding up. Though none of the rocks in either slide was huge, they could have done considerable damage.

I was beginning to see *serranos* in ever-increasing numbers. Once I'd learned not to fear them, I found Ecuador's natives to be the most interesting sight in the Andes. Indians throughout South

America wear distinctive clothing. This varies not only from jungle to mountains to coast but also from region to region inside those zones. I saw new costumes almost on a daily basis. Sometimes these were variations of what I'd seen the day before. Other times the outfits had little in common with anything I had ever seen. I was able to identify only two universal ingredients in Andean dress. One was that almost every *serrano*, man or woman, wore a hat. Within any given area, there were normally two styles, one for each gender, but those styles varied greatly from region to region.

The piece of attire that varied least was footwear, almost always a pair of sandals with soles made from automobile tires. These left tire tracks in the most extraordinary places! Before I knew their source, I more than once wondered how these imprints had come to be in some of the places where I saw them. Most of my potential explanations had to be discarded when I saw tire tracks on the dirt floor of a small grocery store, accessible only through a very narrow door! That discovery finally led me to solve the mystery.

Throughout the Andes, it was common to see Indian women occupied with a mysterious activity while walking along the roadside. At first it had seemed that they were amusing themselves with a toy that combined the attributes of a child's top and a yo-yo. However, that impression didn't survive when I got a closer look. By means of a process that would capture attention as a circus act, they were spinning yarn from raw wool with a wooden spindle shaped much like a child's top. After a pencil-like distaff was inserted into it, the device was attached to wool threads and dropped, spinning, to the height of the user's knees. There it would twist wool fibers into yarn and roll the finished yarn around the stick by a process I could never figure out. This tool required considerable dexterity, especially when used by someone moving at a fast walk or even a jog. It wasn't an activity for someone who has trouble walking and chewing gum at the same time!

South of San Lucas, the *serranos* appeared to have chosen their outfits from a Hollywood wardrobe room. They all looked more like witch doctors than the one who had treated Hamaca in Las Playas. The men had a single pigtail that hung to the waist. They wore black ponchos and black knee-length trousers. Some sported short leather chaps, and most had wide, black leather belts and matching machete sheathes, both freely decorated with metal studs.

Communication can bridge the gap created by differences between people, but no such factor mitigated the fierce appearance of the *serranos* near San Lucas. None spoke Spanish, or at least none consented to do so with me. Equally disconcerting, there was no reaction – physical, verbal or emotional – when I spoke to them. Almost everyone I passed in that area seemed either drunk or mentally impaired. More than once I encountered people who silently glared at me, their facial features frozen in unfriendly expressions. Knowing how terribly – and for how long – white men had abused Andean *serranos*, I wondered if they automatically disliked Caucasians.

On the other hand, perhaps they were merely stoic, and I was reading too much into it. That theory, however, didn't explain why the expressionless eyes showed appreciation and envy when shifted to my mares. Until then, I'd always felt pride when people admired Hamaca and Ima, but suddenly I wished my mares could be temporarily less attractive.

In San Lucas – true to my worst fears – there was no hay to be found. I located a leading citizen and left my mares in his care while I took the bus north to Saraguro. There, I'd been told, I would find a North American missionary who had an alfalfa field. Along the way, the bus broke down, and during the course of repair work, I caught a ride with a passing truck. This second vehicle also broke down, and by the time repairs were finished and Saraguro was reached, it was late afternoon.

The missionary lived just outside town, and I set out on foot, in semi-darkness, to find him. It took a while. People simply pointed the way, and I had to ask frequently to be sure I was on the right track. I was impressed when almost everyone spoke of the man with affection and respect before pointing the way to his home. Once there, I discovered that his small alfalfa field produced barely enough for his own purposes. Even so, the missionary generously gave me a bundle. Realizing that it wasn't as much as I needed, he directed me to a neighbor who sold me more. Between the two sources, I acquired enough to get my horses through the night.

While waiting for the bus to San Lucas, I was invited to have dinner with the missionary's family. He and his wife were both medical doctors. They had forsaken the comforts and financial rewards that would have been theirs in the States in order to establish their mission and medical clinic in the Ecuadorian Andes. There they were raising their children and tending the physical and spiritual needs of the local poor. I enjoyed their company tremendously. It was a rare treat to catch up on news from home and to speak and hear English.

The bus arrived two hours late. Half-bus and half-truck, it was well suited to Ecuador's highlands. The front half looked like a school bus and was packed full of *serranos*. The rear portion resembled the bed of a truck and contained "baggage," to use the term loosely. There was everything from machinery to firewood to live animals. Baskets of fruit and vegetables along with trussed-up goats, chickens and pigs were coming from or going to the area's open-air markets.

Feeling like one of the gang, I threw my bundles of alfalfa into the cargo area and found a seat in front. My fellow passengers – with stone-faced expressions – subjected me to the Andean version of the silent treatment. Any other behavior would have been a surprise, especially after the wordless encounters I'd experienced throughout the day.

Upon my return to San Lucas, I was invited to stay with the man who had watched Hamaca and Ima in my absence. My host was as talkative as my fellow passengers on the bus had been the opposite. His words did little to ease my troubled mind.

"Your life is at great risk, *señor*," he stated bluntly, shaking his head sadly.

"How's that?" I asked, suspecting what might be coming.

"Broad daylight robberies are common around here. Traveling as you are – alone, unarmed, with two desirable horses – you make an irresistible target."

"Are there any precautions you'd recommend?" I asked, intending to quickly change the subject if this conversation was good for nothing more than unsettling me.

"There are none you can take, traveling as slowly as you are. Every bandit within miles will know you're coming."

"I haven't had any problems so far."

"Lady Luck has been good to you, *señor*, but she can easily withdraw her favor."

After I saddled the horses the next morning, I strapped on my Bowie knife for the first time since Olmos. It was a melodramatic gesture, of little good other than psychological. I had never used such a weapon and would choose not to in almost any circumstance I could imagine. But very similar statements could have been made by those in charge of America's nuclear arsenal, and that had, nonetheless, been an effective deterrent. Right?

That day's travel took us twelve miles to Saraguro. The trip was routine, except for the fact that the mares and I ascended to our highest altitude yet. Crossing the mountain range between San Lucas and Saraguro, we reached an altitude above 10,000 feet without problems.

It was Thanksgiving. For me, the day had almost passed as any other. In the absence of reminders from radio, television and family members, I hadn't been aware of its approach. As it turned out, however, I had an invitation to a traditional holiday dinner, issued the previous evening by the wife of the missionary near Saraguro. Thanks to her kindness, I was scheduled to share this North American holiday with other North Americans.

My hosts kept a stallion in the only livestock enclosure on the mission. As a consequence, Hamaca and Ima spent that afternoon tied to a hitching rail, and they didn't particularly care for it. The resultant fidgeting seemed to fascinate people who were strolling past.

Shortly after Thanksgiving dinner was served, there was a knock on the door.

"The horse of the *señor* just dropped something on the ground."

Anxiously, I stood up and hurried outside to find that Hamaca had finished her grain more quickly than I'd expected and had taken off her feed bag. I picked it up, smiled, thanked my informant and rejoined my hosts at the dinner table. Three mouthesful later, there was another knock from another bearer of important news.

"The horse of the *señor* is chewing on its rope."

Reluctantly, I got up from my dinner and walked outside to find that Ima was mouthing her leadline but hadn't broken through a single fiber. I said a polite thank-you (no smile this time) and returned to my meal. A short while later, yet another knock announced the impending delivery of further fast-breaking news.

"One of the horses of the *señor* just stepped on the other one's foot."

I walked to the window, looked out to verify that all was well and sat down again. It was only a short while before the next knock came.

"This is getting ridiculous," I said, irritated to be causing, even indirectly, these many interruptions of my hosts' Thanksgiving meal.

"I think it's cute," the lady of the house said with a relaxed grin.

"Cute?" I asked, making a distressed face.

"Sure," she said. "Our neighbors have heard there's a tall, lanky *gringo* in town, and they want a look at him."

"Well, if you don't mind it, I don't," I said, not altogether truthfully.

The knocks on the door continued throughout the afternoon, becoming less frequent after the bolder folks in the community had satisfied their curiosity.

Only someone who has been a long time without an appetizing meal – or his fill – could appreciate how very much I enjoyed that dinner. The best company I'd had since Piura magnified the pleasure. That Thanksgiving, I completely forgot my cares for the first time in a long while. The meal was the most familiar I'd had since leaving the States, complete with roast turkey, bread stuffing, corn, mashed potatoes and gravy. True, the pimento-stuffed olives and cranberry sauce were missing, and there was neither football to watch nor a television set on which to watch it. Otherwise, though, I experienced a classic Thanksgiving holiday.

More than any before it, that particular Thanksgiving reminded me of blessings for which I was truly grateful. Sitting in the company of people who had given up so much in order to help others, I realized that I, too, was in the midst of a clash between spiritual and materialistic values. My worldly possessions (except for Hamaca and Ima!) easily fit in two duffel bags. I had never owned less, nor had I ever so enjoyed living.

Having seen the attention Hamaca and Ima attracted, the missionary decided it wouldn't be wise to leave them tied near the road at night. He offered to let my mares share the corral with the family's stallion. To prevent him from making advances, the stallion was chained up at one end. To restrain Hamaca and Ima from visiting him, they were tied to a tree at the opposite extreme.

That night, I slept in the mission's medical clinic, several hundred yards from the house. There were no other occupants, and I anticipated a good sleep in a comfortable bed. Unfortunately, that wasn't my destiny, in spite of the fact that my bed was wonderfully cozy. As night progressed, the seeds planted by my previous host began to sprout. My thoughts dwelled on long-simmering worries about bandits and horse thieves. I was awakened by every noise, no matter how slight, immediately suspicious that rustlers were at work. A half-dozen times I made my way down the pitch-dark corridor to peer through the picture window that overlooked the corral.

Just as one of these dark, eerie walks ended with me standing in front of the oversized window, I was startled by a series of what sounded like gunshots. I half expected the glass in front of me to shatter as bullets crashed through. Then common sense overpowered my fears, and I realized that someone had set off a series of firecrackers, probably as part of a celebration.

Morning dawned with me still among the living and both mares still tied where I had left them the night before.

Hours later, a stone's throw from where I started (see page 162).

CHAPTER 19

Tschades of Tschiffely!

Hoping to be on my way as early as possible, I saddled Hamaca while breakfast was still on the stove. Then I tied her where she'd spent the night and answered the ringing of the mission's dinner bell, morning version. Twenty minutes later when I went back outside a maddening scene greeted me. Hamaca was backed up to the still-chained stallion. The saddle was turned under her, and she was covered with muddy hoof prints. Even if she hadn't been pregnant before breakfast, her status may have changed by the time I finished eating!

To this day, I'm not certain how Hamaca got loose. I always used a knot designed to prevent horses from untying themselves, and her lead rope wasn't broken or damaged. Most likely, a good Samaritan concluded that she was tangled up when he saw the heart rope I used to keep her from pulling. Intending to set things straight, this do-gooder must have untied her. At that point, Hamaca – never trusting of strangers – could easily have spooked and pulled free.

A crowd of people stood around, chuckling. I myself failed to see the humor. The previous day, my Thanksgiving dinner had been interrupted a dozen times for no good reason, but when I really needed help, yesterday's busybodies just stood around and watched Hamaca getting bred!

By that time, Hamaca had worked herself into good shape and was becoming fitter with each passing day. In that condition, being on the trail in the early – or even middle – months of pregnancy shouldn't pose a problem. If Hamaca *was* pregnant, the problems would come after we were back in Los Gatos. Pregnancy, after all, would rule her out of the Tevis Cup in order to give birth to a foal that wouldn't even be a pureblood.

My appetite had been on strike all the while I'd been in Ecuador, mainly because I disliked the food there. On the day I left Saraguro, however, my stomach growled and rumbled unceasingly, begging for more of what it had received the day before. The meal at the mission had awakened my appetite, but only briefly. By the following morning, it was asleep once more, not to reappear until provoked by the culinary delights of Quito.

From Saraguro we traveled to Oña and in the process established our latest altitude record. We reached nearly 12,000 feet on

177

Carbonsillo Pass. It was the first time there were noticeable effects. I became slightly light-headed. My nose produced a trickle of blood, and my energies flagged. The horses became sluggish, and Ima produced huge and frequent yawns. This was in line with the general rule of thumb that oxygen deprivation begins to take effect at 10,000 feet above the elevation to which one is accustomed. Only two weeks earlier, the mares and I had been in Piura, barely above sea level.

At those heights, I got my first look at one of Ecuador's distinctive *paramos*. These are high plains, well above the timberline and clothed mostly in scrub brush and tufts of hardy grass. Called *altiplanos* in Peru, these cold and rainy places are reputed to be a favored haunt of bandits. We made it across without misadventure and at day's end dropped down into the town of Oña, still well above the tree line. A quaint little village, Oña must have been near a quarry because most of its buildings were made with blocks of stone. If one didn't look too closely, this gave the place a wonderful medieval flavor. To add to the novelty, the mares spent the night in a corral they could enter only by descending a flight of stone stairs.

Had there been an alternative, I wouldn't have asked Hamaca and Ima to tackle the stairway. It was steep, and the heights of the steps varied by as much as a half-foot. To add to the hazards, the top of each step was narrow and uneven. Most horses have difficulty descending stairs, but Ima was a notable exception. Hamaca, on the other hand, frantically tried to take more than one step at a time. In the process, she shaved a bit of hair and skin from the backs of both hindlegs. The following morning, going up, the stairs were no problem.

My frustration with the meandering ways of the *Panamericana* came to a head that day. It seemed that I never traveled more than a few miles north without also winding and doubling back toward the east, the west and even – a surprising number of times – the south. My goal was to go north. There had to be a way to do that more than a fraction of the time!

For quite a while, I'd been sorely tempted to explore the mule trails I'd seen intersecting the highway. Initially, I had worried that any particular crossing might be part of a trail that would take me where I didn't want to go. I had been repeatedly assured, however, that these were basically a single trail that crossed and recrossed the *Panamericana*, leaving and then rejoining it after saving miles of twisting and turning. I was ready to give them a try.

Few things in life have been as easy as I thought they should be, but the discrepancy has seldom been as marked as it was that day. I selected a trail that seemed to be in particularly good shape, and near the highway, it was. Before long, however, the mares and I found ourselves sliding down a steep, slippery channel worn into solid rock. Shortly thereafter, we were precariously walking a narrow ledge protruding from the face of a sheer mountain wall.

Farther along, Hamaca and Ima had a chance to put into practice what they had rehearsed that morning. They had to climb steps of heights between six inches and two feet. These had been worn into solid rock by thousands of hooves during centuries of use. I don't know what I would have done if it had been necessary to descend that stairway, rather than climb it. I'm not sure the mares could have done so, but they might not have been able to retrace their steps back to the highway, either.

After quite a long while, I began to wonder if I might have selected a trail that wasn't going to rejoin the highway. Eventually, though, it did. Once back on the *Panamericana*, I tried to guess how many miles of roadway had been bypassed. Even my most liberal estimate fell short of justifying the effort expended. I knew I didn't want to try another mule trail if they were all that difficult, but the siren call of the shortcut still beckoned. Perhaps I had chosen an unusually difficult segment of trail. It wouldn't do to make a final decision based on such a small sampling. One more "mule trail" was all I needed to teach me why they weren't called "horse trails" and to persuade me to stay near the highway.

Apparently, however, I was persuaded without being entirely convinced. Just before the town of Zuzudel, I spotted a particularly enticing shortcut. I could see the entire trail from where it left to where it rejoined the *Panamericana*. It was all downhill and in good shape, with a moderate slope. Best of all, it cut a considerable distance from the route followed by the road. I couldn't resist. After all, this one was foolproof. Well, not quite!

About twenty yards along, the three of us suddenly began sliding in grease-like mud. The horses locked their legs. I did the same, and we skied a good thirty yards before I managed to stop. Hamaca then slammed into me, which stopped her. Finally Ima crashed into both of us, and the excitement was over. That did it! I was finally and firmly resolved against further shortcuts, period.

As we were passing the *Hacienda* Zuzudel, I noticed an empty corral and approached the main farmhouse to ask where my mares and I might spend the night. The result was as I'd hoped. A very pleasant gentleman showed Hamaca and Ima to an adobe corral they would have to share with several sheep.

When the mares sampled Zuzudel's water, they tentatively sucked in a mouthful and quickly let it drain back out. Nothing could convince them to try it again. I washed out their water trough and refilled it to no avail. Suspecting that the water tasted bad, I mixed molasses into a bucketful. Both mares normally considered molasses a treat, and they hopefully smelled this mixture but refused it.

Served cured hay – compliments of the *hacienda* – the mares found their dry meal incompatible with dry mouths and throats and ate little. This fussiness was new, and it irritated me. Then I was served a cup of tea, and forgiveness came into my heart. Even after I'd added ample sugar and squeezed several lemons into a cup of strong tea, the water's foul taste dominated. When my host saw that I didn't like my tea, he was more understanding than I had been with Hamaca and Ima. He apologized for the taste of Zuzudel's water and offered me a glass of milk. Unfortunately, it had been boiled as a precaution against tuberculosis. *Albright's Book of Useless Facts* had a new entry: boiled milk is not among the world's great delicacies.

That afternoon, I was shown adobe structures at Zuzudel that were over two hundred years old. Built before the American Revolution, they were still in use. In the States, we speak disdainfully of a "mud hut," but how many of our tract homes will be serviceable after a similar time?

The next morning, the mares still hadn't taken a drink and had barely touched their hay. Concerned, I set out at first light, my foremost goal being to find drinkable water. At best, this wouldn't be available before the next valley. Getting there meant we first had to follow the road up and out of the valley where we had overnighted.

Like an airplane taking off, we began a long climb, steadily gaining altitude until we were inside the low-lying clouds that had filled the sky above us. After still more climbing, we emerged above the clouds, under sunny skies. Below us was a white sea. Here and there peaks protruded, looking like islands with foam lapping at their shores. It was a sensational, majestic scene that disappeared when the clouds rose and enveloped us again. Visibility was cut to a twelve-foot radius, and the humid air was bone-chilling. In spite of the little I'd been able to drink, thirst was the last thing on my mind. I hoped it was the same for Hamaca and Ima.

Though exercising strenuously, I remained chilly until the sun finally managed to break through. In Peru's deserts, that same sun had been an enemy to be avoided at all costs, but in the Andes, it was fast becoming a welcome friend. The Andean Indians once worshiped the sun, and I could easily see why. The thin air of their world could be penetratingly cold, but the sun's beneficial effect was immediate. The instant it bathed me in its rays, I was warm and comfortable. If it passed behind a cloud, even briefly, I was immediately chilly.

Later, pearly white clouds drifted over, high above, their outlines harsh and linear. Looking like frozen explosions pasted in the sky, they were gigantic, their shapes constantly changing. I'd never realized how many aspects clouds could have. Depending upon circumstances, they huddled in the valleys below us, drifted lazily through the sky above or wrapped us in their embrace. They might be thin and wispy or thick and fluffy, white or boiling black, smooth or jagged, a single entity from horizon to horizon or a collection of puffs. The variety was endless.

At the bottom of the next valley – actually an extremely rugged canyon – we came upon a rushing river that swirled and leapt around the fantastic rock formations it was endlessly carving. Hamaca and Ima were fascinated, but refused to get close enough to drink. Raised in one of the world's driest deserts, they had never imagined water in such quantities or behaving that way. Without the equivalent of books or television – to tell them what existed beyond their experience – they must have wondered what might be coming next. What came next was water falling from the sky. Ima, true to form, tried to stop the rain by swishing her magical tail. Initially, this tactic seemed to work. More than once, the rain started and fizzled out, giving Ima good reason to believe *she* was stopping it. Soon enough, though, a cloudburst gave her a massive dose of humility.

Over the next few hours, a series of downpours started and stopped, going from dry to deluge without transition and stopping without tapering off. At times, we were in glorious sunshine while nearby areas were in the grip of a raging storm, or vice versa. Once the edge of a rainstorm was so precisely delineated that rain fell on Hamaca's forequarter while her hindquarter remained dry. Amazed, I stopped Hamaca half-in and half-out of the rain, turning my head back and forth to confirm that this *was* actually happening.

For the second time we were on the *páramo*, with the difference being that this time we'd spend the night, in the *town* of La Jarata, which turned out to be nothing more than four huts. One had been abandoned, providing ready shelter for Hamaca and Ima. Even though protected from wind and rain, both mares were so cold that they showed no interest in water and hardly ate. This was their second consecutive night of semi-voluntary fasting, but neither looked the worse for it.

Inside one of the other huts was a restaurant where I ate dinner. Including the kitchen, dining area and a little room at the back, the whole enclosure didn't measure more than twenty feet square. It was filthy, and I asked that my dinner be cooked *very* thoroughly, still clinging to the hope that sufficient heat, applied for enough time, would kill any germ.

During dinner I was regaled with stories of truckers shooting up the place during the night shift. Those stories still fresh in my mind, I hesitated when invited to spend the night. After considering the alternatives, however, I accepted. I was shown to a miniature (for me!) bed in the back room. Desperately needing sleep, I lowered myself, fully clothed, onto the tiny, lumpy mattress. No matter how I arranged myself, some body part or another was cantilevered in thin air. The resulting aches and pains woke me periodically, insisting that I roll over and abuse my other side for a while.

The wall between me and the dining area was a single layer of planks with sizable gaps between. All night long, truckers came and went, and I was roused from my slumbers by their noisy arguments. It was like trying to sleep in the middle of a "Save the Earth" conference involving radical environmentalists and unemployed loggers. Just when one group went on its way, another arrived, anxious to compare opinions on some volatile subject or another. The resulting discussions speedily evolved into serious disagreements, and more than once, I peered through gaps in the wall to satisfy myself that the participants were unarmed.

Morning didn't dawn so much as it just showed up. La Jarata was cloaked in an opaque fog, a thick one judging by the dull, gray color of the sunlight that filtered through. The air was icy cold, and I found Hamaca and Ima huddled together in a corner of their hut, their food barely touched. Both mares had white dewdrops condensed on eyelashes, forelocks and the hair in their ears. For some reason, this struck me as enormously funny. Though I think it's silly to assign human characteristics to animals, it truly did seem that both mares were offended by my laughter.

When I realized that I had similar dewdrops in my beard, my laughing abruptly ended, and I saddled up in preparation for moving on to Cumbe. At that altitude, the countryside was stark and the land good for little. The roadside was dotted with flocks of goats tended by dark-skinned shepherds with staffs and flowing garb. Repeatedly, I had the impression I'd wandered into biblical times.

In Cumbe, I had my first taste of out-and-out rejection by an entire town. Few would return my greetings or answer my questions. No corral owner would even consider allowing my mares to spend the night. I was turned away by several private citizens, the town's political chief, an *hacienda* owner and finally the local priest. Beyond town, we finally found hospitality at a small *hacienda*.

"Come in! Come in!" said my excited host-to-be after I briefly explained my journey and asked about possible accommodations. "You and your horses are more than welcome here."

Surprised by his enthusiasm, I thanked him and described my poor reception back in Cumbe.

"It would appear that fate brought you here!"

This last declaration puzzled me greatly, but I didn't get a chance to follow up. The man was rushing about, doing what was necessary to establish Hamaca and Ima in an adobe corral. The first step was to move two tiny, tame deer he kept there. Not much more than twelve inches at the shoulder, the deer fit comfortably into a nearby cage covered with chicken wire.

Our host brought hay while – at his instruction – I lugged pails of water and emptied them into a bathtub in one corner of the corral. Hamaca and Ima took a keen interest in both the hay and water, evidently feeling the effects of their self-imposed deprivation.

"Yes, I'm sure of it. Fate has guided you to my *hacienda!*" The man repeated his curious assertion after he had finished tending to his deer.

"What do you mean?" I asked. "Why would fate bring me here?"

"It's very rare for a man to travel through many countries with horses, don't you think? Well, it just so happens that such a man on a journey similar to yours stopped here when I was a boy. In those days, this was my father's *hacienda*, and the man stayed with us on his way to North America. His horses stayed in the same corral as yours. So, you see, it's *my* turn to be *your* host. That's why fate has brought you here!"

I wasn't sure I agreed with these conclusions, but it certainly was interesting that I'd received such unfriendly treatment in town only to discover a stranger who seemed overjoyed to see me.

"Do you recall this traveler's name?" I asked.

"Oh, no, *señor*. That was a long time ago, and as I remember, his name was peculiar and difficult to pronounce. However, I do remember one of the horses' names. It was Gato."

"Was the other named Mancha?" I asked, incredulous.

"Yes! Yes, I believe it was!" he responded excitedly. "Do you know this man?"

"Yes, I do," I answered, "or at least I know *of* him. His name was Tschiffely, and he's very famous."

By all appearances, I was – at that very moment – following in the footsteps of A. F. Tschiffely! Not only that, but my mares were lodged in a corral where Mancha and Gato, two immortals of the equine race, had once spent a night.

"And now you're recreating this man's famous ride," I was told. "It must give you great satisfaction."

I was proud, and I think justifiably so, of what I was accomplishing, but to mention my achievements in the same breath as Tschiffely's seemed like blasphemy.

"Even if I succeed in doing everything I plan," I said, "Tschiffely rode many times as far as I will."

"He was a man, and you're still a boy," my host asserted, slapping me on the shoulder, "but you're going to grow up fast on this journey, and you might be surprised at what you'll accomplish. Someday you will realize your merit and be very happy with yourself."

I smiled, pleased by his optimism and trying not to let my pleasure show. Maybe, in a sense, fate *had* guided me to this friendly *hacienda*. Clearly, I wasn't there because of any planning on my part. In fact, I had done everything I could to be somewhere else!

We said no more on the subject, but Mancha, Gato and Tschiffely stayed in my mind. Amie Tschiffely was my hero, and it was pleasing to be compared to him, even if undeservedly. Furthermore, what my host said was true: many of the differences between us were those typical between a man and a boy. Maybe I *would* be surprised at what I'd accomplish.

The night was still young when my sleep was interrupted by … what was it? A couple of times, I fell back asleep and was reawakened. When my tolerance for these interruptions had worn thin, I found my flashlight and turned it on. The beam of light revealed that large rats had invaded my room. I climbed out of bed and hung my saddle and bridle beyond the rodents' reach.

Who knows? I mused, only half-awake. *Perhaps I'm being honored by a visit from descendants of a rat that once chewed a strap on Tschiffely's saddle.* Be that as it may, I would have happily put an end to his – or any other rat's – family line if given the chance. The desire to accomplish this grew stronger every time I was awakened by the sounds of these sizable rodents scurrying across the floor.

In the morning I put the saddle and cargo on Ima for the first time. Her hooves were looking much better, and she'd become surprisingly fit. It was time she carried her share of the load. The new order of march had Hamaca tied to Ima's saddle and third in line for the first time. I should have known better than to make a major change just then. Hamaca and Ima had been explosive all week, at times so charged up that I could barely control them. Perhaps it was the strain of constantly being confronted with new experiences, and maybe it was just excess energy. Whatever the reason, I shouldn't have changed their routine while they were in that state of mind.

With Ima no longer behind her, Hamaca went into blind panic every time traffic passed. Unconcerned about motor vehicles since Piura, she knew cars wouldn't hurt her when she was second in line, but might it be otherwise when she was third? Evidently she didn't think it significant that Ima had survived two weeks in that same position.

Many are the tales of horses rescued from burning barns only to escape their handlers and run back inside. Like those horses, Hamaca had become her own worst enemy. I saddled her with the cargo and reinstated her old, familiar spot in the line of march, but the damage was done. She was insane with fear and continued to endanger all of us whenever vehicles passed, which was often, owing to a dramatic increase in traffic. During one such episode, Hamaca tore the leadline from my grip as she and Ima charged past me on opposite sides. The rope tied between Ima's halter and Hamaca's saddle caught me across the chest, tipping me backwards. I saved myself a nasty fall by grabbing it and holding on. For a moment, everything was a confusing tangle. I flopped inelegantly, like wet laundry on a clothesline in a strong wind. Somehow, I retained my grip on the rope, but subsequent efforts to stop my mares confirmed that a man's strength is nowhere near that of two horses. Ultimately, the rope was ripped from my hands, and I was flung to the ground. The impact ripped my Levi's and my hide at the knees.

Almost instantly back on my feet, I saw Hamaca and Ima in wild flight down the middle of the highway. I gave chase, fearing that I'd never manage to catch them before a vehicle hit one or both. Luckily, a pedestrian spread his arms wide and blocked their path. When they stopped, he took hold of the dragging leadline. Despite Hamaca's suspicious snorting, he held on until I arrived. Out of breath, I profusely thanked the man between gulps of air.

"Is there anything more I can do?" he asked.

"Yes, thank you very much, there is," I answered, having decided that my problems with Hamaca were far from over and that I needed to get her under control without further delay.

Quickly, I untied Ima from Hamaca's saddle and handed her leadline to the helpful passerby. Before my breathing returned to normal, I had untied the cargo, lowered it to the ground, adjusted the saddle and snugged up the cinch. To tell the truth, my blood pressure was a little high. Otherwise, I might not have dared ride Hamaca in her mood, even though it was probably the safest thing to do in the long run.

As soon as the saddle was well secured, I mounted Hamaca and rode back and forth, waiting for traffic. When it came, it provoked a battle that put both our lives in jeopardy. By the time our struggle was over, I'd convinced Hamaca that cars were nowhere near the problem I could be! My mission accomplished, I stepped down, transferred the saddle to Ima and reloaded the cargo. While I cleansed the wounds on my knees with chlorinated water from my canteen, I thanked my helper once more. Then I swung onto Hamaca's bare back and started down the road, the rope burns on my palms and the abrasions on my knees vigorously competing for my attention.

My frame of mind quickly improved. It was pleasant to be *back in the saddle again*, if such can be said of riding bareback. I had planned to walk farther, but if Hamaca had enough surplus energy to make trouble, she had enough to carry me. As long as her self-discipline was absent, it would be my job to impose a substitute, something best done from horseback.

After all, traffic was only going to increase as we approached and entered Cuenca, the third largest city in Ecuador.

CHAPTER 20

True *Cold War* Spirit

Cuenca was the most modern city I had seen since Piura. Located in a forested valley, it was founded in 1557 atop the ruins of an ancient Inca city, Tomebamba. Its attractions were many, but for me, one stood out above all others. Cuenca was home to a famous cavalry detachment known as the *Cazadores de los Ríos*, and word was that their hospitality was second to none. The mares and I reached the cavalry fort in the late afternoon. Arrangements for us to stay there were to have been made by the commander of the garrison in Loja, but no one seemed to be expecting me. Starting with the guard at the gate, I slowly worked my way up the chain of command, meeting only blank stares from people anxious to make me someone else's problem.

Finally, I got as far as the officer in charge. While explaining my situation, I mentioned that I had come from Peru. Considering the growing animosity between Peru and Ecuador, it was unwise to volunteer that particular information, and I should have known better. Suspicion immediately clouded the eyes of the officer in charge who did what any good military man would have done under the circumstances. He took the matter to a higher authority. The post commander made his decision without emerging from behind the impressive door to his office. The solution to my problem, he decreed, would be for me to go into town and get permission from District Command Headquarters.

An hour later, I walked into district headquarters. My distinguishing characteristics – aside from my height, of course – were a week's growth of beard, holes ringed with blood in the knees of my jeans and a large Bowie knife hanging from my belt. In spite of all that, I was treated with considerable courtesy and granted written permission to rest for two days with the *Cazadores de los Ríos*.

After caring for the horses, the first item on my agenda was a shower. I was filthy, and whenever I thought about it, I started itching as if I was wrapped in fiberglass insulation. The greatest luxury I could imagine was a long, hot shower. I knew better than to hope for hot water, of course. I hadn't found any of that – except in my tea – since Piura.

The fort boasted an indoor shower, and I looked forward, at least, to less frigid conditions than I'd found outdoors in Loja. I'm sure that would have been the case, too, if only there had been glass panes in the windows.

The following day, I ran errands, did my shopping, left my laundry for washing, planned my itinerary and sent grain ahead, the same basic routine that preceded each new leg of my journey. I also purchased a used packsaddle. It was ill-maintained but serviceable once I had the cinch and some leather straps replaced.

After I returned to the fort, I borrowed a typewriter and dedicated myself to writing letters and finishing another in my series of articles for *The Peruvian Times*. While I was thus involved, the post commander approached me with great purpose. Obviously, he had important matters to discuss.

"You are invited to be the guest of honor at the officers' luncheon tomorrow afternoon," he began. "All the officers are hoping you can be there. It isn't often we get the opportunity to discuss current events with someone from the States."

"I'm honored by the invitation," I responded, having stood up and barely resisted the urge to salute. "You mustn't expect too much from me, though. I've been out of touch with the news for months."

"No doubt you have some very interesting opinions, and I look forward to hearing them," he said, ever so politely. "You must promise to be there and to join our discussion."

On my way to the post office that afternoon, I could think of little except the impending luncheon. In my mind it was shaping up as a formidable event. I looked forward to it but was also apprehensive. I wondered what sorts of questions I'd be asked and whether I would have the answers … or at least be able to make intelligent conversation.

During the luncheon itself, this self-inflicted pressure increased tenfold. The event was formal, and I had neither the attire nor the knowledge of etiquette to go with fine china, rows of silverware, linen napkins and the tinkling of crystal glasses. Perspiring soldiers – elegantly dressed as waiters – rushed here and there in response to orders from the officers. One took a special liking to me, probably because my few requests were delivered politely and in a tone of voice indicating that I'd be grateful for his efforts. By contrast, the officers would ask for something – say a glass of water – and then follow up with: "Off with you now! Bring it to me as quickly as if you were a rocket!"

I was seated at the head of a table from where I was ceremoniously introduced and applauded. Next we were served a splendid meal, and, finally, it was time for the much-awaited discussion, which was initiated by the post commander. By all indications, his choice of subject matter was popular. Three years after his assassination, John F. Kennedy was still prominent in the hearts and minds of Latin Americans. Few North American presidents had even come close to equaling Kennedy's incredible popularity with the millions who lived from Mexico to Argentina.

Under the careful orchestration of the post commander, the discussion touched on the Bay of Pigs, the Cuban Missile Crises, Kennedy's civil rights record, the Peace Corps and the Alliance for Progress. Though participation was lively, I had the feeling we were skirting whatever was foremost on most minds in the room. This hunch was confirmed after the post commander excused himself and retired to his quarters. Those left behind immediately zeroed in on the heart of the matter.

"Do you think Jacqueline Kennedy will marry *Señor* Onassis?" one of the officers asked me.

"Do you think she should?" another probed, without waiting for my first answer.

To tell the truth, I'd never given the matter much thought, but my companions evidently had. This subject was discussed for at least as long as all the others combined. The intense fascination grew from a single, unacceptable thought: the widow of the great John F. Kennedy might lie in the bed of another man. It was a notion deeply offensive to these gentlemen's *machismo*.

✶✶✶✶✶✶

Most of the time, I'd had to force myself to be courteous with the reporters and photographers who besieged me in Peru. Crossing into Ecuador had put a welcome end to the time-consuming interviews and photo sessions, and my initial reaction had been: *goodbye and good riddance*. However, I soon came to realize that the baby had been tossed out with the bath water. All that publicity had produced useful by-products, and without it, doors were often opened with suspicion or even slammed in my face when I needed to rent a corral or buy hay.

In the absence of reporters chasing after me, it appeared that I'd have to chase after them, and Cuenca seemed like a good place to start. After the officers' luncheon, I visited the office of the city's largest newspaper, *El Diario*, and chatted with a reporter who nonchalantly asked questions and took photos.

The following day brought a prominent article about my ride. It read, in part:

"Before his visit to *El Diario* came to an end, the young North American asked us to express his gratitude to the many people of Ecuador who, in one way or another, have helped him with his adventure...." At that point, the writer had added an unbiased editorial comment: "This country of ours is home to an exceptional people."

During the week to come, I would, indeed, meet people who were *exceptional*, but not in the flattering sense the *El Diario* reporter had in mind!

From Cuenca to Azogues, the road was relatively level, making for a relaxing day. The journey was all the more pleasant because I was riding instead of walking. The cherry on the sundae was that Hamaca and Ima behaved perfectly, probably because, at my request, they had been given Vitamin B injections by the *Cazadores de los Ríos* veterinarian. I had often heard that these would sooth frazzled equine nerves, and, indeed, that seemed to be the case. The mares didn't change overnight from lions to lambs, but they lost the neurotic edginess that had begun to typify their behavior.

Many times I had been promised that I'd find people friendlier as I moved farther north, but my experience during the coming week proved the opposite. With notable exceptions, the people seemed less hospitable with each passing day, a trend that began in the town of Azogues. There I had a particularly difficult time finding accommodations for the mares, and my stay was marred by a series of unpleasant episodes.

For dinner I chose a seemingly quiet restaurant that shared a single room with a bar. When I sat down, the bar was empty, but I carelessly overlooked an important indicator of what was to come: the bar was several times the size of the restaurant. Soon after I ordered, the bar filled with blue-collar workers and university students. On a birds-of-a-feather-flock-together basis, both groups congregated and began drinking.

Not long after my meal was served, it was disturbed by a series of anti-American speeches in which the workmen and the students seemed to be trying to outdo one another. Much was made of U.S. involvement in Vietnam, and there were accusations of "economic imperialism" against Ecuador. My thoughts went straight to my conversation with the German administrators at Casa Grande.

Perhaps it was time to take seriously their assessment of America's popularity! I chewed faster, intending to go elsewhere as soon as possible.

"A lot of Johnnies [9] are dying in Vietnam," one of the students said, looking directly at me, "and they deserve it."

I couldn't be certain the remark was directed against me personally. It was even possible that it was an overture of sorts. After all, it was the era of the hippies, and after three months on the road, I looked like one! However, if I joined the discussion, the speakers wouldn't like what I had to say, and I earnestly tried to give the impression I didn't understand Spanish. That tactic backfired when it led to some rather rude comments about how Americans never troubled to learn other peoples' languages.

I left the instant my meal was finished, but I soon felt equally unwelcome in the rest of Azogues. The streets were full of foul-mouthed guttersnipes who delighted in making fun of my height and whatever else lent itself to their taunts. I hadn't encountered such profanity before. It was uncommon to hear Latin American youngsters publicly using foul language, and I was troubled by the vulgarity even more than the mean-spirited teasing.

In a way, my reaction marked me as a hypocrite. After all, my own vocabulary had degenerated terribly since I'd begun my ride. A day seldom passed when I didn't launch into several long and heartfelt reviews of every bad word it had ever been my pleasure to learn. In my own defense, I can only say that my personal and powerful prowess with profanity was practiced in private - not proffered in public.

Because I naively expected to somehow put a stop to the endless problems and difficulties that plagued me, I was the perfect candidate for frustration. Invariably, this was closely followed by the need to express myself forcefully and eloquently. Afterward, the memory of this behavior distressed me, and I sincerely longed to correct it. Many times I resolved that my use of profanity would cease and desist, and sometimes I kept these well-intentioned resolutions for as long as an hour or two. Usually, though, I broke them much more quickly than that.

In his book, Aime Tschiffely described his own musings on this very same subject. His reflections came while he briefly had the company of a fellow rider, identified only as "Mr. W.":

191

> "Most horsemen, horsebreakers, and open-
> air men have a special vocabulary of their
> own. Now a horse did something wrong,
> again the pack slipped, the trail was rough,
> or a thousand similar things and happenings
> demanded suitable remarks at short inter-
> vals. I remember soon after we set out
> together Mr. W. giving me a moral lecture
> about my strong language, assuring me that
> if I thus continued I should become so used
> to this horrible, useless and degrading habit,
> that I should never be able again to mix with
> decent people."

When upset with myself after one of my tirades, I sought conso-
lation in the belief that few men, under the circumstances, could
have held themselves in check. Tschiffely had similarly consoled
himself, pointing out that his friend:

> "... had not been long with me before he was
> very efficient in the use of my private vocab-
> ulary, and, thanks to his knowledge of the
> language, I was able to add a few very origi-
> nal and expressive words to my repertoire."

My next outburst of colorful language came when I went to check
on Hamaca and Ima. Neither was where I had left them and their
corral gate was wide-open, left that way, no doubt, by one or more
of the town's street urchins. Skillfully I tracked Hamaca and Ima,
though not by following marks on the ground. It was faster and
more reliable to ask and then go in the direction people pointed.
After all, loose horses on a city street were a sight that got noticed
and remembered. Furthermore, there seemed little danger that anyone was pointing out the trail of some other escaped horses.

By the time I found my mares, they were no longer footloose or
fancy-free, having been captured by two stern-faced policemen who
insisted that I buy a chain and padlock to avoid any further such
episodes. This being the second time my mares had been carelessly
set free, I had already decided to invest in exactly such a security system. In fact, I made the purchase and installation immediately after
returning the mares to their corral.

Throughout my journey, I had felt a self-imposed obligation to tolerate unwelcome spectators. Not so, however, that night in Azogues. I wanted nothing more than peace and quiet for both the horses and myself. Repeatedly, I asked the audience around the corral to leave us alone, but the more I worked to disperse the crowd, the more it grew. The number soon topped out at more than a hundred.

In view of the anti-American sentiments heard during my dinner, it seemed prudent not to go beyond asking people to leave. Scalding words and strong-arm tactics were out of the question on a practical as well as a moral basis. There was one incident, though, which transcended such considerations.

Upon finding the corral's gate chained and padlocked, two young scamps crawled under it in order to chase Hamaca and Ima. I asked them to leave and got no acknowledgment that they'd heard. Adding volume and severity, I repeated myself. That was good enough to slow their pursuit of the mares but failed to stop it. It was time for words to give way to actions! I grabbed each boy by an arm, slung one over each shoulder and carried them out of the corral. This resulted in giggling and other indications that they were having a wonderful time. When I set them down, I made it rough enough to take the fun out of things!

Such problems, it turned out, were not destined to end when I left Azogues. Most nights thereafter, crowds gathered around my rented corrals. Unfailingly, someone would ask to see the mares move. Hoping they'd go away afterward, I usually accommodated them by catching Ima and gaiting her back and forth on the halter. I always chose Ima for this purpose because she was better-gaited, more-spectacular and more-likely to make a good impression. In retrospect, this proved the truth of Marie Ebner von Eschenbach's [10] famous quote: "We are so vain that we care for the opinion of those we don't care for."

Unfortunately, these command performances never relieved the congestion around the corral. A few people might leave, but new arrivals more than made up for departures, and those who had missed the first show would clamor for another. If I didn't accommodate them quickly enough, they were only too glad to take matters in their own hands. The boldest would whistle, yell, wave arms or throw pebbles to get the horses to move and show their gaits. It went beyond rudeness.

Hamaca and Ima needed to eat, rest and sleep, and this harassment meant that they couldn't. Not until night had fallen and the crowds had at last dispersed, would the horses finally have a chance to relax. I watered them for the last time around 9:00 and often found them only beginning to eat at that late hour. Between 3:00 and 6:00 A.M., we'd set out for the next town where I would feed them immediately upon arrival. Hungrily, they'd begin to eat, but it was never long before an audience gathered and put an end to that.

Under the best of circumstances, horses eat and sleep poorly in unfamiliar surroundings. With the agitation provided by inconsiderate crowds, Hamaca's and Ima's difficulties were compounded. It didn't take long to reach the point where I was close to declaring my own personal war on rude and obnoxious people!

In Peru, I had been warned that the Andean *serranos* would tax my patience. Though it initially seemed these warnings were proving accurate, it turned out that I was failing to distinguish pure Indians from *mestizos*, whose ancestry is a mixture of bloods, usually European and Indian. Once I could recognize the difference, I found that the Indians were almost never the source of my difficulties. More standoffish than any other people I'd ever met, they seldom showed me even the slightest courtesy. However, the worst discourtesy I suffered at their hands was to be ignored when I spoke to them, and in many cases, this may have been nothing more than a matter of language.

The far-more-numerous *mestizos* were the ones who refused to leave us in peace, and they were the ones who asked the questions. Every night, in every town, I was asked the same questions, in the same words and the same sequence:

"Where are you going?"

"How far do you travel each day?"

"Where do you plan to spend the nights between here and Quito?"

I usually tried to avoid giving specific answers, just in case the inquiry was designed to gather information for a robbery attempt. I told all but a few people that I came "from the south" and was going "to the north." If people persisted, I'd go so far as to inform them that I had come "from Peru" and was going "to the United States." I was amazed at how easily vague answers could turn aside specific questions. To my dismay, however, I never found a similarly effective way to avoid further questions on a whole host of other subjects, such as financial ones.

"How much did the horses cost?"

"I don't remember," I'd respond evasively.

"Well, how much did the big one cost?"

"I don't remember."

"Well, how much did the little one cost?"

"I don't remember."

"Well, approximately how much did they cost?"

"I don't remember! I don't remember!"

"How much are you earning for this ride?"

"Nothing."

"Do you want to sell your horses?"

"No."

"Do you want to sell the big one?"

"No."

"How about the other one?"

"No."

"How about your knife? Do you want to sell it?"

"No."

"Do you have anything for sale?"

"No. No. No."

Next would come expressions of doubt concerning my plans and procedures.

"Are you sure it's possible to go all the way to the United States on horseback?"

"How will you cross the ocean?"

"Are you sure you haven't been traveling in trucks or trains most of the time?"

"Why don't you take an airplane?"

"Why don't you use mules?"

"Why do you feed your horses this?"

"Why don't you feed them that?"

Next the helpful observations.

"Did you know that horse is cut on the jaw?"

"Did you know the other horse is cut on the leg?"

"Did you know...?"

One by one, every blemish would be noticed by dozens of eyes and pointed out by half as many mouths.

Answering those questions was like trying to fold an octopus into a tidy bundle. Every time I thought the job was done, another arm would flop out. When the questions mercifully ceased, the advice began.

"The big horse needs new shoes."

"The little horse needs new shoes, too."

"You travel much too far every day."

"You should travel farther every day."

"You shouldn't scrape them with that thing (curry comb); it will make them sick."

I nearly went crazy having the same conversation over and over again. There was so little variation that the whole procedure seemed to have been scripted by a sadistic researcher interested in how much I could stand and for how long. These conversations weren't confined to my nightly stopovers, either. Whenever and wherever I ceased moving, someone would approach, and the questions would start. Most of the time I answered and explained, but when I was going to be less than cordial with a particularly boorish character, I'd tell people – in true *Cold War* spirit! – that I was Russian. The benefits were twofold: I avoided making a bad impression for my country while simultaneous discrediting an archenemy.

That night in Azogues, my hotel mattress was full of fleas, and not long after midnight, some noisy rats infested the tack I had stacked on the floor next to my bed. It was so dark I couldn't actually see them, but my ears told me they were there. With all the self-control I could muster, I felt the floor with my hand until I located one of my boots in the midst of the scurrying and squealing. I then thrashed the area, using my boot as if it were a fly swatter. Unfortunately, my visitors weren't easily intimated.

Having no desire to walk among sharp-toothed rodents in the pitch dark with one bare foot (try as I might I couldn't locate my second boot), I propped myself up on an elbow. Without getting out of bed, I leaned out and carefully unpiled my gear, spreading it out to deny my visitors an easy hiding place. Thus exposed, they disappeared under the door or into holes in the wall.

Before long, though, they were back!

---

[9] It was the only time I ever heard my countrymen referred to as "Johnnies." If one ignored the derogatory tone, it was an appropriate nickname, even a century after Union soldiers in America's Civil War called their Confederate enemies "Johnny Reb."

[10] An Austrian novelist.

CHAPTER 21

"Stop Him! He's an *Americano*!"

Without regret, I said farewell to Azogues early the next morning. The road climbed steadily until day's end, when it dropped down into the quaint village of Cañar. Where the highway entered town, a teen-age boy approached me. His interest instantly put me on guard. I didn't want him and his friends pestering me or the mares, and my intention was to brush him off as harshly as necessary. Before the evening was over, however, I would know this boy, whose name was Guillermo, as a species far removed from the guttersnipes of Azogues. He was shy, pleasant, respectful, soft-spoken and more attuned to other people than most adults.

"*Señor*, you must be Pablito," he said. "I read about you in *El Diario* and have been waiting for you to arrive."

"How'd you know what day I'd get here?" I asked, bringing the mares to a stop.

"I guessed," he said, shrugging his shoulders. "Fortunately, I was correct."

"But how did you know what time to expect me?"

"I didn't. I have been waiting here since lunch."

"And what was important enough to be worth all that?" I asked.

"I wanted to be the first to offer you a place to stay," he paused, evidently trying to decide if he should say more. "I hope you will accept."

When his invitation had been accepted, Guillermo took control of the situation with maturity beyond his years.

"My family's house has no place for your horses," he explained in his quiet voice. "Therefore, I took the liberty of making arrangements for them to stay elsewhere."

"Where?"

"On a friend's patio."

"Patio? Are you sure it's suitable for horses?"

"*Sí, señor*. There's no place in Cañar where your horses will be as safe and comfortable."

Quickly and efficiently, Guillermo led me off the highway and onto side streets before the town was aware of my arrival. It soon became evident that he was making a considerable effort to keep me out of sight. I had a feeling that this wasn't consideration for me as much as it was the desire to have me exclusively for himself.

197

Whatever the motivation, I enthusiastically supported his goal!

Alternately walking and jogging, Guillermo guided me into an above-average residential area, making me all the more curious about the accommodations he had arranged for Hamaca and Ima. The streets were narrow and the houses built against the sidewalk, only a few feet from motor traffic. Between one intersection and the next, the fronts of the houses formed a continuous wall. Each entry was marked by a huge set of double doors. When swung open to admit cars, these rode on metal wheels. Pedestrian traffic passed through a smaller door, cut into one of the large ones. Behind these doors were patios, surfaced with cobblestones. The house – typically two stories with a balcony – surrounded the patio on three sides.

It was hard to believe that someone had offered one of these for horses! From the homeowner's point of view, there were certain inescapable disadvantages, piles of manure for one. From my horses' point of view, the only disadvantage was that they'd spend the night on a hard, cobblestone surface. From my perspective, though, these patios were ideal: flat, safely enclosed and protected from curious crowds.

After Guillermo rang the doorbell next to a particular set of double doors, a kindly looking gentleman swung them open. He cheerfully welcomed us, advising that he had laid in a supply of hay and filled several pails with water in anticipation of our arrival.

While caring for the mares that evening, I noticed that one of Hamaca's rear shoes was loose. On his own initiative, the owner of the house disappeared and soon returned with a blacksmith who renailed the shoe for the equivalent of eighteen U.S. cents. All the mares' needs were met with a comparable lack of effort on my part. By the time Guillermo and I left for his house, I knew Hamaca and Ima were in good hands and had no misgivings about having them out of my sight for the rest of the night.

When I had accepted Guillermo's invitation, it hadn't occurred to me that his offer might have been extended without parental consent. However, when I saw his mother's reaction to my arrival, I knew instantly. Stern looks were directed at her youngest son when she didn't think I was looking. Toward me, she was polite, but her coolness gave the impression that she suspected I'd taken unfair advantage of her son's natural generosity and was there to sponge off his family. I was invited to dinner, but since it had been on the stove when I arrived, I knew the quantities hadn't been calculated with a guest in mind. I declined, muttering something about "other arrangements" and set out in search of a restaurant. Before I left, Guillermo suggested that we meet at the movie theater after dinner.

The evening at the movies was a study in simple pleasures. Guillermo arrived with several friends who were anxious to meet me, and the boy tending the box office, another of my *fans*, refused to allow me to pay admission, resulting in a saving of twelve cents. The feature was North American, B-grade. It had Spanish subtitles and was badly out of focus. The film was also marked with numerous vertical white scratches, which I was told were the result of many trips through ancient projectors. Besides all that, the sound track was distorted and played at an extremely low volume.

In time, the projectionist improved the focus and increased the volume. The sound quality also could undoubtedly have been improved, but there was little incentive. I was the only person who could have understood it, even had it been perfect. Though not very good, the movie was, at least, educational. Poor sound quality notwithstanding, the English soundtrack and Spanish subtitles helped me add to my ever-growing Spanish vocabulary.

In the States, a showing half as bad might have provoked a riot. In Cañar, however, it was appreciated, and I enjoyed it more than most. For me, such diversions were rare. Only because Hamaca and Ima were secure inside their patio had I dared leave them for more than a few minutes.

After the movie, my newfound friends and I strolled through the streets, talking and laughing. I remember thinking that people in Cañar, much the same as those in Olmos, were poor and happy, circumstances which many North Americans mistakenly view as incompatible. In the United States, money is everything, but even with the world's highest standard of living, Americans score lower than the people of poor countries in polls that measure happiness.

In America, most will intellectually acknowledge that less money can lead to more happiness, but very few are willing to prove it. Jobs and careers are all too often chosen for financial reasons. Americans don't feel comfortable following their hearts in a land where going one's own way is looked down upon unless a person makes a fortune in the process.

Guillermo and I returned to his home later that night, under dim streetlights. With my mind free of its normal occupations and preoccupations, I enjoyed an outstanding sleep. I woke early and dressed quietly with the intention of slipping out before the lady of the house woke and felt obligated to prepare breakfast for me. I was too late. Guillermo's mother was already at work in the kitchen, cheerfully preparing a large, delicious breakfast. Her cordial manner indicated a change of attitude, and conversation revealed the reason: she'd read the *El Diario* article and had apparently concluded that I wasn't an opportunist living off other people. It was an unexpected and welcome demonstration of the power of the press!

Before I left Cañar, I cleaned the manure and excess hay from the patio where Hamaca and Ima had spent the night. The owner wouldn't hear of payment, not even reimbursement for the hay he'd bought. Using flowery words, he insisted that the pleasure of hosting Hamaca and Ima amounted to payment in full.

As I was saddling up, I asked for information about the altitudes ahead. The mares' host advised me that the *páramo* we had crossed before dropping down into Cañar was 14,500 feet, the highest point anywhere along the road to Quito. If that was true, the mares and I were well adapted to heights and had no reason to fear altitude sickness.

During coming days, I verified and reverified that particular altitude before finally accepting it. I couldn't believe we had reached such an extraordinary height without seeing some sort of marker. Evidently, altitude markers were the responsibility of the same nonexistent people who posted "Falling Rocks" and "Poisonous Plants" signs.

I prepared to leave Cañar with no sense of urgency. The ride ahead of me that day was an easy one. According to the military in Cuenca, it was a mere twenty miles to Chunchi. I didn't, therefore, pay much attention when the mares' host insisted that Chunchi was farther than I'd be able to ride in a single day. Nonetheless, a small, nagging doubt was planted and began to grow. A few miles out of Cañar, I began to see *serranos* walking or riding their mules along the road. Assuming they should know distances better than people who traveled in vehicles, I asked how far it was to Chunchi. I got an answer that was vague but reassuring. Just for good measure, though, I decided to reconfirm it a few times.

"Right up here just a little ways," the *serranos* would answer. "Once you get to the (and here each person named his favorite landmark: a gas station, a long grade, a turn in the road, etc.), it's just a little farther."

The days to come would reveal that these types of answers are typical of people in the *sierra*. No matter how near or far one's destination may be, the locals will invariably name a landmark from which it's "just a little farther." The problem is the distance to the landmark in question! Perhaps something in the *Quechua* [11] tongue leads to this peculiar habit, or maybe it comes from the *serranos'* notion that it is impolite to deliver bad news.

When passing a group of *mestizos*, I asked for *their* estimate of the distance to Chunchi and got an answer that conflicted with what the *serranos* had said and coincided with what I had heard in Cañar. By noon, the mares and I had gone over twenty miles, and the Indians were still insisting that Chunchi was "just a little farther" while the *mestizos* begged to differ. By then, I had a pretty good idea who was right. It seemed I was once again in the same predicament I had encountered on the way to La Toma. The cause, too, was the same: as-the-crow-flies military charts, no doubt prepared for the air force!

I was amazed by the ease with which the mares' gaits gobbled up the miles and handled the climbs, especially considering the altitude and the sizes of their burdens. Ima was carrying a hundred pounds of gear on the packsaddle. Hamaca was carrying over two hundred and fifty pounds between rider and gear. Throughout the afternoon, we made such progress that I began to believe we might make it to Chunchi in spite of the distance. That was wishful thinking!

By the time night and rain simultaneously began to fall, we had come about thirty-five miles, to a desolate *páramo* not far north of Gun. [12] There wasn't the faintest sign of another human being, and I pressed on, hoping to find a better place before I stopped. It took a while, but I finally spotted a forlorn house and corral nestled almost out of sight at the base of a hill. I approached the owner and asked if I could rent his corral for the night. Without a word, the man led his cow from the corral, tied it elsewhere and gestured for Hamaca and Ima to move in.

What seemed like unbelievable hospitality turned out to be well-developed commercial instincts. No sooner were the mares inside the corral than the man collected his outrageous fee, up front. While my money was being stuffed into his pocket, I asked my host where I might purchase feed.

"Your horses will have to do without feed tonight, *señor*," he said with great formality. "I have none to sell you. Believe me I would if I could."

I believed him!

"For that matter, I have nothing to offer for your personal consumption, either," he added.

"It won't hurt me to miss a meal," I said, "but I would like to find something for the horses. Do you think your neighbors might have anything?"

At that point, I wasn't sure there *were* any neighbors.

"I can take you to a man who is far more prosperous than I," my host said. "He might be able to help you."

With that, he lit a kerosene lantern and guided me along a narrow trail, which climbed the nearby hill. In the dark, I found the footing treacherous. My guide – familiar with the steep, winding path – soon got far enough ahead that I could no longer make use of the faint light from his lantern. Once that happened, I was slowed even more and quickly lost sight of him. A howling wind came up, and I realized the night was unusually dark because of storm clouds filling the sky. I considered calling out but wasn't willing to risk the embarrassment. After all, the man on the slope above me – if that's where he was – was little more than half my size.

Becoming lost in that dark and unfamiliar place was a disturbing prospect. I made my way as rapidly as I could, stumbling from time to time and unsure I chose the correct fork at either of two intersections. Several times I stopped to search for lantern light above me, but I saw nothing. Finally, I crested the hill. My host and another man were standing there, in the doorway of an adobe shack. I hid my relief, and the neighbor invited me inside. For my benefit, his living room was rapidly converted into a general store, where rye grass, rice flour and dried corn were measured out and sold to me.

As he pocketed my money, the neighbor saw the possibility of further capitalizing on my arrival. His hut suddenly became a restaurant and hotel. I didn't want to sleep that far from the mares, but dinner was a temptation I couldn't resist. Mysteriously, I was promised something "very, very special," and a fire was started in the kitchen stove. In the flickering light, the neighbor went to work. When my dinner was set before me, it turned out to be a fire-broiled rodent with all four legs sticking straight up, like a cartoon rendition of something dead. It was, I was told, guinea pig.

Immediately, Carlos Luna came to mind (not that he in any way resembled a guinea pig!). *Don* Carlos was the man who had flown from Lima to bring my geldings' travel papers and represent the *Asociación* at Jorge Baca's send-off in Chiclayo. He was a professor at Peru's most important college of agriculture. While I was in Lima, he'd taken me on a tour of his department, showing me several research projects involving guinea pigs.

These creatures have been widely consumed in the Andes since the days of the Incas, and it was his objective to develop larger strains. The idea of guinea pigs as food had been interesting intellectually. As actual food for my personal consumption, it was quite another matter. Just to be sure it wasn't *Kentucky Fried Rat*, I nonchalantly asked to see the herd from which my dinner had come. Proudly the neighbor took me to a nearby building and showed me a room full of what appeared to be desks with a single drawer running the full width of the top. One-by-one, he pulled the drawers open until I had seen his entire inventory of guinea pigs.

Thus deprived of my best excuse for not partaking, I sampled my meal. Though it sounds trite, the taste was, in fact, similar to chicken, a flavor frequently used to describe exotic meat. The main difference was that the flesh had more consistency. Though it tasted fine, I could find no justification for guinea pig to be considered a delicacy. The price, however, was somewhat helpful in that regard. I almost protested, but considering the number of pounds produced per year by a female guinea pig, I decided the amount might not be all that far out of line.

During the trip back down the hill, I had my hands full. My host offered no help with the two large bundles of rye grass or the burlap bags containing corn and rice flour. He seemed to be waiting for my offer of a tip. Such an offer never came, and neither did his assistance. I was soon huffing and puffing, but the greeting I got from the mares made it all worthwhile. They noisily nickered, glad to see me and their dinner. Except for the rice flour – which they ate sparingly – both mares showed greater-than-usual enthusiasm for that evening's meal. That was as it should have been after their performance during the preceding ten hours.

Having seen his neighbor in action, our host induced me to rent a small "sleeping room" with no windows, no light and a dirt floor for a bed. The lack of amenities didn't stop me from getting a good night's sleep.

At daybreak, my host took me aside and earnestly warned me – as had so many – that I would unquestionably fall prey to bandits, or worse, if I continued on. Buses full of people had been waylaid on the road ahead, he said, and men capable of such boldness would hardly be deterred by a lone man on horseback. One can listen to only so many warnings before their accumulated weight takes effect, and I was uneasy as I set out for Chunchi. The morning's events wound the tension tighter, filling me with foreboding. The countryside was brushy, ideal for ambush, and I was expecting one at any moment. As if to increase my edginess, someone was setting off liberal quantities of firecrackers, at least that's what I hoped they were.

To tell the truth, the detonations sounded suspiciously like gunfire.

Eerie, oriental-sounding music echoed hauntingly through the valleys. I could hear, but not see, people talking in the harsh-sounding *Quechua* language. Soon communication switched to elaborate whistles and birdcalls, filling my head with images of Andean Indians with the characteristics of Geronimo's fiercest warriors. By that time, I was regretting that I hadn't increased my life insurance at the last option!

The various sound effects were all the more sinister because I couldn't locate their sources in the heavy brush. For that matter, I couldn't see anyone, anywhere. When I finally did, I had the explanation I'd been seeking. It was a religious holiday. This became self-evident when I encountered a procession of *serranos* making its way solemnly down the center of the highway. All were wearing bright, festive colors, and the men carried a platform on two horizontal wooden poles. The platform supported a large, crude religious statue. Immediately, I parked the mares and myself at the side of the road to show proper respect as the participants marched past.

There was much to set this procession apart from religious observances in the States. First and foremost, the participants – men and women alike – were intoxicated or well on the way. Another was that the religious symbols arranged around the statue combined Catholic icons with those the Andean peoples had worshiped before the Spanish came. It was an extremely curious mixture.

Further along, as I passed through a populated area, I found a carnival-like atmosphere. On one farm, men and women in festive costumes were ceremoniously plowing with a pair of oxen. Each ox was decked out in an ornate blanket and headpiece. The headpieces were adorned with brightly colored flags flying from pencil-sized sticks. When I stopped to take a better look, the celebrants thought I was taking their picture and made an immediate demand for payment. I explained that I was only looking and that my camera was packed away, but the group lost no time in removing the oxen's headpieces and blankets. After that, they ducked down behind their beasts in order to foil what they were convinced was an attempt to *steal* photographs of them. If I'd had quick access to my camera, their actions would have made better pictures than the pose they had hoped to sell me.

Later that afternoon, while passing through a small town, I sensed that I was being followed. Then I confirmed it. At first, it didn't seem all that important. People frequently followed me, hoping to start a conversation. Most of the time, they were polite enough to require some sort of acknowledgement before approaching, and if denied this, they'd give up and go away. But this time was different. The man behind me didn't go away. Instead, he was joined by a companion and then another and another, until there were six, in dirty suits and various stages of inebriation. I comforted myself by observing that the mules they rode were small and scrawny. Meanwhile, I moved Hamaca and Ima into a faster walk and kept my eyes peeled, in vain, for an army post or police station.

At the city limits, I wondered at the wisdom of continuing into the unpopulated area ahead, but what else could I do? Turning back to town also had a downside. The group behind me had grown from one to six in that very town, and given the chance, it might grow even larger.

A little farther along, the leader put his mule into a fast trot and came up alongside me. Making an obvious attempt to sound authoritative, he announced that he was "the Law" in the town I had just left.

"It will be necessary for you to show me your passport and the contents of your bags," he demanded.

"Do you have anything to show your authority?" I asked, turning to look his way without slowing my horses.

"I'm not making requests! I'm giving orders!" was the stern reply.

"How do I know you have the right to give orders?"

"*Señor*, you must stop your horses at once!"

"As soon as I see proof of your authority."

We were temporarily at a stalemate, and neither spoke for a moment. Obviously *the Law* wouldn't or couldn't prove his authority. Considering the size of his *deputies* and the dubious speed of their tiny mules, I wasn't about to be talked down off my horse. My resolve was all the stronger because I had the impression that the men behind us would abandon their mission, unless it proved effortless. The man at my side, however, was the kind who sees things through. His determination made me wonder if I might be the one in the wrong, even though all evidence was to the contrary. In nearly seven hundred miles of travel, no one except border guards had asked to see my papers, and even they hadn't bothered to inspect my baggage. In addition, I had passed hundreds of uniformed representatives of "the Law," and I'd even slept in their jails without any such requests. Now, six half-drunk men, without proof of authority, were insisting that I show them my possessions. If I was stupid enough to obey and if they saw anything worth taking, I was pretty sure about what would happen next.

The leader kept up an incessant stream of chatter about international "law and order," "American imperialism" and "suppression of downtrodden peoples." I was intrigued by the fact that he referred to people from the States as *"Americanos"* rather than *"Norteamericanos."* Trying to defuse the situation, I pointed out that most South Americans would correct me if I did the same. This feeble strategy failed to sidetrack him. *The Law* stuck to his theme, repeatedly ordering me to stop and dismount. I kept the mares a few steps ahead of his mule and double-talked him, hoping he'd tire of the game and go home. Unfortunately, he didn't.

Instead, he suddenly turned his mule and jumped her between my horses, grabbing Ima's lead rope. I was holding the free end, not wishing to risk more broken parts by tying it to my saddle. I stopped Hamaca and turned her to face him. One last time – half-hoping that he would produce a convincing badge – I repeated that no one would see my passport or baggage without proof of authority. Again we were at a stalemate, but my situation had worsened. I was no longer moving, and the other five men were getting in position to surround me.

I jumped Hamaca toward *the Law* and his mule, counting on the fact that she must look pretty big from his vantage point down below. At the same time, I leaned forward in the saddle and shouted at the top of my voice: "Be careful!" The man recoiled, blinking, but didn't release his grip. While he was off-balance, I yanked the lead rope as hard as I could, but he was very strong, and his grip held. Immediately, I rode toward him – until there was slack in the rope – and then turned Hamaca and took up the slack, giving the rope a hard jerk. Again *the Law's* grip held. Immediately I turned Hamaca so the rope's pressure pulled him farther in the direction he was already leaning. That reduced his options to two: let go or come off his mule. He let go.

Startled and angry, *the Law* ordered me to: "Halt or be shot!"

I hadn't seen any firearms, but as I moved the mares off at a gallop, I could feel tingling sensations up and down my spine.

No shot was fired, but the intrepid six came in hot pursuit. When I looked back, I could see the mules churning the air with their short legs, looking like Chihuahuas in pursuit of greyhounds. It might have been laughable were it not for serious problems developing at my end of the chase.

This was the first time I'd had the mares at a gallop, and it showed. They were awkward, excited and difficult to control. Ima's gallop was especially clumsy, and the packsaddle flopped and swayed each time she launched herself into the air and again when she came to ground. The ways things looked, it wouldn't be very long before the packsaddle rolled beneath her. I put thirty meters between us and our pursuers before slowing the mares to a speed that conserved energy yet allowed us to maintain a constant lead. At the slower speed, both mares smoothed out, and the packsaddle rode better. However, my predicament remained serious.

The mules might look ridiculous chasing fresh horses on a relatively flat road, but there was potential for a reenactment of *The Tortoise and the Hare*. At that altitude, the unfamiliar gallop would tire Hamaca and Ima very quickly. Using the right shortcut, some of the mules and riders could close the road ahead of us while the others blocked our retreat. Soon we passed a crew of workers who were repairing the road. My pursuers called to them.

"Stop him! He's an *Americano!*"

I rode by, making deliberate eye contact with each man. Smiling, I greeted them individually, with the most cheerful "*buenas tardes*" I could manage.

The workers were disarmed and each responded with his own "*buenas tardes*." No one made a move to stop me. Farther down the road we repeated the procedure with a group of farm workers, returning home after a day in the fields.

"Stop him! He's an *Americano!*"

"*Buenas tardes.*" "*Buenas tardes.*" "*Buenas tardes.*" "*Buenas tardes.*"

Still farther down the road, we passed a second road crew, this one clearing a rockslide.

"Stop him! He's an *Americano!*"

One fellow, sitting behind the wheel of a big road grader, must not have liked *Americanos*. His head whipped around, and he eyed me intently. A smile and a friendly wave – given as I looked directly into his eyes – briefly deactivated the man, but after we passed, he stepped on the gas and gave chase. This raised a disturbing question: would a man on a road crew respond in such a fashion if my pursuers were not, indeed, *the Law?*

As a participant in this bizarre race, the grader was as superior to my horses as they were to my pursuers' mules. Furthermore, there was no hope of escaping by leaving the roadway. It was little more than a ledge carved into the steep face of a mountainside. The mares and I were confined on the right by the perpendicular cut of the road's uphill side and on the left by a steep downgrade where horses could easily break a leg. Escape was possible only if the mares could outrun the grader, and there was almost no chance of that. In fact, it was far from certain that they'd get the chance to try. At our increased speed, the packsaddle was, once again, threatening to roll beneath Ima.

Rapidly, the grader drew even. Hamaca and Ima seemed to sense that the grader was a threat, and when I urged them to greater efforts, they delivered. We remained neck and neck, speeding pell-mell down the road. Even with her greater burden, I'm sure Hamaca could have gone faster, but Ima was giving everything she had. It wasn't enough. The grader inched ahead, and when his vehicle was past us, the driver cut his wheels sharply to the right and hit the brakes. The grader swerved and went into a slide. The driver was going to block the road or run us down, and he didn't seem to care which! Only a rapidly closing gap remained between the front of the grader and the embankment on the uphill side of the road. I aimed for that gap, and somehow we squeezed through before the grader crashed into the embankment with a loud thud.

By the time the grader had been restarted, maneuvered around and pointed in our direction, the driver must have done some thinking. Perhaps he had remembered that his job description didn't include chasing *Americanos*. Maybe he'd considered the issue of who would pay if he damaged the grader. For whatever reason, he gave up the chase. *The Law* did the same, evidently disheartened when the roadblock, intended to stop me, became an impediment that allowed me to further increase my lead.

Soon thereafter, I passed some high-school students. Though no one was in visible pursuit, I took the precaution of greeting each one with special cheerfulness. Not long thereafter, I noticed two of those same students running after me. They were waving their arms and shouting.

Oh, no! Now they've got kids chasing after me for being an Americano! I thought, enjoying the Keystone Cops flavor of such a possibility.

The students were yelling for me to stop and wait. A quick study of the roadway showed no one else in sight, and I stopped the mares, alert for signs of trouble.

"What was that all about?" the taller of the two wanted to know when they caught up.

I told them the story, whereupon one of them bemoaned the rudeness of his countrymen and offered a night's lodging for the mares and myself.

"Do you think those men were really law officers?" I asked, my mind not quite ready to change gears.

The two broke into laughter, and for the first time, I felt sure that wanted posters offering a reward for my capture were not a likely consequence of the last hour's events.

[11] Quechua was the language spoken in that region under the Incas, prior to the coming of the *conquistadores*.

[12] Pronounced "Goon."

Sliding in grease-like mud (see page 179).

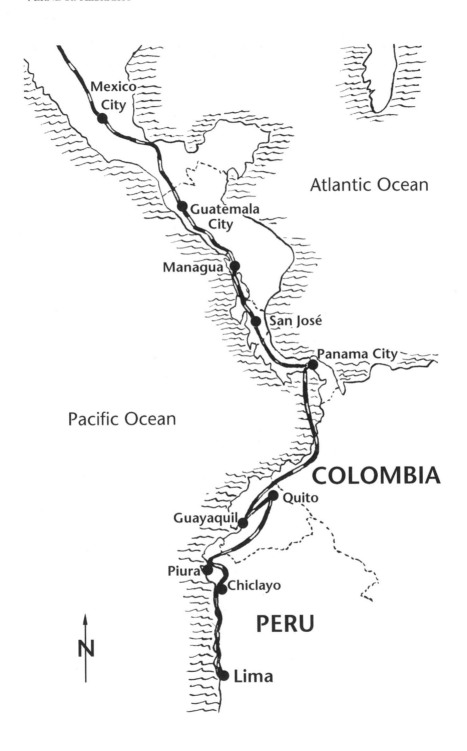

Atlantic Ocean

Mexico City

Guatemala City

Managua

San José

Panama City

Pacific Ocean

COLOMBIA

Quito

Guayaquil

Piura

Chiclayo

PERU

N

Lima

CHAPTER 22

The Outsider

Bound for Chunchi and anxious to hear about my "escape," the two students fell in step with Hamaca and Ima. I slowed the mares, enjoying the company until my escorts unexpectedly turned off the roadway and started down a mule trail. When I didn't follow, they explained that the trail was a shortcut. In my vocabulary, "shortcut" was on a par with "bandit." I didn't want anything to do with either one, and I said I preferred to continue along the road and meet them later, in town. Hearing this, the boys walked back toward me, both talking at the same time and gesturing excitedly.

"Following the shortcut," one pointed out. "Chunchi is only four kilometers from here."

"If you stay on the highway, it's more than twice that far," the other chimed in.

There *was* one other consideration. Every few steps, I'd been looking back over my shoulder. Leaving the highway would probably frustrate any further attempt *the Law* might make to catch me, and that was the telling argument. I gave in and followed. For the two boys, the rugged shortcut was a way to save time and effort. They didn't realize how difficult it was for horses. It used every ounce of energy Hamaca and Ima had left. Both were blowing hard by the time we reached our destination.

In Chunchi, the boys introduced me to a man who offered a corral for my mares. At my insistence, my would-be host went home to clear his invitation with his parents. He returned just as I was finishing up with my nightly chores and guided me to where he lived. Soon after our arrival, it was apparent I had once again accepted an invitation extended without parental consent. I later learned that his mother and father had been gone when the boy went to ask, a small detail he hadn't passed along to me. This created an uncomfortable moment for everyone, me most of all.

Amazingly, the story of my run-in with the six men and the road grader was already circulating in Chunchi, and the parents had heard it. When they realized that their would-be houseguest was the star of that little drama, they quickly warmed to me. The father informed me that my six pursuers were well-known and little-loved bullies. In the absence of a police or army presence in their town, they were self-appointed vigilantes who constantly exercised their nonexistent authority at the expense of others. My refusal to go along with their demands was being hailed as a well-deserved come-uppance, and I was something of a hero.

Since I hadn't been expected for dinner, I dismissed the family's polite objections and excused myself to go to a restaurant. Upon my return, I found my fourteen-year-old host upstairs in the gue-stroom, where I had left my gear. With my Bowie knife in his hand and the sheath strapped to his belt, he was galloping around, as if on horseback. I ducked back – out of sight – and watched, realizing this was his version of my escape. It was worth a good laugh, and I had one, quietly and unnoticed.

The irony of this sensationalized re-enactment was that I hadn't, for a second, considered unsheathing my knife. For one thing, there had been a possibility that my pursuers might actually have some sort of official status. Besides, brandishing a weapon simply wasn't my nature. In fact, I frequently questioned whether my "dagger," as people called it, was a liability or an asset. Undoubtedly, such a for-midable-looking weapon was a deterrent to most petty thieves, but it could also have been an attraction for the more hardened variety. After my height, it was the first thing most people noticed when they saw me, and its impact was shown by many persistent attempts to buy it.

My host and his brother spent the night on hard, wooden bench-es so I could have the double bed where they normally slept. I made a sincere attempt to reverse the sleeping arrangements. When that failed, it became my solemn duty to enjoy the bed enough to justi-fy the boys' sacrifice, and that's exactly what I did. A double bed was a luxury in the South America of those days, and this was the first I'd slept in since leaving the States.

The previous week, to lighten Ima's load, I had sent my sleeping bag ahead with the rest of the excess baggage. That decision had been prompted by the fact that I hadn't once needed it while in Ecuador, but as soon as it was gone, of course, I needed it. Almost every night for a week, I had ended up sleeping on hard, chilly floors because there was no bed or because the one I was offered was too small. Several nights, my saddle blankets had been my only protec-tion against sub-freezing temperatures. They were too short and required me to sleep while folded into the smallest-possible pack-age. A night in that position always left me feeling like the tin man after a light drizzle. However, the accumulated rust disappeared during my night in that glorious double bed.

At dinner in Chunchi, I had discovered that an amazingly accurate description of my *escape* was circulating like wildfire. By the next day, that account had spread far beyond the confines of town. As I made my way toward Alausí, I met strangers who knew almost as much as I did about the events of the previous afternoon. One after another, they stopped me to make fiendishly clever comments at the expense of my pursuers.

One dump truck driver did a double take as he drove past me and then hastily stopped and parked his vehicle on the side of the road. Throwing open the door, he emerged wearing a huge smile and greeting me with warm familiarity.

"I was working with that road crew yesterday afternoon, and I thought you might be interested in knowing what happened after you got away from the road grader," he said.

"Yes?" I said tentatively, wondering if he was, perhaps, best friends with the grader driver.

"Before you were out of sight, the men pursuing you demanded that I take them as passengers and continue the chase in my truck. When I refused, their leader threatened to commandeer my truck by virtue of his 'authority.' Apparently, he didn't know how many friends I have on that road crew!"

The truck driver concluded his narrative with an eloquent facial expression, and I couldn't help but chuckle.

"I don't know what devil made that idiot think I was going to let him use *my* truck to chase such a fine gentleman as yourself," he continued, shaking his head and clucking his tongue.

In the aftermath of the chase, I was famous. Though I tried to downplay my role, no one was having any of it. If I wouldn't boast in my own behalf, there were plenty of others ready to do the job.

"You showed those cretins that they can't bother people anytime they feel like it!"

"There'll be others who will stand up to them now that you've done it!"

"I'm so glad that you had the courage to put them in their places!"

I soon decided that the hard part of being a hero isn't the performance of the deed; it's handling the way people treat you.

******

Back in Peru, I was on the trail early each morning so I could get where I was going before the hottest part of the day. In Ecuador, early starts continued to be advisable, but for a different reason:

mid-afternoon downpours. The rainy season had arrived, and I'd been cautioned that the afternoon cloudbursts could turn torrential – and even dangerous – without advance notice. Proof came when the sky opened up that very afternoon as we approached Alausí.

A few days earlier, I had bought a rubberized, Indian-made poncho. Indians throughout tropical America were using fabric coated with rubber when the Europeans arrived. Never having seen this material, the Europeans were much impressed. So was I. That particular poncho was proving to be the most satisfactory rain gear I'd ever used. It was long and full and discharged its runoff away from my pants and boots.

For a couple of days, I'd been thinking about buying two more such ponchos and modifying them into horse blankets. My North American-made blankets, treated with water repellent, were no match for the cloudbursts we were encountering, and word was that the rain would get worse in days to come. It poured heavily throughout the night, but Hamaca and Ima paid no penalty for my procrastination in replacing their blankets.

"It just so happens that I have the town's only covered stall, behind the police station. It's empty, and your horses are welcome to use it," the Chief of Police told me when I asked where I might board the mares.

The stall was the nicest I'd seen since Piura. It was in excellent repair and had a raised floor that prevented the inside from flooding. Inexplicably, the floor had been surfaced with cobblestones, without regard for the fact that hard surfaces are punishing for horses' legs. Still, my horses would be more comfortable that night than ninety-nine percent of their brethren in the Andes. While I was caring for the mares, the Chief extended a further invitation.

"You're more than welcome to spend the night at the jail. There's a bed in the cell where you should be safe and comfortable."

"If it's not too much trouble … "

"No trouble at all," the Chief interrupted gruffly. "Come on. Let's get some dinner."

We walked to a nearby restaurant and ate a meal far superior to those served when customers were less distinguished than my companion. The outstanding meal was, however, surpassed by the service. Everyone there dropped whatever he or she was doing in order to attend and flatter the Chief. Later, when the Chief asked for our check, he was informed that our meals were compliments of the house. During our meal, the Chief proved to be wonderful company.

He was intelligent, well informed and fond of conversation, an art at which he excelled. Very little escaped his notice. He even knew the details of my "escape" and had some questions on that subject. I'm afraid I was thoughtless when he asked how I had known that my pursuers weren't legitimate police officers.

"A uniform doesn't bestow authority," he said, frowning with disapproval. "Authority comes from a man's character - not from a piece of cloth!"

Carelessly, I had failed to note that the Chief himself wore no uniform, but I recovered in time to avoid any mention of badges, yet another item not in evidence. After dinner, I tagged along on the Chief's nightly rounds, and was soon tired of the nauseating bowing and scraping that began the instant he came on the scene. Assuming that he felt as I did, I was preparing to say a few words on the subject when I realized – barely in time – that the Chief was showing off for me. He loved the elaborate attention and had no doubt that I was finding it very impressive.

It soon became evident that this complex man had many sides to his character. On the one hand, he was among the most personable and entertaining men I had ever met. On the other, he was a tin god who exhibited the worst effects power can have on a man. In his worst moments, he seemed to be one of those stereotypical, old-time southern police chiefs seen in American movies. Methodically he went from store to store, picking up a piece of merchandise in each and asking the price. The price was always the same: "Free, of course, for you, *señor*!"

This forced generosity was accepted as his due, and the Chief never responded with more than a listless: "*Gracias.*" He didn't seem to care what the townspeople thought of him as long as he had "respect," but for some mysterious reason, he wanted my approval. Toward that end, he stood outside, unseen, whenever I entered a shop looking to purchase supplies. After the price had been quoted, he would suddenly appear.

"What?! How much?!" he'd bark at the shopkeeper, who had just given a greatly inflated price.

Instantly the price dropped fifty per cent, to the amount local residents would have paid. In Latin America, merchandise is for sale at a wide range of prices. The lower end is for local residents, and the top end is for foreign tourists. I knew what things should cost and was careful to inform vendors that I wasn't a *tourist* and wouldn't pay *tourist* prices, pronouncing the word with proper contempt. Tourists had the reputation of being easy marks, and if my haggling was to bring results, it was critical to declare "I'm not a tourist!" with great indignation. I got to be very good at it.

Despite my best efforts, though, everyone always tried to overcharge me. Invariably, I stood my ground and beat the price down to where it belonged or took my business elsewhere. However, haggling was tiring and time-consuming, and there were times when the excess charge wasn't exorbitant. On these occasions, I was sometimes tempted to swallow my pride and pay a few extra cents, but with my precarious finances, I just couldn't bring myself to do it.

******

Between Alausí and Guamote, we crossed the *páramo* called Palmira, famous as one of the most distinctive spots in Ecuador's highlands. There – swept by howling winds, at an altitude above 11,000 feet – was a desolate, sandy and cold "desert," looking very much out of place. Actually, the *sand* at Palmira wasn't sand; it was finely ground volcanic cinder. The individual particles clung together, interlocking and stacking in a way that grains of sand could never duplicate. The resulting dunes dominated the landscape, their shapes fantastic and ever-changing. Fierce winds constantly arranged and rearranged this volcanic residue, piling and carving it into fantastic shapes that were blown away, piled, carved and blown away again.

Nature took center stage on Palmira, displaying her impressive ability to change and intimidate. From one instant to the next, the sky became crowded with ominous, dark clouds. What had been a bright, sunny afternoon abruptly turned a flat black color that absorbed rather than reflected light. Next came deafening peals of thunder. Nothing on Palmira happened half-heartedly, not the wind, the thunder or the lightning that followed. Bolts of glowing electricity branched out as they raced through the air and touched the ground, briefly linking earth to sky.

We were caught in a powerful thunderstorm and arrived in Guamote drenched. The rain fell, not in drops but in great, formless masses that seemed to have been poured from a gigantic pitcher. Hamaca and Ima trudged into town, heads lowered, ears back and eyes half-closed. My head, too, was lowered, and my hat was pulled down, though it gave little protection from the sheets of cold rain. The mares needed to be under cover that night, and much perseverance was required before I found and rented a small shed with a thatched roof. My search was complicated by the absence of people in the streets but aided by the fact that people were in their homes and therefore available when I knocked on their doors.

Once the mares were comfortable and fed, I rented a room in a small hotel. By using the word "hotel," I risk conveying the impression of a place that resembles a Holiday Inn, perhaps with carpeted floors, drapes, telephone, television, pool and maybe even a nightclub. The hotels where I stayed lacked those amenities and then some.

In almost every fair-sized town along the *Panamericana*, there was at least one cheap hotel. In the Peruvian desert, these had seldom been more than a single story, but in the Andes, where flat land was at a premium, they were usually two or three. Each floor offered anywhere from four to twelve rooms, the tenants of which shared a common bathroom. The rooms were rectangular, measuring about six feet by ten. The lone piece of furniture was the bed, and it was twin-size, with hard, rough sheets and itchy wool blankets. There were no closets, but guests were sometimes furnished a few pegs (or nails) on which to hang coat, trousers and hat, all this for only a dollar a night.

From Guamote we went on to Cajabamba, where the mares spent the night in the back room of a small hardware store.

******

Except for Palmira, the geography between towns had settled into a predictable pattern. From a small village near a river in a warm valley, we'd climb a chilly mountain, crest the top and descend the other side. In the next warm valley we'd cross a river, pass through a village and then head up into the icy mountains once again. It was a routine with few surprises, and in view of that, I became exasperated at how my timing was so consistently bad.

By that time, I was free to select my overnight stopping place according to the day's developments. Hay and grain were available everywhere, and I was no longer sending it ahead. My objective, of course, was to wind up at night in one of those warm valley towns, but as a rule, I ended up on cold mountaintops. The reason was simple. Unless I reached a valley town at or after nightfall, I'd dutifully convince myself that I could – and should – get to the next valley before stopping. More often than not, I failed.

As I made my way farther north, I entered an area where the population was ever-more-dense but flat land remained scarce. There, the majority of the houses were built on stilts, and crops were grown on the sides of hills. Repeatedly, I saw farmers and their oxen

218

plowing straight up and down steep slopes, without thought of erosion control.

Between the large towns along the highway, there were small settlements called *cantones*. These were picturesque, with narrow streets lined by wooden storefronts that had balconies overhanging plank sidewalks. There was usually a small, old-fashioned train station, visited by trains that arrived behind ancient wood- or coal-burning engines. These belched great puffs of steam and smoke, with all the appropriate sound effects. The overall scene gave the general impression of the early American West, all the more so with the colorfully dressed Indians thrown in. Sometimes, I felt as though I was starring in a cowboy movie, and I amused myself by coming up with appropriate titles: *Gunfight at the Guamote Corral ... High-Altitude Noon ... From Road Grader to Eternity ... The Magnificent Six (And Their Somewhat Subpar Mules!) ... Gone With the Rain ... The Lone Gringo.*

If composed of characteristic Andean music, the soundtrack of my movie could have become a big hit, even if the movie itself wasn't. In fact, I had almost suggested Andean music to George Jones when he asked about Peruvian products that he and I might sell in the States. It would have been a good choice, for this music has since taken the rest of the world by storm, going from practically unknown to quite popular. The music of the Andean Indian is dominated by the panpipe and usually slow, solemn and mournful. In small doses, I find it pleasant and soothing. However, I didn't anticipate its popularity because for me it quickly becomes predictable and boring. Most of my Peruvian friends complain that the haunting melodies induce sadness. That opinion was shared by Baron Alexander von Humboldt, a famous German naturalist who visited Ecuador in 1802 and commented:

> "The people are the strangest in the world.
> They live in poverty on mountains of gold,
> sleep tranquilly at the foot of volcanoes, and
> cheer themselves with sad music."

The attire of the Indian men continued to vary from place to place. Near Cañar, the dress was black trousers and a white sweatshirt-like garment over which was worn a short-sleeved black coat. The hats were shallow and had narrow brims, resembling World War I helmets. A little farther on, the pants and ponchos were red, the hats were of the Tom Mix cowboy-type, and woolly, sheepskin chaps were worn. Many of the *serranos* carried slings, presumably for hunting, though I never saw one used for that purpose. They also carried flutes slung, rifle style, over one shoulder, by means of a strip of leather. Untying one end of the *latigo* produced whips for driving livestock.

The people of the Andes hadn't invented the wheel by the time the Spanish conquered them. Almost five hundred years later, they seemed to have a genetic predisposition against its use. Loads of almost any size or description were carried on their backs. The most surprising such burden I saw was a perfectly good wheelbarrow.

"Is it broken?" I asked the man toting it.

"No, *señor*," he answered, lowering it to the ground and rolling it to demonstrate.

Then he picked the wheelbarrow up, slung it across his back and continued on his way.

Firewood was the cargo I most often saw transported by indigenous people. It was the only fuel available for their cooking and heating, and the land near their villages had long since been cleared down to the last twig. In the absence of conservation or reforestation, journeys of ever-increasing length were and would continue to be required to gather this necessity. Finding and transporting firewood seemed to be the women's duty. I often saw women carrying truly impressive bundles of wood. At their sides were daughters – usually under six years of age – carrying a baby on their backs and leading a toddler by the hand, already training for their bleak futures.

Whether in rural areas or towns, the *serranos*, both men and women, relieved themselves with little apparent concern for sanitation or modesty. The women wore full skirts, which hung to the ground, and when it came time to take care of personal business, they'd just fluff out their skirts and squat down. The nursing of babies was performed in a similarly casual manner.

Ecuador's ethnic totem pole was well-defined, and the Indians were at the bottom. All other groups – especially those not far above them – treated them badly. It was the aspect of Andean life that most disturbed me, but strangely enough, the *serranos* themselves didn't seem to mind. Almost invariably, they appeared content and naturally submissive. Of course, that same was once believed of the American Negro, an illusion fostered by those who supported segregation.

Perhaps due to my "white" skin (and proximity to the top of that imaginary totem pole), the *serranos* assumed I was important. Unfailingly, they stepped aside to let me pass. At first, I reacted by smiling, stepping equally far in the opposite direction, and signaling them to pass first. This made them uncomfortable and obviously failed to deliver the message I had in mind. After a few tries, I gave up.

When they spoke to me at all, the *serranos* addressed me respectfully as *jefe* (leader) or *patrón* (boss). If I asked to be called by name, the invariable response would be: "As you wish, *Jefe*."

******

I have vivid memories of my arrival in Riobamba. The setting was as beautiful as anything I had ever seen. Miles before I got to the city itself, the *Panamericana* was lined with orderly rows of trees and maguey plants. Thus landscaped, the highway descended gently into a green valley surrounded by craggy snow-capped peaks, at least one of which was a dormant volcano.

On the outskirts of town I rode through an upper-middle class neighborhood, which boasted the nicest homes I'd seen since Lima. The sight of such houses started me thinking about what life would be like after my ride. Where would I work? Would I ever live in such a house, and if so, would it be worth what I'd have to endure to pay for it? Adventure was proving addictive. True, it wasn't easy, but the hardest thing I had ever done – by far! – was to endure "everyday life." There, problem solving was equally difficult and much less satisfying, time-consuming and urgent but seldom important.

Some of the local residents were out on their porches and stared at me as I rode past. I stared back, feeling like an outsider, not only from their point of view but from my own.

221

CHAPTER 23

The Last of the True Gentlemen

The mares and I rested for two days at the Riobamba cavalry fort. There I was served tasty, sanitary meals, slept in clean, bug-and-rat-free accommodations, enjoyed intelligent conversation, and even had hot (yes, hot!) showers. Life was good! For two days, my only concern was that one of the sentries might accidentally shoot me, a notion that took root because one nearly did! After nightfall during my first evening at the fort, I was walking toward the stable to look in on Hamaca and Ima. Suddenly I heard a stern voice say: "Halt. Who goes there?"

For some reason, the universal challenge of the sentry didn't hit with much impact. To tell the truth, it seemed silly. I had been there most of the afternoon, and everyone knew who I was. Furthermore, there was enough illumination from overhead floodlights to make for easy recognition of such an identifiable specimen as myself. Since I didn't respond quickly enough, the next challenge was more dramatic.

"Halt, or be shot!"

The sentry had his rifle held at the ready and obviously meant business. *That* had impact! Immediately I stopped and stood in what I hoped was an unthreatening manner. Slowly, I explained who I was and why I was there.

"You may pass," I was told, without a request for proof.

I expected this ritual to end once I had made the sentry's acquaintance, but sentries were constantly rotated, and I never saw the same one twice. As a consequence, I was challenged in the early morning darkness and again after sundown every time I went to care for Hamaca and Ima. Each sentry insisted on going through the whole routine, by the book. It was aggravating, but they were just doing their jobs.

My horses were re-shod, compliments of another resident of the cavalry post who was just doing his job. The blacksmith performed his traditional service without charge. The frequent assistance of blacksmiths was necessary because horseshoes in Peru and Ecuador were made of iron, a far softer metal than the steel used in the States. By the time Hamaca and Ima arrived in Riobamba, all eight of their shoes were worn in half at the toe, and the same would soon happen to the new shoes they acquired there. From time to time, I thought about asking someone to send me steel horseshoes from the States. However, the uncertainty and expense stopped me. International packages to South America were unlikely to arrive and were subject to exorbitant duties and taxes if they did. Overall, it was preferable to put up with the iron shoes, especially since they were usually free. The only serious downside was that Hamaca's and Ima's hooves were becoming honeycombed with nail holes.

******

During my first day in the Riobamba fort, one of the officer's eyes lit up when he saw me. He was the coach of the post's basketball team, which I suspected even before he introduced himself. Having played basketball in high school and college, I was familiar with the way basketball coaches tended to react to my height.

As a young boy, I'd felt no calling to play basketball, but a series of coaches had hounded me until I gave it a try. I was terrible at first, but in high school, I improved to the point where I was named to the Northern Nevada all-star team. My high school teammates and I played for the state championship, falling short of that lofty goal by only three points. Six years later on another continent, it was proposed that I make a comeback. The post's basketball team shared first place in the Riobamba City League and that night would play the team with which it was tied. This particular opponent had brought in an outside player in order to defeat the cavalry in their last meeting, and thanks to me, the cavalry was looking forward to returning the favor.

Having scarcely touched a basketball in five years, I wasn't enthusiastic about putting my rusty talents on display, even less so in a significant game. However, the coach maneuvered me into a position from which I couldn't politely decline. With a sense of impending disaster, I reluctantly agreed to become an Andean ringer.

That afternoon, I had a long list of errands. The coach put a jeep and driver at my disposal to make sure I'd be back in time for an early dinner and some rest before the game. It was wonderful to dispatch my tasks so quickly, but this gesture's side effect was to increase my self-imposed obligation to play well in the big game.

"Don't you think it might be a good idea for us to practice together," I asked the coach.

"That won't be necessary," he answered casually.

"Maybe just for a little while?" I suggested.

"We play to enjoy ourselves," the coach said. "We never practice. That's too much like work."

"I haven't touched a basketball in years," I pleaded. "Is there someplace where *I* can practice?"

"You're taking this much too seriously," the coach assured me, with a wink and a pat on the back.

Shortly before the game, I got my first look at Riobamba's basketball court. It was not what I expected, beginning with the fact that it was outdoors. The playing surface was packed dirt, which had an unfamiliar feel, not to mention that the ball did things it wouldn't have done on a hardwood floor. The silver lining was that the court was smaller than regulation size, a welcome alteration in view of the altitude and my questionable wind.

On all four sides, the court was enclosed by a high adobe wall, limiting the space available for spectators. There was a single set of crude bleachers, adequate to hold only a fraction of those who had come. The remainder of the standing-room-only crowd was crammed into every available nook and cranny.

"It looks like basketball's a popular sport around here," I commented.

"Not this popular!" the coach said with a shrug. "This is the biggest crowd we've had in years. I think most of them came to see you!"

Oh, great! Just what I needed to get the butterflies out of my stomach!

After a short warm-up period, the game got under way, and it was only a few minutes before I changed strategies. I had started as always, by getting position close to the basket and using my height to maximum advantage. After a few easy baskets, I lost interest in that. With such an unfair size advantage, it made more sense to help my teammates do the scoring. Before long, I was doing what the coach had recommended, relaxing and enjoying myself. Even so, there was a wide margin in the final score, and that night I celebrated our win with the troopers from Riobamba's cavalry.

I believe I enjoyed the stopover in Riobamba far more than Hamaca and Ima did. Every time I went to see them, they came right up to me and followed wherever I went, even ignoring the feed I had set out, until after I left. Their actions gave the impression that they were hoping I'd saddle them so we could set out for some new and interesting destination. When we did move on, both mares seemed particularly ready. As for myself, I left the comforts of Riobamba with regret but refreshed and ready for the coming week's trek to Quito.

Hamaca and Ima were looking better than ever. In Riobamba, they had enjoyed peace and quiet for three nights in a roomy, properly bedded stall. They'd even been able to lie down, a rare luxury. Their accommodations were usually too small or too uncomfortable for that. Hamaca had long since given up trying, but Ima had persisted until one night when she stretched out in a very small corral and Hamaca accidentally stepped on her jaw, opening a nasty gash.

The previous week, Hamaca had carried two hundred and fifty pounds every inch of the two hundred miles from Cuenca to Riobamba, at altitudes that were 3,000 to 5,000 feet higher than the highest point on the Tevis Cup trail. If her brilliant performance was sustainable, I just might have an endurance race contender on my hands, especially when she was carrying a rider half my weight.

That day's travel took us as far as Mocha. All day, we had Chimborazo, a spectacular snow-covered volcano, in view. I was in such high spirits that I spent a good part of the day singing at the top of my lungs, ever-vigilant and ready to postpone my performance at the first sign of an audience.

An opportunity to do a good deed made the day memorable. While on a long, straight stretch of highway, I could see a bundle lying in the distant roadway. My attention was first attracted by the way vehicles were swerving to miss it. As I drew closer, I realized that the *bundle* was a man, apparently unconscious, in the middle of the road. Cars, trucks and buses zoomed by within inches of him. The potential for tragedy seemed to have no effect on the passing drivers, but I couldn't go on without doing something.

I stopped Hamaca, dismounted, waited for a lull in the traffic and walked out into the road. To my considerable relief, the man was breathing. I slowly rolled him on his back, taking care to avoid movements that might aggravate internal injuries if he had any. The instant he was on his back, my nose informed me of the reason for the man's predicament and why there was so little sympathy for him. He reeked of a variety of odors, the worst being urine and the sour breath caused by the over consumption of alcohol. The combined smells were literally nauseating.

The man's intoxication was so complete that he didn't stir when I took hold and slid him along the ground and out of harm's way. While thus occupied, I began to see how disgusting a man I was rescuing. He was filthy, and I had to fight a powerful revulsion that made me want to leave him where he lay. I could *feel* the germs crawling up my hands and arms, but I persisted long enough to slide him off the roadway and leave him in the shade of a large bush. The instant this was done, I took my canteen and a bar of soap and

225

thoroughly scrubbed my hands, over and over again.

It wasn't uncommon, especially in rural areas, to see men sleeping off a drunk wherever they had fallen. Though this particular case was the most dramatic, I'd seen many such situations. In the days that followed, the sad sight of unconscious men lying about became commonplace. Intoxication came to be my automatic assumption, exactly as it had been for the drivers steering their vehicles around the man I'd pulled from the roadway.

Later in the day, I passed two bloated mules lying dead at the side of the road. My automatic assumption in their case was that they had eaten one or another of the toxic plants about which I'd been warned.

"See there," I said to a puzzled Hamaca in my most-authoritative voice. "That's what will happen if you don't do what I tell you!"

Then I laughed. A simple statement of fact had come out sounding very much like a threat.

******

The next day, between Mocha and Ambato, we came to a place where the highway department had done some blasting and dislodged enough dirt and rock to block the road. Workmen who lacked any visible sense of urgency were clearing the debris. Thus I became part of an Andean traffic jam, a long-and-growing line of cars, trucks, buses and two black horses. The vehicles around us had no choice but to sit motionless for hours or turn back. On the other hand, Hamaca, Ima and I had other options, one to the left and one to the right. Going downhill, to the left, looked treacherous and might lead nowhere. If we went uphill, to our right, we'd get a view which would show the way around the blasting if there was one. I dismounted, having decided that the climb was more than a horse could do while carrying a rider.

The steep embankment had a deep covering of loose rock and dirt. The mares and I would take a step up and slide most of the way back to where we had started. Having repeated this until we were winded, we paused, our progress pitiful compared to the effort expended. After a short rest, we clawed our way higher, only to have gravity again steal all but a few feet of our progress. In gradual increments, we finally reached a narrow ridge that fell away for two or three feet on each side into piles of razor-sharp rocks.

From that vantage point, I could see a network of trails that seemed to lead back to the highway, beyond the blocked portion. En route, though, we would have to use a narrow, ledge-like trail that offered a nasty fall as the penalty for a misstep. I glanced again at the parking lot below and swung my eyes to the workmen who were clearing the road. Seeing their miniscule progress made the choice easy.

We made it back to the highway and continued on, passing a long line of stationary vehicles pointed in the opposite direction from those we'd left behind. We had saved many hours but paid a price. Both mares were scraped up. The only wound of any consequence was a slice in Ima's left rear fetlock, which swelled up when we stopped for lunch. Fortunately, the swelling subsided as soon as we were again on the move, a pattern that repeated itself for the next few days. The fetlock didn't seem to cause her pain except during the first few steps after standing a long time in one position.

In those early days of December, Ambato was awash in decorations, the first sign I had seen that Christmas was approaching. I hadn't given a moment's thought to the coming holidays, and it was an abrupt transition to be thrust into a full-blown, festive Christmas atmosphere. Windows in residential areas sported brightly lighted trees, decorated with beautiful, handmade ornaments. The nativity scenes, too, were handmade and each had its own distinctive flavor. The shops were full of merchandise, and shoppers were out in force. These manifestations of Christmas spirit were the first familiar sight I'd seen in a long while. Upon reflection, I decided that *some* of life's routines can be pleasant and comforting.

While window shopping that afternoon, I particularly admired an exquisite woodcarving depicting an old-fashioned, high-top shoe. On the tip of the toe, a mouse was perched next to a hole, which was obviously his handiwork. Made from hardwood, it was simple yet rich in character and obviously carved by a highly skilled craftsman. Some years later, on another trip to Ecuador, I bought a similar carving, and it remains among my favorite possessions. This first time I saw one, however, my finances permitted me only to admire it.

Later, I decided to take in a movie. The selection was limited to two, and I chose one, *Dr. Zhivago*, for no special reason. It was a fortunate choice. For over two hours I was transported into a totally absorbing world. I'm sure my reaction was based to some degree on my lonely circumstances, but there was much more than that. I fell in love with Laura and Tonya, identified with Zhivago's passion for writing and found the story enthralling. During the coming months – in those days before videotapes, videocassette recorders and movies on television – I would see a movie more than once for the first time in

227

my life, enjoying *Dr. Zhivago* immensely each of four times.

The next day, after a hard ride, I was on the outskirts of Latacunga when a four-wheel-drive pickup truck stopped next to me on the roadside. The driver, a man about my age, got out looking pleased to see me.

"There can't be much doubt that you're Mr. Albright!" he said in perfect American-accented English as he approached me.

It had been months since anyone had addressed me as other than "Pablito," and weeks since I'd heard even that nickname. Who in Latacunga, Ecuador, could possibly know my name and how? I knew no one within a thousand kilometers.

"Not much doubt at all," was my hesitant reply.

"I thought so," came the answer and a big smile. "My name is Gustavo Moncayo."

He extended his hand, and I dismounted to shake it.

"Are you an American?" I asked, not knowing what to say during a long silence.

"We Ecuadorians consider ourselves Americans," he said good-naturedly, "but not North Americans."

If I hadn't believed I was speaking to another *North American*, I wouldn't have phrased my question as I had, but I didn't get into that.

"How did you know my name?" I asked, unable to contain my curiosity.

"I'm a ham radio operator," he explained. "I've been keeping track of you since you left Chiclayo."

While I was in Lima, members of the *Asociación* had discussed the possibility of setting up a network of ham radio operators to follow my ride. Such a system, they had felt, would keep them advised of my progress, and in remote locations, would be the quickest method for getting help, should I urgently need it. This had been enthusiastically discussed for a couple of days and never mentioned again. I assumed that the idea had been abandoned.

"You're the first ham radio operator I've met since Lima," I told Gustavo.

"The first one you *knew* was a ham radio operator," Gustavo corrected. "To me, it's unbelievable that you've been in such remote areas without having set up emergency contacts with amateur radio operators. That would have been *my* top priority!"

This was said with all the conviction of a true believer, which makes me wonder how I could have been insensitive enough to say what I said next.

"I doubt there were ham radio operators in many of the places where I've been."

Gustavo's expression advised me that I had just contradicted one of life's greatest truths.

"You can be absolutely certain there were," he disagreed. "There are ham radio operators everywhere, and they can help you in more ways than you realize. Be my guest for the evening, and I'll show you."

Gustavo's *hacienda* was far off the highway, and he offered to find more-conveniently-located quarters for Hamaca and Ima. Then he drove ahead and arranged for stalls at a nearby *hacienda*. Once my mares were settled for the night, we left them and started a long drive on a very rough, dirt road. During the drive to his *hacienda*, it became evident that Gustavo was a man who enjoyed his "toys" and had plenty of them. His truck had every accessory the factory offered plus any number of other gadgets, installed after he'd taken delivery. Proudly, he pointed them out, demonstrating most but stopping short of the vehicle's portable shortwave radio.

"I have a little demonstration in mind," he said mysteriously, "but it's going to require the more powerful equipment I have at my *hacienda*."

After dinner that night, I was the guest of honor as Gustavo devoted several hours to his favorite hobby. He had enough radio equipment to fill the small room where it was kept. Having seen his truck, I wasn't surprised, but I was amazed at what a good shortwave radio could do. Effortlessly, Gustavo was able to contact radio operators throughout the United States, and it fascinated me to listen to him. He was intimately familiar with North American slang, including the variety peculiar to the "ham." In view of the very formal and dignified behavior that was typical of South American gentlemen, it made me smile to hear him telling people that his "handle" was "Gus."

After establishing contact, Gustavo would pass along a bit of information about my ride and hand me the mike. *That* part of the procedure wasn't particularly enjoyable. I was embarrassed by the attention and hardly interested in answering questions that weren't much different from the ones I answered all day, every day. Though it wasn't Gustavo's intention, the evening was soon providing more pleasure for him than me. Quickly sensing that I wasn't enjoying myself, Gustavo asked if I'd like to speak to some of my friends and family.

"I don't know anyone who has a shortwave radio." I responded.

"We can get around that little problem," Gustavo promised. "Give me names and the cities where they live."

I hadn't spoken with anyone from home since I'd left. International phone calls were very expensive in those days, and even a small number of them would have been budget busters.

"Who else?" Gustavo asked after writing down my mother's and father's names and the city and state where they lived.

I gave him more names, tantalized by the prospect of speaking with family and friends but holding my excitement in check, in case Gustavo was raising expectations he couldn't fulfill. After all, my parents had neither a shortwave radio nor access to one. The same was true of everyone else on my list.

Gustavo patiently searched the airwaves for *hams* located near the cities I had listed. Each time he found one, he briefly indulged in polite conversation and then asked if there was any chance of putting through a "phone patch" call. This required the party on the other end to connect his radio's speaker to the phone's mouth-piece, and the mike to the speaker in the phone's earpiece. As simply as that, a ham operator in the States could *patch* me into a phone call. If local, the call would cost nothing. Considering that this was also the cost of the transmission carried by the radio, it fit my budget beautifully!

With a persistence that was very much appreciated, Gustavo whittled away at my list. After many tries, he found a radio operator close enough to Joe and Pat Gavitt that the call was local, and he duplicated that feat so I was able to speak also with George Jones. For the call to my parents, he found someone close enough that the man kindly offered to pay the long distance charges. Thus, I was able to talk with the most important people in my life. It was an evening that would long be remembered for its pleasures ... and its disappointments.

My love of adventure was shared with no other person in my family, my mother least of all. She had been opposed to my journey and would have forbid it, if that had been within her power. This was partly because she felt South America was dangerous and partly because she couldn't see how an intercontinental horseback ride would help me get started with a career.

Throughout my journey, I had written regularly to my parents to assure them that I was alive and healthy and to inform them of developments along the way. However, I didn't provide as much detail as I did in my letters that were written at the same time to the Gavitts. Although concerned about my well-being, my parents weren't interested in horses or a blow-by-blow description of life in other countries. Most of the remaining details would only have alarmed them.

On the verge of talking to my parents for the first time in months, I was worried that our conversation might be strained, and, in fact, it was more formal than I would have preferred. My dad was out of town. Mom wished me a merry Christmas. She told me to be careful and to come home safely, and I promised to do my best. I doubt our conversation was any more satisfying for her than it was for me. There was so much to say, but we'd said nothing.

For me, the best part of the evening was Pat Gavitt's excitement over the prospect of riding Hamaca in the Tevis Cup. Her questions came one on top of the other, and she obviously feared I wouldn't get to Los Gatos in time. Joe seemed equally interested and took down the information he needed to make Hamaca's Tevis Cup entry before the deadline.

True to character, George Jones reminded me to keep my eyes open for anything that might have commercial possibilities in the States.

******

About six hundred miles west of Latacunga are Ecuador's Galápagos Islands, where Charles Darwin made what are probably his most famous observations. During his voyage on *H.M.S. Beagle*, Darwin also visited South America where he had the opportunity to observe horses schooled in the Spanish tradition. His following words show that he was duly impressed:

> "A horse is not considered perfectly broken till he can be brought up standing in the midst of his full speed on any particular spot, for instance on a cloak thrown on the ground, or until he will charge a wall, and rearing scrape the surface with his hoofs."

The next morning, Gustavo offered me a chance to see horses trained in much the same fashion as those that had so impressed Darwin. These were on a neighboring *hacienda*, and in his brand-new Ford Bronco, yet another of his toys, Gustavo drove me there. We arrived after some rather exciting cross-country driving and were treated to an impromptu exhibition of what are called "Spanish High School Horses." Designation as a *high school horse* comes from an animal's training. Over a period of years, the two horses I saw that morning had been taught to perform complicated maneuvers, including the discipline known as *dressage*. They and their riders had been trained by European dressage masters and had learned their lessons well. In our modern world, it's uncommon for that much time and training to be invested in a horse, and it was a rare treat to see the results.

Without a misstep, one or the other of the two riders performed each *haute école* [13] movement. The most spectacular was the *capriole*, a movement supposedly developed for warfare, in which the horse jumps straight upward with its forelegs drawn in, kicks out in a horizontal direction with its hindlegs and lands in exactly the same spot from which it took off. As a grand finale, both horses lined up side by side and did the *levade*, raising and drawing in their forelegs before standing balanced on crouching hindlegs.

Afterward, Gustavo took me back to where my mares had spent the night so I could begin my journey to Lasso. To my amazement, his hospitality didn't stop there. He had business in Lasso and promised to arrange the coming night's lodging for the mares and me.

On the drive back from Lasso, Gustavo stopped and gave me directions to the diary farm where he'd arranged for me to spend the night. During our brief roadside chat, he warned me that my greeting at his friend's farm might be a bit unconventional. It seemed that his friend was a bit troubled by my having come from Peru, where there were periodic outbreaks of hoof-and-mouth disease.

In cloven-hoofed animals, there is no known cure for this disease. Symptoms include the appearance of horrible sores in the mouth and between the segments of the hooves. This is followed by lameness and foaming at the mouth, and the end result is death by starvation when the afflicted animal stops eating. Hoof-and-mouth is easily transmitted and highly contagious. Horses and even leather products can carry the virus. The discovery of hoof-and-mouth disease in a single animal calls for the immediate destruction of all cloven-hoofed animals in the immediate vicinity. This is done even if no other animal shows symptoms and even though many are undoubtedly not yet infected. Any less-drastic measure almost always results in the spread of the disease.

That afternoon – true to Gustavo's word – my host and several of his employees met me outside the entrance to his dairy farm. They were armed with buckets of liquid, brushes and very serious expressions. The liquid smelled as if it might have been a very strong vinegar solution, and it was, I was crisply told, effective against the germ that causes hoof-and-mouth disease. After being carefully inspected for sores in their mouths, Hamaca and Ima were subjected to a thorough dousing, scrubbing, re-dousing and re-scrubbing. Next, the saddles, bridle and all other leather tack were submerged in a large drum, filled with the same liquid. As a final precaution, I was asked to deliver my personal leather items for a similar dipping. I responded by handing over my boots and recently purchased belt.

"Is your wallet made of leather?" my host asked.

"Yes," I conceded, "it is."

"We need to dip it also," I was told.

"Will it be all right if I remove the photos and currency?" I asked, as a joke.

"Yes, I suppose so," was the answer, after careful consideration.

All in all, these precautions were the most drastic I'd see until my horses entered quarantine in the United States. Such extraordinary thoroughness was unusual in Latin America, and I was willing to wager that my host was an ex-Prussian army officer. I would soon find that his social skills implied the same. Gustavo's friend was never impolite, not for a second, nor was he polite even once. I passed an extremely uncomfortable evening, constantly sensing his lack of enthusiasm for my visit. Of course, he said nothing to that effect, but volumes can be spoken without words.

My host made not a single inquiry about my travels (not as welcome a relief as I would have expected, considering how weary I was of questions!), and when an employee did so, he immediately sent the man on an errand to another part of the farm. His attitude seemed to be that his employee's questions – as well as my ride – were frivolous. Including those whose hospitality had been bought rather than given freely, I hadn't met another Latin American as lacking in sociability.

An unpleasant night was followed by a miserable day. En route to Machachi, the mares and I had to cross another high, cold *páramo*. I seldom suffer from low temperatures, being kept comfortable in cold weather by the same metabolism that caused me such distress in Peru's deserts. As long as I keep moving, I'm usually comfortable all the way down to freezing and slightly below. On that day, however, owing to wind and humidity, I walked a good distance, wore several layers of cold-weather attire and never for an instant felt warm enough.

That afternoon, I passed within nine miles of Ecuador's most famous sight, Cotopaxi, which at 19,360 feet is the world's highest active volcano. Clouds covered it, completely obliterating a sight that many had told me was fantastic. Near Cotopaxi, I saw huge receiving dishes and later, a sign announcing that these belonged to a NASA satellite-tracking station, located a half-mile off the highway. I considered turning in, having a look around and chatting with my countrymen there, but by that time, I was too cold. My number-one priority was to get off that cold, windy *páramo*.

In that area, the highway was paved. It was one of the few times since I had entered Ecuador that the *Panamericana's* surface was other than dirt or gravel, and I soon saw why. Traffic abruptly became much heavier. Curious motorists slowed their cars and drove past with their windows down, asking questions. In the howling wind, it required considerable effort to understand what was being said, let alone answer before the cars were out of hearing range.

While thus occupied, I noticed a gray Mercedes Benz coming from the opposite direction, slowing down and drifting toward the side of the road. When it stopped and I saw someone preparing to get out, I winced. A conversation at that moment represented time lost before I'd be able to warm up. A moment later, I completely forgot I was cold!

The passenger got out, and I recognized him immediately, even though we had never met. I had so often heard this man discussed in Peru that I felt I already knew him. His name was Luis de Ascasubi, and on the threshold of meeting him, I suddenly turned nervous. Without thinking, I dismounted in order to avoid showing disrespect by approaching him on horseback. *Don* Luis was among the world's foremost experts on Peruvian *Paso* horses. On that subject, he had written the most comprehensive book of its time, offering, among other things, the first scientific description of the gaits that made the breed famous.

Standing before me, he was every bit as impressive as his reputation. With his neatly trimmed, snow-white beard, subdued speech and manner, distinguished accent (he spoke English fluently), and the well-tailored look of a British nobleman, he had the unmistakable aura of someone who was important. I felt as if I stood in the presence of European royalty.

There are many stories about *Señor* Ascasubi. My favorite involves a Peruvian *Paso* breeder from Lima. While visiting Quito, this particular breeder decided to visit *don* Luis, a simple-sounding task complicated by a large problem. The Peruvian had neither *don* Luis' phone number nor his address and could find no listing in the telephone directory. On the odd chance that he might get lucky, the Peruvian flagged down a taxicab and asked the driver if he knew where to find Luis de Ascasubi. At the time, Quito had well over a half-million inhabitants and as Ecuador's capital, was home to many of the country's best-known citizens. Nonetheless, the taxi driver grew suddenly enthusiastic.

"Ah, *don* Luis de Ascasubi," he said, excitedly, "the last of the true gentlemen!"

To my considerable surprise, *don* Luis had long been aware of my ride. Being keenly interested in long journeys on horseback, he'd been looking forward to my arrival in Quito. The evening before, Gustavo had informed a mutual friend, by ham radio, that I was between Lasso and Machachi. When word was relayed to *don* Luis, he decided not to wait until the mares and I arrived in Quito the following day.

After introducing himself, he turned his attention to Hamaca and Ima, walking around them slowly, studying them with his eyes and touching them with his hands.

"Incredible," he kept saying. "It's really incredible. These horses are in excellent condition. If I hadn't seen it, I wouldn't believe it!"

Anyone who would succeed must remember that success is measured by deeds and not by other people's opinions. Nevertheless, this particular assessment was hugely satisfying. I knew from his writings that Luis de Ascasubi's approval was not given often or lightly.

---

13 The French term for the equine discipline known as "high school."

Hamaca and Ima shared their corral in Oña with a collection of farm animals (see page 178).

Guillermo poses with Hamaca and Ima near Cañar (see page 199).

The hospitality of the *Cazadores de los Ríos* was second to none (see page 187).

236

Entering Riobamba, the road was lined with trees and *maguey* plants (see page 221).

Sheep at the *Hacienda* Zuzudel patiently wait and hope for morsels of hay after Hamaca finishes her dinner (see page 180).

All day, we had Chimborazo, a snow covered volcano, in view (see page 225).

237

CHAPTER 24

Sure Shot and Friends

A half-hour after his arrival, *don* Luis de Ascasubi was still standing alongside the road, talking with me and shaking his head in disbelief. I was in no hurry for the moment to end, but, of course, it did.

"I'll meet you on the road tomorrow at the entrance to Quito," he promised.

With that, *don* Luis drove off. I had enjoyed his company tremendously and was anticipating the opportunity to spend more time with him. As it turned out, I didn't have to wait long. Less than three hours after his gray Mercedes departed for Quito, it returned to find me closing in on the last few miles of the day. This time, two men emerged. Upon arriving in Quito, *don* Luis, full of enthusiasm, had gone to visit a friend. While singing the praises of Hamaca and Ima, he became so enthused that he insisted his friend accompany him all the way back to Machachi in order to see the mares for himself.

"Just look at them!" *don* Luis exclaimed, "One would never guess these horses just came through the Andes, all the way from the border, not to mention several hundred kilometers in Peru!"

The two gave my horses a thorough looking over, examining their legs and hooves carefully and making positive comments about their weight, general health and muscle tone. For me, the whole scenario was like a dream. Standing before me was one of the most respected men in the Peruvian breed, and he was in a state of euphoria over something *I* was doing. Never had I felt such gratifying approval. It would have been only slightly more satisfying if I'd had an equally glowing evaluation from Amie Tschiffely himself!

For some time, Luis de Ascasubi had loomed large in my mind. It had been a defining moment for me when I first read his book. Prior to that, I'd read everything I could find on the Peruvian breed, but there was precious little. Now and then I found a brief article, and in desperation, I once fought my way through one breeder's college thesis on the subject. The problem was that everything I found had been written for people already familiar with the breed.

For centuries, ownership of Peruvian *Paso*s had been confined to a small group, never large enough to warrant the publication of books and articles. Knowledge passed by word of mouth from one generation to the next. Several Peruvian breeders had offered to help me in that same fashion, but living in the United States, I was too far away to benefit from their good intentions. My need for information was finally satisfied by a hot-off-the-press copy of Luis de Ascasubi's book, *El Caballo de Paso y Su Equitación*. In his book, Ascasubi achieved an extraordinary clarity through the brilliant use of analogies that were informative to the connoisseur yet understandable to the newcomer. I enjoyed his excellent writing so much that I read another of his books. The subject was bullfighting, a sport that didn't interest me, but the book provided another glimpse inside the exceptional mind of its author.

Later that afternoon, after *don* Luis had again left, a Ford Bronco passed and stopped ahead of me on the shoulder of the road. It was Gustavo Moncayo, bound for Quito on business. He stopped and handed me a sack lunch his wife had prepared. Before saying good-bye, he also gave me directions to an *hacienda* near Machachi, which belonged to another of his friends.

"Don't worry! You'll be welcomed more graciously than you were last night," he said with a smile, after hearing of my experiences the previous night.

I found my destination with no difficulty, and just as I turned off the roadway and started through a gate, I was met by four ranch hands. They carried buckets brimming with a familiar, vinegary-smelling liquid. This particular solution smelled much stronger than the one used the night before, but my worries were dispelled when I was told it would be applied to the mares' hooves only. With the assistance of large scrub brushes, the men set about their task. Quickly, the familiar routine moved to where the men dipped my tack and personal leather items, though they didn't go so far as to request my wallet. Apparently ranchers near Quito shared an acute fear of hoof-and-mouth disease. In view of that, it was a testimonial to their outstanding hospitality that any of them allowed my horses to stay at their farms.

After the mares were comfortably settled, my host drove me to Quito for an evening tour. I liked Ecuador's capital from the very first instant. It was full of atmosphere, extraordinarily beautiful and destined to be my favorite of all the cities I would visit during my journey. A thing of beauty in and of itself, the city was ringed by mountains, and on a clear day, at least three snow-capped volcanoes enhanced the view. Almost anyone from anywhere in the world would have appreciated Quito, but my approval was magnified by my having been away from such a sophisticated level of civilization for a long time.

239

The drive through town was thoroughly enjoyable, with the notable exception of one incident. My host's automobile was stopped at a traffic light next to a plaza when it was engulfed by an unruly mob of demonstrators. Social protest was a popular activity in the mid-1960's, and apparently, this was as true in Quito as elsewhere. Hundreds of demonstrators filled the plaza and clogged the surrounding streets, bringing traffic to a standstill. These protesters were fired with enough emotion to be dangerous. The more insolent leaned against cars, and the most brazen sat on hoods and trunks. Thus trapped, the occupants of cars sat quietly in their vehicles, windows rolled up and doors locked. Not a single driver touched his horn or did anything provocative. It was an ideal time for practicing self-restraint!

Despite the signs carried by the demonstrators, there was nothing to reveal what was going on, at least not to someone who didn't already have a pretty good idea. As time passed and the threat of violence diminished, I relaxed enough to ask what was being protested, fervently hoping it wasn't *North American imperialism*! My host flew into a rage and answered at a volume that was anything but discreet. Agitated, he went on at length with a description of his country's problems, jumping from subject to subject until I was lost. There was little doubt that he could be heard outside the vehicle, and not wanting to add fuel to the fire, I sat quietly and didn't respond to his words.

When the demonstrators had dispersed and we were moving again, my host grew even more agitated.

"You are courageous, my friend," he marveled, "tackling such a journey alone ... and on horseback!"

"Most people have been very kind," I answered, hoping to sidetrack a discussion I'd already had too many times.

"I'm not sure you fully understand," he took his eyes off the road to stare hard at me.

"If you mean bandits..." I began.

"Actually," my host interrupted, "I was speaking of the current political climate. Serious violence could erupt at any moment. I'm absolutely convinced of that, to the point that I keep a submachine gun in my bedroom for protection. You must be very careful and draw as little attention as you can. *Norteamericanos* aren't necessarily welcome in this country right now!"

Later that evening, my host took me back to his *hacienda* in Machachi, and before drifting off to sleep, I thought about his warning. Having already traveled a considerable distance in Ecuador, I felt that he was exaggerating the perils, but I also knew from first-hand experience that there *was* danger. More unsettling still, the next nation in my path was a death trap for its own citizens, to say nothing of a passing *gringo!*

Just beyond Ecuador's northern border was Colombia. Those were the days before that country's all-powerful drug lords had come to the fore, but the climate for large-scale defiance of the law was already well established. As I approached her southern border, Colombia had been subjected to a reign of terror (known as *La Violencia*) perpetrated by murderous gangs for two bloody decades. This *violencia* had begun as a guerrilla war between Liberals and Conservatives. Tragically, the sustained lawlessness encouraged the formation of large, well-organized bandit gangs. Since World War II, these murderous gangs had slaughtered tens of thousands.

Often espousing communist ideals and sustaining a facade as political guerrillas, the bandit leaders were well known on Colombia's national stage. Publicity conscious, most had nicknames – such as "Revenge" and "Sure Shot" – which might have seemed comical to someone not contemplating a horseback trip through their lairs. Boastful and colorful nicknames aside, however, these men were to be taken very seriously. They had even been known to attack military posts in retaliation for campaigns against them.

According to an article in *Time* magazine, *La Violencia*, since 1948, had been responsible for almost a quarter-million deaths. That number equals the losses suffered by the U.S. military during all of World War II! Another measure of *La Violencia's* scope was the claim that, during some years, the bandits' ill-gotten gains actually exceeded the budget of Colombia's national government. The situation had improved in the years immediately preceding my ride, prompting me to hope I might be able to ride safely through at least part of Colombia. Exactly how, where and if this might be done was difficult to decide, especially based on the sparse and unreliable information available.

Even if I decided to chance it and ride across Colombia, there was the question of how to proceed once I got near Panama, where the Pan-American Highway would simply end. Between that point and the place where the highway began anew lay one of the world's most infamous obstacles to travel, an impenetrable jungle known as the Darien Gap. [14] By the time of my ride, there was a long list of adventurers, going back to early Spanish explorers, who had tried to cross it and failed. Even as determined a traveler as Aime Tschiffely never seriously considered attempting the Darien, opting instead to load Mancha and Gato onto an ocean-going freighter and bypass it. [15]

Taking inventory: Ecuador was potentially hazardous, the first crossing of the Darien Gap wasn't likely to be made by a man with two desert-bred horses and up-to-date information confirmed that Colombia was still one of the most dangerous places on earth. These factors prompted me to make a sudden and dramatic adjustment in my intended route. With one single bold move, I would sidestep the Darien Gap and avoid Colombia, altogether. Though I was perfectly willing to continue on horseback as far as the Colombian border, that would have put me in a location from which I couldn't execute my new plan.

I had always planned to go around the Darien by ocean-going freighter, as Tschiffely had done, but I had another option, one that hadn't been available to him. That night in Machachi, I began, for the first time, to seriously consider the idea of flying the mares from Quito to Panama City. An airplane would be the fastest way to get back to covering ground on horseback and would regain some of the time I had lost. The big problem would be the cost. It was a given in those days that shipping by air was more expensive than shipping by sea. On the other hand, going by freighter would involve secondary expenses – such as getting to the coast – which might bring the final total even higher than airfreight.

Within reason, the higher cost of airfreight could be justified by another consideration, the well-being of my horses. During an importation from Peru, I'd already had experience transporting horses by freighter, and those particular horses didn't completely recovered for months. Aboard ship, horses must be confined to shipping crates, where they can't move or get relief from bracing themselves against the ship's rolling motion. Furthermore, they normally lose their appetites while at sea.

Clearly, an airplane was the best choice, if I could afford it. To reach a final decision, I needed to do some comparison shopping. Unable to do that until I reached Quito, I had gone as far as I could that night in Machachi. The time had come to sleep, but I couldn't. I was feeling guilty … or perhaps inferior!

Intellectually, I knew I shouldn't measure my accomplishments by what Tschiffely had done. Even if I had ridden every step of the way from Chiclayo to Los Gatos, my journey would have amounted to only half of his, and my goal had always been even more modest than that. But suddenly I was preparing to do even less.

From the beginning, I'd known that time constraints would require my horses and I to travel farther in vehicles than under our own power. So far, though, I'd come all the way from Chiclayo on horseback. The only exception had been those few miles near La Toma, where I accepted a ride in a truck to get off a roadway made dangerous by repair work. If I boarded an airplane, my perfect record would be gone. The prospect of flying to Panama felt like the first scratch on a shiny, new car.

I'm sure Hamaca and Ima had no such thoughts that night. They had their own problems, caused by being corralled in a spacious bullfight arena, normally used by our host for testing his fighting bulls. The arena was over a hundred and fifty feet in diameter and surrounded by a high, thick, circular adobe wall. Both mares were uneasy there, especially when unidentified sounds originated unseen beyond that wall. They also seemed unsure of how to behave in a place that offered so much room.

Hamaca and Ima would habitually select – by what criteria I do not know – a particular spot in each *corral* big enough to offer a choice. It took them a while to choose this place, but once selected, it was where they spent their time, as if they were safer there. When their feed was elsewhere, it didn't alter this behavior. They might completely ignore what I provided for them in favor of scraps or growing grasses found where they were, or they might just stand and gaze longingly, from a distance, at their hay. At best, they would walk over, take a mouthful and walk back to where they felt safe before chewing.

Whenever I put them in new quarters, I did my best to guess the location Hamaca and Ima were going to prefer, but I never got very good at it. Usually, when I returned after my dinner, I'd find that the mares had scarcely touched their feed. More than once, I was strongly tempted to leave the feed where it was until hunger drove them to it, but invariably I gave in and moved it, knowing they'd begin eating the instant I did so.

That evening in Machachi, my persnickety mares had a huge area from which to choose, and I moved the feed three times before they were satisfied. In the middle of the night, I was awakened by the sound of rain drumming on the roof. I went out to the arena and – just as I had thought – found the mares comfortably sheltered against the wall in a spot where it protected them from the wind-driven rain. Their feed was across the arena, out in the open.

Hamaca and Ima greeted me with hungry nickers, and I moved their feed for the fourth time. When I got back to the house, my host was standing at the door in his nightshirt. He couldn't imagine why I'd gone out in the middle of such a miserable night. After listening to my explanation, he shook his head and smiled broadly.

"You're a good 'daddy' to your two 'daughters'," he commented, patting me on the back.

How true, if I do say so myself!

14 While the Darien Gap has narrowed since my ride, the Pan-American Highway (at the time of this writing, 1999) still hasn't been completed in that region, further confirming the difficulties involved.

15 Tschiffely twice embarked his horses, first around the Darien, to avoid the jungle, and later around Nicaragua, to avoid a violent revolution.

The intrepid six came in hot pursuit (see page 206).

CHAPTER 25

Where Hemispheres Meet

The next day I staged a private horse race, pitting Hamaca and Ima against the clock. With at least a weeks' rest scheduled in Quito, it seemed the perfect time to see how they handled a vigorous workout. We ended up covering thirty miles in four hours, at altitudes ranging from 8,500 to 11,500 feet. I was well pleased, especially since nine of those miles were traveled on city streets, in traffic.

At the entrance to Quito we were met, as promised, by *don* Luis de Ascasubi and – an unexpected but pleasant surprise – Gustavo Moncayo.

"*Don* Luis has arranged for your horses to stay at the best horse facility in Quito," Gustavo informed me after the three of us had greeted one another.

"There might be one or two others that are better," *don* Luis corrected, with his usual passion for precision, "but you should find it satisfactory."

That said, the two men bracketed the mares and me between their vehicles, with *don* Luis leading and Gustavo following. Our motorized escort took us directly to the large, elegant, brick-walled *Colegio Militar Eloy Alfaro*, Ecuador's West Point. To my delight, Hamaca and Ima arrived in wonderful condition. Several hours at a brisk pace had only invigorated them.

Don Luis had arranged for the mares to stay – at an extremely reasonable price – in the academy's stable with the cavalry horses. While a couple of troopers and I prepared the stalls, we were entertained by snippets from a good-natured debate between Gustavo and *Señor* Ascasubi. Gustavo started it.

"You always say that my shortwave radios are no more than toys," he said, "but without them, we might not have met up with Verne."

"It wasn't the radio that was driving on the road the night you saw him," Ascasubi countered. "It was you. What did the radio have to do with it?"

"The radio kept me advised as to where he was," Gustavo offered.

"I knew that because of letters from friends in Lima, and a stamp – don't forget – costs a fair bit less than those fancy radios of yours."

Back and forth they went, Gustavo bidding for at least a small concession and Ascasubi doggedly refusing to grant it.

Once the mares were comfortable, *don* Luis apologized for

245

conditions that made it impossible for him to host me in his home. Gustavo advised that he had arranged for me to stay with a Hungarian friend of his, a man everyone called *Señor* Negro because of his unpronounceable first name. After I was delivered to the Negro home, I got myself cleaned up and went into town to see if I could find affordable air transportation. My afternoon started out well. The cost of flying Hamaca and Ima to Panama was well within my budget. The bad news was that both Ecuador and Panama, it turned out, suffered from Latin America's instinctive need to wrap everything in paperwork and tie it with red tape. To quote the airline freight agent: "Both countries have a few requirements for horses that travel by air." Basically, each mare would need a certificate from the Ecuadorian Ministry of Agriculture in order to leave Ecuador and another from the Panamanian Consul in order to enter Panama.

It sounded simple, and that's what worried me. In Latin America, simple-sounding tasks are invariably otherwise. On top of that, the holiday season would slow the normal snail's pace of Latin American officialdom. With such low expectations, I didn't figure to be disappointed. However, if I had known what I faced, I might have been tempted to tackle Colombia's bandits and the Darien Gap instead.

It required four twelve-hour days filled with endless paperwork to get the exit papers from Ecuador's Ministry of Agriculture. The instant they were issued, I took them to the Panamanian Consul, as instructed. When I presented them, the consul looked at me with undisguised disdain.

"I can't accept this document!" he said, as if I was trying to put something over on him.

"Why not?" I asked.

"How do I know the signature is genuine?" he answered my question with one of his own.

"How do you know any signature is genuine?" I made it three questions in a row, then four. "Isn't it enough that the document has all the official seals and stamps from the Ministry of Agriculture?"

"But how do I know the signature is genuine?"

I found myself wondering if the record for consecutive questions in a dialogue was within our reach.

"What must I do to make the signature acceptable?" I asked.

"You'll have to go to Ecuador's Department of Exterior Relations and have them authenticate it," he demanded.

When I arrived at the Department of Exterior Relations, I was informed that they couldn't authenticate the signature.

"We have no way to be sure this is genuine!" the clerk huffed as if I was a fool not to have realized that. "The signer is a veterinarian at the Ministry of Agriculture. First, the Vice-Minister of Agriculture will have to authenticate the veterinarian's signature. Then we can authenticate the Vice-Minister's signature."

The potential for a hilarious Abbott and Costello routine was obvious, but I wasn't laughing. For the third time that day, I spent money on a taxicab in search of a solution to a stupid problem.

"The Vice-Minister of Agriculture doesn't authenticate the signatures of our veterinarians," I was next told. "His lawyer does that, and then the Vice-Minister can authenticate the lawyer's signature."

And the lawyer will want a fee for his services, as well as the Vice-Minister for his, I thought. *Then there will be a third fee to have the Department of Exterior Relations authenticate the Vice-minister's signature and a fourth fee to have the Consul of Panama authenticate the whole damned mess. And scientists still say no one has ever perfected a perpetual-motion machine!*

Years before – on my jeep trip – I had arrived at the Argentine border station to find a most interesting sign on a wall. It simply said: "*Energía y Corrección,*" which best translates as: "Energy and Accuracy." The man in line ahead of me was a German, apparently traveling South America's back country on a limited budget and for a long while. He read the sign aloud in a booming voice and added his own spontaneous comment: "At last!" I laughed so hard that the Argentine immigration official felt it necessary to subject me to some extra-rigorous questioning before he admitted me. Since then, I habitually visualize appropriate signs for government offices, not just in Latin America … though I reserve my ultimate creativity for that fertile environment. My creation for Quito's Ministry of Agriculture was: "Two Problems for Every Solution!" I had walked in looking for a solution and left with two new problems. The first: what demands would the lawyer make before he consented to authenticate the veterinarian's signature (perhaps this was where the vet's mother would come into the picture?)? The second: where was the lawyer's office? No one had been able to provide directions. If I thought the lawyer's office might be nearby, I had another think coming. All three *authenticators* were located at different extremities of Quito. In my dark mood, I became convinced it was a plot to keep taxicabs in business.

When I arrived at the lawyer's office, I was told I'd have to wait two weeks for one of his assistants – the one in charge of authenticating signatures – to return from Christmas vacation. With consummate skill, I alternated back and forth between my most winning ways and my finest righteous indignation. As a result, alternatives suddenly appeared, and the veterinarian's signature was verified in the astonishing time of only two days.

Theoretically, the task had been reduced to simply retracing my steps. As is the case with most things in life, this was more easily said than done. Everywhere I went, the only person who could help me was out of the office. Trying to save time – and cab fare – by phoning ahead was impossible since Quito's telephone system was out of order most of the time, and government offices didn't answer their phones, anyhow. When I finally presented the papers and signature authentications to the Panamanian Consul, he calmly dropped his next bomb.

"Even if I issue a permit for your horses to enter Panama," he said matter-of-factly, "they could still be quarantined as long as forty days if you arrive without the prior permission of the Panamanian Ministry of Agriculture."

"And how do I get that?" I asked, cringing.

Half an hour later, I rushed off an emergency cable to Panama, requesting "prior permission," exactly as the Consul had instructed. Ten days and two follow-up cables later, I still had no response. The three cables had cost more than I normally spent in a week.

If I ran into similar delays at each of the eight borders ahead, paperwork alone would add three months to my journey. Conceivably, I could arrive too late for the Tevis Cup even if I didn't cover another inch on horseback!

I also discovered that Ecuador had its own version of the dreaded *Peruvian Factor*. This became self-evident when I set out to get Hamaca and Ima inoculated against tetanus. Since Piura, my repeated attempts to accomplish that simple feat had been foiled because tetanus vaccine was unavailable. While we were in the Andes, this hadn't seemed crucial because there was little possibility of tetanus in that climate. However, the danger would be acute in Panama, meaning that tetanus shots had finally risen to the top of my *Things To Do* list.

Even in as large a city as Quito, an entire morning of searching produced no tetanus vaccine for horses. The alternative was to use the vaccine intended for people. Since a horse needed many times the human dosage, this was painfully expensive and required me to scour nearly all of Quito's pharmacies. None carried more than a few doses, which was understandable in a place where tetanus was-n't a problem. Finally, vaccine in hand, I hired a veterinarian to administer it. He did a satisfactory job of injecting Ima, but when Hamaca's turn came, he attached the needle incorrectly to the syringe. When the vaccine began to leak, he blithely continued pushing the plunger until he had squirted all of it on the outside of Hamaca's neck.

"Don't worry," he said, rubbing the site of the attempted injec-tion with an alcohol-soaked cotton puff. "I'm sure I got enough in her to do the job. She should be immune."

His attitude was typical of most easy-going South Americans ("If at first you don't succeed, the hell with it!"), but I was neither easy-going nor South American. I wanted to be sure. After many more hours – and dollars – I collected enough vaccine for a second try, during which another vet managed to put the precious liquid *inside* Hamaca's neck.

With sensational weather bathing the area in warmth, it was the perfect time to enjoy Ecuador's splendid capital. Having gone from too hot (in the desert) to too cold (in the Andes), I was delighted with what people in the States would have called "Indian summer," a late burst of warm weather during a season that otherwise resem-bled fall. Quito is located about fifty miles south of the equator, where the earth's northern and southern hemispheres meet. Typically, the equator (after which Ecuador was named) is known for very hot temperatures, but Quito's location at 9,350 feet moderates the climate. Outside of certain brief seasons, such as the one in progress, Ecuador's capital has cooler weather than one might expect.

During my first week and a half in Quito, every second of every day was filled. Each night I'd fall into an exhausted sleep, dreaming of enough leisure time to stop and smell the roses. Once things slowed down, though, I gained insight into what it must be like to look forward to retirement and then have nothing with which to fill one's days. Quickly, the inactivity became as heavy a burden as the overload that preceded it. I was starved for company, and the fact that it was nearly Christmas didn't help. Ironically, however, I did everything I could to avoid people.

"Hey, Giraffe," someone would inevitably shout whenever I went out in public.

My contribution to Quito's Christmas spirit was to be the ideal butt for jokes. It seemed that almost everyone enjoyed making rude comments about my height, and many followed me for blocks in order to indulge their creativity. The few who restrained themselves did so only to improve their chances when they approached me to beg for money. Surrounded by people wherever I went, I was conclusive proof that unwelcome company is no antidote for loneliness. Repeatedly, I was reminded of a little couplet written by actress Diane Varsi:

"Go away and don't bother me.
Can't you see I'm lonely?"

Varsi was a successful actress – tired of invasions of her privacy – who abruptly stopped making movies and left Hollywood in the midst of a promising and profitable career. This unusual act briefly attracted an even greater abundance of the scrutiny she sought to escape. More than one gossip columnist indulged in amateur psychology, quoting Miss Varsi's little verse to prove she wasn't thinking clearly. Why else would anyone voluntarily trade the magical world of Hollywood for a "life of obscurity"?

I agreed with the gossip columnists in one respect. Diane Varsi's couplet did explain why she left Hollywood, but not because it was nonsense. There have been many times when it made perfect sense to me, and December of 1966 was one of them.

Of course, some people's company was welcome, and one of them was Gustavo Moncayo. Just before Christmas, he came to Quito and remained for several days. During his stay, he found time to visit me every day. I still remember those visits as extremely pleasant, though I can't recall much of what we did or talked about. Friends find pleasure in simple activities, and we were becoming good friends.

One memorable afternoon, we dropped in on one of Gustavo's friends, a man who procured exotic animals for zoos and pet stores. The man specialized in boa constrictors and anacondas. Proudly, he told us that he had a particularly good inventory on hand, in cages located inside the garage.

"Would you like to see them?" he asked.

My answer was affirmative and enthusiastic.

"I'll wait out here," Gustavo said without further explanation.

Maybe his words were intended as a warning. I'll never know, but I do know that when I entered the garage, I was nearly overcome by the same smell that my host didn't seem to notice. Almost immediately I thanked Gustavo's friend for the opportunity to see his snakes and insisted that I felt guilty taking so much of his time. He graciously assured me that he had all the time in the world and that it would be his pleasure to show me every single one of his snakes. It was clear I couldn't avoid offending a very nice man without taking the complete tour, and I wasted no time before getting started. Scarcely breathing, I moved quickly from crate to crate, asking only enough questions to satisfy a minimum standard of politeness. Mercifully, my sense of smell soon tuned out the worst of the odors. At that point, I slowed down enough to notice that the snakes, though big, were not as large as I had expected. I asked if they were smaller than the average.

"Not at all," I was told. "These aren't anywhere near the world records, but they're good-sized. Were you expecting them to be larger?"

"I've heard they sometimes kill animals as large as a pig or crocodile, and that gave me the impression of something a bit larger," I said, making allowances for the man's pride.

My host looked disappointed.

"They must be wonderfully efficient," I added.

Gustavo's friend opened a cage and grabbed the occupant behind the head.

"Pick him up," he instructed. "Don't worry. The only way he can hurt you is to bite, and I won't let him."

I was amazed at how hard it was to remove the uncooperative serpent from his (or her?) cage. Extremely solid and heavy, the snake had a way of making itself difficult to lift. After a considerable struggle, I finally hoisted the reptile clear of its cage, and it began to flex its powerful muscles. The portions I held in my grasp swelled and turned rock hard. My hands were forced open no matter how hard I squeezed. Groaning with the effort, I returned the snake to its cage, having come very close to dropping it. It was easy to imagine the fate of any small animal that found itself in the grip of such a powerful reptile. My host had made his point. The snakes were every bit as big as they needed to be!

Providing me with another interesting day was a visit to Luis de Ascasubi's lovely *Hacienda* Guachalá. *Don* Luis picked me up in the early morning and drove me there, giving me my first ride in a Mercedes Benz. In those days, the Mercedes was uncommon in the States and aside from the Rolls Royce, had no competitor for the title of finest automobile on earth. It was a long-anticipated thrill to finally ride in one. Because we traveled on a cobblestone highway, I

251

couldn't fully appreciate the fabled Mercedes' ride. I had no idea how a lesser automobile might have sounded and ridden under the circumstances, but the Mercedes didn't strike me as anything special. I felt terribly let down. It was a precursor to the rest of my day.

Guachalá straddled the equator north of Quito. It was a truly magnificent place, complete with fighting bulls, finely bred horses, an elegant house, superb gardens and a man-made lake stocked with bass. On those beautiful grounds, *don* Luis envisioned the eventual construction of a luxury resort where guests would sleep in the northern hemisphere and breakfast in the southern.

There were many breeds among the horses in Guachalá's stable. These included so-called *Peruvians*, generations removed from imported stock and showing unmistakable signs of outside blood. *Don* Luis pointed out ways in which he believed them superior to the animals being produced in Peru. I thought the opposite. Ascasubi's *Peruvians* were fine, as far as they went, but they didn't go far. My disappointment, which I feared he could sense, was based on what I didn't see more than what I saw. They were nothing special, lacking the exquisite touches that make Peruvian *Paso*s unique. There was no flair, nothing to fascinate the eyes and mind.

On the drive back to Quito, *don* Luis became similarly disappointed in me. It was *the* defining moment in our relationship. He would never again show the interest and warmth he had shown up to that point. The change came after our conversation revealed something I thought he already knew: that I had led Hamaca and Ima a good portion of the way to Quito. I hadn't tried to hide that, nor do I think he believed I had. He seemed to consider that leading the mares, in and of itself, had been a form of dishonesty. At first I tried to make him understand my reasons, but he refused to acknowledge their validity. I soon stopped the justifications, too proud to beg for his approval. There was a hollow feeling inside me. Never had anyone – even my own father – withdrawn approval with more devastating effect. It was difficult to accept that this had happened because of an action that I felt should have reflected credit on me.

Don Luis remained cordial and correct, but never again did he show any sign of emotional investment in my project. I saw him only seldom during the rest of my stay in Ecuador. [16] The loss of *don* Luis' frequent company was softened by the sterling hospitality of my host, *Señor* Negro, and his wife. Received in their home with the utmost in warmth and kindness, I greatly appreciated being part of their household. As Christmas drew near, their preparations gave me a sense of participation in something that otherwise seemed to be passing me by.

Early on several mornings, while most of Quito slept, my Hungarian host and I had driven to the country club for a brisk gallop on two of his polo ponies. That may seem a strange activity for someone taking a vacation from an intercontinental horseback ride, but it was totally different from my everyday activities on the trail, and I found it relaxing.

Señor Negro gloried in testing his driving skill and the cornering ability of his two imported sports cars. Many times he drove me down the winding road from his hilltop home, tires squealing as he negotiated the tight corners. As my knuckles turned white, he'd speak the words that sent chills down my spine.

"I could have taken that corner *much* faster. Let me show you on the next one!"

With that, he'd stomp on the accelerator, just before a particularly sharp turn. Nowhere along the trail had I feared for my life as I did on those occasions. Once I came to recognize the capabilities of the cars and their driver, I found some small enjoyment in these demonstrations, but I concealed that information from *Señor* Negro, lest it inspire him to go even faster.

I would have enjoyed continuing to stay at the Negro home, but they had guests invited for the holidays, and I needed to vacate the guestroom. It was hard to leave, especially two days before Christmas, but on December 23rd I moved out. Thanks to the intervention of Gustavo Moncayo, a room was made available to me at the military academy, where Hamaca and Ima were stabled. The price was the same charged to students, which was very little. My new lodging place was a four-patient room in the academy's hospital. This unorthodox accommodation was offered because nothing else was was available. Even it might have been in use but for the fact that the cadets and instructors were on leave for the holidays. The loneliness of these new accommodations was interrupted by a visit from Gustavo Moncayo on the eve of Christmas Eve. I don't know what he'd heard from *don* Luis, but he knew that all was not as it had been.

"Don't worry about it," he told me. "*Don* Luis can be very drastic. It's his nature to find fault. He's generous with criticism and stingy with praise, but he's a wonderful man who thinks better of you than you realize."

Gustavo took time from his busy schedule to borrow a friend's shortwave radio and arrange phone patch calls to my parents as well as Joe and Pat Gavitt. Afterward, he had bad news: he was returning to his *hacienda* and wouldn't be back in Quito until after I'd left for Panama. With sadness and regret I said my last *good-bye* to him. Not since Juan Luis Ruesta in Piura had I felt so close to anyone. In years to come, I would often think of him, and in his absence, my days at the Academy grew longer and lonelier.

The Academy was where I spent my remaining days and nights in Quito. A maintenance man was on duty by day, but I saw little of him, and everyone else was on Christmas vacation. In the early mornings, while the neighborhood was quiet and deserted, I took long walks. After the streets began to fill with people, I'd return to my room and kill the rest of the day reading.

For economic reasons, I laid in a stock of groceries. Once or twice, I had lunch in a restaurant, but invariably breakfast and dinner were eaten in my room, mainly because – whenever the maintenance man wasn't there – I couldn't have get past the locked doors.

After dark, it was eerie to be the only person in such a large building. Each night, I walked down unlighted, deserted corridors to the shower, trying not to imagine danger lurking around every corner and behind every door. However, I had limited success in controlling my overactive imagination. More than once, I almost doubled up on my deodorant and skipped that spooky walk, but I always gave in to the habits my mother had installed during my youth. Afterwards I couldn't resist wedging a chair back securely under the doorknob on each of my room's two doors.

A week before, one of my daily trips to the Panamanian consul had brought welcome news. A cable had arrived giving the "prior permission" I needed to enter that country with my horses. In a state of euphoria, I was ready to depart immediately, but waiting for the cable was replaced by waiting for my flight. The airplane that would take me to Panama was busy elsewhere. The only available information was that it could arrive on very short notice and that I needed to be available at all times because I might be contacted only hours before it left for Panama.

Initially, it had seemed I would easily be in Panama and on the road again before Christmas. The airline's agent had assured me that my flight would leave no later than December 21st. It didn't. After that, I received five additional promises, all subsequently unfulfilled. Twice, I actually rode to the airport, only to be informed that the plane hadn't arrived as scheduled. Each time I went to the airport, I had to arrange for a veterinarian to meet us there and give final clearance for Hamaca's and Ima's departure. Next I'd pack my gear, check out of my room, pay my bill at the military academy and ride my horses to the airport.

When the plane didn't arrive, I'd reverse the entire process, leaving the airport, riding back to the *Colegio Militar*, getting permission from the *comandante* to stay a little longer, exchanging dollars for *sucres* – since I had purposely run out of Ecuadorian money in anticipation of leaving – and rushing to the open-air market to buy hay and grain before it closed.

My next scheduled departure was noon, January 2nd. Skeptical after my previous experiences, I phoned the airport control tower bright and early that morning. The news was good: the plane had been on the ground in Quito for several hours and had filed a flight plan for Panama. That was all I needed! In no time, Hamaca, Ima and I were at the airport. This time, lo and behold, the airplane was actually there, not only the plane but the pilot, too! In fact, he arrived a full hour and a half before the scheduled departure time. Such uncharacteristic punctuality turned out to be less mysterious than I originally supposed. The pilot was North American.

The aircraft was loaded with cargo, except for a space at the rear of the fuselage, obviously intended for my horses. However, the mares' shipping crates were nowhere to be seen. I phoned the freight agent, and he promised to send them immediately. Shortly after that conversation, I called the freight agent again to notify him of a second problem. There was no livestock-loading ramp. This was finally delivered two hours after our scheduled departure. It was nothing more than planks, placed side-by-side and held together with cleats, and its length was only a few feet more than the distance from the ground to the plane's cargo door. In addition, there were no protective railings. Again I called the freight agent.

"We won't know if it's too steep until it's actually put in place," he explained patiently.

"My horses will have to grow claws to get up that ramp," I said, growing colorful as my patience grew thin.

"Don't worry," I was assured.

I bypass all intermediate stages and go straight into full-fledged panic whenever a Latin American tells me not to worry. I know from vast experience that this means he or she has no idea what to do next and is stalling in the hope that someone else will figure it

255

out. *Someone else*, in this case, would have to be me. The only loading ramp in Quito was too short and could hardly be stretched. What to do?

Finally inspiration struck, and I made arrangements to borrow a large flatbed truck that was parked near a hanger. When the time came, I planned to use the flimsy ramp to load Hamaca and Ima onto the bed of the truck. Then the truck could be parked near the airplane's cargo door, and the ramp could be run between them, at an angle that would make loading relatively safe, if one ignored the lack of safety railings. Once my horses were in the aircraft's cargo hold, the only remaining task would be to secure them in their crates. At last, we would then be ready to go, none too soon for my taste!

The customs agent didn't deliver the horses' health certificates to the official airport veterinarian until almost three hours after scheduled flight time. Forty-five minutes after that, the latter gave the horses clearance to fly. Everything was ready, or at least it would have been if my baggage (sent from the Military Academy almost five hours earlier) had arrived. I called the Academy and was promised that my baggage would arrive in fifteen minutes, which it did. As it was being unloaded, I saw the pilot walking toward me, presumably to announce our imminent departure.

"Mr. Albright," he said calmly, "I'm afraid I have bad news."

South Americans hesitate to deliver bad news. For one thing, they consider frankness impolite. For another, they believe that any situation will work itself out, given enough time, thereby eliminating the need to displease their fellow man. Furthermore, getting down to the crux of the matter, what wisdom is there in passing along bad news to someone a foot and a half taller than you are? For all these reasons, it took a North American to bring me the news.

"The flight has been postponed until 8:00 tomorrow morning," the pilot continued.

"Why is that?" I asked.

"Well, the truth is that the cargo on board is the incoming cargo. There isn't anyone available to unload it, and apparently there won't be until late tonight."

"Do you think the plane will really go out tomorrow?" I asked.

"Can't guarantee it," he said cheerily, "but I think so, yes."

"Is there somewhere I can leave my baggage rather than send it back and forth again?"

"Our company doesn't own any facilities here," the pilot said, "but I can look after it for you, if you like."

I thanked him and saddled up for the ride back to the Academy. All the way, I sat grimly on Hamaca's back without once giving any indication of where she should go. She proved that we had covered that particular route too many times when she made all the right turns in all the right places, all by herself. When my mares came to a stop in front of the stable where they had spent almost a month, I roused myself, spoke with the *comandante*, made arrangements for the three of us to stay a bit longer, rushed to the bank, exchanged money, rushed to the market, bought horse feed, rushed back to the Military Academy, fed the mares and trudged to my old room, which was just as I had left it (the maintenance man wasn't fool enough to invest his time until he was sure I was airborne!).

Then I just sat and simmered.

16 After I finished my ride, I saw *don* Luis whenever the two of us were in Peru, but he continued to hold me at arm's length. Years later, when I was at the International Exposition in Manizales, Colombia – with José Antonio Onrubia's horses – I arranged for *don* Luis to be invited as a special guest. While he was there, we were briefly drawn closer by our mutual efforts to translate his book into English and get it published in the United States. However, the distance between us reappeared and grew larger when we disagreed over how that should be done.

Ascasubi's book had been critical of the Peruvian horse's deficiencies, and accurately so. I had no quarrel with the need to work toward improving the breed. My objection was that the book – actually a collection of essays, written over a period of years – repeated the same criticisms, almost word-for-word, in two or three different sections. I wanted to remove the repetition. *Don* Luis insisted that not a single word be changed, and we never resolved the resulting deadlock.

CHAPTER 26

A Man, A Plan, A Canal, Panama

The next day, I wrote a progress report for the newsletter of the American Association of Owners and Breeders of Peruvian Paso Horses. It was the first "official news release" I had sent to the United States in months. After my experience with the geldings, I had decided to wait until something had been accomplished before calling further attention to myself. Publicity was one of the objectives of my ride, but I had already publicized one failure too many.

Years later, when I re-read that letter, the first thing I noticed was the handwriting. It was difficult to read, but there was good reason. I wrote it from inside the vibrating belly of an airborne C-47 cargo plane. My desk was a wooden crate next to shipping stalls containing Hamaca and Ima. We were on our way to Panama after our plane had departed Quito a mere two hours behind schedule.

The takeoff had been unique in my experience. Because of the Quito airport's 10,000-foot altitude, the air was thin, and aeronautical law restricted the amount of weight that planes were allowed to carry. Our craft was carrying so much cargo that its fuel had to be limited. Becoming airborne required full throttle and every last inch of runway. With the engines running flat out, the racket in the cargo hold was deafening, and my mares' reactions were my major concern of the moment.

Begrudgingly, the pilot had given me permission to ride in the cargo hold during takeoff, and I was determined to stay there throughout the flight. Several times the co-pilot was sent to bring me to the cockpit, and each time, I convinced him to let me stay where I was. I wanted to be close by if Hamaca or Ima acted up. Problems were unlikely, especially after the airport vet had injected both mares with tranquilizer, but better safe than sorry. My outlook on flying with horses had been influenced by an incident of some years before, involving a well-known horse on its way to the Olympics by air. During flight, the animal went berserk and escaped its shipping crate. The horse's destruction was ordered by the pilot when its crazed thrashing threatened to destroy the plane in mid-air. The unenviable task of carrying out these orders fell to the animal's handler who had to use an axe, the only lethal instrument available.

Our World War II vintage aircraft compared to a passenger plane the way an ancient, beat-up, half-dead truck compares to a brand new luxury car. Whether on the runway or in the air, the ride was rough and the racket deafening. The bare minimum of time and money had been invested in maintenance, and everything rattled, vibrated or hummed. On top of that, there was no noise insulation. Even shouting at the top of our voices, the pilot, co-pilot and I had difficulty hearing one another.

Once we were at cruising altitude, the rush of air past the cargo door added to the other sounds. Obviously, our craft was far from airtight, and I wondered if I should be concerned. If the cockpit was pressurized and the cargo hold wasn't, what would happen to the mares and me? Upon further reflection, I relaxed. It was unlikely that this particular aircraft could fly high enough to require pressurization!

Throughout the flight, Ima was obviously under the influence of her tranquilizer shot, but Hamaca remained surprisingly alert. The sides of their shipping crates were high enough that the mares were hidden from one other. In Ima's semi-conscious state, she seemed perfectly happy eating from the hay net I'd hung in front of her. Every few minutes, however, Hamaca stretched high enough to nervously glance inside the neighboring crate. Once she had verified that Ima was still there, she would return to eating until the plane made its next sudden movement, again causing her to wonder if anything was going on next door.

Instead of proceeding directly to Panama in a northwesterly direction, our plane was flying southwest toward Guayaquil, where it was scheduled to land and have the fuel tanks topped off. Taking off and landing are the most hazardous moments of any flight, all the more so with livestock involved. I wasn't thrilled about having two takeoffs and two landings shoehorned into our short flight, but the pilot set us down smoothly in Guayaquil, and the second take off – in the more buoyant air at sea level – was far less stressful than the one in Quito. Once we were again airborne, the next scheduled stop was Tocumen, just south of Panama City.

After departing Guayaquil, the C-47 climbed above a layer of clouds. Once we were beyond Ecuador's airspace, the clouds made it impossible for me to know if we were flying above Colombia or the Pacific Ocean. By then, my report was finished, and there was nothing much to do or see, so I indulged my imagination. It's said that males tend to think in military terms, and at that moment, I was a good example as I fantasized that we were making highly unusual bombing runs over Colombia. Whenever Hamaca or Ima would relieve herself, the urine would collect in a pool near the cargo door.

There it would sit until the plane banked into a left turn. At that point, our liquid payload flowed through the gap beneath the doors and – I sincerely hoped – onto the heads of those murderous gangs below!

No sooner did the C-47 come to a stop near a hangar in Tocumen than the cargo door was opened. I looked out to see a group of men hands on knees, gathered around one of the plane's front wheel assemblies. They were watching steaming, red fluid gush onto the tarmac. A chill passed through me when one of the men on the runway responded to my shouted inquiry by confirming that the liquid was, indeed, brake fluid.

"What happened?" I asked.

"Bad luck," he said, as if this were a highly technical answer.

It *was* bad luck, no doubt, but not nearly as bad as it might have been. If that same brake line had burst during landing, the results could have been disastrous. The plane might not have been able to stop before the runway ended or might have been sent into an out-of-control spin.

Still standing in the cargo doorway, high above the ground, I saw a man emerge from a nearby building and walk toward me. When he was directly below, he spoke. It was difficult to hear through the surrounding din. I clearly understood his self-introduction as the local manager for the airline, but I hoped I'd misunderstood the rest.

"Could you please repeat that?" I asked.

"I'm sorry, *Señor* Albright," he yelled through the megaphone created by cupping his hands, "but there isn't a livestock loading ramp available here. You have to make your own arrangements to get your horses unloaded."

I hadn't misunderstood, after all!

"When a passenger plane arrives," I probed, "the airline has an obligation to provide a stairway or a ramp so people can get off the plane, doesn't it?"

"*Sí Señor*, but..."

"Well then, I believe your airline has a similar obligation to provide a ramp for my horses."

"We might possibly be able to borrow a set of passenger stairs from one of the other airlines," the manager offered.

"Stairs!" I shot back. "Horses can't use stairs. You need to find something suitable for livestock."

The manager silently shook his head in disagreement, arms folded across his chest.

"How can the plane continue to Miami if I can't unload my horses?" I tried a mild threat.

"We won't be unloading the rest of the cargo until tomorrow," he called my bluff. "You have plenty of time to make arrangements."

There was more discussion back and forth, followed by silence. I stood in the C-47's doorway, looking down. The airline manager stood on the tarmac below, looking up. Our negotiations had reached a stalemate, but we both had reason to look for a compromise. He wouldn't benefit from a delay in the flight's continuation to Miami, and I didn't want my horses aboard that hot, stuffy aircraft any longer than absolutely necessary. We agreed to split the cost of renting two forklifts for the unloading, an operation that was about to provide some of the most harrowing moments of my entire journey.

On one side, the mares' shipping stalls were just a bit too tall to fit through the cargo door in an upright position, though the other side cleared easily. Brought aboard while empty, the stalls had been leaned sideways when slid through the door. The mares had been loaded inside them after both they and the crates were aboard. Since the unloading was to be accomplished with forklifts, there was no way for Hamaca and Ima to leave their crates until they were safely on the ground. This presented a challenge: how to lean the crates – with horses inside – to fit them through the cargo door?

A team of workers was assembled, and together we were able to slide the crates and occupants over to the door. It took six of us to lean Ima's crate and slid the back end through the opening. There it hung in mid-air, still tilted to one side, while the forks from one of the lift trucks were placed beneath it. The lift truck was at a right angle to the side of the crate, meaning that both forks were touching the bottom on one side but neither supported the opposite side. We eased the crate farther through the door, my crew and I pushing from our end while the forklift driver supported the rear of the crate.

Because of the rounded shape of the fuselage, the crate's top cleared the doorway while its bottom still rested on the threshold. This allowed us to stand it upright and secure its position while the second forklift took up position between the first and the aircraft. After a moment, Ima's crate was raised slightly so that it no longer rested on the airplane. High above the ground and with her tranquilizer wearing off, Ima began to fidget. Her container rocked back and forth while I held on, desperately trying to stabilize it and calm her at the same time.

Before the forklifts began lowering their burden, I stepped onto the first two metal forks where they protruded beyond the base of Ima's container. I intended to ride down with the crate for the purpose of keeping it and its occupant steady. Knowing the typical Latin American concern for animals, or lack thereof, I also hoped my presence would encourage caution on the part of the forklift drivers. Considering the way some Panamanians felt toward North Americans, this may have been ill-advised!

The forklift drivers did their best to synchronize the descent so the two ends of the crate moved at the same speed. Apparently that was more difficult than it seemed. One forklift was constantly ahead of or behind the other. The crate would slant one way and the other, wobbling back and forth whenever Ima began scrambling to keep her balance. Several times I was sure my horse and I were about to be spilled onto the pavement below. Not until it was deposited on the runway was the crate anywhere close to level. Even then, my job was only half done. I faced a repetition of the entire procedure, and unloading Hamaca worried me. With one success behind them, my crew would be overconfident. In addition, they would be feeling rushed because other work awaited them, and the unloading of my horses was taking much longer than they had anticipated.

Undoubtedly, I contributed generously to the bad name we Americans have in Panama as I constantly raised my voice to slow Hamaca's unloading. Even at that, it wasn't long before her crate was safely on the runway next to Ima's. For this second unloading, we had made a small change in our procedure, using only one of the lift trucks. It was a considerable improvement.

The next hurdle was the big one. Officials of Panama's Ministry of Agriculture didn't hesitate to quarantine incoming livestock for as long as forty days if they saw anything they didn't like. Fortunately, both mares passed their physical inspection with flying colors, and their papers were pronounced to be in perfect order. My own travel documents, however, were incomplete. The hang-up was that I couldn't be admitted to Panama without showing my ticket for passage back out of the country.

"My horses are my ticket out of here," I explained.

"That isn't satisfactory, *señor*. The law very specifically requires you to have a ticket for commercial transportation out of Panama."

"If someone enters Panama in his personal automobile," I said, feeling very skilled in the Latin American art of negotiation, "you surely don't require him to have a ticket for transportation elsewhere. His car is his transportation, and my horses are mine."

"Almost everyone who comes to Panama has feet, *señor*, and we still require a ticket to leave the country. Walking isn't considered satisfactory for international travel, and neither are horses."

Checkmate! I resolved the problem by purchasing an airplane ticket to Costa Rica. Shortly after being admitted to Panama, I was able to return the ticket for a refund, minus a small service charge. Now then. Immigration was satisfied. The Ministry of Agriculture was satisfied. All that remained was customs. With my meager possessions, I didn't anticipate problems, but I hadn't counted on the inventiveness of the bureaucratic mind. The customs official informed me that I must make a cash deposit to guarantee the mares wouldn't be sold in Panama without the payment of applicable taxes. I protested as politely and reasonably as I could in my increasingly exhausted state. The deposit would have taken every dime I had. I kept that information to myself, however, as border officials are trained to spot and deny entry to people in danger of becoming destitute while in their countries.

Moments later, I could hardly believe my good luck. Out of the blue, I was informed that I could enter Panama and then appeal the deposit in Panama City the following day. Pleased with this development, I still wondered: if I could be trusted to attend to this matter in Panama City, why wouldn't they take my word that the mares were not for sale? Of course, I didn't present that question for the consideration of the customs official. Better I should leave well enough alone and do my negotiating in Panama City the next day. As the entry stamp was placed in my passport, I was once again sternly warned not to travel with the mares until the issue of the deposit was resolved.

Before leaving the airport, I wanted to get some Panamanian currency, and that quest led me to a money exchange window in the main passenger terminal. After standing in a slow-moving line for the better part of a half-hour, my turn finally came. I placed fifty dollars in cash on the counter in front of the teller. He responded by giving me a quizzical look.

"What exactly would you like to do with this money, *señor*?" he finally asked.

"I'd like to exchange it for Panamanian currency, please," I responded, wondering how there could be any question.

"This *is* Panamanian money!" he snapped, pushing my fifty dollars back to me and dismissing me with a click of the tongue and a wave of his hand.

As I'd soon see for myself, the money circulating in Panama was largely U.S. in origin. Panama also minted its own money, and throughout the country, the two were circulated without distinction. It was quite common to receive change and find a mixture of both nations' currency and coins. The Panamanians officially called their monetary unit the *balboa*, after one of the first Spanish explorers in Panama, Vasco Nuñez de Balboa, but it was common to hear people refer to North American money as *balboas* and Panamanian money as *dólares*. The designs were different, but the sizes, shapes and values were identical. In fact, the coins were interchangeable in vending machines.

It was dark by the time I got directions to my night's lodgings. The route I was given would cross several runways. I couldn't believe I'd be allowed to lead horses across a busy international airport, especially in pitch darkness, and I was hesitant to even attempt it. The alternative, on the other hand, involved several miles of plowing through thick, jungle-like growth, and I finally decided to give it a try, half-expecting airport security to send all available officers with orders to surround and take me prisoner. To my surprise, however, no one took the slightest notice of us, even though planes were landing, taking off and taxiing all around. My worries about Hamaca's and Ima's reactions to the airplanes turned out to be groundless. That morning they had been in the Andes, and since then, they'd seen so many strange things that they took little notice of one more.

My mother had always insisted I look both ways before crossing the street, but at each runway, I went her one better, looking both ways and also up! Mom would have been proud, but I decided – all things considered – that it would be best if she never found out about this particular exploit.

Our host for the night was a porter I'd met at the airport. For a small fee, he let me sleep in an old tool shed and provided an adjacent fenced area for Hamaca and Ima. The mares dined without enthusiasm on the only feeds available, yucca and wild grass. Neither was particularly appetizing or nourishing, but as they had spent a good part of the day eating hay on the airplane, the consequences wouldn't be serious. The following day they would rest while I went to Panama City to resolve the issue of the deposit.

While in Panama City, I would find better feed.

CHAPTER 27

Empty Jail Cells

Panama lay ahead of me. In a sense, it was a case of history repeating itself. Long before the building of the canal, it had been Panama's destiny to be in the path of North Americans. In one of the most spectacular incidents, during the California gold rush of 1849, thousands of fortune hunters took the shortcut across Panama, hoping to arrive in the goldfields ahead of those who sailed around Cape Horn. During the first half of 1849, up to three thousand Americans at a time were stockpiled in Panama City. This was because ships from America's east coast delivered gold seekers faster than west coast ships could pick them up after they crossed the isthmus.

All in all, I was impressed with Panama City when I went there early the next morning. While it didn't have much charm, it was cleaner, more modern and more efficient than cities to the south. At the headquarters of Panamanian customs, I was informed that deposits were always required on big-ticket items brought into the country by tourists. The government had too long been short-changed by those who sold such items and skipped the country without paying taxes, or so I was repeatedly told.

More than once, I carefully explained that I was there to ask that this requirement be waived in my case because of special circumstances. However, all officials with whom I spoke ignored my attempts to discuss that possibility. One after the other, they pressured me to pay the deposit. Since the value of my mares was more difficult to establish than that of, say, an automobile, I was asked for an outlandish sum. It was more than had been requested at the airport the night before and, in fact, more than I had. To make matters worse, this deposit could be returned – if I'd had that much in the first place – only after I crossed into Costa Rica. I'd have to stable my horses there and travel all the way back to Panama City, I was told, to "apply" – the use of that word was most distressing since it implied Panama's ability to say "no" – for a refund. Approval of my application could take days.

No doubt I could have negotiated a much-reduced deposit, but that would have left me wasting time and money to get my refund. During the previous night's tossing and turning, inspiration had come to me, and I had a proposal that should satisfy everyone's concerns. All I had to do was find someone who'd listen. My proposal was that a condition be attached to the visa in my passport, requiring me to exit Panama with both Hamaca and Ima. Once they allowed me to plead my case, I convinced the officials that this would protect Panama's interests as effectively as a deposit. All the while this condition was being written next to the visa in my passport, I mentally patted myself on the back, pleased with my ever-improving ability to negotiate. Of course, this self-congratulation required that I ignore the potential problem inherent in the deal I'd struck: what would I do if one or both mares suddenly died? In that case, I might face paying taxes I didn't owe or living in Panama for the rest of my life!

When I emerged on the street, I was surprised to see women carrying umbrellas, even though there wasn't a cloud in the sky. At that early hour, the umbrellas were closed, but by mid-morning, with no rain yet in sight, they were being opened, and I realized they were parasols, to provide protection from the blazing sun. The parasols seemed quaint and colorful, but they also confirmed that I was in the tropics and would suffer accordingly.

The remainder of a very hot and humid day was spent preparing for the next leg of my journey. There was shopping to be done and laundry to be dropped off, and finally, there was the matter of accommodations for the following night when I returned with Hamaca and Ima. Finding lodging for horses in a metropolitan area would be difficult, and it seemed wise to make arrangements ahead of time. After several inquiries, I was referred to a *Guardia Civil* post on the outskirts of town. The officer in charge invited me to bring my mares the following evening for an overnight stay in the post's stable. He also helped me select nightly stopping places for the coming week. Afterward, I bought grain, divided it into seven equal portions and sent it ahead by bus.

U.S. currency and coins weren't the only familiar items in my new surroundings. I no longer had to mentally convert metric units into their U.S. equivalents. Panama had done the job for me. Instead of kilometers, meters, centimeters and kilos, everything was measured in miles, feet, inches and pounds. Dealing with familiar weights and measures seemed out of place in Latin America. By then, I was comfortable with the metric system and proud to understand it.

It was out of the ordinary to get so much done in a day, and I was in high spirits during the bus ride back to Tocumen. Free from worry for the first time in weeks, I found my smile coming easily, and this encouraged my fellow passengers to engage me in an enjoyable conversation. Even the mares seemed to sense I was having a good day, and they rushed over to the fence to deliver an enthusiastic greeting. After that, they followed me, staying as close as the fence would permit and nickering from time to time. It would have been nice to believe they were happy to see me, but I suspected their reaction would have been different without the bag of grain I was carrying!

For reasons known only to themselves, Hamaca and Ima had been off their feed in the days immediately before our flight. In Panama, they continued to eat poorly, almost certainly because I was unable to find a familiar variety of hay. The inevitable result was that they were a bit sucked-in at the flanks.

In addition, the edge was off their physical condition after the long delay in Quito. While there, I had taken them out for exercise, but not enough to keep them in top shape. To avoid stress during their first days in the sweltering heat and humidity of the tropics – and with apologies to *don* Luis de Ascasubi – I planned to lead my mares as much as possible for the first few days. It seemed a reasonable precaution now that they were in an environment where their bodies were adjusting to different feed, water, bacteria, climate and who-knows-what-else.

The next day, January 5th, we traveled twenty-five miles from Tocumen to Panama City. My recollections of that day center on sauna-like heat and jungle-like vegetation. Although I had technically been in the tropics throughout my journey, this was the first time my surroundings had been tropical. The mares and I were no longer in dry, hot deserts or crisp, alpine mountains. Instead, we were in hot, humid lowlands, surrounded by blood-hungry insects and thriving vegetation. All things considered, I was grateful I had mares from the desert rather than geldings from the sierra!

All the while I was in Panama, I was bathed in perspiration twenty-four hours a day. My metabolism – the same one that made me comfortable in freezing temperatures – now worked against me. Sweat poured into my eyes, saturated my clothing, collected on the surface of my skin and then dripped on the ground, responding to the pull of gravity. This perpetual coating of liquid couldn't provide the relief for which it was produced because perspiration cools by evaporation, a process that can't take place in moisture-saturated air. In response, my pores would open even wider, increasing the flow of perspiration on the apparent theory that more would succeed where less had failed.

When I removed my clothing at night, I would carefully hang each item where air freely circulated all around and even inside it. The next morning, despite this effort, every shred was still as wet as when I had taken it off. Soon I was covered with an irritating heat rash. Hamaca and Ima suffered similarly. Within days, their coats were blemished where they had rubbed away the hair while trying to relieve the excruciating itch of insect bites and other skin conditions. Hamaca, plagued by itches of unspecified origin even in the cool Andes, was constantly scratching herself against any solid object she could find. She was dripping wet most of the time and drank water in unbelievable quantities. Ima suffered less but suffered, nonetheless.

When I rented my first hotel room, the bed had a bottom sheet, a pillow and no other bedding. Unaware that this was standard bedding in all but air-conditioned hotels, I headed for the reception desk to ask that this oversight be corrected. Before I got there, however, common sense kicked in, and I made an abrupt U-turn. Why ask for more bedding? Even a top sheet, all by itself, would have been excessive.

Panama was much more expensive than South America. When I went to pick up my laundry, the bill was quite a shock, especially compared to what I had been charged in Peru and Ecuador. Laundry was one more chore I'd have to start doing for myself. In the absence of laundromats, the job would have to be done with a bar of laundry soap and a bucket (or sink) full of water. I pictured myself, the great adventurer, scrubbing and wringing my clothes by hand. Oh, how the mighty had fallen! Wasn't it the Greeks who said: "Whomever the gods would destroy, they first make him do his own laundry"?

After spending a comfortable night at the *Guardia* post, Hamaca, Ima and I set out at 3:00 A.M. The early start was calculated to miss rush-hour traffic while crossing the Panama Canal on the Thatcher Ferry Bridge. While in Ecuador and Peru, I'd often been asked, frequently by well-educated people, how I planned to cross the Panama Canal. Though I didn't have the precise answer, the question always struck me as silly. Surely, I had thought, crossing the canal would be relatively simple. I later learned, however, that the recent completion of the Thatcher Ferry Bridge had marked the first time the Pan-American Highway crossed the canal. Before that, crossings were made on the ferryboat system from which the bridge took its name.

In the pre-dawn hours, I arrived at the famous canal, a man with a plan, about to cross Panama's most famous landmark. I was reminded of what may be history's most-famous palindrome, 17 coined in Theodore Roosevelt's time to describe the decisiveness with which he pursued the construction of the Panama Canal. It read: "A man, a plan, a canal - Panama!"

Unfortunately, in the darkness, I wasn't able to get a good look at what had often been called one of the wonders of the world. I could see only the lights along the waterway and on a freighter passing by. I strained unsuccessfully to see more, thinking to myself that in broad daylight the sights below would have produced awe. As it was, they produced only squinting, a technique that I hoped would help me see better. It didn't, but what I did see as I approached the bridge was an American flag. It was the first time I'd seen the Stars and Stripes in a long while, and a strong feeling of patriotism unexpectedly seized me.

As I drew closer to the Thatcher Ferry Bridge, I noticed that traffic was much heavier than expected. When I saw the speed of the cars and the erratic behavior of the drivers, I came to the sobering realization that my safe arrival on the other side was anything but guaranteed. Was this why people had asked how I'd cross the canal? Had they known something I was only just discovering?

Several hundred yards before the bridge, I was passed by a Canal Zone police officer in a squad car. He parked in front of me, emerged from his car and waved me over. It seemed all wrong to see an obviously North American policeman so far from home. Instinctively, I anticipated being told that I couldn't ride across the bridge.

"Yesterday afternoon, I saw you and your horses, and I figured you'd be crossing the bridge about this time," the officer said, his manner businesslike. "I'm here to escort you across. Once you're safely on the other side, maybe we can talk for a few minutes."

Before I could thank him, he slid behind the wheel of his car and waved me past. Hamaca was carrying my empty saddle, and I stepped into the stirrup and swung onto her back, remembering the lesson I had learned about controlling her in heavy traffic. After the mares and I passed him, the officer pulled the squad car in behind, dome lights flashing, and illuminated us with his spotlight. Apparently Panama's drivers are much the same as North America's when they see a policeman observing them. Motorists crossing the canal at that moment drove in an exemplary fashion, obeying the speed limit and extending every courtesy to one another ... and to me.

269

Once we were across, our escort passed and pulled off the road, thereby indicating where I was to meet him for the talk he'd mentioned. It turned out that he was the owner of a half-Arab, half-Peruvian mare. Thanks to the ripple effects of a conversation between Gustavo Moncayo and a ham radio operator in Panama, he'd been aware of my ride for weeks. Upon seeing me the day before, he had immediately realized who I was.

"It was a lucky coincidence for me that you were here today," I said, feeling relieved.

"It wasn't a coincidence," he answered. "I made it a point to be here."

"Well, I appreciate that tremendously," I responded, smiling. "You can't imagine how I was dreading that crossing."

"I think I can," he said with a smile of his own. "My horse and I have been in some tight situations in traffic down here, and I definitely wouldn't want to ride across Thatcher Ferry Bridge without an escort."

This man was one of the few Americans I'd seen since leaving the States. I was terribly pleased to have met him, and not just because he probably saved my life! After being exposed to Latin America, I had begun to wonder if we North Americans were truly guilty of what our detractors said about us: that, as individuals, we could seldom find the time to help others. The actions of a certain Canal Zone Policeman had emphasized that people in the States – like everyone else in the world – are individuals and often very kind ones.

After saying thanks and good-bye to my uniformed guardian angel, I continued toward the town of Chorrera. All day, I marveled at something I knew beyond the shadow of a doubt and yet found difficult to accept: while headed toward Costa Rica, I was traveling west, not north, and I would continue in that direction for days. [18]

Along the road near Chorrera, I met a gentleman named Isaacs who was very much an *aficionado* of Peruvian horses. He spotted me from his car, immediately realized who I was and pulled over to talk. His first words were that he lived nearby and would be only too happy to offer his stable to the mares and his guestroom to me.

Guided by *Señor* Isaacs' car, I soon turned off the highway, and still following, proceeded along a driveway toward a small stable. Halfway there, we passed a very large, artistically shaped pool. Its construction was crude, with rough concrete sides and bottom. The bottom was a ramp, gently sloping from ground level to a depth of about seven feet and maintaining that depth throughout the main body of water. The water was dirty, and it was my guess that the pool was used infrequently.

"You are most welcome to go for a swim," *Señor* Isaacs offered later, having noticed the way I was eyeing his pool while perspiration dripped from my chin. "I don't change the water often because my family doesn't swim much, but it's treated with chemicals and is perfectly safe."

He didn't seem surprised to hear me ask if Hamaca and Ima might swim in my stead, but he asked me not to start until he could bring his children to watch. It was well worth the wait to see their eyes widen as I led my horses into the pool and turned them loose. Both mares were prim, proper and puzzled at being set free in such an unlikely place. They stood, barely moving a hair. Then Ima accidentally splashed Hamaca, who created a good-sized wave as she surged in the opposite direction. That broke the ice and put an end to dignified behavior! The two had a great time cooling off and romping in the water, much to the delight of *Señor* Isaacs, his children and myself.

Once I had the horses out of the pool and dried off, I was shown to a large stall with a thick layer of bedding on the floor and plenty of hay in the manger. There, I left my mares dozing and showing little interest in their hay, while I showered and changed clothes. When I was presentable, *Señor* Isaacs took me to a small restaurant in Panama City. To my surprise, the two of us were shown to a table for twelve, and before I could ask why, we were joined by a group of men who shared our passion for Peruvian horses.

Apparently, some sort of ham radio network was still operating in my behalf. Over the airwaves, a Panamanian reporter had learned that my journey would soon bring me to his country. Intrigued, he had gathered information for an article, which was published in a major Panama City newspaper just prior to my arrival. The men I met that evening had read it and made plans to surprise me – which they certainly did! – with a special dinner and reception. Had it not been for *Señor* Isaacs, I would have passed through undetected, missing out on a splendid evening.

Afterward, *Señor* Isaacs offered to take me to a stable in the Canal Zone and introduce me to some North Americans who were also interested in Peruvian horses. The prospect of being among my countrymen sounded like the perfect end to a perfect day.

The Canal Zone, or "*yanqui*" sector, as its detractors called it, was like a piece of the United States that had been scooped up and transplanted. Almost all of the people who lived there occupied a portion of Panama's territory without the slightest intention of ever being part of its culture and society. Never have I met kinder people of any nationality than some of the North Americans in the Canal Zone. The police officer who escorted me across the Thatcher Ferry Bridge was a good example, and there were others, too. However, when I saw *Señor* Isaacs being treated as if he wasn't there, in spite of his own warmth and enthusiasm, I had the feeling that this kindness was not often extended to Panamanians.

It had been troubling me deeply that Hamaca and Ima were showing no appetite for the various kinds of hay I'd been able to find in Panama. Even the hay *Señor* Isaacs had provided – undoubtedly the best available – hadn't been to their liking. Alfalfa was what they wanted, but alfalfa grows poorly, if at all, in tropical climates, and I had given up all hope of finding it. Hence, I was very pleasantly surprised to see dried alfalfa being fed at the Canal Zone stable. I was anxious to purchase a few bales until I learned it was imported from the States and priced at nine dollars for a very small bale. By the time I shipped it ahead, each meal would have cost five dollars, which was more than I could possibly afford.

When we reached *Señor* Isaacs' home that evening, he – without asking – drove me directly to the stable, knowing I'd want to check on Hamaca and Ima. When I got out of the car, he asked me to help him carry something. Smiling, he opened the trunk, and I looked inside, touched to see that he'd secretly bought a bale of alfalfa for me in the Canal Zone.

The next day Hamaca, Ima and I traveled twenty-seven miles to Chame. I alternately rode and walked, trying not to overtax my horses or myself. That night, I slept in a hotel room while Hamaca and Ima stayed in a rented stall at a stable. Renting stalls and staying in hotels would be more common in Panama than in South America, probably because there were fewer isolated villages or ranches where lonely residents felt impelled to welcome wandering strangers.

I walked more than I rode during those first days in Panama. When I did ride, it was without a saddle because Hamaca and Ima had developed blisters on their backs. This problem had made its initial appearance in Quito, and at first, I couldn't imagine why. After giving the matter some thought, I blamed the chemical bath intended to protect a certain hosts' cattle from hoof-and-mouth disease. Saddling my mares the day after must have had the same blistering effect as wrapping an area in bandages after treating it with liniment.

Soon after the blisters first surfaced, the hair on them fell out. Never having seen anything like it, I was deeply concerned and feared some mysterious disease until I gave the matter more-careful consideration. Fortunately, the symptoms quickly disappeared, and the hair began to grow back. I dismissed the incident from my mind until, in the harsh conditions of Panama, the mares began to pull away from currycomb and brush when I was grooming the area covered by their saddles. My response was to ship my saddles and cargo ahead by bus and to ride only sparingly and bareback. As a further measure, I gave my mares saltwater treatments to toughen and heal their suddenly delicate hides. Despite these precautions, it would obviously be days before I could ride much or use my saddles at all

******

Learning to appreciate Panama's beauty took time. The flat panoramas didn't appeal when I was newly arrived from a place where spectacular mountains could be seen in every direction. However, I eventually came to regard the lush and abundant greenery, and occasional ocean vistas, as suitable compensation for what had been left behind.

Panama's flatness may have been less attractive, but it was certainly easier to negotiate than the laborious climbs and descents of the Andes. Nothing else about Panama was less difficult than Ecuador. The steamy heat was almost beyond endurance. The addition of carnivorous insects and their blood-sucking cousins made Panama the worst trial yet, especially for Hamaca and Ima. Countless winged insects landed on their bodies, and countless others, without wings, crawled up their legs. Together, these pests nearly drove both mares insane. One particularly ferocious fly ignored insect repellent to inflict painful bites, tearing out tiny chunks of flesh and creating wounds that wept for days until the hair fell out. I considered myself blessed that these winged meat-eaters showed no appetite for me!

The next day, I'd been on the road for two hours when the top of the sun began to inch above the horizon. Before that sunrise was complete, a car pulled off the road and out climbed a tall, obviously North American cowboy.

"Verne Albright?" he asked, already sure of the answer and preparing to introduce himself.

"Yes," I responded, nodding my head.

"I'm Bob Green. Do you remember me, by any chance?"

"I certainly do."

Two years earlier, when I had been president of the American Association of Owners and Breeders of Peruvian Paso Horses, Bob and I exchanged a whirlwind of letters between California and Panama. We hadn't found much about which to agree, and I wondered if we were about to do any better. The two of us had breakfast at a small roadside restaurant. Bob insisted that it be his treat, proclaiming with a laugh that he was a man who could disagree without being disagreeable. While we talked, Hamaca and Ima munched grain in a run-down corral under a nearby highway bridge.

Bob and I picked up where our correspondence had left off, debating the virtues of the pureblooded Peruvian *Paso* versus the outcross produced by mating a Peruvian with an Andalusian. He accurately pointed out that the outcross was more versatile. I countered that the outcross was "jack of all trades and master of none."

"Crossing a laterally gaited breed with a diagonally gaited breed," I insisted, "is akin to mixing black and white and hoping not to end up with a nondescript shade of gray."

Bob laughed in disagreement, indicating that he was enjoying our good-natured exchange as much as I was.

Later that morning, another car pulled onto the shoulder of the road ahead of us and produced two more Americans, in this case a married couple, named Brown, that I had met in the Canal Zone.

"Boy, are we ever lucky!" the man said enthusiastically. "We drove all the way from Panama City on the off chance that we might find you and get to see your mares."

"We remembered your interest in alfalfa," his wife added, "and brought you a bale."

"Thank you very much," I responded, touched by their kindness. "Sounds like *your* good luck is *my* good luck, as well."

After admiring Hamaca and Ima, the couple drove ahead to leave the alfalfa at the police station in Antón. Later, during their return to the Canal Zone, they stopped again.

"Your hay is waiting for you," the man informed me. "Incidentally, the Chief of Police in Antón is a friend of ours, and we put in the good word for you. I'm pretty sure he'll be offering overnight accommodations for you and your horses."

Mr. Brown had a way about him, and it left little doubt that he had numerous friendships with Panamanians. It was a thought that made me like him very much.

******

Upon arrival at the police station in Antón, I received the predicted invitation.

"There's a fenced area in the back where your horses will be safe for the night," the Chief told me with a smile and a pat on the back, "and for you, I have the safest bed in town."

With those words, he gestured toward one of the jail cells. Despite the fact that I'd slept in such accommodations before, there was something threatening about the substantial steel door. It struck me as easy to close but very difficult to reopen.

"When the new guard comes on duty at midnight, be sure to explain that you are our guest. We wouldn't want him to lock you in," the Chief teased, when he left for the night.

Aware that the Chief was trying to get a rise out of me, I, nonetheless, thought it would be a good idea to stay alert for the changing of the guard. As tired as I was, though, I feared I'd be out for the night as soon as my head hit the pillow. As a precaution, I swung the heavy door wide open to emphasize my status as a voluntary guest. This precaution notwithstanding, I was troubled by an elaborate nightmare about waking in a locked cell with a new guard on duty. The plot revolved around my futile efforts to convince this stranger that I was passing the night in a cell of my own free will.

Fortunately, the following day began promisingly when I opened my eyes to find the heavy steel door still standing wide open.

17 A palindrome is a word or phrase spelled the same forward or backward.

18 Most North Americans believe that Panama runs north/south and the canal east/west. In fact, the reverse is true.

Chapter 28

The Pores Pour

Prior to Panama, my initial suffering in harsh, new environments had eventually subsided. On my final day in Peru's deserts, I easily tolerated the hottest temperature I had yet encountered. In Ecuador's Andes, I soon ceased to experience discomfort or limitations caused by altitude. Panama, however, was another matter! There, my misery increased rather than lessened, and the same was true for my horses. Hamaca and Ima were affected by the same factors that have always tortured livestock in the tropics. I seldom saw a decent-sized horse in Panama's rural areas, and when I commented on this, I was informed that repeated attempts to introduce larger horses had failed. The offspring of imported stock shrunk to match the tiny native horses in a few generations, a result of the climate, the poor feed and most of all, the parasites. [19]

As a supplement to my use of insect repellent, I dutifully searched for ticks every single night (anyone who has ever done this on a human head will appreciate the challenge represented by an area the size of a horse!). The problem with ticks and mosquitoes wasn't only the diseases they carry, but the antibodies such diseases leave in the bloodstream. Blood tests could detect those antibodies, meaning that even if a horse had never shown symptoms or was completely cured, a blood test might brand him a carrier. I wouldn't be able to bring Hamaca and Ima into the United States if they tested positive on any of the required blood tests. [20] It created excruciating tension to know that at any moment my horses might acquire antibodies that amounted to a death sentence. Mexico, where I would be while awaiting clearance to enter the States, would insist on their destruction if they tested positive. Worst of all, there would be no way for me to know if my horses had the antibodies until they were in quarantine because only government laboratories in the States could perform the necessary tests.

All of this combined to create an atmosphere in which I never thought I was doing enough. Every night, I prepared an *humo* near the mares to clear the area of insects, something I learned to do by watching the stable masters at ranches that raised prize livestock. The technique was simple: spread a layer of sawdust or slightly moist vegetable matter, usually straw, on top of hot coals. If done properly, this produced a limited but steady supply of smoke. An *humo* was very effective against flying pests, such as mosquitoes, and though I was never able to confirm this, I was told it also repelled ticks.

Because of ticks, I declined all offers to turn my horses loose in grassy fields. As much as possible in the tropics, I also tried to avoid riding through any greenery that reached above their hooves. Other precautions also found their way into my repertoire. For example: freshly cut hay was as likely to contain ticks as nutrition, and I soon learned to immerse it in water long enough to ensure that clinging ticks would seek oxygen by floating to the surface. There I was waiting to terminate them, with extreme prejudice!

In addition to the insects that might transmit disease, there were many that could inflict other kinds of damage. There was one fly that would lay an egg in the wound created by its bite. This egg would hatch into a parasitic worm that fed on its host's living flesh, creating an ever-growing, usually infected sore that refused to heal. When I became aware of this danger, I decided that insect repellent was not enough. I tried an insecticide with a label that claimed, inaccurately as it turned out, that it was mild enough to be applied directly to a horse's hide. Next, I hit upon the idea of bathing Hamaca and Ima in disinfectant. This repelled insects more effectively than anything else I tried and had the added advantage of being fatal to eggs deposited on or near the surfaces of their bodies. The downside was that disinfectant aggravated their skin, but in the end, I preferred mild skin irritations to the alternative.

By the end of our second week in Panama, both mares were covered with rashes, weeping insect bites and ugly raw spots. Constant bleaching from a combination of sunlight and disinfectant had dulled their once-lustrous coats, Hamaca's to a faded yellow-black and Ima's to a drab reddish-black. The speed with which they were losing weight was another concern. Any hay I could find was either declined or eaten without enthusiasm and only long enough to take the edge from their hunger. The days when I could buy good grain and hay were behind me. There didn't seem to be any sort of grain mixture available at an affordable price, and in a country where countless varieties of grass grew without cultivation, few bothered to plant good hay. Every afternoon, once the mares were settled in their accommodations, I traveled far and wide, looking for anything the mares might eat. Strangely enough, they preferred corn stalks to all else, in spite of my laborious attempts to find something, anything, more nourishing.

In the town of Aguadulce, the mares had their first taste of *pangola*, a grass reputed to be the tastiest and most nutritious of

Panama's forages. I bought the best I could find, but Hamaca and Ima went on a hunger strike until I finally brought corn stalks. Near the town of Divisa, I asked for and received permission to cut some *pará* grass from experimental fields operated by the local agricultural school. I peddled miles to the fields on a borrowed bicycle and – using a borrowed sickle – cut enough *pará* to fill two gunnysacks. While tying the bags on my borrowed bicycle, I was offered a ride by the driver of a pickup truck that was towing a small trailer. The man was evidently a Good Samaritan, picking up people as he went, and he already had so many riders that no room was left in the pickup's cab or bed.

Following the driver's instructions, I loaded the bike, the bags and myself into the trailer, where I joined another overflow passenger. Once we were roaring down the bumpy, gravel road, I noticed that only a stick and some wire attached the trailer to the truck's bumper. Worse yet, the stick seemed to be working its way loose! Dust raised by the tires was so thick that the driver didn't see my frantic gestures. His attention was riveted to the task of driving much too fast for the condition of the road. I got out the very next time we stopped. The other man in the trailer continued his ride after the driver pooh-poohed my warning and did nothing to improve his failing trailer hitch.

Despite having been obtained at the risk of life and limb, the *pará* grass was eaten sparingly. I waited several hours, hoping Hamaca and Ima would give it a fair trial, but they held out, winning our battle of wills and obliging me to set out in search of corn stalks.

Before long, I was considering taking a bus to the Canal Zone and purchasing alfalfa, a move that would have played havoc with my budget. Fortunately, I discovered an easier, less expensive solution: chicken feed and sugar cane. At a small cattle ranch just south of Soná, the mares dined on those delicacies and gave rave reviews to both. The best thing about chicken feed was that its name described its price. The drawback was that it sometimes had grit among its ingredients. I made absolutely certain this wasn't the case with the brands I bought. Though beneficial to a chicken's digestive system, grit could cause serious colic in a horse.

I had never thought of sugar cane as horse feed, but once my eyes were opened, I was surprised to see how frequently it was fed to all kinds of livestock. Having come from huge sugar cane plantations, Hamaca and Ima had apparently eaten it before and readily ate it again. Not terribly nutritious, cane was widely available and would provide a stable diet while we were in the lowlands. Like the parent of many a finicky eater, I gave up trying to get my mares to eat what was good for them and settled for having them eat.

As a further bonus, sugar cane was often available at mid-day. Even when we were far from farms and towns, I could usually find a few stalks spilled along the highway from trucks on the way to sugar mills. To provide a special treat in the middle of the day, I would select an undamaged stalk and hack it into edible chunks. It would have been nice to live off the land by gathering the best stalks scattered along the highway. However, the horses wouldn't have eaten them, except as an occasional treat. When mature enough to be harvested, cane stalks are woody and fibrous. To be eaten in quantity, sugar cane had to be cut prematurely, while still tender. Such cane could be found only at outdoor markets.

Even the sugar cane and chicken feed didn't satisfy *all* of Hamaca's needs. She had what can best be described as a "grazing instinct." This often caused her to ignore a nutritious meal, preferring to nibble at whatever wisps of grass she could find. In Ecuador she often *grazed* on straw protruding from adobe walls, where it was readily available, being a basic ingredient in adobe bricks. At times she persisted in doing this even after I provided perfectly good meals. Once or twice, she had stayed at this grazing so insistently that I finally tied and fed her where the nearest wall was out of reach.

This peculiar behavior reached its extreme in the Panamanian town of Guabala. There I was offered the use of an outside porch when I could find no other accommodations. I tied my mares to the posts that supported the porch roof and set a meal before them. Anticipating a good night's sleep, I unrolled my sleeping bag and lay down on top of it, needing no covering in the heat. I dozed off quickly, the sounds of my mares' chewing being more relaxing than any music. Suddenly, I was jarred awake by a sinister new sound. Hamaca had decided to graze on the thatched porch roof, and was plucking clumps of tough, sun-bleached grass from high overhead. I quickly jumped up and put an end to that. No sooner was I back on my sleeping bag than the tearing sounds began again. This sequence of events was repeated over and over, and I soon longed to tie Hamaca elsewhere but had no available alternative.

Two mornings later, I looked in on the mares, after a much better night's sleep in Santiago. The afternoon before, I had provided a stack of particularly tender sugar cane along with some very reasonably priced feed pellets. I was astonished to find that both cane and pellets had vanished. From the amount of manure on the ground, I could see that Hamaca and Ima had eaten more than usual, but it didn't seem possible they'd eaten *that* much! Since we were scheduled for a day's rest in Santiago, I had given them a huge amount, intending it to last two days. Certainly some of it had been stolen!

Promptly, I brought a duplicate of the previous night's meal. This time I kept a close eye on things, periodically checking the corral throughout the day and night. Every time I looked in on them, the mares were eating, and to my amazement, they had devoured every last scrap by the next morning.

Those two days of gorging went a long way toward filling out my mares' hollow flanks. As for my own flanks, they continued to grow leaner as my appetite dwindled in Panama's oppressive heat. My thirst, on the other hand, was unquenchable. Fortunately, the roadside was dotted with stands where one could buy a *pipa*, which was a green coconut. These were served with a hole cut through the shell and a straw inserted for drinking the cool, sweet water inside. They were a great pick-me-up. As a bonus, the mares enjoyed snacking on the soft coconut meat once the liquid was consumed and the shell broken open.

With the mares facing so many hardships, I walked more than I had originally intended, hoping to conserve their strength and preserve their health. From Panama City, the mares and I traveled three hundred agonizing miles in thirteen days, with only one day of rest. We made nightly stops at one or another of the towns along the Pan-American Highway, each of which seemed to offer its own particular brand of hardship. [21]

[19] These same factors had prevented the introduction of high-quality cattle. Most beef animals I saw were *Cebu* (also called: *Zebu* or Brahman) cattle. Originally from India, this tough breed thrives in hostile environments.

[20] One of which was for piroplasmosis, a condition prevalent in Panama.

[21] As difficult as it was, travel in Panama would have been even more so if I'd made my ride a few years earlier. Before the Pan-American Highway was completed, overland travel meant fording rivers, many of which became impassable during the rainy season. Just before my ride, the United States had financed the construction of numerous bridges, big and small, that provided Panama with an all-weather highway.

CHAPTER 29

Bellying Up To The Bar

Picking up the chronology of my trip through Panama: I left my jail cell in Antón in the early morning. In no particular hurry for one of a few times since I'd started my trip, I didn't get on the road until mid-morning. A mere two hours later, I reached my destination in the town of Penonomé, twelve miles down the road. Correctly anticipating the shock of coming from the cool Andes to the hot tropics, I'd scheduled a short day.

Along the highway in Penonomé, I passed a small, roadside restaurant with a large sign proudly proclaiming its grand opening. There was something else on the sign, the words: "American-style Hamburgers"! My mouth watered at the thought, but I decided not to subject myself to almost-certain disappointment. Several times in Peru and Ecuador, I had ordered hamburgers and regretted it. If it was true that U.S. restaurants did little justice to Hispanic cuisine, the Latin Americans exacted full revenge with *their* version of the hamburger. Nonetheless, the sign *had* said: "American-style."

In a hurry to get Hamaca and Tina settled, I continued on to the home of a man to whom *Señor* Isaacs had referred me. The man proved to be extremely hospitable, offering a spacious stall for the mares and a bed in his home for me.

"My wife is shopping in Panama City," he said, "so I can't offer you lunch. However, just yesterday, an excellent restaurant opened up downtown. I've already tried it and highly recommend the food."

"Is that the place that advertises American-style hamburgers?" I asked.

"One and the same. It's owned by a countryman of yours."

"A North American?"

"As a matter of fact, yes."

American-style hamburgers prepared by an American! It was too much to resist. I had the rest of the day to kill, and, if nothing else, there must be a good story behind a man from the States opening up a restaurant in the boondocks of Panama. I found the restaurant doing a booming business, filled with locals who were animatedly talking with a man who was obviously the North American owner. I took great delight in seeing how much they seemed to like him. Though most Americans I saw in Panama spoke little, if any, Spanish, this particular man could speak it as if it were his native tongue.

281

Periodically everyone around him broke into riotous laughter at some remark he made. He could have changed the future of American-Panamanian relations by simply teaching social graces in the Canal Zone.

"This is the second day of my grand opening, and you're my first American customer," he said after he came over to personally wait on me. "Something tells me you'll also be the first person to order the specialty of the house?"

"Would that be the American-style hamburger?" I asked, with a smile.

"That it would."

"I haven't had a hamburger for a long time, and I don't want to be disappointed," I teased. "Are they any good?"

"Try one," he urged. "You'll feel like you're back in the States."

"In that case, I gotta have one!"

I wasn't disappointed. True to the owner's word, when I closed my eyes and savored the sandwich that practically symbolizes the United States, I could almost imagine I was back home. That historic moment combined the grand opening, the first American customer and (amazingly!) the first hamburger ordered. I had to pay anyhow! Nevertheless, I came back a short while later and splurged, ordering a second burger. Eating them one at a time like that, I prolonged the pleasure for the best part of two hours.

The next day, I rode and walked to Aguadulce. At Bob Green's suggestion, I'd been hoping to rest a day there with a friend of his who raised racehorses. Knowing that racehorses are fed only the best, I envisioned Hamaca and Ima burying their heads up to the eyes in an unlimited supply of alfalfa. However, the man was out of town, and my mares spent the night tied to a tree in a mosquito-infested backyard, nibbling half-heartedly at hay that didn't appeal to either of them.

I stayed the night in a hotel, where my sleep was repeatedly inter-rupted by someone outside the hotel, playing music at an unbeliev-able volume. The culprit had speakers powerful enough to project music into every nook and cranny of the small downtown area. To my despair, the music featured endless repetition of tedious refrains, as if a phonograph needle was repeatedly getting stuck in the same groove. I couldn't imagine any circumstances under which I would have enjoyed it, least of all when I was exhausted after a long, hard day. As my first line of defense, I stuffed my ears with cotton from my bottle of vitamin pills. When that did little good, I buried my head under my pillow, but all that accomplished was to make me perspire. Twice, I angrily got out of bed, dressed and charged outside, determined to eliminate that aggravating racket or not come back alive!

Aguadulce's buildings were mostly masonry, and the music reverberated, echoing from every wall and seeming to originate from a thousand places at once. Again and again, I established what had to be its source only to find that it was coming from elsewhere. Finally, I gave up, which was just as well considering how tactful I wasn't feeling.

Three unremarkable days later – after stops in Divisa and Santiago – the mares and I were invited to spend the night at a small cattle ranch just south of Soná. It rained that evening, and at first, I welcomed the precipitation, anticipating that it would cool what had been an extremely hot day. Instead, the rain had the same effect as pouring water on the hot rocks in a sauna, and the air was soon more oppressive than ever. Despite that revolting development, I got an excellent night's sleep, thanks to a fan and a ten-foot-long bed. My hosts amused themselves and me by placing two five-foot-long mattresses end to end, creating the first bed I'd ever had that was too long for me.

The fan kept me comfortably dry for the night, but the instant I got up and began preparing to push on to La Arena, I was again coated with perspiration. Immediately, I noticed a painful stinging sensation, and a quick inspection revealed that both of my arms were covered with tiny crisscrossed cuts. Thinking back, I realized that these microscopic wounds had been inflicted the day before by grass, and not the kind I used to cut on weekends. In fact, this particular grass had turned the tables and cut *me*!

Hamaca, Ima and I had spent the previous day in country covered with dense, broad-bladed grass that grew six to eight feet tall, right up to the edge of the highway. When vehicles approached from only one direction, they were able to give us space along the edge of the narrow road, but simultaneous traffic in both directions forced us into the roadside grass, in spite of my reluctance to take Hamaca and Ima into tick territory. While plowing through the huge, stout blades of grass, I had disregarded the razor-sharp edges. The consequences were countless minute cuts, inflicted without any immediate sensation but remarkably painful a day later.

On our way to La Arena, we were in the same kind of vegetation for a second straight day, and its density increased until it was impenetrable. At that point, the mares and I were forced to pound the edge of the concrete highway and take our chances with the traffic. This kept Hamaca and Ima beyond the reach of ticks and saved me from being constantly nicked by the knife-edged blades of grass. Those gains, however, were made at a cost. We were constantly harried by traffic, and pounding the hard surface was hard on the horses' legs, even though I got off and led them.

Panama was the first country in Latin America where I had seen semi-truck-and-trailer rigs. The drivers seemed unaware of the effect their vehicles can have on horses, and most didn't move over when they passed us. The roar of their engines was deafening, and the huge trailers created powerful wind currents that pushed and pulled at us. It surprised me that Hamaca seemed unconcerned when one of these giants passed within a few feet of us, all eighteen tires screaming and sending chills up and down my spine. That was a welcome change from her shenanigans in Ecuador's traffic.

I spent the next night in a small storage room behind a combination general store and saloon. After buying supplies at the general store, I glanced into the adjoining saloon. The store had been unremarkable, but the saloon was a different story. I stepped inside to take a better look. Hardly an expert on drinking establishments, I was pretty sure I'd never see another like it.

At that moment, there were no customers. Neither were there stools, chairs or any furnishings other than an extraordinarily tall bar. If I had bellied up to it, I would barely have been able to see over, not to mention that I would have had very sore shoulders if I'd spent much time resting my elbows on the top. The bartender stood on a raised floor on the opposite side. He reminded me of a judge looking down on a defendant.

"Why is the bar so tall?" I asked.

"You'll know as soon as you see a customer come through the door," the bartender answered with a mysterious smile.

The saloon had two doors. The one that connected it with the general store was unremarkable. The other, which opened onto the street, could easily have admitted a truck.

"Couldn't you just tell me why everything is so big around here?" I asked.

"You'll soon see," he assured me.

I looked down at the packed dirt floor and up at the ceiling, high above me. It was a puzzle worthy of Sherlock Holmes. In a land where few were taller than I had been in the fourth grade, here was a saloon of dimensions that dwarfed me. True to the bartender's promise, the mystery was solved with the arrival of customers. They rode through the spacious door on horses and proceeded to the oversized bar where they were served while still sitting in their saddles.

"May we buy you a drink?" one said when he noticed me.

"Thank you very much," I responded, "but I don't drink."

The man looked at me, his face carefully twisted into an expression indicating that my answer meant I couldn't be trusted.

"A soft drink?" he offered.

"That sounds wonderful," I accepted, stepping up to the bar after speculating about what he might think if I went to get one of my horses first.

The bartender overlooked (so to speak!) the fact that I appeared to be a child standing on his knees in a hole. He leaned forward and reached down to hand me a cola.

The next morning, Hamaca, Ima and I headed for Puerto Vidal. All day, we were in wilderness and moving further from civilization with every step. Suddenly and unexpectedly, conveniences such as electricity and indoor plumbing were nonexistent, except in the largest villages, and I found myself once again among Indians. Just north of Soná, the highway had changed. Since I had first seen it, Panama's *Panamericana* had been a straight line, surfaced with concrete, knifing across terrain that was invariably flat. Suddenly, it had turned into a crude dirt road winding through rolling foothills, surfaced with rocks that ranged from the size of a dime to that of a baseball. Often there was no reasonable alternative to walking on those rocks, and by the end of the day, my mares and I were hobbling on tender feet.

From Puerto Vidal, we limped and scrambled on to Guabala. By then, we were a sorry-looking crew, all three perpetually bathed in sweat and the mares' coats more faded than ever. My new, bright-red shirt, a gift from Mr. Isaacs in Chorrera, had turned pale under a layer of caked salt. Both mares were covered with weeping bites and ugly bare spots. Hamaca's *armpits* were peeling and cracking for some unknown reason, and both mares remained drastically underweight. Worst of all, Ima had a foreleg that stiffened whenever we stopped moving. This limited her willingness to walk around during the night and made her hobble noticeably when she did. So far, she had been able to work out of her stiffness each morning, but her malady caused me a great deal of worry. If it worsened, I'd be brought to a halt yet again! Regardless, there was no shortage of people who wanted to buy my mares.

"Are they for sale?"

Those words were spoken constantly, from the doorways of

houses, restaurants and stores, from passing cars and from people who suddenly appeared out of nowhere and came running up behind me. My days were endlessly punctuated by the words: "Are they for sale?" I'm proud that I always answered in the negative without once asking what sort of price might be offered. Though my adventure had a commercial side to it, my priorities required that I first finish what I had set out to do, despite the fact that Central Americans often paid more for Peruvian horses than my countrymen did. In fact, they had been known to pay enough that, even after handing over Panama's taxes, I would have been ahead of the game, compared to what I'd clear in the States.

There was another consideration as well. Central America had imported Peruvian horses off and on for almost two centuries, and yet all that remained were a few partbloods. I wanted my mares to be sold where their descendants would be pure.

Shortly before dark, on the road between Puerto Vidal and Guabala, another man took a strong interest in my horses. Like many others, he approached me. Unlike the others, he had no thought of buying. Instead, he had noticed that the mares and I looked as if we might be interested in some rest, relaxation and good food. He introduced himself as a close friend of the Motta family, which didn't help much because I'd never heard of them.

"The Mottas have a large cattle ranch right along the highway just outside Remedios," he told me, "and they'll no doubt welcome your visit. You and your horses will be comfortable and very well-fed there."

His proposition sounded marvelous. After three hundred miles with only a single day's rest, the ranch sounded like the right place for a break ... and all the better if the horses could eat well. It felt a bit strange, however, to be receiving this invitation from a man who had no apparent authorization to issue it.

"I plan to visit the Mottas this evening," the man continued. "Shall I tell them to expect you? When will you arrive? Tomorrow?"

"God willing," I answered, using a typical Latin expression.

I thanked my benefactor, and he went on his way after giving me directions to his friends' ranch. My plan was to drop in on the Mottas the next day. If they seemed surprised to see me, were less than enthusiastic about having guests, seemed worried about hoof-and-mouth disease or short on facilities, I would immediately continue on. If they welcomed me with open arms, I'd thank my lucky stars!

After an overnight stay in Guabala, the mares and I traveled a mere ten miles the next morning. At the *Hermanos* Motta cattle ranch, we were received every bit as cordially as promised. The Motta's invitation was so enthusiastic that it seemed *I* was doing *them* a favor by accepting. The mares and I stayed for the remainder of the day and a full day after that.

Hamaca and Ima were offered the run of a huge pasture that would be theirs only, except for three bulls. These, I was assured, wouldn't come near them. I had to admit it would be an ideal way for the mares to rest and fill their stomachs. Nonetheless, owing to my fear of ticks and mosquitoes, I asked if it would be possible to put them in a stall. The Mottas assured me that the danger from parasites was nil and that the grass in their pastures was of an extremely high quality.

Furthermore, the pastures were well-trimmed as a result of constant grazing by twelve thousand head of *Cebu* cattle. In such short grass, the ranch's spraying program had eliminated parasites. That being the case, I decided to give Hamaca and Ima the chance to enjoy some freedom and to graze to their hearts' content. Considering, however, that a single tick could render a horse ineligible to enter the United States, I resolved to inspect them three times daily and bathe them a like number of times with disinfectant.

Letting the mares graze in a large, open area was like a magic potion. They had again been eating without enthusiasm and had been constantly uneasy. Accustomed to the desert where they could see for vast distances, they had been uncomfortable in a country where vegetation blocked the view and prevented them from identifying the sources of strange noises and unfamiliar smells.

Once they were loose in the huge pasture, the mares seemed more at ease than at any time since leaving Ecuador. Both immediately showed a strong interest in the tender grass. Hamaca indulged her grazing instinct to the fullest, and for two days and nights, I seldom saw her with her nose out of the grass. It was delightful to see her satisfying her peculiar need in a way that was nourishing, and under circumstances where she wasn't destroying someone's roof! Ima, too, ate voraciously but not as constantly as Hamaca. During her spare time, she added a new dimension to her many-faceted personality. Cautiously at first, she tried out the role of bully, and she liked it so much that she soon embraced it heart and soul.

When the *vaqueros* rode in for lunch, they turned their cowponies loose to graze for an hour or two. Offended, Ima boldly staked out the choicest section of the pasture and wouldn't allow the intruders on it, even though she'd eaten her fill. Ears back, she would rush toward the pasture's rightful residents and turn her hindquarters as if to kick. Due to a combination of fortunate circumstances, she got away with it.

Doubtlessly, those cowponies had done a whole lot more fighting than Ima, and they were almost certainly better at it. Not only that, but they had right on their side, Ima being the *real* intruder. Happily for Ima, they were philosophers. They looked around, noted that the pasture was very large, considered the fact that they were tired and hungry, decided that matters of the stomach should take precedence over matters of the ego and went elsewhere to do their grazing.

With success behind her, Ima decided to branch out in her new career. She next targeted the three enormous *Cebu* bulls with which she and Hamaca shared their pasture. In terms of potential for disaster, this was a move on a par with Hitler's invasion of Russia. I suffered through some very tense moments when I first saw Ima pin her ears back and make a sudden charge in the direction of the giant *toros*. They turned to face her, weighing twice what she did, outnumbering her and equipped with built-in weapons for which she had no defense. She stopped her charge and stood glaring but made no further move in their direction. I hoped her bluff had been effectively called. Far better she should lose face than tangle with those bulls!

Full of confidence, Ima repeated her charge even more boldly than before, and the bulls turned tail and beat a hasty retreat. For the second time that day, I wondered if my mares wouldn't be far better off in a stall.

"Do you think it would be safer if I put them in a stall?" I asked one of the Mottas. "They like to be together and will need only one."

Señor Motta laughed and informed me that the little drama I'd just witnessed had already been acted out countless times when I wasn't looking.

"The bulls are accustomed to being herded by men on horses, and they won't challenge her," he said, reassuringly. "Besides, she has natural cow sense."

Yeah, but does she have bull sense? I asked myself, turning my attention to the pasture again, just in time to see the bulls retreat once again before Ima's latest exhibition of swagger. Chuckling to myself, I wondered if perhaps she and not Hamaca might turn out to be my Tevis Cup horse. The willingness to do a hundred miles at top speed, after all, is a matter of attitude as much as anything else.

Following our stay at the Motta ranch, we made it as far as the town of David, near the Costa Rican border, in two more days. Along the way, Hamaca's and Ima's faith in me was put to the test. By then, my two mares gradually had come to trust me without any apparent reservations. As a result, they would go anywhere I asked, trailing along behind me so faithfully that they even tried following me into stores and homes, much to the delight (or consternation) of onlookers. In northern Panama, however, we came face-to-face with a series of bridges that promised to challenge this blind trust and gave even me a bad case of the chills.

The roadway on most of these bridges was composed of heavy-duty, steel grates, which allowed my mares to look straight down into the canyon or river below their hooves. When we came to the first of these, I was prepared for a long struggle or even the necessity of finding a way into the deep canyon below and up the other side. To my amazement, Hamaca and Ima calmly followed me across, their attention directed downward, showing signs of caution but not distress.

On bridges of other designs, they carefully made their way around or across gaping holes in the roadway, where chunks of concrete had dropped out or planks had broken. I think these bridges scared me more than them. More than once I gave myself goose bumps worrying that a chunk of concrete or a plank might give way beneath one of my horses.

On the way to David, I slept for two consecutive nights in settlements so small they had no names. Both nights the best accommodations I could find were concrete floors, which were made only slightly more comfortable by liberal doses of aspirin. The first night, I hitchhiked forty miles to and from a small ranch where I bought hay and grain. Hamaca and Ima ate only a few stalks and kernels before turning up their noses at my offering. The following evening, again in search of feed, I traveled twenty miles as a passenger on a tractor with no lights and too much play in the steering. I stood on the frame behind the driver and held on for dear life while he wandered all over the highway, turning in at a series of ranches. At the third of these, I was able to buy feed, and my chauffeur then brought me back to my horses.

Once daylight faded, I took the utmost care to avoid standing in front of the tractor's single rear-facing reflector, the only warning other drivers would see before they were on top of us in the semi-darkness. Considering our snail-like pace and lack of lights, I wanted those drivers to have as much advance notice as possible. Our round-trip took over an hour and cost only a pittance, though it had also required risking my life. I arrived back at the mares' corral, quite pleased with my dedication. After paying my fare, I presented the mares with the fruit of my considerable efforts, the best horse feed available in the area. They hardly touched it. If someone had offered to buy them at that moment, he could have had both at rock-bottom prices.

Throughout the two-day trip to David, the road was surfaced with large round rocks that caused a great deal of slipping and stumbling. To spare the horses, I walked. On downhill stretches, my toes were jammed against the fronts of my boots, and this cost me three toe-nails, a recurrence of a problem caused by wearing shoes that were too small when I was a boy. As for the horses' feet, Hamaca and Ima arrived in David with only four horseshoes between them, of which all had worn paper-thin and then broken on the rocky roadway. Once I was settled, my first priority would be to find a farrier.

David was a hard day's ride from the border with Costa Rica. While there, I was to be a guest at the Governor's *finca*. This had been arranged by the chief of police in Antón, *if* he'd kept his word. Standing before the Governor's inviting mansion, I hoped he had. I knocked on the door, and a man emerged from a nearby building. In a soft voice, he explained he was in charge and asked why I was there. I was carrying a letter of recommendation from the Police Chief in Antón, and I handed it to him.

"The Governor is out of town with his family on vacation," the man explained. "No doubt, he'll be distressed when he returns and finds that he missed you."

It soon became evident that the man in charge was finding it dis-tasteful to turn me away. Twice I started down the long driveway, and twice he called me back to explain that the Governor would have attended me splendidly if only he had been there. Each time, I did my best to release him from his self-imposed guilt. Made uncomfortable by *his* discomfort, I assured him that I understood. Finally, however, the man insisted on finding a way to be of help. Expressing regret, he explained that he could offer nothing more than rustic quarters for the mares and myself. I was perfectly happy with that prospect and assured him so.

The mares were turned loose in a well-kept pasture, and I was shown to a tool shed beneath a water tank. My host returned moments later with a chaise lounge, which he offered in lieu of a bed. I thanked him and asked where I might find a horseshoer. He could do no more than refer me to someone who might know. The man who might have known, didn't, but he was able to refer me to someone who referred me to someone else. While going from one person to the next, I stopped by the office of the Costa Rican Consul to ask about requirements for getting Hamaca and Ima into his country. He said I needed my Peruvian health certificate, my Ecuadorian health certificate, the one issued when I arrived in Panama and another from a private veterinarian in David, dated no later than the day before I crossed into Costa Rica. It was no surprise when the Consul advised that – for a healthy fee, of course – he would have to "authenticate" all four health certificates.

Since there was a veterinarian's office nearby, I quickly made an appointment to have the mares examined later that afternoon and then resumed my search for a farrier. My quest finally led me to the only farrier in town. He was an elderly gentleman who coldly advised me that he no longer practiced his trade. I had to practically beg before he consented to come out of retirement.

Since he was no longer practicing his profession, the farrier had neither horseshoes nor nails. I had to forego an afternoon of badly needed rest in favor of hitchhiking to Concepción. There, after much searching, I was able to find and buy two sets of horseshoes, the first steel shoes I'd seen since leaving the States. To my dismay, this little shopping trip took the best part of the afternoon. When I finally brought shoes, nails and mares to the farrier, he proved too feeble to remove the old shoes. He worked, perspired and swore, but made no progress. Part of the problem was that he was using only a machete and a short-handled hammer that was closer to a toy than a tool. Finally I could stand his ineffectual bumbling no longer and offered my help.

The old farrier reminded me that he was shoeing my horses only as a favor and gratefully handed me his tools. I proceeded to remove the shoes, placing the machete against the crimped end of the nails and striking it with the little hammer to cut them off. The machete was dull and made of soft metal, and the pathetic little hammer lacked weight, balance and leverage. Clipping the ends of the nails could have been accomplished in seconds with a rasp and clippers, but equipped as I was, it took a quarter hour. Removing the shoes took a like amount of time, using the claws of the hammer. My shoer at home would have done it in a few seconds, with tongs.

Then I turned the job back to the farrier. Trimming the hooves and nailing on the new shoes would require his expertise, and I resolved to be patient no matter how long he took. He had no hoof clippers, as it turned out, but that was no problem. The last set of shoes had worn out so quickly that the hooves had scarcely grown. All that was really necessary was to nail the new shoes in place.

The old man bent six of the first eight nails he tried to drive, and I watched in silent frustration as he took a half-hour – and burned most of his energy – putting on one of the eight shoes. At that rate, he'd still be working on my horses when the winner of the Tevis Cup crossed the finish line! Figuring I could do no worse, I convinced him to oversee me while I shod the mares, myself. All in all, I didn't do a bad job for my very first try.

When my labors were over, I took Hamaca and Ima to the veterinarian's office where he examined them and issued health certificates. Then I rode to the Governor's *finca*, turned the mares loose in their pasture, ate dinner at a nearby restaurant and returned to my lodgings, well after dark. Looking back and forth between my humble tool shed and the Governor's mansion, I couldn't help but wonder how the evening might have turned out if I had arrived when the Governor was in town. On second thought, I decided I was glad things had worked out as they had. My afternoon of much-needed rest had been consumed by the trip to Concepción, the horseshoeing episode and the visit to the vet. In the main house, I'd have had inescapable social obligations. As it was, I went to bed early and slept marvelously, every bit as well as I would have in the finest house on earth.

From David to the Costa Rican border, forty miles, Hamaca, Ima and I traveled by truck. The day before, I had made the acquaintance of a trucker who kindly offered to take us there without charge. Knowing that the mares' new health certificate was valid for only one day, I was only too happy to accept.

When my horses and I presented ourselves at the Costa Rican border station, the Ministry of Agriculture official refused to let us cross.

"These aren't the correct health certificates. You need to have health certificates from the official *government* veterinarian in David, not a private veterinarian," the man insisted.

"But your Consul in David informed me just yesterday that these were all I needed."

"In fact, these are unnecessary. All we require is a health certificate from the government veterinarian in David."

"That means I have to ride eighty miles because of a mistake that's not my fault," I complained, when it became obvious I wasn't going to talk him out of it.

"Not at all, *señor*," I was told. "You can take the bus."

"With horses?" I asked, unwisely sarcastic.

"We can keep your horses in our quarantine facilities until you get back," came the helpful answer.

"But won't the government veterinarian need to examine them?"

"Show him the certificates you already have, and he'll issue the ones we need."

"Be sure to have the Costa Rican Consul authenticate the certificates before you leave David," another official added.

Briefly, I teetered on the verge of arguing further. How ridiculous could things get? The government veterinarian didn't even need to see my horses in order to issue a health certificate. He could do so based on papers I already had, yet the border officials wouldn't accept those same papers! I was drawing in enough air to express my objections when I realized it would be unwise. The man in front of me had the power to place additional obstacles in my path if I angered him, and he was already looking somewhat irritated. I was going back to David, like it or not.

My newfound friend with the truck had not yet left on his return trip to David and was happy to take me along. During the drive, he commiserated, describing far-worse inconveniences to which he'd been subjected at various borders. I'm sure he intended for his stories to cheer me up, but they only made me feel worse. His experiences seemed to erase all hope that I would ever be able to avoid wasteful paper shuffling.

"I don't believe I should be charged another fee since the four I paid yesterday were unnecessary," I announced when I brought my freshly issued government health certificate to the Consul in David for authenticating.

"I must be paid for every document I authenticate," he answered, looking at me with bored, half-hooded eyes.

"But the ones you authenticated yesterday were for nothing," I stood firm.

"All five of these certificates are required to cross the border," he insisted, staring off to his right from between eyelids that had narrowed even more.

"Why didn't you tell me that yesterday?"

"You didn't ask."

"I most certainly did. I asked for all requirements to cross the border."

The Consul turned and started toward the door of his office. Once he was inside, I knew he'd be unavailable to me for the next day or two, at best. I relented and agreed to pay. The Consul couldn't resist exacting a small measure of revenge.

"Come back in four hours," he said, his eyes advising that the price of further complaining would be to wait even longer.

The episode's only saving grace was that it reminded me of a humorous incident described by Aime Tschiffely in the book he wrote about *his* ride. As I left the Consul's office, it was consoling to savor the way Tschiffely had gotten the better of one petty bureaucrat who stopped him in a remote town, asking to see a permit for his firearms. Though authorized to bear his weapons, Tschiffely didn't have the specific paper requested. Furthermore, acquiring that paper would have required retracing his steps to a city several days behind him. Feeling certain that the official standing before him couldn't read, he calmly handed over a hotel receipt. The receipt bore an impressive-looking signature and the imprints left behind by a series of rubber stamps. The official studied it carefully and returned it with a polite: "Thank you, sir." Once again I felt inferior to my hero. After all, *I* had a receipt for the horseshoes, and it, too, was covered with marks left behind by rubber stamps. Sadly enough, times had changed. The men overseeing my border crossing could read.

Who says education is such a wonderful thing?!

Bandits closing in and the packsaddle is slipping (see page 207).

CHAPTER 30

The Way to San José

After having Hamaca's and Ima's new health certificates authenticated, I caught a bus to the border town of Paso de Canoas. I arrived at 8:00 P.M. and immediately presented my new papers, half-expecting the authorities to come up with further requirements. Instead they smiled and told me I was free to cross the border. Quickly, before they could change their minds, I removed my mares from the quarantine facilities and began my projected weeklong trek to San José, Costa Rica's capital.

The first thirty yards of my renewed travels passed through a covered area, which resembled an oversized carport. It was there that people bound to or from Panama would leave their vehicles while they went inside to deal with Costa Rica's formalities. Every parking space was filled, and a line of cars, coming from Costa Rica, waited for spaces to become available. Rather than wait his turn, one driver had bypassed the line and was slowly driving through the parking area, hoping to pirate the next available spot. The waiting drivers were glaring at him, undoubtedly wondering what gave him the right to escape the long wait he was helping to create. Everywhere I looked, I saw cars with U.S. license plates. For some reason, a swarm of U.S. citizens was headed into Panama. I could see Americans everywhere, most looking tired and grumpy. A steady stream entered the border station and stood in long lines, waiting to present their documents.

"What's going on?" I asked one man who was striding purposefully past. "Why are so many Americans coming into Panama tonight?"

"You haven't heard about the revolution?" he asked, without slowing his pace.

"What revolution? In Costa Rica?"

"No, in Nicaragua."

The answer came from another man. The first had kept walking, ignoring me after answering my first question. The second man was more relaxed and came to a stop, eyeing my mares.

"Is this revolution still going on?" I asked.

"Actually, the excitement seems to be over," he answered, "but you never know when things might heat up again."

"What happened?" I asked, wanting more details. "I've been out of touch with the news for a while."

"There was an attempted coup. The revolutionaries took North

295

American hostages, and the government closed the borders. No one could get out. It took a few days to restore order and get the hostages released. This morning the borders were reopened."

"Looks like every American in the country decided to leave at the same time," I observed.

"This isn't half of them," the man said, chuckling. "There were more that went north than south."

"How bad was it?" I asked.

I remembered that Tschiffely had bypassed Nicaragua to avoid a revolution in progress. Nicaraguans devoted a lot of their time to such activities, and I was worried about how *I* might be affected.

"It was scary. I'd recommend staying out of there for a while," he informed me sternly.

The heavy traffic and the darkness made it inadvisable to go farther that night. I rented a nearby corral and reconsidered an invitation from a Panamanian border official. Seeing how badly my day had gone, the man had kindly offered to let me sleep in one of the border station's back rooms. Belatedly, I took him up on his offer.

Hamaca, Ima and I started out bright and early the following morning. During that and the next few days, I had the invigorating feeling I was making tremendous progress. For one thing, I had traveled far enough west to enter a new time zone, a milestone I celebrated by setting my watch back. A more substantial kind of progress was the one hundred and fifty miles the mares and I covered during our first four days in Costa Rica. It was our fastest push to date and was made possible by several factors. My horses were adjusting to the tropics. They were eating better, and their various afflictions were disappearing. Their backs had recovered and again permitted them to carry me and the baggage. I supplemented the saddle blankets I was already using with four more, two under each saddle. These lifted both saddles and made them cling less securely. Constantly, the riding saddle slid and shifted, forcing me to keep my weight perfectly balanced at all times.

Though we broke our previous four-day record for distance, we were traveling no faster than usual. The added progress came from spending longer hours on the road and from my decision to call upon Ima for her first saddle duty. Before then, she had carried the cargo and packsaddle but never me. I began by riding Ima only a couple of hours per day. As often happens with horses, she took on an unexpected personality when ridden. The attitude she had shown toward the bulls and cowponies at the Motta ranch was suddenly directed toward me! If she didn't want to do what I asked – which was frequently – she didn't hesitate to question my authority. It took several battles for us to reach an understanding, and she sulked about the outcome for a week. Her attitude soured to the point where I suspected she was sticking her tongue out at me when I wasn't looking.

Throughout that first day in Costa Rica, I passed endless banana fields. In the process, I gleaned two new entries for *Albright's Book of Useless Facts*. Fact number one: bananas grow upside down. I already knew that they grew in clusters because that's how they come from the supermarket. The surprise was that the free end defies gravity to grow upwards from the stem, unlike any other fruit I'd ever seen. Fact number two: while on the trees, the banana clusters were protected from birds by clear plastic sacks. I had no idea how the sacks worked. They were hardly substantial enough to resist a sharp beak. I could only speculate that their purpose was to deny landing spots within reach of the ripening fruit. As I rode past mile after mile of bananas, I couldn't help sympathizing with the men who put those sacks in place. They had a job infinitely more mind-numbing than the ones I'd been fleeing when I hatched the idea for my ride.

The bananas I saw were always a rich green color, indicating that they were far from being ripe. Harvested green and allowed to ripen on their way to market, they finally – if all went well – turned yellow just before being sold, peeled and eaten. The timing of the harvest and subsequent shipment had to be precise lest the bananas arrive at their destination mushy and overripe.

At the end of our first day in Costa Rica, the mares and I were most hospitably received at a small cattle ranch. Early the next morning we continued on, passing another thirty-five miles of banana fields before reaching a plantation workers' settlement, complete with both residential and commercial districts. There I rented a room at a dingy hotel. The mares stayed a couple of miles away at yet another small cattle ranch. I managed to find carrots in the marketplace that evening, much to Hamaca's and Ima's delight. They had eaten chopped carrots by the bushel at the Military Academy in Quito and seemed happy to be served something familiar. Unlike humans, horses generally dislike variety in their diets. Furthermore, their bodies have a difficult time adjusting to changes in feed. During the previous week, Hamaca and Ima hadn't dined on the same fare for two successive nights, having eaten sugar cane, corn stalks and two tropical grass hays called *imperial* and *gigante*.

Once convinced that ticks didn't hang out in short grass, especially if it had been sprayed, I had turned Hamaca and Ima loose in a couple of carefully selected pastures. Quickly, they decided that grazing was a tedious way to scrape up a meal, and not even Hamaca remained all that enthusiastic about it. When loose in pastures, both mares would quickly cease grazing and come to me when I showed up with whatever hay I had found.

There were other signs that my traveling companions were adjusting to the tropics. Countless inoculations from insects had "immunized" them, and their once-severe reactions to bug bites were fast becoming a thing of the past. Too, they were taking on a more rounded appearance, amazing in view of the distances we were traveling. Proving that human beings are impossible to satisfy, I found myself wishing they'd gain weight faster, overlooking the fact that few horses working as hard and eating as poorly would have been gaining at all.

To speed up their weight gain, Hamaca and Ima were going to need better feed. Thus, it wasn't only the anticipated cooler temperatures that had me looking forward to Costa Rica's high country. It was also my feeling that better quality hay and grain would be available there.

The low country of Costa Rica was semi-jungle, a type of terrain I had never before seen. Lush vegetation grew right up to the roadside, forming a substantial barrier for anyone who sought to enter the dense broadleaf evergreen forests. The undergrowth was so thick that it foiled my searching eyes when I tried to see past the edge of the road. From behind that impenetrable veil of green, unseen monkeys and birds gave forth stereotypical jungle cries and shrieks.

When the sun was out, I caught glimpses of exotic-looking creatures, including iguanas, sloths and anteaters. When it rained, no living thing, aside from people, could be seen anywhere. When the rain ceased, tiny, spectacularly colored birds would abandon their hiding places, speedily darting from bush to bush as if verifying that everything was all right.

Every plant and tree was different from any I had ever seen. The twisted, gnarled trees were coated with moss, and long, thick vines hung from their branches. One of the more common plants that huddled beneath the trees had enormous leaves. People caught in a sudden downpour would pick one and balance it on their heads, taking on the appearance of ants hard at work. These unique umbrellas were effective, readily available and disposable without harm to the environment.

Often the only sign of mankind was the highway itself, and even that trace of civilization would have disappeared if nature could have had her way. Everywhere, vines crawled into the roadway as if hoping to reclaim it, but passing traffic cut back the fast-growing greenery and kept the jungle at bay.

Electrical storms were a daily (and nightly) event, complete with roaring thunder and awesome lightning. The latter was particularly unwelcome at night when I had sneaked off to the far corner of a clearing to take care of personal business. As often as not, my privacy would disappear when the area was suddenly illuminated bright as day by a bolt of lightening. Fortunately, darkness would return before anyone could see me blushing!

The weather that year was unusual, or at least, that's what the local folks said. I was suspicious, as I always am when told by locals that their weather is usually better. Throughout my travels, few have ever told me otherwise, and it's hard to believe that I have so seldom happened upon typical weather. At any rate, heavy rains came when I didn't expect them and caught me unprepared. My sleeping bag and other items of supposedly unnecessary gear had again been sent ahead. Having been told that the rainy season was over, these "unnecessary" items had included my waterproof poncho. Driven by necessity to follow the lead of the locals, I found that those huge leaves were a whole lot better than nothing.

My traveler's checks, passport and horse certificates were kept dry by wrapping them inside several layers of banana leaves. Everything else got soaked on a daily basis. Never had I seen such enormous raindrops! When they landed on hard surfaces, they splattered, producing visual displays that looked like the explosions of miniature artillery shells. When they hit standing water, a geyser erupted, resembling the detonation of a tiny depth charge (it *must* be true that men think in military terms!). For hours on end, these huge drops pelted my horses and me, hard enough to sting and often enough to discourage.

One morning, after an all-night rain, I came upon a flock of buzzards. Looking thoroughly disheartened, they were standing with their wings extended and their backs positioned to soak up every available ray of sunshine. When I drew near, they hopped away, wings still wide-open. I greatly enjoyed their clumsy efforts to escape on foot without folding their wings, which would have interrupted the drying process. Lacking the oily feathers of waterfowl, the buzzards were soaked to the skin. They knew more rain would soon fall and were anxious to dry off and get airborne before that happened. If they didn't find a meal soon, they might have to do without or search on foot!

Among the area's greatest curiosities were the tiny living creatures swimming in puddles left behind by the rain. These seemed to be tadpoles but were so small I couldn't be sure. Whatever they were, I wondered where they came from. And how did they survive when the puddles dried up? I'm sure there were naturalists who could have answered those questions, but without their input, I was baffled. [22]

During our third day in Costa Rica, we started into the Talamanca Mountains and in three days climbed from sea level to 11,000 feet. The first day, for most of forty-two miles, we paralleled a river. Its steep descent created several picturesque waterfalls, of which no two were alike. They were wide, narrow, lofty or low. The water might plummet in a single cascade, or in several, and might be airborne all the way from top to bottom or atomized into mist by protruding rocks on the way down. The variety was fascinating.

Determined to spend that night in the town of Buenos Aires, [23] I broke my own rule and traveled after dark. In other countries, I wouldn't have risked it, but there, I didn't hesitate. Costa Rica had a reputation as one of the most peaceful nations on earth, and while there, I never once felt threatened by my fellow man.

Just outside Buenos Aires, I met a pleasant young North American Peace Corps volunteer. He offered his help and began by arranging for my horses to spend the night in a vacant chicken coop. The structure was small but provided protection from the intermittent rain. After Hamaca and Ima were settled, my newfound friend drove me around in his Jeep, helping me round up their dinner. Hoping for quality feed at that altitude, I was able to find only crushed corn and sugar cane. In response to my requests for alfalfa, oats or barley, I was told that farther along I'd find all three in abundance.

My Peace Corps friend provided a sleeping bag and made arrangements for me to pass the night in a tool shed. I shared those accommodations with another "stray dog," a young Englishman traveling on a budget as limited as my own.

******

Some of my Peruvian friends taught me what amounts to a very pure form of "racism," a word that provokes automatic horror among most North Americans. My friends' racism differed from the classic North American version in several important ways, most particularly in that it was completely an intellectual activity and didn't justify even the slightest mistreatment of other races, nor did it refuse to recognize exceptions to the rule. Simply stated, it said: certain traits go hand in hand with certain nationalities.

In the States, too, there are many who believe this, but few will openly admit it these days. This seems to be an attempt to compensate for a history during which black people and other minorities have been treated deplorably. In an attempt to erase the shame, Americans have gone from oppressing certain so-called *inferior* races to denying that there are differences. One can justifiably argue that these differences are more learned than genetic, but denying their existence has its origin in political rather than scientific reasons.

In the case of British people, I had always found them to be extraordinary conversationalists, intelligent, well spoken, well informed and thoughtful. If there were exceptions, I suspected that they weren't allowed out in public or, at least, weren't granted passports. I hadn't yet met one, and the young man who shared that tool shed in Buenos Aires wasn't the first.

"You know," he said after we had talked a while, "you're the first American I ever met who knows how to travel."

"What do you mean?" I asked.

"Well, when Americans are young they plunge into their careers, and most don't get around to traveling until they're older," he began. "That's backwards in my mind. People should travel when they're young. That way the things they learn can be put to good use and for a long time."

His tone was neither accusatory nor insulting, and the remark sounded like no more than a simple comment about a puzzling phenomenon.

"Furthermore," he continued, "when Americans travel, they stay in the best hotels, eat at the best restaurants, take guided tours and otherwise isolate themselves from the local culture. What's the point of traveling if that's the way you do it?"

This description struck me as particularly applicable to the Americans I had seen in the Canal Zone. Nonetheless, I felt honor-bound to defend my countrymen.

"I think younger Americans usually travel in their own country," I began cautiously, trying to duplicate my companion's calm, thoughtful tone. "It's cheaper, for one thing, and at that age, people don't have a great deal of money."

"Yes, but even in their own country Americans travel in cocoons, instead of really opening themselves up. Look at their idea of camping.

They go into the wilds with campers, trailers and all the comforts of home. You, on the other hand, seem to know how to rough it."

"You mean like sleeping in a tool shed?" I laughed.

"Yes, exactly! That sort of thing really gets one absorbed into the local culture, don't you think? My idea of camping is going into the mountains with as few provisions as possible. I drink the water that's there, pick berries to eat and try to live off the land. I watch and listen to the birds and animals, instead of the ten o'clock news. My purpose is to leave my familiar, everyday life behind and have a different sort of experience."

I remarked that I hadn't had a "familiar, everyday" day since arriving in Peru months earlier. We both laughed. From there, our conversation branched out, touching on many other subjects.

22 There is a similar phenomenon in California's deserts where the first heavy rain in years will create temporary pools full of brine shrimp. Shrimp eggs remain viable in dry sand for very long periods of time. When immersed in water, even after many years, they hatch, and the new shrimp lay more eggs before the water dries up.

23 Not the one in Argentina, of course.

We used only one of the lift trucks to unload Hamaca (see page 262).

CHAPTER 31

The Peak of Death

The next day, between Buenos Aires and San Isidro del General, I saw *algarrobo* trees, but the seedpods were different from the Peruvian variety. Nevertheless, remembering how much Hamaca and Ima had enjoyed *algarrobo* in Peru, I gathered a handful of the string bean-like pods. The mares briefly sniffed them and rapidly turned their attention elsewhere.

As had been the case every day since I'd crossed into Costa Rica, a large percentage of the oncoming cars bore U.S. license plates. Apparently, the recently failed coup in Nicaragua was still generating a steady stream of fleeing Americans. From inside their "cocoons," to quote my British companion of the night before, few of my countrymen waved back at me. I guess they didn't think it was as special to see another North American as I did, or maybe they were still unsettled by their experiences in Nicaragua. I hoped the situation would stabilize by the time I got there. Flying or going by ship to Honduras were options I couldn't afford. If circumstances demanded, I could stay in Costa Rica until Nicaragua was safe, but another major setback would deal fatal blows to my budget, timetable and enthusiasm.

Hamaca's and Ima's enthusiasm also seemed to be on the wane. Once eager to see what was over the next hill or beyond the next curve, they now wanted to stop at every farm or ranch we passed. Evidently, it was their way of being "barn-sour," even though they had no "barn." When a horse is barn-sour, its overriding ambition, whenever taken out to work, is to return to its barn, stall, paddock, pasture or corral. As long as its living quarters can be seen, the horse will try to head in that direction at every opportunity. Fortunately, this normally ceases once the *barn* is out of sight.

Hamaca and Ima, however, had no permanent residence. Anyplace and everyplace might be their barn. With a dreamy, hopeful look in their eyes, they never failed to turn toward any suitable lodging place they saw. They weren't terribly insistent, only enough to lead me to the conclusion that there were worse things than barn-sour horses that had only one barn.

Some of the horseshoes I'd nailed on in Panama didn't long remain in place. In fact, I had to re-nail one of Hamaca's just two nights later, and as we neared the town of San Isidro, faint clanking

303

sounds told me that two of Ima's were loose. Apparently, my first horseshoeing job had left much to be desired.

Not far outside San Isidro, the roadbed was freshly surfaced with crushed rock. After stepping on a few sharp edges, Ima began to hobble and hang back, intent on stopping. A quick check revealed that she had thrown a shoe, and from there on, Hamaca and I literally towed our tender-footed companion, which brought no joy to any of us. The following morning, Ima's hoof was tender, but after a visit from a proper blacksmith, everything was back to normal.

There were reports of anthrax in the vicinity, and I took the precaution of having both mares immunized. I didn't want even the slightest risk of a disease so deadly that it comes to mind under the heading of "Weapons of Mass Destruction." Anthrax affects most animals, especially grass eaters, in addition to humans, and history records epidemics that killed unimaginable numbers of both.

Later, I was walking through San Isidro's central plaza, lost in thought, when a young street urchin came running toward me.

"*Señor! Señor!* There's a man over there who wants to talk with you!"

"Where?" I asked, slowly coming out of my reverie.

"Over there ... at the bar ... across the plaza."

I wasn't feeling sociable and didn't care for being summoned like that. Fearful of getting stuck in a long conversation with someone who was intoxicated, I thanked the boy and continued on my way, watching as he dejectedly returned to the bar. The degree of his disappointment indicated that he had probably been promised a reward for delivering me. Shortly thereafter, the same youngster – filled with fresh enthusiasm – approached me once again, at a dead run.

"*Señor!*" he called weakly, out of breath.

I stopped.

"That man wants very much to speak with you, *señor!* Please go. He's a North American, and he seems very sad."

It turned out that the man in the bar was indeed a North American, an ex-soldier who freely admitted to having deserted rather than be sent to fight in Vietnam. He hadn't been home for a long time and wanted to know what was happening in the States.

"You couldn't have asked a worse person," I responded. "I've been gone since August."

"I've been gone a lot longer than that," he commented. "From what I read, the war has become very unpopular. Is that true?"

I gave him a thumbnail sketch of what little I knew.

304

"Has there been any talk of pardoning deserters?" he asked, hesitantly.

"Not that I've heard."

During the conversation that followed, I concluded that I was talking with a very melancholic individual. However, his eyes lit up when he found out that I was on my way to San José. That prompted a long dissertation on the glories of Costa Rica's capital.

"How long do you plan to stay there?" he finally asked.

"Two days."

"You better plan on more than that," he admonished with a wink and a grin.

Next, he lectured me on the wondrous qualities of San José's women. He must have had Irish blood because he could definitely paint an intriguing picture with words. When he'd said all he had to say, he finished by declaring: "The women of San José are the world's best kept secret. They're absolutely delightful."

Having said this, he suddenly seemed tired of talking and began drinking, with the apparent intention of drowning his sorrows. I excused myself and started for the door.

"Don't forget I predicted it," he called after me. "A girl will smile at you in San José, and you'll be there a lot longer than two days!"

I chuckled, not entirely in good humor. Lengthy delays and the women of San José weren't on my agenda. I had no intention of getting sidetracked by romance. My recent divorce had been very painful, and not enough time had passed.

Between San Isidro and San José stands the imposing Cerro de la Muerte, the Peak of Death. Its summit at nearly 11,000 feet is the highest spot on the Pan-American Highway in Central America. From that lofty perch, I was told, the view would be well worth having to climb 9,000 feet in twenty-seven miles. For one thing, I would have the rare opportunity to see both the Atlantic and Pacific oceans at the same time.

The forbidding mountain had come by its macabre name honestly, having killed many a traveler. Whenever someone heard that I intended to ride the hundred miles between San Isidro and San José, he or she felt compelled to pass along his or her entire repertoire of Peak of Death legends. Temperatures there could plummet without warning, so quickly that many a traveler had frozen to death in a standing position. The most spectacular incident featured a virtual forest of such bodies, once found near the summit. I didn't bother to ask if frozen horses had ever been found, standing or otherwise. If they had, I didn't want to know!

According to his writings, Aime Tschiffely had heard virtually the same stories thirty years earlier. In both his case and mine, time spent in the Andes had conditioned us to respect but not fear the dangers of mountain travel. However, I packed my warmest clothes and the horse blankets at the top of my duffel bag, where they were quickly accessible.

Before the road was built, the journey across Cerro de la Muerte must have been extremely hazardous, and under the right conditions, it undoubtedly still could be. After all, the summit was 4,000 feet higher than the spot in California's Sierra Nevada Mountains where forty-two members of the famous Donner party died as a result of winter storms.

On the morning I pulled out of San Isidro, my thoughts were diverted to more immediate concerns. Once again, I was suffering the effects of dysentery, the price of a new, more relaxed attitude toward what I ate. Central America had seemed clean and sanitary, compared to South America, and I had been lulled into lowering my guard at mealtimes. My punishment was a case of what Latin Americans call *turistas*, in honor of its tendency to target visitors rather than locals.

The trip over Cerro de la Muerte took three days, instead of the four I anticipated, but it was every bit as difficult as promised. The road was paved with cobblestones, forcing Hamaca and Ima to seek their footing on a hard, uneven surface that turned slippery every time it rained. To lighten my mares' burden on the treacherous cobblestones, I did a fair bit of walking and quickly came to appreciate the difficulty of climbing 9,000 feet on such a surface. Even at that, I'm sure it was easier for me in boots than it was for horses wearing slick, steel shoes.

The countryside was beautiful and the views spectacular, though I never found a point from which I could see both of the world's largest oceans. I did, nonetheless, once look down on the Atlantic within ten minutes of having seen the Pacific. It was disappointing because both ocean views were remarkably similar. I would have had almost the same experience if I had looked at the Pacific to my left, turned a hundred and eighty degrees and then looked at it to my right.

Latin America is often called the "land of startling contrasts." On Cerro de la Muerte, that description seemed like an understatement. In the lowlands, I had perspired even while sitting motionless. On the Peak of Death, I shivered even during hard exercise. The desire for a happy medium had me enthusiastically looking forward to San José's reputedly delightful climate, so much so that I was spurred to efforts that cut a full day from my schedule.

Among those who had told me wonderful things about San José was Marco Vinicio Alvarez, a young Costa Rican I'd met at the border station in Panama. The two of us hit it off immediately. Obviously without intending to, Mary Catherwood described us perfectly when she wrote: "Two may talk together under the same roof for many years yet never really meet, and two others at first speech are old friends." On the night we met, we chatted for a long while, held together by the enjoyment we derived from one another's company. Before he continued on his way, Marco Vinicio gave me his address and an invitation to stay with him when the time came.

Upon arrival in San José, I settled the horses in a public stable and set out to find Marco Vinicio's home. It was wonderful to see him again, and his exuberant greeting indicated that the feeling was mutual. However, I was concerned to find him living with his mother and sister, especially after having been invited into other homes where not everyone welcomed me. Fortunately there was no repeat. The Alvarez family was extraordinarily close, and whatever one wanted was automatically important to the others. Both his mother and sister laughingly threatened me with dire consequences if they found me still in town after I departed their house.

It was better than being in my own home. The family was always available to talk but never once pressed conversation upon me. Mrs. Alvarez made up the spare bed in Marco Vinicio's room for me, and also told me that I was welcome to use her sewing room anytime I wanted a private place to read, write letters or just relax. She also served me three delicious meals, plus afternoon tea, every day. She was offended the one time I ate in a restaurant, which I had done rather than oblige her to prepare a meal at an irregular hour.

Marco Vinicio's mother was easily one of the most agreeable people I had ever met. I never saw her differ with anyone over anything, with one exception. When I called her son "Marco," in the interest of good old Yankee efficiency, she politely but firmly set me straight. Marco Vinicio was always called by both his first and middle names, she explained. [24]

It soon became evident that the American deserter in San Isidro had been right about my spending more than two days in San José, but not because of some smiling girl. I had arrived in Costa Rica's capital on a Friday evening and couldn't start processing my horses' next round of health papers, for entry into Nicaragua, until the following Monday. I had no idea how long that process might take, but I'd obviously be around longer than originally planned. It quickly became a welcome delay. I thoroughly enjoyed every second of my new friend's company, finding him intelligent and perceptive. Except for when I was writing letters, I didn't spend a moment in the room his mother had so considerately reserved for my privacy. Marco Vinicio's company was too good to waste.

"Aren't you fed up with the remarks people make about your height?" he asked, after having spent only one afternoon with me, "I'm tired of it already, not to mention the stupid questions about your ride!"

Marco Vinicio himself studiously avoided interrogating me. He respected my privacy and recognized my need to make a slow transition to civilization after so much time alone. As a result, I found myself telling him more about my adventures than I had told anyone else.

Without once making demands, Marco Vinicio somehow managed to include me in everything he did, even asking me along on a visit to his girlfriend's home. Trying to be respectful of *his* need for privacy, I declined that particular invitation. Marco Vinicio sensed my reasons and repeatedly insisted I come. I held out for a while and finally relented.

I'm grateful things turned out that way ... because that afternoon a girl did smile at me!

---

[24] This practice is common in Latin America, as I should have remembered after spending time with José Antonio Onrubia and Juan Luis Ruesta in Piura.

CHAPTER 32

Emily

Her name was Emily, and she appeared on the landing at the top of the stairs while Marco Vinicio, his girlfriend and I were talking in the parlor below. She was beautiful and elegant, and even beyond that, there was an aura about her that I liked. I was delighted when she started down the stairs. If I close my eyes today, I can't picture exactly how she looked, but I can recall how I felt. I was filled with anticipation and anxiety. Though more uncomfortable than I had been in a very long time, I wouldn't have traded places with anyone in the world!

As we were introduced, she gave me what can only be described as an enchanting smile, and quite naturally, my thoughts turned to a certain North American deserter in San Isidro. Her eyes sparkled. Her voice was feminine and lilting. Her long, shiny hair framed an angelic face. When I looked at her, Emily reminded me of those very popular girls in high school who had always seemed beyond my reach. Her manner, however, was different.

There's something about Latin girls that makes them friendlier than American girls, I thought when Emily sat across from me and began making polite conversation in Spanish. Before long, I was suspecting that she might not be what I had assumed!

"Are you a North American?" I asked, still speaking Spanish.

"Yes," she said, "I'm going to the University of Costa Rica under the Rotary Club student exchange program."

Needless to say, I had to modify my conclusion that Latin girls were in any way superior to American girls! With the ice thoroughly melted, we had a long and enjoyable conversation, of which I remember only that she was friends with Marco Vinicio's girlfriend, that being the reason she was there that afternoon. The other thing I recollect was the feeling of looking into her eyes. On another occasion, she would tell me an amusing story about those eyes. It concerned the youngest daughter in the family with which she was staying, a four-year-old who one day announced that she wanted green eyes. When it was explained that she would have to be satisfied with what she had, the young lady had turned indignant.

"But Emily has green eyes," she had argued, intending to persist until she got her wish. "Why can't I have them?"

I could see how those eyes might enchant a person! Thoroughly charmed, I couldn't stop talking about Emily after we parted company. Marco Vinicio put two and two together, and I braced myself for merciless teasing. Instead, he offered to ask his girlfriend if she could invite Emily to join us for lunch the following day.

When the four of us gathered the next day, Emily mentioned that she liked horses. Immediately taking advantage of this revelation, I invited her to join Hamaca, Ima and me for a ride. She said yes, and that afternoon we took a bus to the stable where my mares were boarded. Having only one riding saddle, I borrowed another from the stable owner. Later, while we were riding, I noticed that my well-broken-in saddle was more comfortable than the one I'd borrowed for Emily. I insisted on switching and excused myself for not having noticed her discomfort more quickly.

"I'm afraid my social graces are a little rusty. I haven't done much dating lately," I teased.

"Is that because you're always busy having adventures?" she teased back.

We didn't know each other well enough to require a serious answer, but just in case it made any difference, I wanted her to know the whole story.

"No," I answered. "It's because I was married for almost five years."

The look on her face spoke volumes. She had been innocently playing and hardly expected to uncover *that* particular piece of information. With an obvious effort, she tried to hide the letdown she felt, but it showed and refused to go away. Those were simpler, less open-minded times. Divorces were rare and usually regarded as proof that a person had a serious character deficiency.

I had developed a philosophy to help me through moments when people were disappointed in me. Simply stated, it was: *don't invest too much energy in trying to meet other people's expectations.* However, I didn't feel that way toward people who were important to me. I wanted *them* to understand and was willing to give enough information to make that possible. Unfortunately, I didn't know Emily well enough for that, and an awkward silence followed. It took a while for things to warm up again, but by the time we were on the bus back to town, everything seemed to be back where it had been, or so I hoped. Unwilling to suffer uncertainty, I wanted to find out where I stood before we parted company, and I asked if she wanted to go to a movie the following evening.

"Yes, I do," she answered, "but I'm not sure I can. In the Rotary exchange program, we stay with each family for a limited time, and I'm moving in with a new family tomorrow. Before I can go out, I need their permission. Can I let you know in a couple of days?"

In spite of the fact that I had plenty to occupy me, the next two days were among the longest of my young life. I plunged into getting Hamaca's and Ima's papers for Nicaragua, anticipating endless delays and countless problems. Unbelievably, I had the papers in my hands within a day and without any of the usual frustrations. Getting my visa was equally uncomplicated.

With free time on my hands and Marco Vinicio occupied with his studies at the university, I took an afternoon to have a look around, and I liked what I saw. As the national capital and the economic/cultural hub of Costa Rica, San José offered more than its share of interesting sights. In addition, it had the uncrowded, unhurried atmosphere of a small town. The buildings were small and simple. Everyone seemed to know everyone. The economy was basically rural, dominated by the production of bananas and coffee. Most businesses were modest in size, and their affairs were conducted in a leisurely manner. It seemed fitting that the sight most readily associated with San José was its gaily painted oxcarts. To me, these symbolized the pace and informality of life there.

San José was also reputed to be one of the most democratic capitals on earth. Marco Vinicio was fond of telling me that Costa Rica's president was frequently seen walking through town in the manner of any other citizen, without escorts or bodyguards. In fact, the president and other political leaders regularly joined informal discussions with common citizens in the local restaurants and taverns.

Apparently Costa Rica's leaders required less protection than visiting North American college students. At least that's the impression I got when I called Emily at her new residence. She reported that she'd been given tentative permission to accompany me to a movie. However, before we could go, I'd have to meet her new family and pass their inspection. In addition, we would be accompanied by a chaperone.

"Please don't take this personally," Emily added. "It's the Costa Rican custom. They plan to send one of their daughters with us. She doesn't speak English, so our conversations will be private, sort of."

"You can believe this or not," I said, dancing a little jig on my end of the phone, "but I don't mind a bit."

Our chaperone had little impact on our date, aside from making it possible. For her trouble, she received a free dinner and movie, but being very shy, she stayed out of the conversation and preferred it that way. Soon I was paying no attention to the chaperone, little to the movie and all the rest to Emily. As always, it was a pleasure to spend time with this delightful young lady. I couldn't help wishing I had met her under other circumstances. Getting to know her would have been the ultimate luxury, but I didn't have time. Very soon, I would resume my journey, and I dreaded saying goodbye.

The day before leaving San José, I went to visit one of the most interesting men I had ever met, *don* Juan Rafael Cabezas. The day I arrived in San José, I had called his house and been told he was out of town. On the day he was due back, I showed up at his door. Someone I had never seen before invited me inside, and I found that I'd inadvertently crashed a party. Equally as embarrassing, I was considerably underdressed for the occasion, despite wearing the best I had. *Don* Juan's was the only familiar face in a room full of people, and I stood uncomfortably watching him move from group to group while attending his guests. In time, his eyes came to rest on me. He looked puzzled for a split-second before his eyes lit up with recognition, surprise and finally pleasure.

"Well, look who came to my party! Pablito!" he said, hurrying my way with arms outstretched.

I had met *don* Juan Rafael Cabezas years earlier. We were both in Peru, scouring the country for breeding stock to take to our respective countries. Though we were competitors of a sort, I immediately liked him, finding him interesting and admirable. Near his seventies, *don* Juan had developed a keen interest in Peruvian *Paso* horses, and he plunged in with all the enthusiasm of a teenager. He was a pioneer for the breed in Central America, a role for which he was extremely well suited, considering his knack for promotion.

Boisterous and jovial, he was immediately popular wherever he went. His quick wit seldom failed to produce laughter, and he had been such a hit with the Peruvians that I couldn't get anyone to pay me the slightest attention when he was around. Like his famous namesake, he also had a way with the ladies. He continued to charm them at an age by which the fictional *Don* Juan was long dead. With great solemnity, he once corrected me, saying: "Pablito, there is no such thing as an ugly woman. They don't exist." Little wonder that women enjoyed his company!

Don Juan enthusiastically introduced me to several guests, men who were also *aficionados* of Peruvian horses, and we stood talking, mostly about my ride. After a while, another man joined our group.

"You must be Mr. Albright," he said in excellent English.

"Yes, I am," I said, unable to imagine how anyone in San José could know my family name. I doubted that even *don* Juan knew it.

The man gave me his name, which I'm ashamed to say I don't remember.

"I'm the National Secretary of Agriculture," he further introduced himself. "I haven't met you, but I signed health certificates for your horses a couple of days ago. I trust our service was satisfactory."

"More than satisfactory," I answered, wondering if he was *really* the Secretary of Agriculture or a prankster, preparing a laugh at my expense. "You can't imagine the problems I've had with paperwork in some countries. It would be wonderful if everyone from here on could be as efficient and gracious as the people in your office."

"Maybe I can do something about that," he offered, and his manner convinced me that he was who he said he was. "Stop by my office tomorrow afternoon. I'll be happy to write some letters of introduction for you."

"I won't be able to do that," I explained reluctantly. "I'm leaving tomorrow morning."

"Well, then," he said graciously, "come in first thing, at 9:00, and the letters will be prepared on an urgent basis. You can be sure they will save you more time than you'll lose by briefly delaying your departure."

I thanked him with as much sincerity as I could muster. Frankly, I couldn't see what good would come from letters of introduction, and I wasn't pleased by the prospect of starting my next day's journey after having wasted the morning.

When it came time for dinner, a very formal affair, I tried to excuse myself, but the host wouldn't hear of it. *Don* Juan insisted that I sit next to him and concentrated his full attention on me, asking about the details of my journey. He seemed genuinely interested, and after I answered his many questions, he put his finger on one of my two greatest concerns.

"By now, you must be running low on money," he said.

"That and time," I told him. "If I'm going to put one of these horses in the Tevis Cup, I need to be in Los Gatos in less than two months."

"I can arrange for you to get a free truck ride as far as Nicaragua," he said, thoughtfully. "Would that help?"

"It would help a great deal," I answered, "and I'd be very grateful."

"What do you plan to do about Nicaragua?" he asked.

"I hope to ride at least halfway across," I responded. "I've been interested in Nicaragua since I was in high school, and I really want to see what it's like."

Don Juan's face became serious, but he said nothing.

"Why do you ask?" I questioned. "Do you think it might be dangerous?"

"Not necessarily," he said, "but if the situation gets bad, you must find a safe place and stay there. I'm sure you can appreciate the danger of traveling on horseback during a revolution!"

The most important part of *don* Juan's promised truck ride to Nicaragua was that it would get me there quickly. Having realized that I couldn't possibly afford to do otherwise, I was faced with the need to cross that country by land, revolution or no revolution. Reliable information was hard to come by, but the consensus was that tensions inside Nicaragua might flare up again at any moment. Hardly a day went by without rumors that the border would soon be closed again. I wanted to be inside Nicaragua – if not all the way to Honduras – before that happened!

If the borders were closed while I was still in Costa Rica, I'd be locked out, but if they were closed after I was in Nicaragua, I'd be locked in. Given a choice, I preferred the latter because, circumstances permitting, I could then find a way to the threshold of Honduras where I'd be several hundred miles farther along when the borders reopened. Once inside Nicaragua, I could decide how to proceed. If I sensed danger, I could hunker down and wait for a truck going my way. Otherwise, I intended to ride at least as far as Managua.

"Where are your horses stabled?" *don* Juan asked. "We can meet there tomorrow afternoon at about 1:00. I'll bring my truck, take you and your horses to the stockyard and find a ride for you."

With those words, *don* Juan ended the conversation about my ride, and we moved to other subjects.

The next morning, I went to the office of the Secretary of Agriculture. Since *don* Juan wasn't picking me up until early afternoon, I was considerably more relaxed than if I'd been losing time. Nonetheless, I went more out of courtesy than self-interest. Try as I might, I couldn't see any advantage to letters of introduction.

I was glad I wasn't riding north that day because the Secretary's secretary took a very long time to prepare the letters. It was nearly noon by the time the Secretary himself finally handed me the small stack. By then, each letter was neatly signed and placed inside envelopes, which bore colorful emblems. There was one addressed, by name, to the Secretary or Minister of Agriculture in each nation I had yet to enter, including the United States.

"These will introduce and recommend you to my counterparts," he told me. "I think you'll find them helpful."

I thanked the Secretary at great length. His unsolicited kindness was not the sort of treatment I had come to expect from Latin American officialdom, and I was grateful, whether or not it would do any good. After I left his office, I put the letters in with the rest of the paperwork I carried in my duffel bag and promptly dismissed the whole incident from my mind. At that moment, I had no way to anticipate the difficulties with which I would soon be confronted. Not fully understanding Latin America's ways, I didn't dream that this packet of letters would save me from having my ride brought to a permanent halt, well short of its destination!

Hamaca, Ima and I were picked up later that day, Friday, February 10th, as promised. *Don* Juan personally drove us to the stockyard. There, he exuberantly solicited the driver of every truck in sight, looking for someone to take the mares and me farther north. I was no better off after he'd spoken to all of them than I'd been before he started. His cheerful attitude unchanged, *don* Juan waited for more trucks to arrive. When they did, he spoke to each new driver with an enthusiasm that gave no hint of how many times he'd already been turned down. His persistence was finally rewarded when he found me a free ride with a commercial cattle truck deadheading to Las Cañas, a hundred and fifty miles to the north. I would have preferred to wait for someone going farther, but I kept that information to myself. I was grateful for *don* Juan's efforts and thanked him accordingly.

Our ride pulled out at 6:00 P.M. after which the truck crawled steadily and slowly along winding mountain roads until 3:00 A.M. By that time, the driver couldn't keep his eyes open and answered my silent pleas by pulling over to sleep. I have no idea how long the two of us dozed, sitting upright in our seats, but at some point the motor fired up, gears ground noisily and we continued on our way.

Upon arrival in Las Cañas at 7:00 A.M., I was offered a further ride with a different driver in another of the same company's trucks. The second truck left almost immediately for the town of Liberia, farther north. Hamaca and Ima switched vehicles without touching the ground. The drivers skillfully maneuvered both trucks until they were rear to rear with the livestock doors facing each other, and I

led the mares from one vehicle to the other, the three of us carefully stepping across the gap between.

The drive to Liberia was through flat country, allowing us to
travel seventy-five miles in an hour and a half, far faster than the
previous evening's one hundred and fifty miles in twelve hours. We
arrived in Liberia at 8:30 and were in town only long enough to eat
breakfast. Afterward, I strapped the saddle on Ima, mounted up and
started down the road with Hamaca following. Despite the poor
night's sleep, I felt fresh after those restful days in San José.

During that first day of renewed travel, we made excellent
progress, even without considering the distance covered by our
overnight truck ride. Our destination was the town of La Cruz, and
for most of the day, we had an impressive volcano in view. I had
already seen several volcanoes, of course, but all had been dormant.
The volcano known as Arenal was clearly different. A small, pearly
white cloud crowned the tip of its cone, and above this towered a
huge, boiling, gray-black pillar of smoke.

I don't know which amazed me more, a live volcano or the fact
that no one else seemed interested in it. Throughout the day, I saw
people going about their daily routines without a glance at the spec-
tacle I found so absolutely captivating. The sight of an active volcano so impressed me that I couldn't imagine why there weren't
crowds watching and taking pictures. The answer, of course, is that
the locals had seen their fill of this and other volcanoes.

Later in the day, a strong wind dispersed the column of smoke,
filling the air for miles around with smog … instant Los Angeles,
without the cars. Once the wind died down, the gray-black column
formed again, and as day's light faded, I could see a reddish glow
projected upwards from inside the cone.

Costa Rica had several active volcanoes, the most famous of
which was Irazú, located only twenty-five miles from San José.
There was a paved road all the way to the top of its 12,000-foot
crater, and it was one of the country's most important tourist attractions. Long dormant, Irazú had flared up and sent tons of ash and
cinder into Costa Rica's capital a couple of years before I rode into
town. Magazine accounts reported that volcanic ash fell like rain,
and people had to cover their noses with handkerchiefs to filter the
air they breathed. Rooftops, especially if flat, had to be constantly
swept to prevent the accumulating weight from causing cave ins. By
the time I saw her, Irazú had been minding her manners for well
over a year.

The next day I rode from La Cruz, Costa Rica, to La Virgen, Nicaragua. The border crossing was pleasant and efficient. As the Costa Rican Secretary of Agriculture had promised, Nicaragua's officials were accustomed to having animals cross their borders and the procedure was well-established and well-understood. While at the border, I asked and was told that the recent revolution had been centered in the capital city of Managua. But for news reports, most people in rural areas wouldn't have known anything was afoot.

The first few miles in Nicaragua were no different from the last few in Costa Rica, except for the tension that gripped me. Nicaragua's history of bloody revolutions was very much on my mind, but I saw nothing other than people going about the routines of their daily lives. Everything was serene and *normal*, and I soon made up my mind to ride at least as far as Managua unless there were dramatic changes. That was the decision I very much wanted to make.

There was something exhilarating about the first time Hamaca and Ima trod where Mancha and Gato had not. Somehow, it seemed important to accomplish something Tschiffely hadn't. Potentially, it represented some small compensation for the many times I'd felt inferior to him.

The weary travelers arriving in San José (see page 307).

CHAPTER 33

Going the Wrong Way and Loving It !

Soon after crossing the border, I got my first look at Lake Nicaragua, the world's tenth-largest body of fresh water. The statistics of this huge lake are mind-boggling: fed by over forty rivers, it contains over four hundred islands, has a length of about a hundred and ten miles, an average width of thirty-six miles and is as much as two hundred feet deep.

Lake Nicaragua, the theory goes, was once part of an ocean bay, which also encompassed Lake Managua to the northwest. Along the coast west of these lakes is a string of some forty volcanoes. Over the centuries, these disgorged enough material to seal the mouth of the bay and convert the area into an inland basin dominated by a huge lake. That would explain why Lake Nicaragua is home to the world's only freshwater sharks, swordfish and tarpon. These and other ocean creatures are said to have adapted as the salt content of the water slowly declined to the point where it is no longer considered saltwater. The lake's history includes incidents involving pirates and gold-seeking "forty-niners" bound for California.

It's common to say that pirates sailed the "Seven Seas," but that number ignores those who flew the Jolly Roger during forays into Lake Nicaragua. This was possible because the lake is accessible from the Caribbean Sea via the San Juan River. In the 16th and part of the 17th centuries, pirates sailed up this river and raided lakeside towns. These activities ceased only after fortifications were built along the river to deny access to unwanted visitors.

Just as some fortune hunters took the shortcut across Panama to California's goldfields, others crossed Nicaragua. North American millionaire Cornelius Vanderbilt offered a travel package along a route that proved to be the fastest and most reliable of all. Travelers on the "Vanderbilt Road" normally embarked in New York, went south along the east coast and crossed the Caribbean Sea. At the mouth of the San Juan River, they were transferred to smaller craft for the trip to Lake Nicaragua and across the lake to its western shore. From there, a short trip by stagecoach took them to the Pacific Ocean, where they boarded ships bound for San Francisco.

Even before the Vanderbilt Road, Nicaragua had been strong competition for the isthmus of Panama, whenever an interoceanic canal was under consideration. When finally ready to build a canal, the U.S. proposed a treaty with Colombia, providing for its construction. In those days, Panama was part of Colombia, and Colombia's congress – badly split over the issue – dallied in ratifying it. At that point, the U.S. opened negotiations with Nicaragua, to explore the possibility of building the canal there, instead. Fearing that Nicaragua would be chosen, revolutionaries in Panama seceded from Colombia, some say with U.S. assistance. Declaring itself an independent republic, Panama then signed the treaty that assured the canal would be built there.

In high school, I had read much that attracted my attention to Nicaragua. My favorite incident involved a little-remembered North American named William Walker. Walker was a filibusterer. Today that word describes someone who tries to talk a piece of legislation to death, but in Walker's time, it described North Americans who fomented insurrections in Latin America.

After leading a failed attempt to take over Baja California and declare it an independent republic, Walker was invited into a Nicaraguan revolution by one of the factions. He was bankrolled by Americans hoping to take over Cornelius Vanderbilt's interests there. As a result, he put together an impressive string of military victories that culminated in his becoming president. He held that office less than a year and was ousted by a coalition of other Central American nations, backed (no surprise here) by Vanderbilt. Defeated, he was sent back to the U.S.

Later, he returned to Nicaragua to pursue his dreams and again was captured and deported. On his way to Nicaragua a third time, he was captured by the British and turned over to the authorities in Honduras, where he was executed.

******

Shortly after I got my first look at Lake Nicaragua, thick clouds of tiny flying insects interrupted my musings. These pests didn't seem interested in a meal. None bit my horses or me, but they congregated around us in such numbers that I was inhaling them with every breath. I knew my mares were doing the same when they began snorting the way a horse will do after breathing in something other than air.

I swung my arms and swatted in every direction, with no improvement in the situation. Next I urged Hamaca and Ima to a faster pace, but that only made matters worse. The exertion soon had both mares gulping much-needed air, along with its winged contents. In spite of everything I tried, we remained surrounded by these dense swarms. Likely, we would have been harassed until nightfall if a strong breeze hadn't come up and driven our tormentors away.

We spent the night at an *hacienda* on the shore of Lake Nicaragua, within sight of the lake's largest island, Ometepe, about sixteen miles long and half that wide. Neither the length nor the width of this island is particularly impressive, but its height is. Ometepe is home to Siamese-twin volcanoes, Concepción and Madera, the taller of which towers some 5,100 feet above the water's surface. Both were majestic and had the classic cone-shape that comes to mind when people think of volcanoes. Originally separate, the two volcanoes gradually became linked together as lava poured out over the centuries and formed an island around them.

The next day, we made our longest one-day push, fifty-three miles from La Virgen to Granada. This was barely more than half the length of the Tevis Cup and admittedly in much-less-rugged country. Nonetheless, I was encouraged to see how easily the mares handled it. More and more, I was coming to believe that Hamaca was capable of representing her breed very nicely in the Tevis Cup.

At a cattle ranch near Granada the mares ate their most unusual meal to date, silage, intended for cows. This was prepared by mixing wheat and corn – both the grain and the chopped stalks – with a special molasses. The resulting mixture was stored in deep, concrete-lined pits where fermentation took place, permeating the air with a strong, sweet odor. This process enhanced the taste and made long-term storage possible without loss of nutrition. When served to my mares, it was still warm and fermenting. Though assured otherwise, I was worried that such a meal, well tolerated in cattle's multiple stomachs, might provoke colic in horses, *if* they'd even consent to eat it. Hamaca and Ima ate it enthusiastically, and afterward, under my watchful eye, suffered no ill effects. Nevertheless, I avoided feeding silage again and certainly wouldn't recommend it as a horse feed.

The next day, we traveled thirty-one miles to Managua, and on the outskirts of town, I found a public stable with available, side-by-side stalls. When I heard the price, I was convinced it had been tripled to take advantage of my being North American. I took the time to speak to several people who boarded horses there and found that I had been asked no more than the going rate. It was my first clue that Managua was frightfully expensive. The cost of living in any particular Latin American country seemed directly related to its proximity to the United States. The closer I got to home, the higher the prices. I had seldom spent more than a dollar a night to have the horses lodged in a stable, and this fee always included feed and cleaning of their stalls. In Managua, I wound up paying two dollars for the most humble of stalls with no such amenities, and that was only because I agreed to clean the stalls daily, feed and water the horses myself and provide my own hay and grain.

Everything else turned out to be proportionately expensive. The hotel, no better than those where I'd been staying, cost three times as much. In Ecuador, a few pennies bought dinner, but in Managua, the simplest restaurant meal cost a dollar. These increasing expenses were a constant reminder that I needed to start looking for a faster way home lest I run out of money before I ran out of miles.

Once my mares were comfortable and cared for, I set out toward the center of town, on foot. Initially I was edgy, knowing that Managua had been the battleground during the recently failed revolution. My anxiety, however, soon evaporated. I saw no evidence of violence, past, present or future. People were busy in their day-to-day world and were as friendly and helpful as their cousins elsewhere in Latin America.

Though no one knew it, violence of a different kind was lurking just beneath the surface, but it wouldn't strike until long after I was gone. Six years later, an earthquake would level whole sections of Managua, damaging the downtown area so badly that officials considered rebuilding the city elsewhere. Violence of a more familiar variety would follow the earthquake, and the government would be taken over by the communist *Sandanistas*. No sooner did the *Sandanistas* take power than the *Contras* began their counter-revolution. But on that beautiful afternoon, as I walked toward downtown Managua, those horrible events were still behind the veil that hides the future.

My first look at Managua had been from the stable on the outskirts of town. Even from that far away, it was an interesting city. The most architecturally innovative building was the International Hotel, which I often heard described as a pyramidal structure. I would have called it a "stair-step" design, myself, but that didn't make it any less eye-catching, especially amongst the surrounding Spanish colonial buildings. Time and again, the locals took delight in finding excuses to breathlessly inform me that Howard Hughes had rented the entire top floor of the International Hotel and was secluded there. I was doubtful at first but later saw a story in *Time* magazine, which confirmed that the reclusive billionaire was most likely where the Managuans said he was.

On my long walk to town, I had occasion to negotiate a few prices and made ample use of my "I'm not a tourist" disclaimer. However, that protestation was questionable. The sights I was most curious to see were on the itinerary of every tourist in town. It was only human nature to be curious about a battlefield, especially when the battle had been fought only recently. From my reading, I knew that the elegant Gran Hotel had been the epicenter of Nicaragua's most recent revolution. Asking for directions several times, I managed to find my way. At first, I saw nothing that would indicate how fortunate I was not to have been there a couple of weeks earlier. After a while, I stopped looking for evidence of the revolution and started noticing that people going in and out of the Gran Hotel looked elegant and well-to-do.

"Do you see where the bullet holes have been repaired?" the man standing next to me asked.

Once my attention was directed to them, I easily saw the freshly plastered spots in the Gran Hotel's facade. They stood out because the touch-up paint covering them didn't quite match the rest of the building. It was a sobering sight, one that emphasized dangers I might face at any moment. Leaving the Gran Hotel, I headed for the bus station to retrieve my gear, as always sent ahead by bus. Back at the border, I had left my baggage with two guards, requesting that they put it on the next bus to Managua. The two men had refused money to pay for the shipping charges.

"We know the drivers," one had told me. "Any of them will be happy to do us a favor."

"I appreciate your kindness, but I should at least give you money for the freight," I had insisted, always happy to save money but nervous about the prospects for receiving my bags if I didn't pay.

"This will be our little contribution to your success," one of them had insisted.

If the guards had done as promised, my bags would be waiting at Managua's bus station. I arrived there just as my gear was being unloaded from an incoming bus. It was an extraordinary coincidence that spared me handling and storage charges and seemed to indicate that it was my lucky day. Within minutes, there would be further evidence to that effect. I gathered my heavy baggage, lugged it out to the street and began waiting for a taxi. Preferring a dilapidated vehicle with a lower price, I let the clean, shiny cabs pass. Quite unexpectedly, a huge intercity bus stopped directly in front of me, and the door opened.

"Where are you heading?" asked the smiling driver.

I recognized the bus and driver that had brought my baggage from the border.

"I'm on my way to look for an inexpensive hotel," I answered, idly wondering why the bus was leaving the station without passengers.

"Would you like a ride?" the driver asked. "This vehicle is on its way for repairs, and I can drop you off at a hotel that offers very comfortable prices."

"That would be wonderful!" I replied, coming aboard with my bags. "Thank you very much."

I have no idea why the driver went out of his way to be so kind. Perhaps the border guards had said something? Whatever the reason, he took me to a well-chosen economy hotel, cheerfully engaging me in conversation all the way. At a traffic signal, a chauffeur-driven Mercedes Benz stopped next to us. A very haughty-looking man was seated in the back, alternately looking back and forth between his newspaper and the unwashed masses outside. As the only passenger on a fifty-five-seat vehicle, I could look down on him, in more ways than one. After all, my vehicle was larger and more expensive than his, and I had a chauffeur, too!

The next morning I set out to do the paperwork necessary for my horses to enter Honduras and El Salvador. I began by presenting the letter from Costa Rica's Secretary of Agriculture. The resulting service was sensational, erasing all doubts as to the usefulness of those letters. The mares were inspected within hours, and their health certificates were issued that same evening. In the meantime, I got my own visas for both countries, making that day the most productive I'd ever spent with Latin American officials.

It was time to again seek publicity, and between trips to government offices, I went to the headquarters of Managua's leading newspaper. There I spoke with a reporter who made an appointment to meet me the next morning at the stable where Hamaca and Ima were boarded. The following morning, after our interview, the reporter – who doubled as his own photographer – asked to take photos of me on one of the horses. I obligingly saddled and mounted Hamaca. She, however, was in a less-accommodating mood than I.

Feeling her oats after a day's rest, she resisted my efforts to guide her where the newspaperman wanted us. In the brief struggle that ensued, her hindlegs slid out from under her. Abruptly, she was in a sitting position with hindlegs collapsed and forelegs fully extended, supporting her forequarter. In a flash, she was back on all four feet, with me still on her back, the whole maneuver having taken only seconds. The reporter/photographer – as I learned when I opened that evening's paper – was incredibly fast with his camera. He had managed to get a shot of the sitting Hamaca with me holding a handful of mane to keep from sliding off.

My journey often had been marked by loneliness, but the solitude I'd felt since San José was becoming acute. I had greatly enjoyed a certain young lady's company, and I missed her, even though I barely knew her. Leaving Emily behind, with no prospect of ever seeing her again, had begun to seem like a terrible mistake, more so with each passing day.

Twice daily, I made the long walk to the stable, looked after my mares and walked back to town. Soon I was no longer eyeing the penthouse of the International Hotel, wondering if Howard Hughes was really there, and dangerous revolutionaries were the furthest thing from my mind. My thoughts went where they pleased, and it pleased them to dwell on Emily. These reflections came complete with a soundtrack, a ballad that had a melody and lyrics as haunting as my own sentiments. Called *Once Upon a Time* and sung by Tony Bennett, it was available on a jukebox in the hole-in-the-wall restaurant where I ate three meals a day. For a nickel a play, I listened to it over and over, awash in feelings. Finally I'd had enough! If Emily was interested, I had to see her again. Every reasonable argument lined up against it, but I had earned one small luxury, and that was the one I wanted.

Smitten though I might be, I wasn't so far gone that I was willing to risk traveling all that way only to find Emily out of town or otherwise unavailable. Likewise, I didn't want her displeased by my interest, a distinct possibility if I simply showed up on her doorstep. With all this in mind, a plan of action came together. The second step would be a phone call. The *first* would be to practice and refine what I wanted to say … and to work up my nerve! When I was at last satisfied with my rehearsal, I made the call, my heart pounding and my mouth dry.

"It would be nice to see you again," said the melodious voice on the other end of the line, "but I can't guarantee that it will be worth such a long trip."

"I'm not sure I understand what you mean," I responded.

"Well, for one thing, I have other commitments this weekend, and we might not be able to see each other much," she said. "The only time I'll be available for sure is Friday night."

In another week, I'd be too far away to even consider going back. It was now or never.

"A true adventurer doesn't need guarantees!" I chuckled, boldly trying to conceal my nervousness. "All he needs to know is that he's not dealing with the impossible."

"That much I can promise," she said, erasing my nervousness with just five words.

I floated down the street to the bus station and bought a round-trip ticket on the overnight express. The accountant in me protested the expenditure but had already been overruled. With time on my hands, I took a leisurely walk to the stables. There I cared for Hamaca and Ima, paid to have them cared for in my absence and left my duffel bags for safekeeping. Finally I walked back to town, ate dinner and boarded a bus for the long, overnight ride to San José.

Advised by Emily of my impending arrival, Marco Vinicio Alvarez met me at the bus station the next morning. He insisted I stay with his family again, which made my short visit reminiscent of my previous stay in San José. The similarities included one I didn't welcome: I spent little time with Emily. Before I knew it, I was again having a difficult time saying good-bye. I had thought that seeing Emily again might lessen my longing for her company, but it had instead made matters worse. Given the option of staying a bit longer, I would have gladly taken it. Unfortunately, Emily had classes during the days, and her evenings would be filled with preparations for a Rotary convention in Guatemala City, three days hence.

"You know something?" she said, eyes twinkling as we said good-bye on her doorstep. "If you put your horses into a fast gallop, you might get to Guatemala City while I'm still there."

******

Knowing how lonely I felt, Marco Vinicio kept me company when I went to the bus station that afternoon.

"Too bad you weren't able to spend more time with Emily," he commented. "You went to a lot of trouble to come back, and it was hardly worth the effort."

"Oh, it was worth it!" I declared, denying the extent of my own disappointment. "It isn't the quantity that counts. It's the quality. Right?"

"Do you think she likes you?" he blurted out.

"She likes me, but I have no idea how much," I began. Then I told him of her parting words.

"Too bad my horses can't get me to Guatemala fast enough," I concluded with a grin.

"Maybe there's a way," Marco Vinicio was suddenly very serious. "Just in case, this is the name of the hotel where she'll be staying."

He wrote on a piece of paper and handed it to me. It wouldn't be possible for me to get to Guatemala City in only two days, but I carefully folded the paper and put it in my shirt pocket. Then it was time to concentrate my attention on the good friend who stood before me. Though I didn't know it at the moment, he would be one of the few I met on my ride who would stay in contact. For many years, he and I exchanged an annual letter or two, usually around Christmastime.

Later, on the long bus ride to Managua, it occurred to me that Emily's idea might have possibilities, especially if I didn't take it literally. Maybe that was what Marco Vinicio had been thinking when he gave me the name of her hotel.

It was a long shot, but if I took the mares to Guatemala City by truck, I might see Emily yet again!

❖❖❖

Heads lowered, we pushed through the sheets of rain (see page 217).

CHAPTER 34

If It's Tuesday, This Must Be El Salvador

Long after midnight, the bus dropped me off on the outskirts of Managua, and I slept a couple of hours in my sleeping bag next to the mares' stalls. By the time the sun was up, I had ridden Hamaca and Ima to one of Managua's largest stockyards. Having decided to take my best shot at seeing Emily again, I hoped to quickly find a truck that had delivered cattle and was northbound without a load. My best hope, of course, was a truck bound directly for Guatemala, but that was a lot to ask. My proposed journey involved the territory of four nations, and I'd be doing well, indeed, to get a ride as far as Nicaragua's border with Honduras. Guatemala City would most likely be reached by stringing together a series of rides. With Emily due to be there in two days, I had no time to lose, but nightfall found me not an inch farther north. An entire day had gone by, and not one northbound truck had called at the stockyard.

After dark, I took Hamaca and Ima to another stockyard, where I was told a truck from Estelí was scheduled to arrive. I slept on the ground next to the night watchman's shack after asking him to please wake me upon the arrival of any truck, bound for anywhere at all. Adding to the previous fifteen hours of disappointment, not a single truck arrived. It wouldn't have been necessary for the watchman to wake me if one had. I dozed lightly, alert for the slightest sound. Innumerable times, I woke, haunted by the persistent feeling that time was on the wing while I was accomplishing nothing.

The next morning, much discouraged, I returned to the first stockyard, where daytime traffic was heavier. Early, several local and southbound trucks arrived, unloaded their cattle and departed. Then nothing. While I waited, a northbound jetliner passed overhead. I watched until it was out of sight. Tomorrow, same time, same place (with allowances for Latin American efficiency), another would probably fly over, pointed in the same direction, and Emily might well be on board. Would she perhaps be looking out the window and wondering about a man with two horses traveling along the highway below?

A short while later, I was sitting on the fence talking with the stockyard's *jefe* when a truck with Guatemalan license plates drove past. The *jefe* – fully committed to helping me – began shouting and waving his arms. I jumped down from my perch and enthusiastical-

327

ly added my efforts to his. The driver, however, drove by without realizing that he'd briefly seemed to be the answer to a fellow human's prayers.

Half an hour later, my stomach convinced me I should take time to eat. Hoping the *jefe* wouldn't permit a ride to escape during my absence, I briskly walked several blocks to a grocery store. On the way back, I noticed the same Guatemalan truck that had passed earlier. It was parked at the curb, and I checked around until I located the driver.

"Please *señor*, are you heading to Guatemala anytime soon?"

"Yes, in about an hour," the short, lean man responded, a little hesitantly. "Why?"

"I'm looking for a ride to Guatemala City," I continued. "I need to get there as quickly as possible, and…"

"Your problems are solved, *gringo*," the man cut in. "I'll be more than happy to give you a ride."

"There's one small complication," I continued. "I have two horses. Is there, by any chance, room for them, too?"

The trucker hadn't expected that last piece of news, and a puzzled expression froze on his face.

"It's very important to me," I wasn't too proud for some pleading.

"What's the hurry?" the trucker asked, brow still furrowed. "Are you going to a horse show?"

"This is a matter of the heart," I said, hoping Latin Americans were truly as romantic as I'd been told. "I need to get to Guatemala City so I can spend some time with a young lady who is going there for a short visit."

"Oh, yes. Now I see," said the driver, his face broadening into an understanding grin, "and how soon do you need to get there?"

"She arrives tomorrow and stays for three days."

"And then she goes home?"

As I nodded in the affirmative, the man's grin faded, replaced by a look of concern.

"I can't possibly get you there that quickly, *señor*," he said slowly.

"How long does it take to drive from Managua to Guatemala City?" I asked, not wanting the conversation to stop.

"If I were traveling alone I could be there by tomorrow evening, provided there are no mechanical problems," he stated confidently. "But there will be delays crossing three borders with two horses."

"I have all my papers in order," I blurted out, confidently. "We shouldn't have any difficulties at the borders."

At that moment, I honestly believed what I was saying, but only because I wanted to. Crossing three borders without problems would be a miracle!

"I earn my living with this truck," the man said. "I can't afford to be delayed."

"If there are delays caused by me or my horses, just leave us wherever we are at the time. You can simply continue on without us," I offered.

"Even if we get across the borders smoothly, there is no guarantee we can get to Guatemala City before your lady friend has gone. We could have mechanical problems, and if we do, it might delay us for days."

I stopped short of offering to help with the repairs. As anxious as I was to have this ride, there was no way for me to overlook my mechanical ineptitude. The driver came up with more reasons why we probably couldn't accomplish what I had in mind, and I stopped responding after the first few. Unless I was mistaken, he was caught up in the magical spirit of romance and had decided to help me, but first, he wanted me to understand that our chances were only so-so. Once he came to the end of his long list of potential problems, his grin returned.

"As long as you understand that I can guarantee nothing, I will try to get you to Guatemala City in time to see your lady friend," he pledged.

"Thank you very much!" I said, feeling intense gratitude.

"My name is Fernando," he said, extending his hand. "They call me Pablito."

Less than an hour later, we set out, hoping to speed through four countries in a mere thirty-six hours. Like a tale out of a storybook, it appeared that I might see Emily again!

Later in my life, I would learn that the journey can be as satisfying as reaching the goal, but when I was young, I was in a perpetual hurry. It was a congenital defect. As far back as I can remember, I feared that failure to reach a goal quickly might mean failure to reach it at all. With that disposition, I found it exciting to be facing the prospect of moving so much faster than usual, not only toward Guatemala but also toward Los Gatos.

It had often seemed that *time* was one aspect in which my ride was more difficult than Tschiffely's. For the most part, no cars or trucks passed him, with their speed emphasizing that in hours they'd be in cities he wouldn't reach for days. Likewise, he didn't have airliners overhead, mocking him with the fact that they'd arrive before the day was over at destinations he wouldn't see for a year or two. I envied Tschiffely's freedom from a deadline and had grown to hate the pressure created by mine. Only much later did I realize that this pressure was self-inflicted. Except for the stretch between Managua and Guatemala City, there was never all that much to gain by being in a rush, but I couldn't help myself. I hurried, even though I hated it. However, with Emily standing at the finish line, the race to Guatemala promised to be pure joy, unless I didn't get there in time.

On the way to Honduras, the truck suffered two minor breakdowns. Both were quickly fixed, thanks to Fernando's considerable mechanical skill, but the combined delays cast doubt on whether we'd reach the border before it closed for the night. If we didn't, we'd suffer a twelve-hour delay only two hundred miles after getting under way. If we crossed into Honduras that night, Fernando's plan was to drive as far as El Salvador before sleeping, and I spent two hours on the edge of my seat, willing the truck to go faster and the clock slower. Fortunately, we made it and sailed smoothly through the formalities necessary to exit Nicaragua. Unfortunately, just a few hundred feet away, serious problems waited.

"You lack one of the certificates that are required," the representative of the Honduran Department of Agriculture told me.

"But I have everything the Consul in Managua said I'd need," I protested, using familiar-sounding words.

"You must have misunderstood," I was told. "There's one paper missing."

"What must I do to get it?"

"Take the horses off the truck, leave them in quarantine and go to the Honduran Ministry of Agriculture in Tegucigalpa."

"And what do I have to get there?"

"A health certificate."

"But I have a health certificate," I argued. "Look. Right here at the top of this paper it says: 'Health Certificate.' It was issued by the Nicaraguan Ministry of Agriculture and has been authenticated by the Honduran Consul."

"Unfortunately, that isn't the one I need."

As far as I could make out, the hitch was that I had arrived by truck, instead of on horseback. Apparently, this called for a certificate I hadn't needed when riding across borders. From the corner of my eye, I could see Fernando preparing to tell me I was on my own. When he did, I wouldn't be entitled to the slightest protest. I had promised to step aside if my horses and I caused any sort of delay. Fernando could hardly be expected to detour sixty miles to Tegucigalpa, spend the night, wait for me to get a health certificate the next day and return to pick up Hamaca and Ima. My glorious dash to be at Emily's side was over before it had begun!

I wondered if my letter from the Costa Rican Minister of Agriculture might help, but I couldn't imagine how. Stupidly, I decided not to trouble to dig it out of my duffel bag. That decision was probably the worst I made during my entire trek.

I badgered and begged, but to no avail. The official never wavered. It was maddening. Once again, I couldn't help wondering about the purpose of a health certificate issued without inspecting my horses. Concluding that the idea was simply to collect a fee, I concocted a possible solution to my predicament.

"What would happen if I paid the fee for that paper ... right here?" I asked.

The official leaned on the counter, bringing his face close to mine.

"I think that can be arranged," he said, in a confidential tone of voice.

The hair stood up on the back of my neck. Without meaning to, I had offered a bribe! And he had accepted! In all my many dealings in Latin America, I hadn't once offered or paid a bribe. I believed it was wrong, and I stuck by that belief, even though it undoubtedly contributed to the suffering I had unfailing endured at the hands of Latin American officialdom.

"How much is the fee?" I asked, stalling for enough time to make my decision.

The man quoted an amount so small that it hardly seemed a suitable reward for corruption. Nonetheless, I remained hesitant. After all, it wasn't the amount that made bribery wrong. The more I thought about it, however, the more I discovered how easy it could be to rationalize bribery. After all, these officials were paid so little that everyone knew they had to supplement their incomes. Bribery was an accepted and routine part of Latin American life. Everybody did it. Abruptly, I became angry with myself. It had always been one of my pet peeves that people could so easily rationalize their wrongdoing. If I was going to do this, I should at least have the integrity to admit it was wrong! I felt Fernando's hand on my shoulder.

"What are you going to do, *gringo*?" he asked. "It would be a shame to miss that pretty lady waiting in Guatemala City. If you need, I can loan you some Honduran money, and you can pay me back in dollars."

He was trying to speed up my decision, and it worked. I pictured Emily and paid the bribe. The Honduran official knew a good thing when he saw it, and he extracted additional "taxes" that would also wind up in his pocket. As an encore, he demanded a fee for a "custodian," who would ride in Fernando's truck as long as we were in Honduras. This escort was a uniformed, submachine gun-toting soldier. Stern-faced beneath his steel helmet, he rode in the cargo area with the mares. He was young with an enthusiasm that marked him as new at his job. In time, he would undoubtedly acquire the same bored look worn by other custodians I saw aboard other trucks while we were in Honduras.

The Pan-American Highway passes through southwestern Honduras where that country is reduced to a narrow corridor between Nicaragua and El Salvador. At that point, Honduras is barely more than a hundred miles wide. In about three hours, we were across and parked for the night, barely short of El Salvador. Fernando had selected a field where other truckers were already stopped, waiting for the border to open the next morning. I unloaded Hamaca and Ima and walked them back and forth until they had thoroughly stretched their legs. That done, I tied them to the side of Fernando's vehicle and began wondering how I was going to find hay. Luckily, the hay found me when I noticed a mule carrying a mountain of grass among the trucks. The man who led him was looking for cattle haulers who needed feed.

"This hay is freshly cut," he told me when I asked why it was so expensive.

"Freshly pulled" would have been a more-accurate description. The overpriced *hay* was nothing more than eight-inch grass, pulled up by the roots apparently from a muddy field. Putting the lie to the claim of freshness, the mud on the roots had hardened to the consistency of sandstone. I dreaded removing it but knew I'd have to. Following two consecutive nights of insufficient sleep, I took a very dim view of laboriously removing this dried muck by hand, but the sooner I started, the sooner I'd be done. It was slow going, and after I'd been immersed in my stimulating chore for some time, Fernando handed me a machete.

"You work too hard, *gringo*," he said. "Why don't you just cut off the roots?"

Of course! I was so tired that I lacked the energy to come up with even such an obvious solution to a simple problem.

The next morning, to avoid complications that might result from

332

trucking the horses into El Salvador, I saddled up in anticipation of riding across the nearby border. When the custodian realized that I'd be taking the mares out of his sight, he grew suspicious and sternly forbade it. I asked him if he wanted to ride along on Ima, but he didn't. Mustering my best powers of persuasion, I explained that I'd ridden all the way from Peru, and with a theatrical flourish, I opened my passport and pointed out the various entry and exit stamps.

"These mares are going to the United States," I assured him. "I have absolutely no intention of selling them, but it will cost me extra money if I take them across the border in a truck."

After sternly warning that I'd find myself in very serious trouble if I tried to cross the border without both horses, the custodian relented. Not wishing to delay Fernando, I skipped breakfast and started out while he was still eating. Ilamaca was bursting with vigor after her long rest, and since our ride was short, I didn't hold her back. The quick rhythm of hoofbeats had an urgent sound in the half-light of sunrise. Emily would be in Guatemala City within a couple of hours. With any luck I should be there by the time the sun rose again. The thought filled me with excitement.

I was in and out of El Salvador's border station in less than half an hour. Instead of a hard time, the officials inside gave me smiles and kind words. Quickly, I started down the highway, intending to move fast until I was beyond where I could be seen from the border station. If Fernando hadn't caught me by then, I'd slow my horses until he did. No sooner had I formulated my plan than Fernando made it obsolete by driving past and gesturing that he'd be waiting up ahead. A mile farther down the road, I quickly loaded the mares back into his truck. Soon thereafter, we were again speeding – if thirty miles an hour can be called *speeding* – toward our destination. I was nearer Guatemala, but the worst difficulties were ahead, not behind.

In Managua, I had taken care of all paperwork necessary to enter Honduras and El Salvador. I hadn't dreamed, at the time, that I'd so soon be arriving in Guatemala, and I had neither Guatemalan health certificates for the mares nor a visa for myself. I had kept that little piece of information from Fernando for as long as possible, but the time had come to tell him. To my relief, he wasn't upset.

"We can have a Guatemalan consul issue you a visa and authenticate your horses' health certificates," he calmly informed me. "I know where there's a consul near the border. We'll stop and have him take care of everything."

Having come clean with Fernando, I sighed, naively assuming

that I had just cleared the day's worst obstacle. Relieved, I sat back in my seat and focused my attention on the sights of El Salvador. The first thing to command my attention was the abundance of pistol-packing *campesinos*. They were everywhere and looked like gunslingers on the streets of Tombstone.

Mostly primitive looking, their pistols resembled the sidearms of America's Wild West days. There were also a few rifles, but the easily carried revolver was the weapon of choice. Almost everyone, it seemed, had one holstered in plain sight. Never before had I seen anything quite like it, and I said so to Fernando. He merely grinned and commented that firearms were a routine sight in El Salvador. Proof of that came when we stopped at a roadside tavern.

The world inside that tavern was straight out of nineteenth century Dodge City. Most of the men wore clothing and hats reminiscent of North American-style cowboys. The result looked as if a Hollywood movie director had orchestrated it. Every detail was perfect, right down to the sign above the bar, which read: *All customers must check their firearms with the bartender. They will be returned when you leave.* My first impression was that the sign was a gag, but the number of pistols passing back and forth between customers and bartender dispelled that notion!

As the day wore on, we continued to draw ever closer to our destination, and I began to actually believe I was going to see Emily. Aside from a few small glitches, things had gone smoothly. Could my luck hold out? I feared the answer might depend on whether I was referring to *good* luck or *bad* luck.

Getting to the Guatemalan consul required us to turn off the highway and drive twelve miles out of our way. When we arrived, the consul's secretary greeted us with bad news: her boss didn't issue visas. For a moment, I was sure I had misunderstood. A consul who doesn't issue visas, I thought, would be the equivalent of an accountant who doesn't do math.

"We aren't authorized to issue visas here," the secretary repeated. "The nearest consul who does that is twenty miles farther down this road. I doubt that he'll be open by the time you get there, though. Most consuls close for business about this time of day."

Additional miles of bad road, perhaps for nothing. I was afraid to look at Fernando. A further detour would be a bitter pill for him to swallow. He'd been an unbelievably good sport, but he had to be nearing the end of his patience. I wouldn't have been surprised if he had washed his hands of me, right then and there. Unfortunately, that was his intention. He raised a fist to the height of his chest, with the clenched fingers facing him and the back showing to me. Then he commenced to extend the fingers, one by one, as he spoke.

"Look," he said, "I have to be in Guatemala City tomorrow morning to pick up a load [the first finger jumped to attention] ... that means I must get to the border before it closes at 6:00 this afternoon [a second finger joined the first] ... Guatemala has a law that prohibits transporting livestock after dark [yet another finger was extended] ... there will likely be delays and additional requirements to cross the border into Guatemala [a fourth finger popped up] ... and the consul's office will probably be closed by the time we get there [he unfolded his thumb]."

"I just remembered something," the secretary offered, helpfully. "The consul is a doctor, and he attends his consular duties at his medical office. He may be available, after all."

"Another thing," Fernando added, as if he hadn't heard. "I can't afford the gasoline for all this extra driving."

Having run out of fingers – at least on his upraised hand – Fernando had dispensed with the visual aides.

"Look, I'll pay for the gas," I offered. "Please. It's only twenty miles."

With Fernando, I always discussed distances in miles because they're longer than kilometers, meaning there are fewer between any two points.

"One way," Fernando reminded.

I could see him gearing up to give me more reasons why my rush to Guatemala City was doomed, and I drew in a deep breath, preparing to answer them. Unexpectedly, Fernando's grin returned.

"You really want to see this girl, don't you?"

My head nodded up and down, and suddenly, Fernando's spirit of romance seized the upper hand over his common sense.

"All right, let's see if we can get you a visa," he said, "but remember, you're paying for the gas!"

It was 3:00 in the afternoon when we arrived at the second consul's office. He was there and turned out to be a very pleasant man who efficiently rendered his services in a matter of minutes. With a visa freshly stamped in my passport and a "verification" attached to each of my mares' health certificates, we set out for the Guatemalan border.

"This will be the most difficult border," Fernando warned me. "Guatemalan officials are famous for being difficult."

He wasn't the only one who thought so. In Costa Rica, *don* Juan Rafael Cabezas had also warned me about the Guatemalan border. On his way to a horse show, he once arrived there with a truckload of horses and a briefcase full of paperwork. In spite of his thorough preparations, he had to backtrack a hundred miles to get a document not required to cross any other border in Central America.

When we were a few miles from the border, Fernando stopped his truck. We had discussed it and agreed to repeat the tactic used with such success at the previous border. With time running out, I quickly unloaded the mares and saddled Hamaca.

"Good luck, *gringo*," Fernando called as I set out on horseback.

A minute later, his truck sped past, with him smiling and waving. I couldn't stop a chill from running down my spine as I watched the now-empty truck disappear down the road. Now that he was free of us, Fernando could easily leave us behind if there was the slightest delay at the border station. This was one crossing that *had* to go smoothly. To my everlasting surprise, it did! Hamaca, Ima and I crossed the border without a hitch, and a mile or so beyond, I loaded the mares into the truck again. As far as I knew, the last obstacle would be getting my horses past the seven police checkpoints between the border and Guatemala City.

In those days, Guatemala had a serious cattle-rustling problem and had implemented stringent measures to get it under control. One of these forbade any transportation of livestock after 6:00 in the evening. According to Fernando, it had never been clear whether horses were included under this ban. Officers at the seven checkpoints would make that determination, and they had a reputation for taking everything to an extreme.

At 6:15, already past the deadline for livestock hauling, I reloaded Hamaca and Ima, an act that exposed Fernando to serious problems. Why he took this risk in my behalf, I'll never know for sure. I sensed that, in part, he didn't like the police and enjoyed putting something over on them. However, I truly believe that what he did was in the name of romance. The closer we came to Guatemala City, the more it seemed to please him that I might make it in time to see Emily.

Fernando had a plan for dealing with the police. It was simple and lent itself to plausible deniability if discovered. To implement this plan, I helped him fasten a large, rainproof, canvas cover over his truck's cargo area. This took nearly a half-hour, but when we were finished, no sign of my mares was visible from outside the truck.

"Trucks don't have to stop at police checkpoints if they aren't carrying cargo," Fernando had explained with a grin and raised eyebrows. "You aren't paying me, so your horses are personal effects - not cargo. That means we can drive right past, and no one will be the wiser unless they send a patrol car after us."

"You should have been a lawyer."

We'd be fine as long as the police didn't stop us. During the next hours, we drove past the first check point, which had a fully loaded cattle truck detained in its parking area, and then the second, third, fourth, fifth, sixth and seventh, without once attracting attention. Later, Fernando spent an hour repairing the generator, which had failed, causing the headlights to grow dim. When we were rolling again, it first appeared that his repair had been unsuccessful, but down the road a ways the lights began to grow brighter. Just outside Guatemala City, we passed an erupting volcano, which lit up the dark sky like a distant artillery battle. I laughed at the analogy that had automatically come to mind. It was time for another notation in *Albright's Book of Useless Facts*: men *definitely* think in military terms!

But men also think in romantic terms. The huge display of nature's fireworks seemed to be celebrating my timely arrival against all odds. Thanks to an extraordinarily kind Guatemalan trucker, I had made it, ahead of even my most optimistic schedule. I was going to see Emily again.

337

Chapter 35

Hello. Goodbye.

Hamaca and Ima spent the night tied to the truck in Fernando's backyard, eating dried corn stalks, and I slept nearby in my sleeping bag. Before dawn the next morning, Fernando woke me.

"*Gringo*," he said, using the affectionate nickname he'd given me, "the fairgrounds aren't far. Go there and ask for Humberto Morales. Tell him you're a friend of mine, and he'll arrange a stall for your mares at a very reasonable price."

With that, he gave me directions.

"I'll never forget what you did for me," I told him.

"It was my pleasure," he said, beaming and reaching up to pat my shoulders with both hands.

Having bid Fernando good-bye, I rode to the fairgrounds and made arrangements for the mares to stay there. Then I checked into a humble hotel that was more expensive than usual because it had a private bathroom, hot water and a telephone. After a thorough shower, I called a surprised Emily at her hotel. She and her fellow Rotarians were about to have breakfast, and I was invited to join them. Their hotel was one of the nicest in Guatemala City, and even though dressed in my best clothes, I attracted more than a few stares as I walked through the lobby. If I hadn't been Caucasian, I would have been intercepted long before I got to the dining room.

Emily and I sat at a table with a half-dozen girls from Costa Rica, all of them Rotarians. When the waiter came, she ordered *huevos pateados*, and the poor man just stood there, looking puzzled. His pen was poised above his order pad, but he wasn't writing. With elaborate courtesy, he asked if she could please repeat her order. After she did so, he was no closer to knowing what she wanted. I was no better off; Emily had just ordered "kicked eggs"!

"They don't use that expression in Guatemala," one of her companions explained in Spanish. "Here they call them *huevos revueltos*."

Scrambled eggs! A chorus of laughter went up.

"That's why we all love Emily so much," one of the other girls explained to me. "Not many North Americans try so hard to do things the way we do."

I think that's one of the reasons I'm so fond of her, I mused, jaws clenched to prevent this thought from taking verbal form.

After breakfast, Emily and I had a moment alone in the lobby.

"Yesterday was my only free day," she told me. "Most of today and tomorrow are pretty well filled. I feel terrible after the effort you made to get here so fast."

I must have looked as disappointed as I felt.

"If it doesn't seem terribly self-serving," she continued quickly, "I can see you when I have free time. It won't be much more than an hour here and there, but if you don't mind…"

"That would be great," I responded. "Are you busy right now?"

"Yes," she said, "but I'll be free between noon and 1:00. We can meet in the lobby at noon."

Thus we planned the first segment of our "catch-as-catch-can" tour of the city.

******

During our noontime stroll through the downtown streets of Central America's largest city, I gave Emily the only gift I could afford. It was a poster, advertising an upcoming event, and it was beautifully done. Since copies were pasted on walls everywhere we went, I caught her admiring them more than once, and I couldn't resist offering to get one for her. It was something I never would have thought of doing under ordinary circumstances, but then again, so is bribery.

To protect them from people with intentions such as mine, the posters were affixed high above the sidewalks, out of most people's reach. I selected one that was in particularly good shape and standing on tiptoe, began working it loose. It was attached to the wall with numerous dollops of paste, and I was obliged to move slowly and carefully. Never more tempted to hurry, I did a good a job of controlling that urge. I was embarrassed by the stares of passersby, and I feared the sudden appearance of a policeman who detested North Americans. None too soon for my taste, I was rolling the poster into a cylinder and handing it to Emily.

Between 3:30 and 5:30, we took a municipal bus to one of the city's many parks. There we sat on a bench and talked, taking baby steps toward getting to know one another. It astonished me that so much pleasure could come from such a simple activity. While we were talking, I noticed a beggar approaching prosperous-looking tourists. He wasn't having much luck. Without thinking, I waved him over and gave him a handful of coins. It wasn't much, but it was more than I had to spare. He smiled and thanked me. To someone who knew how little attention I normally paid to beggars, it probably would have seemed that I was trying to impress Emily. My motive, however, was simpler than that: I was happy, and I wanted to share it.

On the bus ride back to Emily's hotel, we passed through an intersection dominated by a replica of the Eiffel Tower. Smaller than the original but sizable, nonetheless, the structure had been a gift from France. It towered over the intersection, one foot on each of the four corners, and traffic on both streets passed directly beneath its main structure.

Too soon, it was time to say good-bye once more. At her invitation, I accompanied Emily when she and her fellow Rotarians from Costa Rica went to the airport. We stood in the lobby, surrounded by a flock of Guatemalan lady Rotarians who were chaperoning the visitors. Awkwardly, we tried to make conversation, not knowing one another well enough to do a good job of it. Too soon, it was time for her to board her flight.

"Well, goodbye. It was nice to see you again. Good luck on your trip home."

With those words, Emily turned and followed the other passengers. Suddenly she stopped, turned, walked back to me, raised as high as she could on tiptoe and kissed me on the cheek. A cooing sound of approval came from the chaperones. Even though they were the official guardians of her virtue, the gesture was so innocent that they approved. One of the ladies seemed to sense my loneliness after Emily had disappeared through a door.

"What a jewel she is! I can see why you love her," she said softly.

"I don't know her well enough to love her," I said sadly, "but I like her *a lot!*"

Unable to see Emily's plane on the runway and anxious to be alone ("Go away and don't bother me. Can't you see I'm lonely?"), I walked outside. Searching for a view of the runway, I circled the terminal and came to a place where a high embankment made it possible to climb onto the roof. There, I was able to sit, pretty much out of sight, with a commanding view. For a very long time, I sat with my legs dangling over the roof's edge, compelled by nervous energy to swing them back and forth. I could feel their weight pulling my spirits downward. Before long, my legs ceased to swing, and a feeling of exhaustion came over me. I suddenly felt stupid, sitting there with nothing to see but an ordinary airplane sitting on a runway. Finally the ordinary airplane began taxiing toward its take-off position.

After the plane had become airborne, shrunk to a tiny size and disappeared from sight, I was still sitting there, unable to summon enough energy to move. Finally, I jumped down from the roof and slowly ambled toward a distant bus stop. I never dreamed that the plane about to land was Emily's! Shortly after take off, engine trouble had been detected, and the San José bound plane had reversed course. Unbeknownst to me, Emily would spend an additional day in Guatemala City. Unfortunately, she had no idea how to reach me. It was the ultimate irony. After all the effort I'd put forth to spend only four hours with her, I could have added a full day if only I'd known she was there.

******

Having spent more money than usual during the previous two days, I got permission to sleep at the fairgrounds in an empty stall next to my mares. For dinner, I walked to a small grocery store and bought a sack full of bread rolls and fruit. Dejectedly, I sat in a small park in front of the store and slowly ate, lost in thought, hardly noticing the simplicity of the evening's menu.

My eyes had been bigger than my stomach, and I still had two rolls left after my appetite was satisfied. While wondering if I should purchase something to supplement these for breakfast, I noticed a stray dog watching me. His sad eyes said he was hungry, and his protruding ribs confirmed that he'd been that way for a long time. I broke off a piece of roll and threw it to him. He gobbled it up and came a step closer, licking his lips and watching my every move with plaintive eyes. I threw another piece and another until the rolls were gone. Ten minutes later, the dog was still standing there, with a hopeful expression on his face. I bought more rolls and fed them to him, moving slowly to make our mutual pleasure last. In another mood I wouldn't have even noticed such a mongrel, much less sympathized with him.

Inexplicably, the episode with the dog helped me switch gears. For too long, I had been sidestepping important decisions. I was at a fork in the road and needed to go one way or the other. If I was to arrive in time to properly prepare Hamaca for the Tevis Cup, there was no time for more travel on horseback. On the other hand, if I wanted to ride farther, it was imperative I borrow the necessary money. Of course, a bank loan was out of the question. My only hope would be to contact friends or family members, request a loan and offer Hamaca and Ima as security. If I was going to borrow money, I needed to get started. Going around in circles – trying to make up my mind but never quite succeeding – was a luxury I couldn't afford. My financial reserves would soon dwindle to where I couldn't get home if my requests for a loan were denied. I was down to less than two hundred and fifty dollars. Expenses were gobbling up thirty dollars a week, often more. At that rate, I'd be penniless before I reached Mexico City. Then what? If I asked, my parents would wire money. However, as dead set as they had been against my ride, asking them to rescue me was unthinkable.

The way I had come to life in Emily's company was food for further thought. I asked myself why I was sometimes so desperate to prolong what had already been a wonderful adventure. Was it because I wished to lengthen an enjoyable experience, or was I escaping the pain of my divorce and the loss of my children? In all probability, it was some of each. I truly loved adventure and would undoubtedly need to indulge myself from time to time in the future, but it was time to put the pain behind me and put my life back together.

On the following day, I'd make a final decision and stick to it. Period!

Bombs away under the door (see page 260)!

CHAPTER 36

Decisions, Decisions

The next morning I took a long look at Hamaca and Ima, and what I saw was not good. During the past week, I had seldom done more than glance at my horses, never really studying at them. That morning, it was as if I was seeing them for the first time in a long while. They looked like anything but candidates for the Tevis Cup. Concerned about their weight, I'd had them tube wormed by a veterinarian in Managua. Since then, they had worked less and eaten more than usual, and I'd been expecting an improvement in their appearances. If there was one, I couldn't see it.

In my wallet, I carried a photo of Hamaca, taken before we left José Antonio Onrubia's *hacienda* in Piura. When I compared that image to the mare standing before me, I could see dramatic differences. Hamaca looked emaciated, and her once-shiny, seal-slick coat was dull, bleached and rough. Her mane had grown to shoulder length but was shaggy and irregular. Of course, these superficial changes were of limited importance. After all, the Tevis Cup wasn't a beauty contest, and the mares would be as beautiful as ever once they'd been settled in Los Gatos for a while. However, the challenge of the world's most demanding hundred-mile race would be far too difficult for an animal not in prime condition. If I didn't soon get Hamaca on a steady diet of the best possible feed, she'd be running on empty when she tackled the Tevis Cup. My original plan had been to arrive at least two months before race day, but that had been before I knew how much the rigors of the tropics would affect my horses. While I could honestly say that Hamaca and Ima were fit and in good spirits, I had to admit that our journey had taken its toll. Two months wouldn't be enough time to renew Hamaca, not if I wanted her at her best.

Nevertheless, I couldn't stop wrestling with the pros and cons of riding farther before I resorted to vehicles. Not usually a person who thought a decision to death, I found myself doing exactly that. In the back of my mind, I feared that cutting my ride short by two months might leave me with a sense of defeat later on. If my accomplishments were falling short of my expectations, it was because nothing had gone as I'd expected. False starts, unexpected delays and expensive stumbling blocks had steadily drained my meager supplies of time and money. Time was the more critical loss. There was always the possibility of borrowing money, but I couldn't borrow time.

343

I remembered the wonderful impression Hamaca and Ima had made on *don* Luis de Ascasubi when he first saw them, two months earlier. Since then, hundreds of miles, countless poor meals and plenty of other tribulations had been endured. Through it all, Hamaca and Ima had kept going with absolutely no sign of giving in. There was no doubt that both mares could (and would) walk every last mile to Los Gatos and even beyond, if I asked it, but was there any point in pushing them further? What was left to prove after such a heroic display of endurance?

And what about myself? Would choosing to travel by vehicle mean I was a quitter, or was it time to get on with my life? If I'd learned anything, it was that I was an *adventurer*, but not necessarily a *wanderer*. Since I'd begun my ride, each morning had brought the feeling that I was living a worthwhile life in an interesting world. However, that coin had another side. For months, everything and everyone had been disposable, here today and gone tomorrow. Increasingly, I missed having consistent, dependable people and routines around me.

Last but not least, I was a man who had nothing beyond two horses and the money in his pocket. It was time to think about my financial future. And so the final decision was made. Hamaca, Ima and I would step up our pace and finish our journey in the fastest manner consistent with my finances. From the beginning, I had planned to transport my horses in vehicles at some point. The only questions had been: when and how? Now that the time had been chosen, it remained for me to find an affordable method, no small challenge for someone with the princely sum of two hundred and fifty dollars at his disposal.

Duties, fees and quarantine expenses at the U.S. border would consume about half of my remaining funds, and crossing from Guatemala to Mexico wouldn't be cheap. That meant two horses and I had to travel two thousand four hundred miles for what a week of frugal living had cost in the days before my ride. It would be a worthy challenge to end my adventure.

After caring for Hamaca and Ima, I headed for the Ministry of Agriculture, ready to tackle the paperwork for entering Mexico. An hour earlier, I'd been dismayed by how far I still had to go, but during the bus ride to town, my perception did a complete flip-flop, and it suddenly seemed that I was almost home. Within a day or two, I could be in Mexico. After that, only one border separated me from my homeland.

The Ministry of Agriculture was located in the *Palacio Nacional*. The building's Spanish colonial elegance was marred by the presence of armed guards. Palace Guards in Peru and Ecuador had been more decorative with their swords, brightly colored uniforms, shiny black knee-high boots and glistening medieval-style helmets with feathery plumes. Standing at attention with eyes straight ahead, they seemed to have stepped out of a bygone century. The Guatemalan guards were of the functional variety. They wore camouflaged combat fatigues and carried submachine guns. Their manner was alert and businesslike. No one got past them without undergoing a thorough search. Evidently, they were looking for weapons and bombs, a well-advised precaution in view of recent terrorist activity.

I slowed my walk as I approached the half-dozen guards who flanked the main door. They had detained two ladies and were carefully going through purses and shopping bags. Once that was accomplished, they turned their attention to *my* approach and gave me a thorough looking over. The victim of a guilty conscience, I found myself hoping there was no recently issued all-points bulletin for a tall *gringo* who had removed a poster from a downtown wall.

As I drew closer, I slowed my walk and looked at the guards, waiting for instructions. One of them swung his arm, impatiently gesturing for me to go on in and be quick about it. Not until I was in the huge lobby did it occur to me that I was carrying my bulky sweater, rolled up in one hand. Little imagination would have been required to picture a small submachine gun hidden inside. I wondered why I hadn't been searched and could only conclude that the guards trusted *gringos*. Now *there's* a dangerous activity!

My visit to the Secretary of Agriculture's office was as pleasant as government red tape could possibly be. When I presented my letter from the Secretary in Costa Rica, his Guatemalan counterpart cordially insisted on supplying me with his own letters of recommendation.

"I wouldn't want you to think Guatemalan courtesy is in any way inferior," he said, with a broad smile, when I protested that he needn't trouble himself.

Soon afterward, I was presented with three letters. Two were addressed to the Secretaries of Agriculture in Mexico and the United States. The other was of the *To Whom it May Concern* variety. It asked officials in Guatemala to extend me every possible courtesy, and as a result, I received one-day service on my horses' health certificates. Just like that, I was ready to enter Mexico. All that remained was to get there. The Secretary of Agriculture had suggested that I look into traveling by rail, and after some comparison shopping, I found that the train was, indeed, the way to go.

Rates were printed in the railroad freight manual, together with a statement that they are not subject to negotiation. However, freight was divided into many categories, and horses didn't exactly fit into any of them. After initially trying to charge the highest possible price, the freight agent suddenly switched sides and helped me qualify for the lowest rate offered for *any* type of freight. This laudable enthusiasm for saving me money appeared as soon as he became convinced that I was truly short of money and not just cheap.

"There are several technicalities we can exploit to further reduce the amount I have to charge you," he told me, getting into the spirit.

"Such as?" I encouraged.

"By making a few adjustments in the routing and scheduling, I can charge less than the cost of a straight-through trip. Of course, that means layovers and changing trains, but the savings will more than compensate you."

"Sounds good to me."

"One of the peculiarities of our freight rates is that making the trip in three stages rather than straight through is much cheaper. Permit me to show you."

By the time all was said and done, that was only one of several loopholes we exploited. None made much sense to me, but they all saved me money. What the heck, the Guatemalan railway deserved whatever it got (or didn't get) after allowing its freight rates to be set by the same genius who wrote the IRS tax code!

"Too bad you weren't in Guatemala City a couple of weeks ago," the agent said when our transaction was finished. The twinkle in his eyes indicated that he was working his way toward a punch line.

"Why is that?" I dutifully played the straight man.

"Because one of the local television stations offered fifty dollars to the first person over two meters tall who came into their studio. You must be more or less that height, no?"

"Ten centimeters more," I said, mentally spending the much-needed money.

Throughout my ride, my height had been unrelentingly inconvenient in many ways besides the teasing it provoked. That made it all the more discouraging to have missed a golden opportunity to take advantage of it for once.

"The prize money was offered for four days, and nobody claimed it," the agent said, shaking his head and unwittingly rubbing salt in my wound. "There aren't many people that tall in Guatemala."

In order to get the best possible price, my departure was booked on a train leaving the following day. That left me free to spend the afternoon doing something I had long dreamed of, touring Antigua, 25 which had been Guatemala's capital until an earthquake destroyed it in 1773. Thereafter, the corridors of power were moved to Guatemala City.

In its heyday, Antigua was the most important seat of government between Mexico and Peru, and it survives as a world-famous tourist attraction. Its spectacular ruins, only partially restored, are a virtual museum of Spanish colonial architecture. As a bonus, Antigua's man-made beauty is enhanced by its location near the bases of towering volcanoes.

Unable to afford the super-deluxe tourist treatment, I took public transportation to Antigua and there joined an inexpensive guided tour. The tour was memorable, but I met a tourist who was even more so. He was a North American with a spine so misshapen that he was permanently stooped, almost at a right angle. To add to this handicap, the man's knees didn't lock until they were recessed far behind the feet below them. He could walk only with the aid of two canes and his wife. Boarding and exiting the bus was a monumental task that seemed to take him forever. I found myself feeling immense sympathy, not as much for the handicap as for the way people must react to it. I could see the members of our tour group becoming increasingly exasperated with the long delays. Ever more openly, people sighed and impatiently fanned themselves whenever we were obliged to wait.

As the tour dragged on, the man tired, and his movements became slower yet. At the last stop, we had a seemingly interminable delay while he boarded the bus. When he was finally seated, the rest of us boarded speedily, anxious to be under way. It was our fate, however, to sit in the hot, stuffy vehicle because our driver – bored with the long wait – was engaged in a conversation across the street. While we waited, one of the members of our group, a fellow North American, walked up behind the gentleman who had so often delayed us. She was nervous, and it had obviously taken considerable effort to work up the nerve for what she was about to say.

"I can't begin to tell you how much I admire you for getting out in public and enjoying your life, even though it's so difficult for you," she said, after reaching out and touching his bent and stooped shoulder. "I think it's wonderful. I really do."

As if on signal, everyone chimed in, enthusiastically seconding what had been said. I'm positive that hardly anyone had been feeling that way during the long, hot afternoon, but apparently the lady's words had made them think. At a time when I often heard Americans accused of lacking sympathy for others, I felt very proud.

******

I was up before dawn the next day and rode Hamaca, with Ima following behind, to the train station in nearby Pamplona. At 11:00 A.M., the mares and I boarded our train for the first leg of our three-day trip to the Mexican border. Everything went as scheduled, ending with an on-time arrival in the city of Esquintla at 3:00 in the afternoon. Our itinerary called for the mares and me to stay overnight and board another train the following day when we would proceed as far as Mazatenango. There we would lay over again before continuing on to the border at Tecun Uman late on the third day, a Saturday.

That first day, Hamaca and Ima had a boxcar all to themselves and made their trip in luxury, alternately eating and dozing. At first, I rode with them, just to be sure they adapted to train travel. After I was sure they were traveling well, I joined the engineer in the cab of the locomotive during one of our many stops. He and I had an extremely pleasant conversation, despite the difficulty of making ourselves heard above the roar of the engine. When we arrived in Esquintla, the engineer seemed as sorry as I that our time together was at an end. He confirmed this impression by insisting I join him as he drove a World War I-vintage switch engine back and forth, reorganizing his train's boxcars. Shouting in order to compete with the racket produced by the half-century-old locomotive, the two of us continued talking. We were friends by the time he'd finished rolling the engine back and forth, unhooking the freight cars that were staying in Esquintla and locking on to new ones bound for cities farther down the line.

Among the boxcars uncoupled and parked on sidetracks was the one containing Hamaca and Ima. As its only contents, they had spent the entire trip in the tight confines of a small pen and were full of pent-up energy. In anticipation of our overnight stay, I turned them loose inside their car, giving them room to roam and lie down.

Later, when the engineer was about to depart, he came to the mares' boxcar and insisted that I accompany him to meet the stationmaster. Apparently my reaction was transparent.

"It will be well worth your time," I was told. "He can do favors for you if he feels like it."

The engineer and I had been exchanging jokes earlier, and I'd remembered two more I wanted to tell him. As a result, we arrived at the stationmaster's office laughing so hard that neither could speak. When we had composed ourselves, the engineer introduced me.

"Take good care of this little *gringo*," he said, reaching above his head to pat me on my shoulder. "We want him to have good memories of Guatemala."

After the engineer had said good-bye and excused himself, I discovered the stationmaster to be a man of few words. He did little to encourage my attempts at conversation, and rather soon, I excused myself and made my way back to the mares' boxcar. There I opened one of my duffel bags and dug into my provisions for a can of Sterno cooking fuel, a pan, a spoon and some groceries. Just outside the boxcar, I lit the fuel, prepared dinner and ate it. I was unrolling my sleeping bag when the stationmaster paid me a surprise visit. My first impression was that I was about to be scolded for cooking near the boxcars.

"You must be in a hurry to get home," he began, more relaxed than before. "If you like, I can send this boxcar to the border with tonight's nine o'clock train. That should get you there before dawn tomorrow and save you two days."

"Wonderful!" I responded. "Thank you."

"I hope you'll have good memories of the Guatemalan people," he said, still smiling, "including me."

The stationmaster was wrong about saving me two days. His little favor would actually put me three days ahead of schedule. My original itinerary had me arriving at Mexico's border after it closed Saturday night. In order to avoid paying the premium crossing fees levied on Sundays, I had planned to lay over a day. Thanks to the stationmaster, I could skip the Sunday layover, gaining a third day.

The next morning, one overnight train ride closer to Los Gatos, I saddled Hamaca, tied my duffel bags on Ima's packsaddle and rode to the border. After finishing with Guatemalan formalities in less than a quarter hour, I crossed the half-mile-long, wooden *International Bridge*. Though the name was accurate, it seemed grandiose for such an unimpressive, run-down structure. I reached Mexican soil by 10:00. In contrast to events on the Guatemalan side, it took twenty-four hours to meet Mexico's requirements, and even then, I wasn't free to go. It was the lengthiest, most complicated and most expensive border crossing yet, and it also cost me one of the three "gift" days I had just been given.

To begin this ordeal, the Mexican Customs inspector instructed me to unpack my duffel bags so he could go through their contents, piece by piece. This required untying, unloading, unlocking, unpacking and spreading out my worldly goods for his easy access. It took nearly an hour. When I went into the customs building and advised that everything was ready, a second man announced that the inspection wouldn't be necessary, after all. I felt like demanding one, fearing a further change of heart after everything was repacked. Fortunately, good sense prevailed, and I kept my mouth shut.

To my dismay, the official veterinarian had to be summoned from Tapachula, a city twenty-five miles away. It took most of the day for him to arrive, glance at my mares, quickly fill out a printed form and charge me a hefty fee for his services plus travel expenses. Then, the customs official blithely demanded a deposit to guarantee I wouldn't sell my horses in Mexico. I'd been through *that* before. Confidently I pulled out my passport, showed my Panamanian visa and proposed the same alternative.

"This is Mexico!" the man told me, "We don't care how things are done in Panama, or anywhere else!"

It had been my intention to next produce my letters from the Costa Rican and Guatemalan Secretaries of Agriculture, but suddenly *that* seemed like a very bad idea! After a great deal of back and forth, I knew why a stalemate is called a "Mexican standoff." Further discussion resulted in my being directed to the man in charge, an elderly gentleman referred to as the *jefe*. The *jefe* was hard of hearing and unbendable. Not open to negotiation, he meant to have his way or to bring my travels to a halt.

"My job is to enforce the law, and that's what I must do!" he announced after tiring of my persistence. "You can either pay the required deposits or get out of Mexico."

Seeing his determination, I wished I could have paid the deposits, but doing so would have left me without enough money to get to Mexico's northern border and collect the refund.

"Please *señor*," I pleaded, "There must be a way for me to cross Mexico without having to make these deposits."

"Either do as I say, or your horses will be confiscated right here and now!" the *jefe* shouted, now furious with me.

---

25 Sometimes called "Old Guatemala City," Antigua is located about thirty miles from the current Guatemala City.

CHAPTER 37

"Your Horses Will be Confiscated!"

When Latin American officials raise their voices, they fully expect all discussion to cease. This was what the *jefe* anticipated, and it's what normally happens. On other occasions, however, I had learned that if I calmly and politely persisted after the shouting, the authority in question would be on unfamiliar ground. Each time I had used this tactic, a rather surprised official had wound up being courteous and even helpful. Latin Americans generally place a very high value on good manners and find it difficult to sustain discourtesy, even when angered. I sensed this would also be the case with the man sitting before me, and I was right. After blustering, the *jefe* softened his stance.

"We have good reasons for collecting these deposits," he said. "Without them, we have no assurance that you won't sell your horses and leave Mexico without paying taxes."

"I assure you that I have absolutely no intention of selling these horses," I said softly. "When I went through Panama, they handled this same situation in a slightly different manner. May I please show you?"

With that, I opened my passport to the appropriate page and showed him my Panamanian visa. The *jefe* picked up the passport I had set before him and returned it without bothering to take a look. With an explosive-sounding sigh, he swiveled his chair around and removed a fat volume from the bookshelf behind him. Silently, he began searching through its pages, reading various passages and following along with his index finger. This went on for such a long time that I wondered if it was his way of telling me our meeting was over. When it pleased him to do so, he gave me a small tidbit of information.

"This book contains the laws and statutes that apply to your situation."

Sighing frequently, he continued searching and studying while I stood there, wondering how this frustrating day was going to end.

"I may have found a solution," he announced, at long last, his finger parked next to a certain paragraph. "If you transport your horses by train and don't unload them until you reach the United States, we can dispense with the deposit."

"Perfect!" I responded. "I was planning to travel by train, anyhow."

"You must fully understand," the *jefe* said, returning his eyes to the book before him. "Your animals will have to board the train here in Tecun Uman and must not touch Mexican soil until you get to … where do you plan to cross the border?"

"Mexicali," I said.

He took out a form and filled in one of the blanks with the word: Mexicali.

"You must not take your animals off the train under any circumstances," he growled. "If you unload them, even for only a minute to exercise them, your animals will be immediately confiscated! They will become the property of the Mexican government, and there is absolutely no process by which you can appeal for their return! Do you understand?"

Fearing my voice would betray my intentions, I gave a quick up and down nod. Somehow, I'd have to deal with this unexpected requirement, but I didn't yet know how. After the *jefe* finished filling out the form, he signed it and made it official by adding the imprints of several rubber stamps. Casually, he half-extended it toward me, making me reach.

"Give this to the men who sent you," he said, standing and offering to shake hands, with the same half-hearted extension of his arm.

"Thank you very much," I said, quickly taking the paper, shaking his hand and leaving his office.

As instructed, I delivered the form to the man at the customs desk. While he filled out yet another form, I wondered if I had jumped from the frying pan into the fire. There was no way the Mexican railway's rates could have been cheap enough for me to buy passage to Mexicali for two horses and myself. I'd have been lucky to be able to afford the ride to Mexico City, but that was my goal, and my rapidly emerging plan was to get that far and visit the Secretary of Agriculture. I'd show him my letters of recommendation and try to somehow convince him to give me special permission to travel by any means I chose (and could afford). My plan had two obvious weaknesses: one, the railroad might refuse to sell me anything less than passage for three to Mexicali; and two, Hamaca and Ima might be confiscated even if I got them to Mexico City. After all, I'd have to unload them before I could visit the Secretary of Agriculture.

The day's unpleasant surprises were not yet behind me. I next learned that Mexican law required me to hire a customs broker for the purpose of drawing up certain documents. When that was finished and paid for, I was handed a folder full of papers, and with that in hand, I went to see about a train ride to Mexico City. The day's first pleasant surprise was that the freight agent didn't once question my request to purchase transportation only as far as Mexico City. In fact, he cheerfully came up with the cheapest possible rate, showing at least as much creativity as his counterpart in Guatemala City. Thanks to his encyclopedic memory, I became the beneficiary of a loophole that allowed my mares to be shipped "express" for less than shipping them as livestock. Under this classification, Hamaca and Ima would ride in the express car, together with packages and crates designated for priority delivery.

When the time came, I loaded my two horses aboard a Mexican National Railway express car, to the dismay of the man in charge, whose job it was to ride in that car and safeguard its contents. His responsibilities were regarded very seriously, and until his replacement took over, he was forbidden to even step outside the car. He even carried his meals with him, in containers. Required to take such considerable pains in the execution of his duty, he understandably didn't welcome manure and urine producing passengers among the packages and crates for which he was personally responsible!

At my suggestion, we put Hamaca and Ima in a corner and fenced them in with the largest wooden crates. This separated them from the cardboard boxes and paper-wrapped packages but didn't properly confine them. A sudden stop would slide the crates around like bowling balls. Too, horses are top-heavy, and the surrounding crates came no higher than their chests. During an emergency stop, they could easily be thrown all the way to the far end of the car. To help prevent this and other mishaps, I intended to ride in the express car, but the attendant wouldn't hear of it, insisting over and over that this was absolutely forbidden. I could see that he was afraid of horses, and I fully expected him to relent under pressure, but he stubbornly held his ground while I tried every argument I could think of. Terribly frustrated, I came dangerously close to candidly pointing out that his fear of horses would make him useless in an emergency.

Ima was what horsemen call a "wood chewer," because of her tendency to gnaw on anything made of wood. As if to bolster my argument for letting me ride in the express car, she began reducing the edges of surrounding wooden crates to splinters. As small slivers were torn from the crates and dropped to the floor, the attendant became increasingly agitated. He didn't know that Ima wasn't likely to do serious damage, and I tried to take advantage of his

353

ignorance. Again I suggested that I ride with him, this time justifying it as necessary to keep my horses from damaging the other cargo. Steadfastly, he refused. By the time the final "all aboard" was called out, I could scarcely bring myself to go to my seat in the passenger car. It was troubling to leave my mares on their own in an unsafe environment, but the good news was that I was under way and still two days ahead of schedule.

Not far down the line was Tapachula, where Hamaca and Ima had to be transferred from their express car to another, attached to a different train. This obviously didn't violate the prohibition against unloading them. Technically, however, they *were* briefly unloaded, and I made an interesting observation: no one paid the slightest attention. I could have led Hamaca and Ima away from the train station with little danger of the immediate confiscation that had been threatened. That bolstered my confidence in the prospects for success when I did what I had to do in Mexico City.

The bad news was the ramp provided for loading and unloading my horses. It was shiny, polished steel, okay for a hand truck loaded with boxes, but slippery for horses with metal shoes. Having been warned that there was only limited time to get aboard the next train, I had to get the job done quickly, without pauses during which I agonized over possible accidents.

Both horses did remarkably on the downhill slope. Hamaca descended slowly and cautiously, immediately sensing that the surface was slick. She slid the last few feet without panic and arrived safely at the bottom. The attendant nervously held her while I went back for Ima. Ima slid most of the way but managed to do so without mishap. *So far so good*, I told myself, breathing a sigh of relief. *Look on the bright side. Not many people have horses trained to ski!*

The second half of the transfer was a bit more challenging. Entering the next express car required both horses to use the same kind of ramp, this time with gravity working against them. I climbed to the top of the ramp and from there, did my best to steady each mare, in her turn, by applying a constant pressure on the lead rope. Both lost traction and slid backwards several times. Once they began to slide, there was no stopping until they reached dirt. Fortunately, they were quite willing to attempt the slick incline as often as necessary, and before long, they were aboard. Unfortunately, the attendant also transferred, dashing my hopes that his replacement might permit me to ride with my horses.

The Mexican "express" stopped at every town between

Tapachula and Veracruz, no matter how small. The majority of these stops lasted only long enough to pick up freight or passengers waiting on the platform. In such cases, the conductor sternly warned that anyone who disembarked would probably be left behind. There were also a few twenty-minute stops, during which I made all possible haste getting to the express car and looking after Hamaca and Ima. The express car was at the opposite end of the train from where I was riding, and I really had to hustle. Each time, I came perilously close to not making it back to my seat before the train pulled out.

Whenever I visited the express car, I tried to convince the attendant that I should be riding with him, but invariably he quoted the rule forbidding it. At least once, he came close to relenting, but time worked against me. I had to plead my case between rushing around the platform looking for water, holding the bucket so Hamaca and Ima could drink or stuffing hay into hay nets. This pretty much ruled out tactics such as eye-contact and face-to-face sincerity.

Between visits to the express car, I did my best to make myself less uncomfortable in my tiny wooden seat. *That* was a losing battle. After all, if that television station in Guatemala had been unable to find a single person within four inches of my height, why should trains provide space for *my* legs? The only way to accommodate them was to intrude on someone else's space, and this I did with a profusion of smiles and apologies. I finally settled into a position only slightly less comfortable than sitting on a bed of nails and fell asleep just before midnight. Five minutes later, the conductor woke everyone in the car.

"Ladies and gentlemen," he announced. "At our next stop, this car will be attached to a train bound for Chilpancingo. If your destination is Mexico City, you will transfer to another car as soon as the train comes to a complete stop."

My new seat was even less comfortable than the old one. It was similar to a park bench, and the backrest and seat were made of narrow wooden slats with spaces between. Luckily, some of my fellow passengers had continued on to Chilpancingo, and the new car was less crowded. I had an entire seat to myself, and taking full advantage of the extra space, I lay down, curled up and fell asleep shortly after we were again under way.

The harsh movements of the train woke me repeatedly, but each time, I quickly fell back to sleep. At 2:30 A.M., we made a twenty-minute stop in Oaxaca. Half-asleep, I sprinted to the express car, where I checked, watered and fed my horses. I was back in my seat and asleep even before the train left the station. The next time I awoke, it was 6:00 in the morning. My first thought was that I had been very fortunate to sleep so well. Looking around, however, I saw that sleep had come at a price. The train hadn't budged over the past three-and-a-half hours, and none of my fellow passengers could tell me why. The general consensus was that we should be pulling out momentarily.

After a while, I stepped out of the car and stood on the platform. The conductor was nowhere in sight. Neither was anyone else. If I wanted information, I'd have to step inside the station, but having seen the train depart other stations without warning, I was hesitant to get that far away. After an additional half-hour's wait, a quick departure seemed to be the least of my worries. Alert for signs that the engine was building up steam, I walked across the platform looking for someone who could tell me what was happening.

"Pardon me," I said to the stationmaster. "Can you please tell me why the train had been delayed?"

"There has been an accident, *señor*," he replied. "The tracks ahead are blocked."

"Do you have any idea how long it will take to clear them?"

"None," he answered. "I advise you not to get far from the train. It could leave at any moment, without advance notice."

I found Hamaca and Ima contentedly chewing the last of the hay I'd given them at 2:30. They seemed to consider train travel vastly preferable to anything else I'd put them through. Since boarding their first train in Guatemala City, they had found their diet consistent, the water to their liking, their sleeping accommodations comfortable and the weather inside their cars dry and predictable. On top of that, insect bites were a distant memory. In general, life was good! Best of all, there were no more long days of trudging up and down mountains, across deserts and through the tropics, pushing on, in spite of everything.

Before long, groups of passengers boldly headed for town in search of meals, movies and sightseeing. I was tempted to do the same but wasn't quite bold enough. Like my fellow passengers, I felt certain that clearing the tracks ahead would take a *very* long time. However, I couldn't bring myself to stray far. After all, the penalty for missing the train would be that Hamaca and Ima Sumac would arrive in Mexico City without me, which could easily lead to their confiscation.

Bored and badly in need of exercise, I took a brisk walk, circling the train for hours, until I felt sure I'd sleep that night no matter how uncomfortable my seat might be. Next I read two second-hand paperback novels I had happened upon at a newsstand in Guatemala.

I'd bought them for the week Hamaca and Ima would be quarantined at the U.S. border, but they came in handy sooner than expected.

Holding a handful of mane to keep from sliding off (see page 324).

CHAPTER 38

The Great Escape

Finally, at 4:00 in the afternoon, the "express" pulled out after a delay of thirteen-and-a-half hours. Another of my gift days had been lost. I was moved to reflect on an often-used phrase: "The Lord giveth, and the Lord taketh away." Admittedly I was trivializing the meaning, but the words accurately described the three days I'd been given and the two that had already been taken back. Still, it seemed ungrateful to complain while I was ahead.

Southern Mexico had a long history of violent bandit gangs, and there was a pervasive military and police presence. When Tschiffely had passed through, the Mexican government had provided a mounted military escort. Thirty-some years later, safe travel still required armed protection. All trains – including the one I rode – carried federal troops. There were other precautions as well. I was repeatedly approached by soldiers or police officers who demanded to see my papers. Each time, I was delayed while the pertinent data was painstakingly transcribed into pocket notebooks. Whenever I set out for the express car, someone in uniform would take a keen interest in this unusual behavior. More than once, I returned to my seat without having been able to look in on Hamaca and Ima, because of time wasted during yet another review of my documents.

At one point, the train was boarded by heavily armed Customs agents who brusquely went through the passengers' baggage. Since my gear was in the express car with the horses, I was spared. Nevertheless, I was offended to see the other passengers being bullied. Afterward, I commented to a fellow passenger that the agents' behavior had struck me as rude.

"The Customs people are always like that," he said. "They enjoy their power."

"Are the soldiers that way, too?" I asked.

"By no means. Without the soldiers, no one could travel safely in this area," he said. "We're all very grateful to them."

After that I observed the soldiers more carefully. They were, indeed, different from the Customs Agents. Most were obviously from poor families and were just doing a job, without arrogance or dreams of power. When they rode in our car, they were polite and expected no special privileges. In the absence of available seats, they stood. When passengers offered *their* seats, the soldiers declined in a stoic but courteous way.

The Mexican Railway's second-class travel accommodations left much to be desired. The cars were hot, stuffy and jam-packed. My fellow passengers unfailingly threw their trash out the windows and did their spitting – which seemed to be a periodic necessity – in the main aisle. It was so hot that all windows were wide-open. Depending on the train's relationship to the direction of the wind, hot, gritty air either tore past the windows or poured into the car. I soon realized that spitting through those windows would have been hazardous for everyone, including the perpetrator.

The locomotive spewed rolling black clouds of diesel smoke, and that smell was mixed with odors inevitable among folks traveling for days in extreme heat, without bathing facilities. For relief, I periodically stuck my head and shoulders through the window, but things finally got to the point where I spent as much time as possible on the platform between our car and the next.

In Veracruz, another change of cars awaited. I was uneasy over the prospect of further skiing lessons, but they were unnecessary thanks to some decidedly un-Latin efficiency. Our express car stopped directly across from the car to which Hamaca and Ima were to be transferred, with the doors perfectly aligned. A portable bridge, made of sturdy planks, soon spanned the space between. Immediately, men with hand trucks transferred the crates and packages bound for Mexico City. Next, I led my horses, first Hamaca and then Ima, across.

The attendant in the new express car easily succumbed to my logic and permitted me to ride with him. Once I had braced the horses during a jerky departure and stopped Ima from chewing on the fresh supply of crates, there wasn't much to do. For hours, I sat in the open doorway, my legs hanging out, watching as we rushed toward Mexico City. Bored, I grabbed at twigs and leaves on the trees that flashed past while the hot, dirty wind tore at me. In the early evening, we passed the ruins at San Juan Tíotihuacan. These cover eight square miles and date back to four hundred years before Christ. The numerous structures include several impressive pyramids. In the cold, clear light of day, the ruins undoubtedly showed massive deterioration, but by moonlight, only the absence of lights revealed that the city was uninhabited.

Contrasting with the darkness at San Juan Tíotihuacan, we next entered a huge, brightly lit metropolis. Quickly Mexico City enveloped the train, and before long, the largest city in North

America stretched as far as I could see in every direction. Our train's arrival at the depot brought forth soldiers, policemen and other government officials, creating an environment highly unsuited for breaking the law. I shuddered to think about what might happen when I unloaded Hamaca and Ima.

At that pivotal moment, a freight agent with the impressive-sounding name of Cipriano Maldonado came to my rescue. He appeared out of nowhere and directed the mares' unloading, giving it official status. After that, he volunteered to arrange for Hamaca and Ima to spend the night in a vacant boxcar on an out-of-the-way spur track.

With him directing my every move, no one paid much attention as I led Hamaca and Ima away from the crowds and commotion toward an area that seemed completely deserted. The boxcar in which my horses had been invited to spend the night was parked next to a warehouse that boasted a concrete loading platform. That little feature made it easy to walk my mares into their sleeping quarters and boded well for a quick getaway in the morning. Once Hamaca and Ima were comfortable in their accommodations, I stepped out and slid the door shut.

"Do you want that padlocked?" Cipriano asked, gesturing to the door I had just closed. "I can come by and unlock it for you in the morning."

"I prefer not to," I answered, trying not to show how important this was to me. "Do you mind if I sleep on the loading platform so I can be close to my horses?"

"I can't permit that, *señor*," he said. "This area can be dangerous at night. However, I *can* let you sleep in the warehouse. It isn't used much anymore, and right now it's empty."

Using the same flashlight with which he'd helped me inspect the mares' boxcar, Cipriano guided me into the warehouse. Together, we rolled an empty freight cart over near the door, where it would serve as my bed. From there, I could hear if anyone opened the door to my mares' boxcar.

Having run out of ways to be of service, Cipriano excused himself, saying that he needed to attend to his other duties. I didn't let him leave until I'd thanked him at great length. It was unlikely he'd ever know exactly what his help had meant to me, but at least I made sure he knew I was grateful.

Inside the dark warehouse, even after my eyes adjusted, I could scarcely see. Guided only by my sense of touch, I found the flashlight in my duffel bag. Then, in the feeble light provided by worn-out batteries, I unrolled my sleeping bag on the freight cart and crawled inside. I feared what the next day might bring but was happy to be in Mexico City a full day ahead of schedule.

I woke up with the impression that I had only just fallen asleep, but a look through the windows revealed faint traces of sunlight. Considering the crises I faced, I had slept unbelievably well. I felt refreshed and ready – as ready as I would ever be! – to attempt my *Great Escape*. The interior of the warehouse was still pitch black, and I needed the help of my flashlight to roll up my sleeping bag, brush my teeth and wash up. By the time I emerged from the bathroom, the light of day had begun to pierce the warehouse's high, dusty windows.

For days, I had been dreading the fateful and all-important event that was about to take place. I could still hear the *jefe* at the border. Over and over, my mind replayed his words: "If you unload them … your animals will be confiscated … immediately! They will become the property of the Mexican government, and there is absolutely no process by which you will be able to appeal for their return!"

Once or twice, my pending escape had struck me as an interesting challenge, but only as long as it was off somewhere in the future. Now that it was upon me, it was ominous. The instant I crawled out of my sleeping bag, my respiration quickened, and my heartbeat began hammering in my ears. By the time I opened the door to leave the warehouse, I was full of adrenaline, and my pulse and respiration were accelerated to the point where I wondered if I was the only person who could hear them.

Quietly I poked my head outside and devoured the area with my eyes, trying to be casual. There were some workmen nearby, and they glanced my way when I stepped onto the loading dock. Stretching and trying to move without apparent haste, I crossed the platform, opened the door to the boxcar and stepped inside. Once I had Hamaca saddled and Ima loaded with the baggage, I looked outside again. By then, I half-expected to be confronted by as many soldiers as surrounded Robert Redford and Paul Newman in the final scene of *Butch Cassidy and the Sundance Kid*.

Happily, the scene that greeted me was tranquil and unthreatening. I led Hamaca onto the loading platform and stood there, waiting for someone to challenge my unlawful behavior. Nothing happened, and my anxiety began draining away. It was like Tapachula all over again. No one seemed the slightest bit interested in my actions or even my presence. I could have yelled, "I hope nobody confiscates my illegally disembarked horses," and still no one would have looked twice. Apparently the *jefe's* threats had been empty, issued in the hope of producing compliance through fear. Well, one out of two ain't bad. He definitely produced the fear!

Now that fear's effect was wearing off, I proceeded to bring Ima out of the boxcar. When things remained calm, I decided to get moving before a curious policeman or soldier showed up. I stepped into the saddle and rode away, following a spur track that Cipriano Maldonado had pointed out to me the night before. That spur track led to the Mexico City stockyard, and that was my destination. If I could arrange it, the stockyard would be the perfect place to leave Hamaca and Ima. Among thousands of head of livestock, they'd stand out like a needle in a haystack. Furthermore, if my meeting with the Secretary of Agriculture was successful, the stockyard would be the perfect place to catch a ride, as I had learned in Costa Rica and Nicaragua.

As several of its employees later told me, the Mexico City stockyard was the world's second largest, behind only Chicago's. It looked huge with its collection of corrals, fences and gates seeming to go on for miles in every direction. I planned to quickly arrange for the mares' stay and immediately visit the Secretary of Agriculture, that very afternoon. Unfortunately, things didn't work out that way. Permission to board Hamaca and Ima could only be granted by the superintendent, and he wasn't an easy man to find. Several frustrating hours were consumed by my efforts to hunt him down and arrange a meeting. It was late afternoon, much too late to see the Secretary of Agriculture, before I was finally shown to a corral in a little-used corner of the stockyard.

"There are concrete feed troughs in the corrals, and you can sleep in one of them if you want," the superintendent told me, his smile suggesting I was exaggerating my poverty.

He obviously didn't believe I'd take him up on his invitation. To me, however, the offer was no joke. I was too broke to afford even the cheapest hotel. The feed trough had the width and depth of a large bathtub and was forty to fifty feet long. As a bed, it was a bit firmer than I prefer, but on the bright side, I could stretch out to my heart's content. Still working on a considerable sleep debt, I slept deeply, soothed rather than disturbed by the sound of lowing cattle.

The next morning, my priority became that fateful visit with Mexico's Secretary of Agriculture. To prepare myself, I asked for and received permission to take a shower in the worker's clean-up facility at the slaughterhouse. By that time, I no longer noticed the stockyard's formidable odor. Nonetheless, the smell near the slaughterhouse gagged me. The incineration of waste material – such as intestines and tails – produced so foul an odor that I feared I might be acquiring a scent worse than the one I was washing away. I didn't bring my clean clothes to the slaughterhouse for fear they might absorb the odor there. Instead I wore my old clothes back to the corral, where I changed. That done, I walked to a nearby boulevard and caught the bus for downtown.

******

Strange looks were directed my way when I asked to see the Secretary of Agriculture.

"The Secretary is available only by appointment," I was informed, "and appointments are granted only when absolutely necessary."

Until that very instant, I hadn't realized how bold it was to walk in, especially as shabbily dressed I was, and ask for an audience with one of the most important officials in Mexico's government. Severely deflated, I handed over my "magic letters" from Costa Rica and Guatemala and asked that they be shown to the Secretary, but I feared that this, too, would be a waste of time. My fondest hope was that an assistant might be assigned to see what I wanted.

To my surprise, and that of everyone else, I was invited into the Secretary's private office. There a dignified man shook my hand and asked how he could be of service. The Secretary seemed genuinely intrigued by my adventure, and it was soon apparent that he intended to help me. I was sent to a waiting room and called back into the Secretary's office about an hour later. I found him signing and stamping a stack of certificates and letters. Finally, with a satisfied grin, he signed and sealed the last one.

"No one will bother you if you show them these," he declared as he handed me a large manila envelope containing the valuable papers. "You may travel to your country by whatever means you desire."

Free to go home by whatever means I desired, I soon learned that there was no means I could afford. From dawn to dusk for four days, I never came close to getting a ride. My efforts were concentrated on trucks deadheading after having delivered cattle to the stockyards. I was able to offer no more than token payment, and my only hope was that someone would consider a pittance better than nothing. So far, however, when the truckers heard how little I was offering, every one had declined, most without even making a counter offer. Finally I took the advice of a worker at the stockyard and

363

visited the national headquarters of the Association of *Charros.* [26] This was perhaps Mexico's most powerful horse-related organization, but its busy employees took no interest in my predicament. They told me what I already knew: that it would be almost impossible to find the transportation I was seeking.

Having slowly become convinced that my financial situation was as desperate as I said, the superintendent at the stockyard was the only person to offer help. He made daily visits to the mares' corral and repeatedly advised that, if I wanted, he could find *me* a ride to the border.

"By now you must realize that you will have to go on without your horses," he insisted, "but I can help you sell them."

That was an option I wouldn't consider, but the mere thought left me demoralized. Soon discouragement had me in its grip, and my mood degenerated to where I read a book one afternoon rather than face further rejection from Mexico's cattle haulers.

[26] *Charros* are Mexico's cowboys.

***

The "long" rider after a long day.

CHAPTER 39

Home Stretch

In the midst of this seemingly hopeless situation, I decided to treat myself to a night out, having discovered that *Dr. Zhivago* was playing in one of Mexico City's many movie theaters. Going to see my all-time favorite movie struck me as the perfect way to boost my sunken spirits. The crosstown trip to the theater involved public transportation from one extremity of Mexico City to another. All in all, I faced a fifty-mile round-trip. The multiple transfers among buses and streetcars meant that a single mistake might doom me to being lost for hours, maybe days!

While en route, I obsessively and repeatedly asked directions, fretted, then checked and rechecked by asking other people. Amazingly, I made the trip, saw *Dr. Zhivago* and returned to the stockyard without a single misstep. I arrived back at my feed-trough bed after a highly enjoyable evening. Best of all, I could already tell that I was going to wake up ready to tackle my problems with renewed vigor.

The following morning, I decided to change my objective. Up to that point, I'd been seeking a truck to take my mares and me most or all the way to the U.S. border. I had wanted to get as far as possible with my first ride because, once I left the stockyard, I'd never again have access to so many trucks. On second thought, I decided to seek *any* ride that was headed in my direction. This would allow me to take advantage of the fact that assistance is most-easily obtained in small amounts and in small towns. Alas, when I put this new approach into practice, it produced results as negative as those I'd already had.

Two more days passed. Then suddenly, bright and early on a Saturday morning, there was a glimmer of hope. Two trucks, traveling together, delivered cattle. A chat with the drivers revealed that they had come from Guadalajara and planned to return immediately. Better yet, each had room for one of my mares. Thanks to the intervention of the stockyard superintendent, I was offered a price that was incredibly reasonable. Unfortunately, it was well beyond my budget. I was down to less than eighty dollars, not including what I had set aside for duties, fees and quarantine expenses at the U.S. border. These men wanted thirty dollars per horse.

"I can't pay more than five dollars each," I said, embarrassed to be haggling over a price that was already spectacularly low. "I admit that a ride to Guadalajara is worth much more, but I don't have it."

365

The drivers read one another's expressions before the more rotund responded.

"Make it twenty-five apiece," he countered.

I hesitated for some time before responding.

"I might be able to pay ten dollars apiece," I offered, "but no more. Even at that, I'll probably run out of money before I get home."

The men shook their heads in unison, side-to-side.

"If we were to fill our trucks the rest of the way with cowhides," the spokesman replied, "we could earn ten times that much."

"You're hauling cowhides?!" I exclaimed.

"Yes, but we have plenty of room for a horse in each truck."

"Cowhides?" I double checked.

"*Seventeen tons* of fresh cowhides," I was told.

"Seventeen tons?"

"*Sí, señor.* We just came from the scales."

Seventeen tons of fresh, bloody cowhides! The words echoed in my head. *I must be cursed!*

One of the men threw open the back door of his truck and gestured for me to look inside. The cargo area was open to the sky and surrounded by panels made of wooden stakes and slats. Except for a few feet at the rear, it was crammed full of fresh cowhides, liberally sprinkled with lime. My nose confirmed what my pessimism suspected. The pleasant aroma of tanned leather hovered off somewhere in the future. At present, the scent was ripe and attracting flies. Looking down, I saw reddish liquid dripping beneath both trucks. Even if my life depended on it, I wasn't sure I could get my horses to go anywhere near those trucks. After all, one dried cowhide is enough to convince a horse that a detour is in order. At best, seventeen tons of fresh hides would inspire enough resistance for the drivers to decide that the delay wasn't worth the token amount I could pay.

"Horses won't go near those hides," I sighed. "I'm afraid I've been wasting your time."

I smiled at the men, with considerable effort, and turned to go. Immediately, the price dropped to twenty dollars each, and I received two firm votes of confidence that "we" could get my mares loaded.

"Make it fifteen," I suggested.

After five days of seemingly endless failure, I finally struck a deal. However, I didn't intend to part with any money until *after* Hamaca and Ima were actually on board, not that failure was an option. Getting two horses and myself to Guadalajara for only thirty dollars was an opportunity I couldn't lose, cowhides or no cowhides! There was no way I was going to let the mares veto the deal, but my firm resolve was unnecessary. Both loaded easily, taking only scant notice of the hides. What *did* upset them was riding in separate vehicles. It was the first time since Piura that they'd been out of one another's sight. From my seat in the cab of the lead truck, I could hear them ceaselessly calling to each other, throughout the day and long night that followed.

We drove straight through without stopping, except for fuel, and for the fourth night in a row, I got little sleep. The stockyard's feed trough had been a less than ideal bed. Despite that, during my first couple of nights there, I had managed to ignore its discomforts and sleep well. That ended, however, with the arrival of a lonesome calf that had a bawl louder than the foghorn on the Queen Mary. It hadn't helped that I was also suffering the effects of dysentery, hopefully my last encounter with what the Mexicans laughingly refer to as "Montezuma's revenge."

Three hours after unloading in Guadalajara, I was in the central market talking with a tomato truck driver. He was headed north and had room for two horses. For ten dollars, he agreed to take Hamaca, Ima and me as far as Culiacán, another four or five hundred miles closer to the border. I hesitated because the driver wouldn't be leaving until the following evening, but my indecision was brief. Considering that I wasn't likely to find another ride for anywhere near the price, I offered a handshake to seal the deal, stationed my mares in a rented stall and spent Sunday's remaining hours touring Guadalajara.

It was surprising to find a metropolis with over a million inhabitants and such a charming atmosphere. The city was liberally sprinkled with plazas and parks. A considerable amount of work had gone into their construction and upkeep, and they were well worth seeing. Fountains and statues were everywhere. The trees were beautifully kept and painstakingly pruned. Sometimes brightly colored flower gardens had been arranged and trimmed so their shrubbery and flowers spelled out words and phrases. As often as not, the walkways were paved with beautiful tiles.

With two days to kill, I found time to take in three movies, each of which made a twelve-cent dent in my entertainment budget. None of the three B-grade films were as interesting as the venues where they were shown. Guadalajara had lavishly decorated movie theaters. Inside and out, they were remarkably ornate, a striking contrast to the stark, box-like movie houses I was accustomed to in the States.

Two mornings later, after an all-night ride in the tomato truck, we arrived in Culiacán, and I set out in search of hay. Since Mexico City, I'd been able to get baled alfalfa at reasonable prices. In Culiacán, however, I learned an expensive lesson: Mexican alfalfa is sold on the "let the buyer beware" system. In Mexico, as in the United States, alfalfa was sold by the bale. The difference was that the Mexicans weighed each bale at the time of sale, and the exact price was determined by the weight.

Unbeknownst to me, this motivated some purveyors to pour water into their bales because the trapped moisture increased the weight and, therefore, their income. Leftover bales got the same treatment, at least once a day, until sold. When I opened my bale, the consequences were just beneath the surface, in the form of moldy hay. With my funds at such a premium, it was especially galling to have spent good money on bad hay, and I angrily returned to where I'd made the purchase. Unfortunately, the larcenous pair that had sold me the rotten hay was long gone. I had no choice but to buy another bale from another vendor. Much the wiser by then, I refused to pay until the bale had been broken open for my inspection.

The following day, a Wednesday, I was fortunate enough to catch another ten-dollar truck ride, this one from Culiacán to Ciudad Obregón. On Friday, ten more dollars took us as far as Hermosillo, where I found myself less than four hundred miles from the border with less than eighteen dollars to my name. In the race between my money and Mexico's miles, my money was out of the running.

Joe and Pat Gavitt were poised to come to the border town of Mexicali and trailer Hamaca, Ima and me to their ranch, but first I had to get to Mexicali. Joe and Pat couldn't come inside Mexico, where regulations made it difficult and expensive to bring horse trailers from across the border. Not only that, but the Gavitts had jobs and could hardly drive two thousand miles to bring me to Mexicali and then drive another twelve hundred miles a week later, after the mares were released from quarantine.

Between Hermosillo and Mexicali, I faced indefinite expenses. Aside from transportation, I had to feed the horses and myself, not to mention that I'd have to sustain myself for a week or more while my mares were in quarantine. No matter how I sliced it, I didn't have the money to get to the border without dipping into funds set aside for quarantine and customs expenses, and that I couldn't do. A kindly trucker tried to rescue me with advice frequently given those who are short of money: "Get a job." I had already considered and rejected *that* as impractical. After all, I had no work permit; I knew no one; I was unfamiliar with the Mexican way of doing things; and Mexican wages were so low that they'd scarcely sustain me and two horses, let alone allow for getting money ahead. Besides, looking for a job would have been like looking for a needle in a haystack.

However, the trucker got my undivided attention when he said that he had a specific job in mind. It was immediately available. The pay was extremely interesting, and the trucker even offered to accompany me to the interview.

The haystack was suddenly much smaller!

I waited my turn in the arena, riding Hamaca and leading Ima as so often before (see page 377).

CHAPTER 40

Finish Line!

Within hours, my official title was *"picador,"* but, alas, I wasn't destined to strut before cheering thousands. It turned out that there are *picadores* (courageous, mounted lancers who defy death to joust with the brave bulls), and there are *picadores* (dirty, tired men who defy foul odors to care for frightened cattle on railroad trains). I was of the latter variety, having been hired by a local rancher who was shipping cattle north and needed a second caretaker. My duties were to commence aboard a train that would soon depart for Mexicali. The wages were free passage for my mares and myself. It seemed like an unbelievable stroke of good fortune, but I kept telling myself not to get my hopes too high. After all, there were sure to be bureaucratic obstacles.

My interview and hiring took place at the local railhead, from where the cattle would be shipped. Even before I was hired, I noticed a shed near the tracks that served as a branch office of the Sonora State government. This was under the command of a strutting little popinjay of a man, a government official suffering from small man's complex. It was a truly scary combination and became all the more so when he intervened as I went to put my mares in one of the corrals.

"I'm the Livestock Deputy for the state of Sonora," he introduced himself. "Where do you think you're going with those horses?"

"To Mexicali," I answered.

"Are you aware that you need a special permit to transport horses by train?" he asked, after he'd hauled me into his office, taken a seat and left me standing in front of his desk.

Busy thinking, I didn't comment.

"There are also fees and taxes you have to pay."

His manner was rude and abrupt. It was tempting to tell him that I was fresh out of money but would gladly bequeath him a few inches of height if that would make him feel any better!

"Show me your papers," he demanded.

In response, I pulled out my federal permit. He glanced at it and haughtily handed it back.

"I'm very sorry," he said, his voice revealing that he was no such thing, "but you must have a *state* permit, also. Unfortunately, the office that issues them is closed for the weekend. You won't be able to travel before Monday."

I took a deep breath and drew myself up to my maximum height. The Livestock Deputy looked at me through half-closed eyes, his manner emphasizing that he wasn't impressed.

"But I have a job on *today's* train!" I said firmly.

I regretted the words as soon as I'd spoken them. No doubt the Deputy would next add the cost of a work permit to the fees he intended to collect. Fortunately, however, labor matters were not his concern.

"That's your problem," he said, his eyes looking elsewhere and his voice indicating boredom.

An expressionless clerk glanced up momentarily, then silently returned to his paperwork. Somewhere in the room, a clock was ticking. Getting nowhere in a hurry, I remembered the other papers given to me by the Secretary of Agriculture in Mexico City. Among them, I could surely find one that would grab the Deputy's attention by the lapels and give it a good shaking. I started with the most humble-looking of those papers. From there I would present the increasingly magnificent ones until I got my point across ... I hoped. I pulled out the smallest and plainest paper and handed it to the Deputy. He glanced at it with a weary expression, started to hand it back and did an almost-comical double take.

Looking resigned to a cruel fate, he called the clerk over to have a look. Suddenly everything was "Yes, sir," "No, sir" and "If you like, sir." All problems with the Sonora Livestock Deputy instantly disappeared. Miraculously, I had no taxes to pay, no permits to acquire and no red tape to untangle. My would-be tormentor waved his hand to indicate that I was free to go.

"Don't you need to give me some sort of permit?" I asked, wanting to be sure I wouldn't have problems somewhere down the line.

"Why?" he asked, in a subdued voice. "You don't need it."

The office clerk looked at me and added further explanation: "With that paper *no one* can stop you!"

The departure of the train seemed imminent throughout the long afternoon and night, during which I remained awake and as alert as possible. Landing my new job had been a miracle, and I certainly didn't want to be sleeping somewhere when the train pulled out. Even though anxious to be under way, I was glad to have time to get ready for the trip. First, I would need to prepare some sort of traveling accommodations for my mares and myself. I started with the horses. Their situation was more dangerous because, on the evolutionary scale, their traveling companions weren't all that far removed from the old Texas longhorns. Their horns were a good three feet from tip to tip, with dangerous-looking points that no one had troubled to blunt.

Scheduled to be loaded thirty-five per boxcar, the cattle would fill every available inch, and I was hard-pressed to see how Hamaca and Ima could safely travel in their company. I counted the cattle, did some highly advanced calculations and realized that one of the boxcars would be carrying only thirty-two head. After clearing it with Carlos, my fellow *picador*, I loaded Hamaca and Ima in the last boxcar, tied them at one end and literally built them in, using stout poles to construct a crude but strong fence. Another problem was solved when I came up with the idea of hanging my baggage from the ceiling of that same boxcar. There, at least, my worldly goods would stay clean, dry and untrampled.

At first, I expected Carlos to be able to suggest a place where I could travel and sleep in safety. It turned out that he made the trip on a regular basis and had a standing invitation to sleep in the caboose. There he shared cramped quarters with the brakeman and two more of the train's crew. To my disappointment, there was no room for anyone else, least of all someone my size. Anyhow, I wouldn't have been comfortable sleeping that far from my horses and was determined to find a way to travel in their boxcar.

Each boxcar had an outside ladder attached to one end with a narrow crawl hole near the top, providing the only access once the side doors were shut and locked. After the cattle were loaded, those crawl holes would be the only way into or out of the boxcars. I tried out the crawl hole in the car where Hamaca and Ima were stabled. Even while the train was standing still, it was difficult to slide through the small opening. The instant I was inside, gravity irresistibly pulled me to the floor, a descent I most certainly didn't want to repeat with cattle aboard.

Following a long search, I found a plank that was a foot wide and long enough to bridge the width of a boxcar. Carefully, I slid one end between the slats on one of the boxcar's walls, high above the floor. The other end went between the corresponding slats on the opposite wall, creating a scaffold directly beneath the crawl hole. Having secured the plank with rope, I climbed up to try it out. I could find only one problem. Because of the location of the crawl hole, I hadn't been able to position my platform above the mares' pen. Instead it was at the opposite end of the car, above an area that would soon be filled by cattle with wicked-looking horns. If I had to get to my mares while the train was in motion, it would be difficult and dangerous.

Saturday morning around 4:00, Carlos and I busied ourselves loading the cattle. About an hour later, the whistle blew to announce our imminent departure. Anticipating the surges and jerks that would accompany the train's departure, we two *picadores* made sure every last steer was on its feet. Any that were lying down when the train began to move might not be able to get to their feet, exposing them to being trampled or suffocated. Not only that, but as they fought to get up, those long horns could easily gore the soft underbellies above them.

At daybreak, our train began its twenty-four hour desert crossing to Mexicali. Riding with Carlos on top of one of the cars, I looked out across the surrounding countryside and found myself thinking how commonplace such scenery had become. In general, Americans imagine Latin America as a land of mountains, jungles and semi-tropical landscapes. On my journey, however, I had traveled through desert terrain more than any other.

During the final minutes of each stop, Carlos and I made sure the cattle were all on their feet. Aside from that, there wasn't much to do besides keep our eyes open. Whenever one of the steers went down, we used long prod-poles to move his neighbors and clear a space big enough for him to regain his feet. The rest of the time we rode outside on the roof of a boxcar, talking and eating oranges. Toward late afternoon, the sky unexpectedly darkened and began pouring rain. Boyishly giggling, we ran across the tops of the moving boxcars and slid through the narrow crawl hole into the boxcar that housed my makeshift scaffold. As we sat there visiting and watching the cattle, I became aware that I had unwittingly created a serious social problem.

No feed had been provided for the cattle, yet my horses had been eating continuously. This inequity went unnoticed as long as the steers' stomachs were full, but the situation was changing with the onset of hunger. Restlessly, the have-nots fidgeted as the haves noisily chewed. The steers nearest my mares stood with heads down, staring between the poles behind which special privileges were being flaunted. Before long, pushing and shoving began to put considerable pressure on the protective barrier I'd built. To forestall serious trouble, I decided to feed Hamaca and Ima only when the train was stopped and I could keep the steers at bay with my prod-pole. Fortunately, this strategy worked. Without hay to provoke it, the friction between equines and bovines disappeared, along with the pressure on the fence that separated them.

When night fell, I removed the sleeping bag from my hanging cluster of baggage, unrolled it on my scaffold and crawled inside. Each little jump or sway of the boxcar roused me from my shallow semi-sleep. Hoping to increase my chances of survival, I took a length of rope and wrapped it twice around my body and the plank beneath, before firmly tying it. Even with this crude safety belt, my mind was on the thirty-two full-grown steers beneath me, with their sixty-four dagger-like horns and one hundred twenty-eight hooves, topped by fourteen tons of beef.

The next morning, just before dawn, my career as a *picador* came to an end. I said goodbye to Carlos and unloaded Hamaca and Ima in the small town of Pascualitos, six miles from the quarantine corrals in Mexicali. For the last time on my ride, I saddled my mares, loaded my baggage and mounted up, about to live the final episode of an epic journey. We had done it! The last leg had been less a test of endurance than of persistence and ingenuity, but it had become yet another challenge met and overcome. I had traveled the final fifteen hundred miles on just sixty dollars, not bad for two horses, a man and two hundred pounds of baggage.

As I started down the road for the last time, I was jolted by this sudden end to my adventure. Only a few days earlier, I had been at the stockyard in Mexico City, wondering if there was any hope of a successful conclusion. Now I was within an easy stroll of my homeland. The trip had been arduous and lonely, but in many ways I was sorry it was over. After having worked so hard to bring my ride to a conclusion, I was already starting to miss it. The bad times had faded from memory, leaving behind images of beautiful country, wonderful people and interesting experiences.

By the time we were within sight of the quarantine facility, my curiosity had gotten the best of me. I stopped, dismounted, reached inside one of the duffel bags and withdrew the sealed envelope given to me by Jorge Baca's neighbor just before my departure from Chiclayo. I still remembered the hints he'd given as to the contents, and I wondered how accurately he'd predicted my arrival date. Leaning against Hamaca's saddle, I opened the outer envelope and found three smaller envelopes inside, each one carefully sealed.

The first contained a small painting of Saint Christopher, the patron saint of travelers. To tell the truth, I could easily have suggested a few small improvements in Saint Christopher's service, but

I knew complaints wouldn't be justified. I'd been rescued from dire straits time and again. Whenever forces beyond my control had hampered me, other forces beyond my control had come to the rescue. There had been a solution for every problem, and at times, my luck had been nothing short of spectacular.

In the second envelope I found a letter, handwritten in the cramped, shaky scrawl of an elderly gentlemen. Reading, I found the prediction of my arrival date, *"Noviembre de 1967."* I was at the border eight months earlier than that, but this prediction might have been remarkably accurate if I'd ridden the entire distance, as the letter writer obviously had assumed I would.

The surprise gift in the third envelope was a beautiful, color lithograph. The subject was a famous palomino Peruvian *Paso* stallion named *Mantequilla, and he was as stunning on paper as in life. In a few months, after rest, good feed and grooming, Hamaca and Ima would again represent their breed almost as impressively as *Mantequilla did. In the meantime, the colorful print would serve as a reminder of the virtues of the Peruvian horse and the worth of my traveling companions. Not only were Hamaca and Ima beautiful creatures, but they had more than met my expectations in other ways. We had been through a lot together, and I deeply admired and respected both of them.

Shortly after arriving at the quarantine station, I learned that the requirements for bringing horses into the U. S. had become very complicated since the last time I had done it.

"You won't be able to handle this without a custom's agent," I was informed. "There's really no choice but to hire one."

Reflexively, I drew in a breath of air, preparing to argue that I couldn't afford it. After thinking twice, I stopped myself. This was one border where arguments and letters of recommendation weren't going to help. Getting my horses into the United States would depend on meeting the requirements, nothing more and nothing less. Though I had enjoyed preferential treatment since Costa Rica, I had no regrets about the fact that my country didn't offer it. Instead, I felt secure knowing that the rules were the same for everyone and that decisions would be made objectively, not based on who I was or who I knew.

By telephone, I was put in touch with a customs agent who quickly proved his worth, explaining that, since my horses were registered purebreds, he could get me an exemption from import duties. That single maneuver would save me the equivalent of his rather modest fee. The agent and I spoke on the phone, in Spanish, for another few minutes before he asked my name.

"Albright," I stated, "Verne Albright."

"Good night! Are you an American?" he asked, rapidly switching to English, "I thought you were a Mexican. Welcome home."

"I thought you were too!" I responded, having been misled by his fluent Spanish.

"I wasn't raised in the United States," he explained, "so I grew up being bilingual. Where did you learn your Spanish?"

"In Peru, mostly."

He didn't say where he'd been raised, but it seemed to me that it probably wasn't Mexico. He spoke classical Spanish, and in general, Mexicans spoke their own unique version.

After hanging up, I placed a call to inform Joe and Pat Gavitt that I was at the border and expected Hamaca and Ima to be released from quarantine in five days. Joe had news of his own. A new Peruvian *Paso* breeder named John DeLozier had offered to pick me up in Mexicali and trailer my horses as far as his ranch, two hundred and fifty miles closer to Los Gatos. Joe would meet me there.

The five-day wait while the mares were in quarantine provided lots of time for thinking. Only once during that time did I wonder if I had made a mistake by not riding farther and coming closer to what Tschiffely had done. At long last, that particular fear seemed to have lost its power over me. My mind turned frequently to the *hacienda* owner in Ecuador whose father had played host to Tschiffely. As he'd predicted, I was finally learning to take pleasure in my accomplishment. Considering the time and money at my disposal, I had done a lot. Clearly Tschiffely had done much more, but what I had done still had merit. By my best estimate, I had ridden (and walked) over twenty-five hundred miles.

On days when my attention was turned toward the future, I wondered if I would see Emily again. I had already said goodbye three times, thinking each was the last time I'd see her. Twice miracles had happened, if something can be called a miracle when assisted by so much human effort. [27] At that time, the most I could reasonably expect was a letter. I had written twice since we parted in Guatemala, but I had no way to know if letters from her would perhaps come to the Gavitts' address in Los Gatos.

Two days before my mares were scheduled for release, I met a cattle buyer from Brawley, California. Having heard about me from quarantine officials, he came looking and took me to a restaurant for the best dinner I'd had in a long time. While we ate, he invited me to ride in the grand entry at a combined horse show/rodeo in Brawley, one day after my mares were supposed to leave quarantine.

"I'll be trucking some cattle from Mexicali to Brawley on Friday," he said, "and will be happy to take you and your horses."

At first I was hesitant. For one thing, I had less than four dollars, which – while I waited for John DeLozier – would go further in Mexico than in the U.S. The cattle buyer must have read my mind.

"You can stay at my ranch. That way you won't have any expenses, and your friend won't have to drive as far to pick you up. A camera crew from *Wide World of Sports* will be at the rodeo. I spoke to their boss, and he wants to interview you. Your breed will get national television exposure," he became more enthusiastic as he listed his arguments. "Come on! It'll be like a big 'welcome-home' celebration."

It all sounded good, but the prospect of national publicity for the Peruvian *Paso* was the telling argument. I phoned John DeLozier to ask if he could pick me up in Brawley, rather than Mexicali. John was pleased with the potential publicity and cheerfully agreed to the change of plan.

※※※※※※

The opening ceremony at the Cattle Call Horse Show was the perfect way to end my ride. Just in case I was planning to bask in glory, however, it provided me with a quick, no-nonsense dose of reality.

I was scheduled to appear before the thousands of spectators immediately after the Grand Entry. As my moment in the spotlight drew near, a steady stream of horses and riders exited the spacious arena they had filled during the playing of the National Anthem. When the last rider passed me, going in the opposite direction, it was my signal to head into the suddenly deserted arena, riding Hamaca and leading Ima as I had done so often on our long journey. The huge arena reduced a single horse and rider to insignificance.

The crowd had grown silent as people settled back, waiting for what they'd come to see. During the Grand Entry, the voice that came through the speakers had boomed and echoed as the announcer tried to make himself heard over the roar of spectators. Now that same voice seemed subdued, even bored, and the audience was quiet. I heard the announcer give my name and then mispronounce the names of both mares. I noticed the cameras trained on us as ABC-TV filmed for *Wide World of Sports*. The videotape they were shooting would wind up on the cutting room floor, and when I later went to see about an interview, they would be much too busy to talk with me.

In response to some unseen cue, the spectators broke into polite applause. To them, I was an unavoidable delay before the rodeo started. A man leading one horse and riding another hardly compared with bucking broncos and high-spirited cowboys. My battered hat, faded shirt and worn-out jeans were dull after the arena had been overflowing with colorfully dressed cowboys and Indians. All in all, my "big welcome-home celebration" was a disappointment, but it served to emphasize some important facts. I had made my ride for my own reasons, and it would be a mistake to search for its meaning in the reactions of others. It would be an even-greater mistake to expect any sort of special treatment.

The following morning, John DeLozier arrived with his horse trailer. John was a Peruvian *Paso* enthusiast to whom I had sold horses not long before I left on my ride. He had offered to pick me up because he wanted to discuss his dissatisfaction with one of them. Three things happened as a result of our conversation that day. First: John became my best friend. Second: John's commitment to the Peruvian breed grew to where his Thunderbird Ranch became one of the leading breeding farms in North America. Third: Within a month, John and I traveled to Costa Rica where he bought horses from *don* Juan Rafael Cabezas and I saw Emily again.

Seeing Emily again was only one of many wonderful surprises waiting in my future. By 1985, I would make sixty-five trips to Peru, leading to more wonderful adventures. My memories of those are my most treasured possessions.

But that's another story! Some day, I hope to write it.

---

[27] I was destined to see Emily twice in the next two years. Though it would have been comforting to know that, I'm glad I didn't. It would have ruined two wonderful surprises.

Even the Best-Laid Plans

A little more than a month after my ride ended, one of my most cherished dreams was shattered. Somehow it seemed a fitting end to my journey. Too often its hopes, wonders and successes had see-sawed back and forth with disappointment, unexpected setbacks and even episodes of outright failure. And then, so soon after I won a significant race against time, it suddenly seemed there would be nothing to show for all my effort.

"I'm sorry, Verne," Pat Gavitt told me one morning, after she'd been riding Hamaca for a few weeks. "Hamaca can't begin to keep up with *Marinera. 28 It's going to take her a very long time to recover from the trip."

I slowly shook my lowered head as her words sank in. Less than five weeks before, Pat's husband, Joe, had trailered Hamaca, Ima and me to our final destination in Los Gatos. The upcoming Tevis Cup immediately became the focal point of my life. I dreamed that my ride's final and most important justification would come from Hamaca's success there. The Tevis Cup would be a national showcase for her breed.

Failure is most bitter after a person makes the mistake of anticipating success. To me, it had been a foregone conclusion that Hamaca would make exhilarating progress. But now, after Pat's disappointing assessment, I realized I'd been counting chickens long before they hatched. Pat was among my best friends and was very knowledgeable. It wasn't likely she was wrong, and it wasn't her nature to look on the negative side. She liked both of my mares very much 29 and was as disappointed by Hamaca's failure as I was.

Neither was Pat the kind to shrink from challenges. On the contrary, she had been delighted with the prospect of riding in the famous Tevis Cup on the second Peruvian *Paso* ever to compete. Pat had begun working with Hamaca soon after my arrival in Los Gatos. She was as anxious as I was to get some answers: How were Hamaca's strength and attitude after months of constant stress? Was she in better or worse condition after having dealt with the hardships of her journey? Had the tropics taken too great a toll on a species of animal not intended to live there? Could she be made ready for another major challenge so soon?

To learn the answers, Pat began riding Hamaca up and down California's Santa Cruz Mountains with *Marinera and Julie Suhr.

Though initial indications had not been good, Pat had withheld judgement until she was absolutely certain. It was only after several dozen of these test rides that she conveyed the bad news. The journey had taken too great a toll.

In those days, few North Americans had ever seen a Peruvian *Paso* horse, and many would judge the entire breed by the first few individuals they saw. Thus, we felt a heavy responsibility. What we did would go far toward establishing the breed's reputation, and our goal had always been to finish in the top third. Pat, however, suspected that Hamaca would be hard-pressed to complete the hundred miles within the twenty-four hours allowed.

The long-awaited shot at the Tevis Cup was not to be, and I felt my odyssey had lost all meaning. The truth was that I had lost track of my original goal, which had been to publicize and promote the Peruvian horse. Hamaca and Ima had done their part, but I hadn't done mine! After my return to the States, a few newspaper articles had appeared with no effort on my part, and I made the mistake of sitting back and waiting for publicity, as if this would materialize on its own. It was a while before I realized that I needed to take matters in my own hands. I put together some notes and slides and began making presentations before horsemen's groups, telling my audiences a little about my ride and a lot about the Peruvian breed.

I also wrote articles, some about my ride but most about the breed. These began to be published in national horse-related magazines where they appeared with a regularity that led *Western Horseman* to dub me: "Mr. Peruvian *Paso*." Articles, though, could never fully describe the breed's characteristics. Books would be the best way to do *that*, and I went to work on two of them. The first started as a translation of *don* Luis de Ascasubi's book. When that project came to a halt because of our disagreements, [30] I began work on a book of my own. [31]

Immediately thereafter, I wrote a book telling the story of my ride. Originally that book had been one of my ride's primary purposes, but discouraged by the aftermath, I still hadn't gotten around to it a year later. The first step was to gather the lengthy letters I'd written to Joe and Pat while en route. Rereading them reminded me of details that were already fading from memory and provided the inspiration for a short book, *In the Saddle Across the Three Americas.* [32]

More than three decades have passed since Hamaca, Ima and I crossed the U.S. border at Mexicali. Since then, I've learned that sometimes the best-laid plans can work out better than anyone could have imagined! At the time of this writing, there are perhaps as many as fourteen thousand registered Peruvian *Paso* horses in the United States and Canada. From here, the breed has spread to countries throughout the world. The "Cadillac of Horses" has become the "Rolls Royce of Horses" in England, the "Mercedes of Horses" in Germany, the "Lamborghini of Horses" in Italy and so on.

I don't believe for an instant that the Peruvian *Paso* owes its success to my ride. The breed sold itself on it own considerable merits. However, these horses first had to be brought to the attention of America's horsemen, and it was my pleasure to be among the people who helped do that. [33]

During my ride, a strong and durable bond was formed between the Peruvian breed and a tall, lanky *gringo*. That bond led me to dedicate my life to the promotion of Peru's National Horse. I can't claim to have done this unselfishly because I enjoyed it tremendously. If I could relive my life another dozen times, I don't see how I could live it in a more interesting and satisfying manner.

Of the many paths my life could have taken, the right one for me was the long way to Los Gatos!

[28] Hamaca's training companion, *Marinera, a registered Peruvian Paso, had been the first of her breed to complete the Tevis Cup. Ridden by owner Julie Suhr, *Marinera twice finished in the top ten percent.

[29] In fact, she and Joe later bought Ima Sumac from me. A few months after that, I sold Hamaca to Betty Bowe. With Betty, she lived out a long life, first in southern California and later in Washington state, receiving a level of care that more than compensated her for the suffering she endured on our journey.

[30] See footnote 16.

[31] At the time, I was distressed by influential American owners who were politicking to impose radical changes on the Peruvian breed in the United States. My response was to write *The Peruvian Paso and His Classic Equitation*, presenting the Peruvian horse as a "package" that should be preserved along with its unique traditions, history, standards, training methods, tack and characteristics.

[32] Later lengthened and republished as *Horseback Across Three Americas*.

[33] It was especially gratifying to play a role in saving the Peruvian breed in the late 1960's and early 1970's, when it seemed in danger of disappearing during and immediately after Peru's Agrarian Reform.

Heaven's Gait - A Profile of the Peruvian *Paso* Horse

The doctors told Sharon Reynolds that her riding days were over. A lifetime in the saddle had caused discs in her lower back to deteriorate, and the experience of riding had shifted from exhilarating to painful to downright dangerous. Sharon risked permanent damage and even paralysis if she continued doing what she enjoyed most, riding horseback.

"It was the worse news of my life," she said, "and yet, contrary to my wishes, I had to admit the doctors were right. Every time I rode, it wouldn't be thirty seconds before I'd start feeling those painful twinges. It kept getting worse and worse."

In an unexpected turn of events, Sharon had the opportunity to ride a horse recently imported from South America.

"It was unbelievable! The ride was so smooth it felt as if the horse was floating!" she exclaimed. "There was no pain or discomfort ... just the marvelous sensation of being able to ride again."

What made the difference? Sharon had ridden a Peruvian *Paso* horse. There are horses especially bred for practically any purpose. Clydesdales and other draft horses were created for pulling great loads. Shetland ponies are the perfect size for children. Arabians are admired for their endurance and beauty. Sleek Thoroughbreds race at high speeds, and quarter horses are born to work cattle. Still other breeds are esteemed for the smooth way they cover ground. Peruvian *Paso* horses fall in the latter category. In fact, the Spanish word *paso* refers to the gait that offers the smoothest ride in the equine kingdom.

Don Luis de Ascasubi, considered one of the foremost experts on the breed, once wrote:

> "There are many breeds of ambling horse,
> but only one is a true artist, and that is the
> Peruvian *Paso*."

For those who have yet to understand and appreciate the artistry of Peruvian horses, the *paso* gait may appear just a bit peculiar. Most people are accustomed to seeing trotting horses with legs moving in a diagonal pattern. The left rear and right front hooves hit the ground together, and then the action shifts to the opposite diagonals. This repeated motion, back and forth, produces the bouncing which can causes discomfort and even pain.

By contrast, the Peruvian *Paso*'s inborn gait is lateral. It begins with the rear and then the foreleg of one side, followed by the same pattern on the other side. The legs move individually, and the sequence is such that the Peruvian always has at least two feet on the ground, similar to the way a baby crawls. Unlike the trot, the *paso llano* gait has no aerial phase, with all four hooves in the air, after which the horse's weight comes crashing to earth with jarring impact.

These various factors combine to provide that splendid, gliding ride for which the Peruvian is widely celebrated, but there's more! In addition to smoothness, the Peruvian's way of moving has a unique and spectacular style. The significance of this was best described by Luis de Ascasubi.

"There are times in life," he said, "when one longs for the superfluous. And in this world, dominated by statistics, efficiency and materialism, it's a joy to see [a Peruvian *Paso*] come dancing down the road, rhythmically tapping out his beat, glowing with good humor."

Ascasubi was discussing what the untrained eye might see as "wasted energy," expended as these majestic horses exhibit their *término*. The Peruvian is the only horse with *término*, a unique, graceful and flowing movement of the forelegs. The front knees bob high and the forelegs arc toward the outside as the horse strides forward. It looks something like the arm motions of a swimmer doing the Australian Crawl. Combined with the breed's carriage, presence and energy, *término* completes a beautiful picture, one for which Peruvian horses are justly famous.

Despite any such fame, naturally gaited horses are less-known and less-often-seen than today's more familiar trotting breeds. There was a time, however, when trotting horses were the rarity. In those days it was much more common to see a smooth-riding "pacer," or gaited horse.

Prior to the seventeenth century, most of the world's horses were naturally gaited. In those days, the back of a horse was the best option for travel, and most people rode, whether or not they knew anything about it. It was obviously desirable to ride the smoothest horses available. Horses that trotted (called "bone-shakers") were considered suitable only as pack animals or mounts for servants. Even knights, who required the larger trotting horses for battle, often had naturally gaited horses they rode to the battlefield, leading their "chargers" behind.

During the seventeenth century, the uses for trotting horses increased. Networks of roads were built, and people began traveling in horse-drawn vehicles. Great expanses of land were devoted to cattle

383

raising for the first time. Simultaneously, horse racing gained world-wide popularity. Trotting breeds excel at pulling, working with cattle and racing, and within a single century, the gaited horse shifted from the rule to the exception. It was the most dramatic change horse breeding had ever seen. Even so, horsemen in Peru continued to esteem and breed their naturally gaited *Caballo Peruano de Paso*.

The traditional Peruvian version of the *Caballo Peruano de Paso's* history is under attack, challenged by modern scholars who have dug into the breed's past to uncover enlightening, fascinating and illuminating details. These researchers now tell us that the Peruvian *Paso* is not descended from the Andalusian, but from the predecessor of the Andalusian, also called the Andalusian. If that sounds like splitting hairs, it really isn't. It's a basic difference of opinion over when the Andalusian breed began its glorious history.

Most modern North American scholars say the Andalusian breed was founded in the 1700's, or thereabouts. Most Peruvians differ, maintaining that the modern Andalusian and its predecessor are a single, continuous breed, without regard for radical changes, including strong injections of outside blood. The traditional Peruvian approach sees the Andalusian as having once been gaited. The scholars see those gaited horses as predecessors of the modern, trotting Andalusian breed. The problem with the Peruvian version is not its truth but the fact that it oversimplifies something very complex. It is much more precise, specific and accurate to use the term *Jennet* when discussing the Peruvian's ancestors.

The confusion comes from language. Spanish horses during the conquest and for more than a century afterwards were *types* rather than *breeds*, there being no registries. Horses were identified by the region that produced them, meaning that all horses from Andalusia were "Andalusians," in spite of their differences. Among these "Andalusians" were the Spanish Jennets, sometimes called "mobile thrones," which originated in and around Granada, in the province of Andalusia, and were reputed to provide the smoothest ride of their day. Though called "Andalusians," their more specific name was *Jennet*, which came from the Spanish words "*jinete*" ("rider") and "*a la jineta*" (the style of riding used on smooth-riding saddle horses). Loosely translated "Jennet" means "riding horse," and that's what they were, smooth-riding saddle horses. Their name referred to their function, much the same as today's terms: "jumper," "cowpony" or "endurance horse." Not by current definition a *breed*, they founded the modern Andalusian and Peruvian *Paso* breeds.

Following the conquest, Lima became the most-important city in the Western Hemisphere. It governed most of the continent and for a while, even became the only port through which the Spanish permitted trade with their South American empire. For this and other reasons, the horse first entered much of South America through Lima, where the cream was skimmed off.

The vast majority of Peru's initial breeding stock came from islands and countries bordering on the Caribbean Sea, [34] but the Peruvians contend that the most important ancestors of the Peruvian *Paso* came directly from Spain. Furthermore, they carefully point out that the war-horses brought by the *conquistadores* were mostly trotters and that the ancestors of the *Paso* came in subsequent shipments.

The New World ceased to receive bloodstock from Spain in 1507, the year that country outlawed the exportation of horses because this and other factors were draining its supplies. The Peruvians, however, assert that this ban did not necessarily apply to horses owned by the eminent and distinguished personages that came to Lima. We know, for example, that Pizarro was permitted to import two fine Spanish horses long after exportation had been forbidden. Other powerful administrators and important noblemen who came to Lima, among them some of the finest horsemen of the day, were almost certainly able to bring fine horses that were their personal property. Even if the number of such imports was relatively small, the influence was probably huge, witness the modern impact of Sol de Oro (V). Importations seem to have waned to almost nothing, however, when Peru's high-quality horses became numerous and far-less-expensive than comparable horses in Spain.

The modern-day Peruvian *Paso* owes its excellence to the Spaniards' position as the foremost horse breeders of an era. However, the proud heritage of this breed pre-dates the *conquistadores*. In fact, its origins can be traced back thousands of years.

Long ago and for hundreds of years, North Africa's Phoenicians and Carthaginians let their influence be felt on the Iberian Peninsula, that landmass which is home to Spain and Portugal. Both the Phoenicians and Carthaginians traded extensively with Spain, and the latter's armies campaigned there, using cavalry units that rode North African, mainly Numidian, horses. This introduced foreign stock that mixed with horses already living in the Spanish countryside.

Centuries later, with the conquest of most of Spain by the Berbers and its subsequent occupation by the people who became known as the Moors, the North African influence was accentuated. The Berbers brought with them an early version of the modern Barb, which derives its name from its homeland along the Barbary Coast, North Africa's Mediterranean shoreline from Morocco to Tripoli. The Barb was created by mixing Numidian and Persian horses with others brought to North Africa from Spain by the Vandals. Like the Arabian, the Barb gained well-deserved fame as a great improver of horses, and the cross of the Barb with animals already in Spain [35] produced that country's finest horses, most notably the type known as the Jennet.

The repeated North African invasions were interspersed with another onslaught, that of Germanic barbarians and other peoples. These often came on horseback, riding animals that also became part of Spain's equine gene pool. Centuries later, after the Moors were finally driven from Spain, breeders imported northern and Eastern European horses that were crossed with Spanish horses, a process that established the modern Andalusian. [36]

The Peruvian *Paso* may well have been the first new breed developed in the Western Hemisphere. Thanks to Peru's geographic isolation, it was certainly one of the purest, and it became not only Peru's National Horse but, according to *don* Luis de Ascasubi:

"...the greatest triumph of genetic selection ever achieved by a group of breeders."

Ascasubi went on to say:

"The Peruvian sense of luxury is unequaled. When a Peruvian wants something a certain way, he will not be satisfied with less. I don't think any other people would have had the persistence or patience it took to create this breed. Many breeders in other parts of the world started with similar objectives, but they invariably gave up and changed to an easier goal."

More than any other factor, patience, almost five hundred years of it, is responsible for the excellence of the modern Peruvian breed. That patience has produced a national treasure to rival any taken from Peru by the Spanish. However, patience alone wouldn't have been enough. The other indispensable requirement was integrity. This point was clearly illustrated at a Peruvian *hacienda* I visited in 1964, together with a gentleman from Argentina. After showing us many fine horses, our host brought out a truly magnificent specimen. Both of us foreigners complimented him, and the Argentine expressed confidence that this exceptional stallion would surely be the next national champion. The proud owner thanked him but said he had overestimated the horse just a bit; the animal would place fourth or fifth at best. When asked why, he explained that his stallion had a stride that was a bit short.

"Well then," declared the Argentine, "here's a little secret for which you can thank me when your horse wins the championship. To lengthen his stride, all you need to do is lay cavaletti poles flat on the ground, parallel to one another, like a stepladder. Space these so your stallion's hooves will hit them unless he takes a longer step. In time, he'll learn to increase his stride."

Our host's face furrowed into a frown. Since his manners were impeccable, I'm sure he didn't realize he had the expression of a man who had just detected an unpleasant odor.

He responded: "Well, in the first place that would be cheating according to unwritten rules we have here. Secondly, it seems to me that it wouldn't be wise. If I do as you suggest – and win the championship as a result – a great many mares will be brought to my stallion for breeding. Many of the resulting foals will require this training on the cavaletti poles. According to our thinking, it's preferable for a stallion with a naturally long stride to be the champion so he can pass this stride genetically."

I came away from that experience so impressed that I began to sing the breed's praises as soon as I got back home. Eventually, things snowballed, and North America is now home to more than half the world's population of Peruvian *Paso* horses.

---

[34] Indirectly, therefore, from Spain.

[35] Luis de Ascasubi considered the Barb to be the most important ancestor of the modern Peruvian *Paso*.

[36] The idea that the Friesian, a trotting breed, is also an ancestor of the Peruvian *Paso* originated with Luis de Ascasubi, who even published writings with pictures of Peruvians that he said had reverted back to that particular ancestor. However, injections of Friesian blood into Spanish breeds, if these indeed took place, happened after most, if not all, ancestors of the Peruvian Paso had left Spain and gone to Peru. Knowing Ascasubi's passion for accuracy, I hesitate to discount his theory, but a good case has been made to the contrary.

Spanish terms used in this book

Aficionado – A devoted fan of some particular thing or activity.

Algarrobo – A native Peruvian variety of acacia (sometimes called *huarango* in the south of Peru), which produces a long, yellow seed pod that, when dried, is readily eaten by cattle.

Altiplano – The Peruvian word for a high mountain plain, usually above the tree line.

Americano – Infrequently used to refer to *Americans* in the sense of people from North, South or Central America, not merely those from the United States.

Asociación – Association, in the sense of an organization.

Balboa – The prime Panamanian monetary unit, named after one of the first Spanish explorers in Panama, Vasco Nuñez de Balboa.

Bandido – Bandit.

Bravo – Loosely: "Well done!"

Brío – Though the word *brío* is most often translated as "spirit," it is far from synonymous. In English, we sometimes call a horse *spirited* when it is difficult to handle. In Spanish, there is no such usage. *Brío* refers to a horse's vigor, energy, exuberance, courage, presence and liveliness, and it automatically implies that these qualities are willingly placed in the service of the rider.

Buenos días – Sometimes expressed as *Buen día*, this phrase literally means "Good day." However, it is used only before noon.

Buen viaje – Phrase meaning: "Have a good trip."

Buena suerte – Phrase meaning: "Good luck."

Buenas tardes – Phrase meaning: "Good afternoon."

Charro – The name given to the Mexican cowboy.

Cabalgada – Cavalcade; a gathering of riders.

Caballo – Horse.

Caballo Peruano de Paso – Peruvian *Paso* horse.

Caballo de trabajo – Literally: *work horse*; the Peruvian term for a castrated male horse (gelding).

Campesino – Peasant.

Canton – In Ecuador: a smallish settlement.

Caserío – In Peru: a small settlement; hamlet.

Cerro – Hill; ridge.

Chalan – In Peru: the trainer who works with Peruvian *Paso* horses, from the Arabic word *chalab*.

Colectivos – Taxis that carry as many·passengers as possible, anywhere on a predetermined route, for a standard fee.

Colegio – School; academy.

Comandante – Commander.

Conquistadores – Literally conquerors, this refers specifically to the Spanish soldiers who conquered the Spanish empire in North, South and Central America.

Criollo – Creole; in Latin America: a native person, thing or breed of livestock.

Cristiano – Christian.

De nada – Phrase meaning: "You're welcome."

Despoblado – Wilderness; literally "unpopulated place."

Dólar (dólares) – Dollar (dollars).

Don – A title once reserved for nobility now evolved into a title which indicates respect. Generally, the word is used with a person's given name and thus represents a unique combination of respect and friendliness.

Diario – Daily.

El – The (masculine form).

Estados Unidos – United States.

Equitación – Equitation.

Fiesta – Party; celebration.

Finca – A modest-sized agricultural operation.

Gracias – Thank you.

Gringo – A white person, normally of European extraction; this term is not normally derogatory, and Peruvians often use it as a nickname for their light-skinned children.

Guardia Civil – Name of rural police force in most Spanish-speaking countries.

Hacienda – A plantation or large farm/ranch, which is usually worked by resident labor.

Hermano – Brother.

Hípico – Relating to horses/equines.

Humo – Smoke.

Instituto Cultural – Cultural Institute.

Jefe – Leader.

Kilómetro – Kilometer; approximately five-eighths of a mile.

La – The (feminine form).

Latigo – Whip; cinch; strip of leather.

Latino – Latin.

Machismo – An exaggerated sense of masculine pride; a Latin philosophy in which the male is at the top of the chain of command and privilege.

Mañana – Tomorrow.

Mestizo – A person of mixed ancestry; half-breed; in Andean countries, this often refers to a person with European and native South American blood.

Militar – Military.

Muerte – Death.

Mula – Mule.

Norteamericanos – People from the United States.

Noviembre – November.

Pachamanca – A Peruvian-style barbecue.

Palacio Nacional – National Palace.

Panamericana – The Pan American Highway.

Paramo – The Ecuadorian word for a high mountain plain, usually above the tree line.

Parque – A park; property open to the public for its enjoyment.

Paso llano – The four beat, lateral gait (sometimes called simply: *paso*) which is the trademark of the Peruvian *Paso* breed.

Patrón – Boss.

Picador – Mounted principal in a bullfight who jabs the bull with a lance to weaken its neck and shoulder muscles.

Plaza de Toros – Bullfight arena.

Resistencia – usually translated as "endurance," it implies the ability to *resist* more than just physical work. True *resistencia* includes the ability to withstand just about anything that comes along. In the case of the horses chosen for my ride, it meant that they had to *resist* – in addition to hard labor – disease, hunger, thirst, altitude, extreme climates, unfamiliar feed, insect bites and whatever else they encountered.

Salado – Salty; an unlucky person.

Señor – Mister; sir.

Señora – Mrs.; a married woman.

Señorita – Miss; an unmarried woman.

Serrano – A highlander; in Peru and Ecuador, the term is understood to apply specifically to Indians living in the *sierra*.

Sí – Yes.

Sierra – Mountain country.

Siesta – An early afternoon nap once common in Spanish-speaking countries.

Sol (soles) – The sun; also the prime Peruvian monetary unit.

Sombrero – Hat.

Su – His; hers; its; their; your; one's.

Sucre (sucres) – The prime Ecuadorian monetary unit.

Suroche – Altitude sickness.

Término – The swimming action seen in the forelegs of Peruvian *Paso* horses.

Tio – Literally: *uncle*; this word is often used as a polite was of making a well-liked man into an honorary member of one's family.

Torero – Bullfighter.

Toro – Bull.

Turista – Tourist.

Que le vaya bien – Phrase loosely meaning: "I hope everything goes well for you."

Vaquero – Cowboy.

Violencia – Violence.

Yanquis – A usually derogatory term applied to people from the United States.

❖❖❖

For further information about Peruvian *Paso* horses, contact the website of the American Association of Owners and Breeders of Peruvian Paso Horses at: http://www.aaobpph.org

******

For more information on horses of Iberian ancestry, such as the Peruvian Paso, Paso Fino, Andalusian, Lusitano, Azteca, North American Spanish Colonial Horses and many more, contact:

CONQUISTADOR MAGAZINE & BOOKSTORE
1510 DOVE MEADOW ROAD
SOLVANG, CA 93463
PHONE: (805) 686-4616 or visit their website at:
http://www.conquistador.com
E-mail at: amigo@conquistador.com

Other books by Verne R. Albright, available from Amigo Publications: ***The Peruvian Paso and His Classic Equitation***

The Peruvian Paso Horse in Central America today.
Photo by Jack Greene and courtesy of AAOBPPH.